Manchester Disunited

Other books by Mihir Bose

Football
Behind Closed Doors: Dreams and Nightmares at Spurs
False Messiah: The Life and Times of Terry Venables

Cricket
Keith Miller: A Cricketing Biography
All in a Day: Great Moments in Cup Cricket
A Maidan View: The Magic of Indian Cricket
Cricket Voices
A History of Indian Cricket
(winner of the 1990 Cricket Society Literary Award)

General Sport
The Sporting Alien
Sporting Colours: Sport and Politics in South Africa
(runner-up for the 1994 William Hill Sports Book of the Year)
Sporting Babylon

History and Biography
Bollywood: A History
The Lost Hero
Michael Grade: Screening the Image
Memons
The Aga Khans

Business
The Crash: The 1987–88 World Market Slump
A New Money Crisis: A Children's Guide to Money
Are You Covered? An Insurance Guide
Fraud: The Growth Industry of the 1980s
How to Invest in a Bear Market

Manchester Disunited

Trouble and Takeover at the World's Richest
Football Club

MIHIR BOSE

To my darling daughter, Indira, who was taken to White Hart
Lane at the age of five as an act of baptism and has since said,
'Daddy, when Tottenham don't play, can we support
Manchester United and isn't David Beckham gorgeous.'

First published in 2007 by
Aurum Press Limited
25 Bedford Avenue
London WC1B 3AT
www.aurumpress.co.uk

A catalogue record for this book is available from the British Library.

ISBN-10: 1 84513 121 5
ISBN-13: 978 1 84513 121 0

10 9 8 7 6 5 4 3 2 1
2011 2010 2009 2008 2007

Designed and typeset in Minion and Helvetica Neue by
SX Composing DTP, Rayleigh, Essex

Printed and bound in Great Britain by MPG Books, Bodmin

This book is printed on paper certified by the Forest Stewardship Council as
coming from a forest that is well managed according to strict environmental,
social and economic standards.

CONTENTS

ACKNOWLEDGEMENTS

Many people have helped me in the writing of this book. Some of them would like their help to be acknowledged; others, while willing to talk to me, would not want their help mentioned. I respect that.

I would particularly like to thank Tehsun Nayani of Smithfields, the public relations firm that acts for the Glazers and Rothschild, who, like the classic PR man, helped in many different ways arranging interviews but has preferred to remain the facilitator rather than the man who takes centre stage. John Antcliffe, the former Rothschild man and boss of Smithfields, was also very helpful.

Dermot Desmond, the power behind Celtic, my second team (after Tottenham, of course), helped me understand many of the strands of this complex story that seemed obscure and confusing at the start. I would like to thank Robert Leitao and Majid Ishaq of Rothschild for their time and forbearance and Philip Swatman, intrepid sailor, generous host and old Rothschild hand, for helping me make the necessary contacts.

I cannot begin to say how grateful I am to Mark Rawlinson of Freshfields who proved that not all lawyers start the clock the moment you meet them.

Iain Rodger, former head of communications at Allen & Overy, proved that you can be a PR man for a top legal firm yet help journalists and I am grateful to him both for providing me an insight to the excellent inhouse catering of Allen & Overy and for introducing me to key personnel of his firm including Andrew Ballheimer, Richard Hough, Ed Barnett and Joe Greenan.

Tim, Lord Bell, was, as ever, brilliant in his description of events of which he had first-hand knowledge.

David Bick, despite being a West Ham supporter, brought a great deal of knowledge of football and the City and his readiness to provide a treasure store of information and insights was very useful. Shimon Cohen, another City PR man with a keen interest in football, was also exceedingly helpful.

Andy Holte, Divisional Commander of the Trafford Division, the area which polices Manchester United, gave willingly of his time as did Sir John Bridgeman, former head of the OFT, and a fellow member of the Reform, a club we both cherish so much.

David Davies, Paul Barber, Adam Crozier, Howard Wilkinson, Andy Walsh, Nick Towle, Patrick Harverson, Charlie Methven and Charlie Brook all very willingly let me share some of their memories which proved essential in a better understanding of the story.

I am particularly grateful to Phil Townsend who, when he was the spokesman for the Department of Culture, Media and Sport, did not allude much to the fact that he was a season ticket holder at Old Trafford, but has since proved an exemplary PR spokesman for the club.

Jim White, now a colleague of mine at the *Daily Telegraph*, brought that mixture of fan knowledge combined with an ability to assess objectively the team he supports, an increasingly rare and valuable ability. John Cassidy, the exiled Leeds fan at the *New Yorker*, made available valuable insights and material and Andrew Murray-Watson and Dennis Campbell were also very helpful.

Nigel Phillips is another fan, albeit of Arsenal, who combines extensive knowledge of football with that of the City and readily let me have access to both. My old friend Colin Gibson willingly shared secrets despite the temptation to hoard them for his own memoirs.

Alex Arnall proved a very able researcher, as did Oliver Brown.

William Lewis (then of the *Sunday Times*, now Editor of the *Daily Telegraph*), Jonathan Nortcroft, and Sam Wallace were all exceeding helpful.

Ed Dudley, son of my great friend Nigel, proved both a great cook and a very diligent researcher into Manchester United history. Unfortunately he died just as the book was being completed and it is impossible to convey the sense of loss I feel after a sudden illness laid waste this talented young man.

When I previously wrote about Manchester United I had the help of many people. They included Martin Liu, Martin Edwards, Maurice Watkins, David Gill, Peter Kenyon, John Bick, Ken Ramsden, Sir Bobby Charlton, Mike Edelson, Glenn Cooper, Edward and James Freedman, Keith Harris, Rupert Faure-Walker, David Blake, Greg Dyke, Mark Booth, Martin Stewart, Richard Campbell-Breeden, Tim Allen, Chris Haynes, Peter Leaver, Peter Robinson, Ian Stott, Irving Scholar, Sam Chisholm, Peter Hill-Wood, Danny Fiszman, Neil Bennett, Bodo Mueller, Lennart Johansson, Gerhard Aigner, Fritz Ahlstrom, Guido Tognoni, Patrick Cheney, Graham Kelly, Keith Wiseman, Geoff Thompson, Yasmin Waljee, Peter Crowther, Harry Harris, Michael Knighton, Michael Crick, Roger Brierley and his son, Paul Greengran, David Conn, David Mokades and Rod Dadak.

I have also benefited from the remarkable range of published material on the club. They include the Monopolies and Mergers Commission Report on the failed BSkyB takeover, the financial accounts, which are much more informative than that of most football clubs, and the many books that have been published in the last few years. These include Martin Hannan's *Rock of*

Gibraltar, Michael Crick's *The Boss*, Alex Ferguson's *Managing My Life*, Roy Keane's *Keane: The Autobiography*, John Carlin's *White Angels*, Jimmy Burns's *When Beckham Went To Spain*, David Beckham's *David Beckham: My Side*, Adam Brown and Andy Walsh's *Not for Sale*, Jeff Connor's *The Lost Babes*, Ned Kelly's *Manchester United: The Untold Story* and Eamon Dunphy's *A Strange Kind Of Glory*.

Graham Coster of Aurum Press has proved a very supportive publisher and ably marshalled a fine team. Steve Gove's assistance was also invaluable.

When I first wrote about Manchester United, Caroline Cecil was like Busby's hunt for the European Cup, a treasure I coveted but felt I could never have. But like Bubsy and Ferguson I succeeded and I cannot thank Caroline Bose enough or her marvellous support team led by Melinda Scott-Manderson.

Prologue

THE TERMINATOR ARRIVES AT OLD TRAFFORD

ON FRIDAY 12 November 2004, Manchester United held their annual general meeting at Old Trafford.

In ordinary circumstances the fans should have come to the meeting in good heart, confident that Manchester United were once more the best in England after what for them had been a poor two years. With no Premiership title since 2003, they were eliminated in the first knockout stage of the Champions League by AC Milan. While they had won the FA Cup in 2004 by vanquishing Millwall, it was by their standards a poor consolation.

Then, just two weeks before the board meeting, had come a historic victory over Arsenal, the reigning Premier League champions. Arsenal had arrived at Old Trafford in a record 49-match unbeaten run stretching back to the previous season and were being compared to historic club sides of English football. Beforehand the critics had written off Manchester United's season. But, in a match marked by many controversial moments, United beat the champions 2–0.

The rancour generated in the match spilled over into the tunnel after the match, resulting in 'the battle of the buffet'. As Arsène Wenger and Alex Ferguson confronted each other, somebody from behind Wenger threw pizza, sandwiches and soup from the players' buffet at Ferguson, leaving an ugly red blotch on his shirt, which he had to change before giving his post-match television interview.

But if the victory showed the fans that the old combative Manchester United was back, they came to the AGM full of foreboding. For two years their beloved manager Sir Alex Ferguson, who had brought them so much success, had been at war with the club's major shareholders, Cubic Expression, owned by Irish businessmen John Magnier and J.P. McManus, more famous for their involvement in horse racing than football. Their 28.9 per cent holding had made them the kingmakers of Old Trafford and their battle with Ferguson over the stud rights of the horse Rock of Gibraltar had been so bruising that it had dragged the fans into the argument. During the dispute the Irish had attacked the Manchester United board on a broad front and by raising several issues of how Manchester United was governed and its relations with agents had forced the board to change the way it ran the plc, making disclosures on agents fees that no other club had ever made.

By the winter of 2004 Ferguson's quarrels with the Irish had been settled, but now the fans had a more deadly worry. Another, even more disturbing stranger was threatening their club. What was worse, this stranger was not from over the Irish Sea but from across the Atlantic. Fans knew nothing about him. He had never set foot in Old Trafford. They had never heard from him what his intentions were for United, all they knew was that he wanted to buy their club. They feared that it was United's reputation as the world's richest club that had attracted this predator. The most committed of these fans, who were also shareholders, promptly announced that 'Manchester United Is Not For Sale'. If this was somewhat illogical, given that United was a plc and anybody could buy its shares, it represented the mood of a vocal section of the fans that the club could not be bought – at least not by a man called Malcolm Glazer, whose main interest was a team called Tampa Bay Buccaneers playing the very different sport of American football. As a plc United was very different to Arsenal, say. United's shares were listed on the stock market and therefore offered for sale every day. All a buyer needed to do was ring a stockbroker. But to buy Arsenal's shares, most of them held by the directors, an approach would have to be made to an existing owner and the buying process was known as the matched bargain system where a buyer had to find a willing seller. Not so with United.

Even without such a background, the annual general meetings of football clubs are a curious anomaly. English clubs, unlike those in Spain or Holland, are – apart from Ajax – not owned by the members but are limited companies and can be owned by anybody with money. However, until 1983, this did not produce too many contradictions. Clubs were owned by all sorts of people, generally a local dignitary. Often the local brewer had a large shareholding, as at Ipswich and Oldham, but it did not matter. Under the rules of the Football Association, clubs were not allowed to pay dividends. So while there was always a social divide in football clubs – fans huddled in Victorian terraces smelling of urine while directors sat down in the club's boardroom for a pre-match three-course meal and the chairman parked his Rolls-Royce in front of the main stand – there was no great financial benefit in owning a club, apart from the status it gave the owners in their local community. All this changed in 1983 when Tottenham Hotspur's new owners, seeking money to cover the huge deficit created by a new stand, evaded the Football Association rule by forming a plc which then owned the football club.

The plc was floated on the Stock Exchange. While the Tottenham Hotspur Football and Athletics Club continued to exist, the plc which owned it could behave like any other public company. Other clubs followed the tactic

Tottenham had used, Manchester United copying them in 1991. For fans who saw a football club as part of their extended family, an essential part of their community, there was a new, hitherto unsuspected alien in their world: shareholders from far and wide who owned the plc and expected the club to behave like other plcs. For these shareholders football was no longer a game but a product. These plcs no longer talked of fans but of customers whose needs for products and services had to be catered for.

Many fans who had become shareholders never took to the plc concept. Some Tottenham fans who had bought a few shares in the plc, not as an investment but merely for sentimental reasons – many hung the share certificate in their bathrooms – actually returned their first, small dividend cheques, saying the club should have the money and use it to build a fund to buy players.

Before the arrival of the plc, football club AGMs had been genial affairs in which a benevolent owner surrounded by the manager and coaching staff talked to a few shareholders. Now they were no longer such anodyne affairs but an occasion for the fan-shareholders to express hostility towards the board. AGMs inevitably saw such fans venting their venom at what they regarded as fat cats, overpaid directors only interested in how they could make more money for themselves and their shareholders. This made running such clubs a very uneasy balance. To the shareholders the directors were trying to run the club as a business, promoting the success of the company in the interests of the shareholders. But if, for instance, this led to keeping ticket prices high, fans became angry as they wanted to keep them as low as possible.

Manchester United had tried to square the circle by claiming they were running a successful football club and a successful business. In his chairman's statement for the 2004 accounts, headlined 'Running a Football Club as a Business', Sir Roy Gardner, pictured in braces and wearing horn-rimmed glasses, had talked of treating 'our fans as customers, offering them a good match day experience, and a range of additional products and services which meets their interests'. The report concluded:

Manchester United has built a sound business on the heritage of a great football club and its unique record of success under Sir Alex Ferguson. This year, once again, our committed and loyal staff have worked tirelessly to deliver the high expectations of our fans and partners. This combined with our proven financial discipline and prudent management of the cash generated by the business should continue to provide long term growth for shareholders and further playing success for our fans.

In contrast, United's rivals, who were also plcs but did not have large outside investors, tried to play down their business aspects, pretending that they were still old-fashioned football clubs. The manager attended the AGM, the formal part of the plc business was kept brief and most of the meeting converted into a fans' forum. So after the directors had been re-elected, accounts approved, auditors reconfirmed and other required resolutions passed, the manager would answer questions from the fans about his buying and selling of players, team tactics and what was called the club's 'ambitions', in other words how he intended to win trophies for the club. A few days before Manchester United held their AGM on 12 November, this is exactly what had happened at Tottenham's meeting.

The formal part of the AGM took scarcely half an hour and the club used the occasion to unveil its new manager, Martin Jol. Most of the questions centred round how the new man was going to revive the lost glories of this once great club.

However, Manchester United from the beginning wanted to be different. Their plc was designed to stand comparison with the best listed on the stock market and there was no question of it becoming a fans' forum with Sir Alex Ferguson in attendance. Only once had they tried to break with this pattern. In 2002 Sir Roy, presiding over his first AGM as chairman, had thought it would be a good idea for Ferguson to attend and, after the meeting, take questions from fans. But far from producing harmony, Ferguson had become so annoyed by some of the questions he had faced from one shareholder that the poor man had been subjected to the sort of treatment the manager gave to players who upset him. United's board quickly decided to abandon the experiment.

So, as they approached the AGM, Sir Roy and the board knew they would have a tricky job balancing the interests of fans and shareholders. But their problems were made worse by the behaviour of one of the shareholders and the effect the board feared it would have on the fans. By this time Glazer had acquired 28.1 per cent of the shareholding and was the second biggest shareholder, a short head behind the Irish.

Sir Roy and the board should have been comforted by the way they appeared to have dealt with the Glazers. On 25 October, the day after the victory over Arsenal, the United board announced that it would not support a potential offer from Glazer as it would put the club too heavily into debt and was therefore not in the best interests of the company. The board had every reason to feel that this would put them on the right side of fans opposed to the Glazers. Had they not shown the Americans the door?

However, the board had not told the fans everything that was going on. The Glazers were still at the door furiously knocking to get in, and even after public rejection the board had been in constant dialogue with them.

For days after the 25 October statement telephone lines between the Glazers' home in Palm Beach and Old Trafford had been busy. David Gill, United's chief executive, had held long conversations with Joel, the son of Malcolm Glazer who was fronting the family's effort to buy the club. By now their investment in the club was well over £200 million. They could not sell their shares without incurring a huge loss and they were determined to persuade the board to co-operate with them.

What they wanted was simple: access to the underlying accounts and other financial documents so their experts could look at the numbers and work out the financing necessary to buy the club. Although the public impression was that the Glazers had already made an offer for the club, in fact they had merely discussed certain ways of financing a purchase and sought the board's approval. Access to the books was the key to their approach. In their 25 October statement the board had not disclosed this. But before they made public their rejection of the Glazer approach, they had privately told the Glazers they would not give them access to the books. In their telephone conversations Gill kept repeating this refusal. But the more he refused, the more determined the Glazers appeared.

It was in the middle of these transatlantic telephone calls that the AGM of 12 November came on the horizon. For the Glazers this was too good an opportunity to miss. Joel, and his brothers Avram, known as Avi, and Bryan – all three of whom were involved in buying United – were quick to see what a handy weapon it could prove. It did not take long for the three to decide that they would attend the AGM, not in person but by sending their lawyers armed with proxy cards enabling them to vote.

United first became aware of the Glazers' intentions on Monday 8 November, four days before the AGM. Sir Roy received a letter written by Andrew Ballheimer, managing partner of the London office of Allen & Overy, the law firm acting for the Glazers. Ballheimer told Sir Roy that he and his colleagues would turn up in person at the AGM as the Glazers' representatives and asked United's registrars to check that their proxy cards were in order so that they could use them to vote. The letter also sought reassurance from Manchester United regarding the conduct of the AGM, saying they expected United to continue their past practice of putting all resolutions to the vote by poll and not by a show of hands. This was a procedure tailor made for what the Glazers had in mind.

In most AGMs a resolution is first voted on by a show of hands. This means that a shareholder with one share who has one vote is in effect on a par with a shareholder who has millions of shares. Where everyone approves what is being proposed it does not matter. However, when there is a dispute, an investor with a large shareholding and keen to make his vote count has to stand up and demand a poll vote to give due weight to his shareholding. But when United became a plc they had adopted a rule whereby voting on all resolutions was done by a poll. At the end of the meeting shareholders went to a table where the registrars of the company were sitting and dropped their poll cards into a ballot box. As each card indicated the number of shares the person held, a Glazer holding 28.1 per cent would easily be able to outvote the small shareholders. The United rule would prove very useful for the Glazer representatives, keen to vote but preferring not have to get up and demand a poll vote, thus identifying themselves to a potentially hostile meeting.

If the Allen & Overy letter clearly indicated to the club that there was some nervousness on the part of the Glazers' representatives about being identified at the AGM, it also worried United. They had been told by Manchester Police that there would be demands from fans at the AGM for the Glazers' representatives to stand up and show themselves. If this happened, the anger felt by some fans towards the Glazers might erupt and there could well be a riot.

The board was well aware of how explosive the situation was. Some fans were even threatening a form of urban terrorism against the Glazers. Much is made of the admirable passion the English show for their national game, but this can easily boil over into violence. By now the very word 'Glazers' had many United fans foaming at the mouth. Some of the Glazers' advisers had already been badly mauled. Days after it emerged that they were advising the Americans, J.P. Morgan, their merchant banking adviser, had felt the wrath of the fans. Their offices had been bombarded with hundreds of pizza deliveries and a succession of taxis turned up, claiming they had been booked. These were the polite, even humorous, forms of harassment. In addition less pleasant items had been delivered – condoms, tampons, soiled nappies, even excrement.

Brunswick, the PR firm hired by J.P. Morgan, had a skip delivered outside their offices in London's Lincoln Inn filled with rubbish, pizza delivery men turned up with unwanted pizza orders so did plumbers saying they had been summoned to do work and Brunswick even had to close their website down for a time. Some of the Brunswick men did go to Old Trafford pretending to be ordinary fans although they were probably lucky that the hard core fans at the Stretford End did not recognise them. Paul Ridley, the former *Sun* editor, who had been employed by Brunswick as a specialist sports consultant, was bombarded with so many calls on his mobile phone that he had to change his number. The fans had not subjected Allen & Overy to quite such intense harassment. Unlike Brunswick they did not have to close down their website. Iain Rodger, head of the firm's PR, still had his details on the site, including a photograph. Inevitably his office and secretary began to receive streams of angry, often abusive, telephone calls.

Measures were taken to screen e-mails. If probably 95 per cent were from genuine Manchester United fans who cared for their club and thought the

Glazer takeover was a very bad thing, there were also some very hostile, even threatening, ones. The advisers had also taken other suitable precautions, making sure that the home addresses of the partners and directors, which would normally be listed in Companies House, were removed. For this they had to convince the police and the government that there could be physical danger to them if their addresses continued to be listed.

However, the address of one Manchester United director was well known to the fans, and he had felt the wrath of those who considered contact with the Glazers such a sin that it justified vandalism or even physical violence.

In June 2004 Maurice Watkins had sold some of his shares to the Glazers. As far as he was concerned he had asked his stockbroker to sell shares and the Glazers, looking for stock, had been eager buyers. In such a sale there is no contact between buyer and seller; Watkins did not even know the Glazers had bought his shares until some time after the deal was done. But for many fans it was as if he had stood on Busby Way (the road outside Old Trafford) and hawked his shares to the Americans. He was treated, not as the club's loyal legal adviser and its longest serving director, but as yet another person who had betrayed the club. Not long after the deal, as Watkins was relaxing one Sunday evening with his wife and son, his son spied some hooded intruders run into the driveway and spray paint on his father's Jaguar.

The fans were from a group calling themselves the Manchester Education Committee and openly exulted in their desire to take direct action against anybody who supported the Glazers. A year earlier, when the enemy were the Irish, this group had threatened to disrupt Cheltenham, the showpiece of the National Hunt season. The Glazers' arrival had made them threaten the sort of actions specialised in by animal rights campaigners. These had included an attempt to halt a United reserve team game by invading the pitch dressed in balaclavas and then burning an American flag. It was all part of their pledge to 'render the club ungovernable'.

It was against this background that the United board and its advisers began to assess what might happen at the AGM. The more they thought about it the more worried they got. None more so than Mark Rawlinson, a partner at the law firm Freshfields, who specialised in mergers and acquisitions and had been advising the club for the last year.

Rawlinson, then a forty-six-year-old lawyer, had been born in Manchester and attended Manchester Grammar for a year before his parents moved south. But the club was in his blood: 'I was indoctrinated by my grandfather into Manchester United. I was taken to my first match at the age of ten into what was then called the Cantilever Stand and that was in the days of George Best and Bobby Charlton.'

However until 2003 Rawlinson remained a fan who cherished such associations with the club that came his way. So having seen Paddy Crerand play in the great Busby side of the 1960s he sat next to Crerand that night in Barcelona in 1999 when United won the Champions League, a moment he cherishes with great pride. At that time Rupert Murdoch, with the blessing of the board, was seeking to buy the club and the board was being advised by Rawlinson's partner Tim Emmerson on how to get the deal past the Monopolies and Mergers Commission.

By the winter of 2003 Rawlinson started getting interested professionally in the club. Emmerson had left to join another firm, Millbank, Tweed, Hadley and McCloy, which was just as well since the two men had a reputation for not getting on. Rawlinson now targeted Manchester United with all the thoroughness that Sir Alex Ferguson might to get a player he covets. Rawlinson recalls:

> It came about because of a combination of things. One I saw that the Irish had taken a stake and there started to be speculation about a bid from the Irish, I did a memorandum on preparing for a bid, how to react to it. But I did not know David Gill. I found someone who knew Gill, Rod Carlton (part of Freshfields competition team that had advised Manchester United in 1998). I got David's e-mail address and sent off the memo. I followed it up in two ways. One was with Michael Gradon who was a great mate of mine at P & O (director of commercial and legal affairs). He knew Maurice Watkins. I got Michael to put in a very good word for me with Maurice. The third omen was that I heard that Cazenove (one of the City's most highly regarded investment bankers with an expertise in take-overs) had been called in to help Manchester United. And the guy there who was doing this, I found out, was David Anderson, who used to be at Lazards. I knew David well so again I got him to put in a good word for me. And eventually I got invited along to a board meeting in Centrica's offices in London, where Sir Roy Gardner was chief executive. Although the Glazers were around, I was first called in to deal with the Irish when the Irish started to cause all the trouble after their falling out with Ferguson over the race horse.

Now Rawlinson's focus had shifted to the Glazers and, in the days leading up to 12 November, as the board considered Ballheimer's letter, Rawlinson's great worry was that Ballheimer might identify himself as the Glazers' lawyer at the AGM. Surely all hell would break loose.

On the afternoon of 11 November Rawlinson rang Ballheimer, whom he knew from a deal they had worked on together in Norway back in 1993. However he could not get hold of him and ended up speaking to Joe Greenan, Allen & Overy's head of security. (Rawlinson would later discover that at that moment Ballheimer was on the train to Manchester.)

Greenan, as it happened, was in Prague, addressing a seminar on security and with his thoughts far away from Old Trafford. He had spent nearly a quarter of a century as a military policeman, carrying out surveillance work, investigating drug dealers and protecting VIPs, government ministers, a prime minister during a G8 summit and members of the royal family, before being hired by Allen & Overy to deal with anti-globalisation protests and May Day violence directed at the City.

Rawlinson recalls: 'I said to him, "Look, Man U is handling this very professionally. Turn up at head office ahead of the meeting, we'll get you into the general meeting early, we'll find you seats by an exit, we won't draw attention to you at the meeting. Make sure your car's parked close by so you can get out." The last thing Manchester United wanted was for someone to get hurt.'

Not surprisingly, Greenan wanted assurances from Rawlinson and Beswitherick that Allen & Overy were not going to be identified. 'Don't worry,' said Rawlinson. 'No way is it going to happen. But get there early.'

By Thursday night Rawlinson was himself in Manchester and had fulfilled one of his greatest dreams. Despite the impending gloom cast by the Glazers, Rawlinson could savour the occasion. He had been advising the board for over a year, but this was the first occasion he had been invited to a meeting in the boardroom of the club he had supported since he was a child. Previous meetings had been at the offices of Centrica, where Gardner was chief executive, either in London or Windsor. He recalls his first sight of the boardroom: 'There was a big central oval table with Sir Roy sitting in the centre and many rectangular tables alongside with the advisers seated around them. Apart from me there were David Anderson and Patrick McGee from Cazenove as the advisers at the meeting. In addition, of course, there were the board members, both the executives and non-executive directors.'

Rawlinson went through the ten resolutions that were to be put to the meeting and considered what the consequences would be if the Glazers or the Irishmen voted against a particular resolution. They might, for example, vote not to pay dividends. Later that night Rawlinson, along with the representatives from Cazenove and Finsbury, the PR firm advising Manchester United, and Manchester United's own-in-house PR man Phil Townsend, retired to the Lowry Hotel.

After they had checked in, Rawlinson contacted Ballheimer, Greenan having given him Ballheimer's mobile number. By this time Ballheimer's team had got to Manchester and taken up residence at the Radisson SAS, having considered and then rejected staying at the Lowry. They had also been joined by Greenan who had hurriedly flown back from Prague.

Rawlinson made it clear to Ballheimer that the club would do nothing to frustrate the Glazer lawyers in their mission and was very anxious that it should be a smooth, low key AGM. However, he also wanted reassurance that the Glazers' representatives would not be provocative: 'There will not be a show of hands, we will put all the resolutions to the poll as we normally do. But please do not stand up and make a speech. Keep a low profile. The board is very concerned about having a riot on their hands.'

But, if this dealt with the security fears, what United did not know was how the Glazers were going to vote. They knew the Glazers were determined to vote – so determined that they had proxies in the names of the three Allen & Overy lawyers in case anything happened to one of them. Proxies had been obtained and transfers made in the names of Ballheimer, fellow partner Richard Hough and associate Ed Barnett.

Like most companies, every Manchester United AGM saw some directors retire and others stand for re-election. This time the board proposed to re-elect two existing non-executive directors, Maurice Watkins and Philip Yea. Chief executive of 3i, Yea was chairman of the audit committee and was considered, as the annual accounts put it, to be United's 'senior independent director'. The board also proposed to elect a new executive director, Andy Anson, who had been appointed commercial director earlier that year.

In the previous few days the board had heard that the Glazers intended to vote against the resolutions that would be put to the meeting. Rawlinson recalls: 'In order to get the financing to buy Manchester United they had to have due diligence on the company. They told us that if we didn't give them the information they wanted then they were going to vote against certain resolutions.'

But, while Joel had held out this threat, what the board did not know was how far the Glazers would go. Would they stop at voting off just the three directors or would they vote against all other matters before the AGM? Would they vote against approving the accounts? Against the reappointment of the auditors, PricewaterhouseCoopers? These were issues that had to be approved in order for the company to operate.

There was also another great worry for the board. In the weeks preceding the AGM there had been contact between the Glazers and the Irish. Had the two shareholders, who between them had a clear majority – 58 per cent of the share capital – got together secretly and decided to vote the entire board off? This was Rawlinson's biggest fear: 'I was always more worried that they would not just vote off the three directors but change the whole board. Vote all the directors off, appoint their own directors. Then, instead of having to offer £3 a share to buy the club, they could appoint a new board and just take over the company.'

In fact the Glazer camp was divided on what they should do. Rawlinson and Cazenove had picked up an inkling of this division when they heard City rumours that the advisers had strongly told the Glazers not to pick a fight with the board. Rawlinson told me: 'I had heard of various conversations between the Glazer advisers in the run-up to the annual general meeting, on the lines of, "You guys, you cannot be serious. If you vote the directors off this then becomes very aggressive, very confrontational. It makes it a state of war."'

The rumours that J.P. Morgan and Brunswick advised the Glazers not to vote against the board were to prove correct. Some time that evening J.P. Morgan's Henry Lloyd had made it very clear to Ballheimer that if the Glazers did so J.P. Morgan might have to stand down.

But this advice clearly cut little ice with the Glazers. They had a major investment in Manchester United and the management were not taking them seriously. The board needed to be told who owned the company. The United board might propose but the Glazers would dispose. Yet the Glazers wanted to choose their targets carefully.

As the second biggest shareholder, they were certainly big enough to launch a full-scale war. They could, if they so desired, oppose the approval of the accounts or the reappointment of the auditors. But they knew that if they succeeded they would throw United into chaos, affecting the day-to-day running of the club and jeopardising their £200 million investment in the company. They wanted to flex their muscles, but not go so far as to stop the club from functioning.

As they looked at the agenda of the AGM, they found it more attractive to concentrate on some softer but telling targets. The vote against the three directors was a power play to prove to the board who was boss. They were also much taken by voting against a resolution allowing the board to buy back the company's shares. A routine measure that would normally pass on the nod, were this approved it would enable the board to reduce the number of shares available in the marketplace, affecting the Glazers' ability to buy the club when they finally launched their bid.

The Glazers must have been bemused that their intentions were causing such anguish for their British advisers. In the more robust corporate world of the USA, such power plays would be considered routine. In any case, as the Glazers saw it, if they voted Watkins and company off, it did not mean they would have to leave the boardroom. The articles of Manchester United allowed the board to reappoint them until the next AGM. However, even at this late hour, the board had one last chance to prevent a hostile vote. All it needed to do was open the books to the Glazers.

In his conversations with Ballheimer Rawlinson had picked up the clear hint that if the board gave due diligence the Glazers would cause no trouble at the AGM. When Rawlinson asked Ballheimer, 'What will it take you not to vote against?', Ballheimer replied, 'I don't know but I think access for due diligence.'

Rawlinson explored this possibility with the board but late on Thursday night he rang back to say: 'Sorry, the board cannot give access.'

'What will change their minds?' asked Ballheimer.

'I am not sure,' said Rawlinson, 'Perhaps if the Irish asked us as well.'

Rawlinson's answer showed the crucial role John Magnier and J.P. McManus played in this Manchester United drama.

The Glazers had already been in contact with them and tried to get them to put pressure on the board to grant them due diligence. The Irish had not obliged. Now the board wanted them to endorse the Glazers' request. This would have enabled the board to tell the fans that they had to let the Glazers in to see the books; the biggest shareholder, one the fans already hated, had said so. But the Irish were not keen to play the board's game either: they were just as keen as the board to avoid being blamed by the fans.

But, although the board had failed to get the Irish to take responsibility for opening the books, it hoped instead to get them to vote in its favour and help defeat the Glazers. Indeed, as Rawlinson probed Ballheimer to establish the Glazers' intentions, the board was waiting for a sign from across the Irish Sea that the Irish would ride to its rescue. If they sided with the board, then with the help of other shareholders the board could defeat the Glazers with something to spare. If they sided with the Glazers, it was game over before the match had started. The Glazers would win even if the Irish abstained. Since it is almost unheard of for anything like 100 per cent of shareholders to vote, the Glazers' 28.1 per cent was effectively worth well over 50 per cent and would give them mastery of the meeting.

The Irish were amused by the turnaround in their fortunes. Even a few months earlier they had been the bête noire of the board and the fans. In fact, in the midst of United's Irish war the board had courted the Glazers in the hope they might provide a check on the Irish. But now it was keen to get the Irish back on its side.

However, in all the years since they became shareholders of Manchester United, the Irish had never attended an AGM. In fact, neither Magnier nor McManus had ever visited Old Trafford. This, of course, gave ammunition to fans who could mock them as a pair of horse traders who knew nothing about football and had no right to belong at their club. True, Magnier had never missed a Manchester United match on television, but the Irish saw their buying of United shares as an investment pure and simple. As with all their investment decisions, they left it to their two trusted advisers: the chartered accountant Eddie Irwin and the lawyer John Power. These two had been to Old Trafford, met the board and seen matches. But even they did not turn up for AGMs.

Not that this was an act of hostility. If anything they supported the board. Their practice was to send their proxy in favour of the board to David

Beswitherick a few days before the AGM, which meant the board knew the votes were in the bag even before the meeting started. That was what the board was hoping would happen again this time.

A few days before the AGM, Nick Humby, United's finance director, rang John Power at his offices in Kilmallock. Humby in some ways was the odd one out on the United board. While every other United director proudly broadcast their love and support for Manchester United Humby made no secret of the fact that he was a Southampton supporter. A former finance director and chief operating officer at Pearson Television he had joined United in January 2002 as Group Finance Director, six months after Gill had been made Group Managing Director. Now he asked Power, 'We have not received your proxy yet. Could we expect it soon?'

Power smiled as he heard the question. The question reminded him of what happened a year earlier, at the previous AGM. Then, despite the fact that the Irish were unhappy with many aspects of how the board ran the company, they had given their proxy to the board. Soon after that they were involved in public rows; a letter was written raising issues about corporate governance, conflicts of interest, the relationship between the club and agents, and the role of both Ferguson and Watkins. Humby had tartly commented that he could not understand why the Irish were raising all these questions. At the last annual general meeting they had given the board the proxy and approved the accounts without any questions. His implication was clear: if they had so many questions about how the company was run and the payments being made to agents, surely they should not have voted in favour of the accounts. Once they had done so they did not have the right to question anything.

Now, as Power listened to Humby's plea for the Irish proxy, those comments came back to him. Yes, he acknowledged the proxy had not been sent. As to whether it would be sent, he let the question hang in the air.

Contrary to board fears about a stitch-up between the Irish and the Glazers, there had been no contact between the two before the AGM. However, intermediaries had told the Glazers that the Irish were likely to abstain. While this was reassuring for the Glazers, they were untroubled as to whether they won or not. The very fact that the board was scrambling round to get the Irish on side told them a lot. It meant that without them the board was powerless. And if, at the last minute, the Irish did come to the rescue of the board, it meant the board were totally dependent on them. For the Glazers this was a devastating conclusion, pointing clearly to where power lay at Old Trafford.

It was well past two on the morning of Friday, late evening at Palm Beach, when the three Glazer brothers decided exactly what they would do. They would vote against Watkins, Yea and Anson and against allowing the board to buy back Manchester United shares.

How were the Glazer lawyers going to get to Old Trafford? A few days before the AGM, Iain Rodgers had a chat with Ballheimer and Hough and gained the impression that they expected to take a taxi to Old Trafford, then after the vote stroll along Busby Way and hail a taxi back to the airport. This was clearly not a sensible idea, and with Greenan taking the lead, it was decided that secure transport had to be arranged. A Mercedes minibus was chosen because it looked thoroughly inconspicuous. Very careful attention was paid to who might drive it. A man was chosen who had experience of going into hostile areas and coming out again. He had worked with the police in sensitive cases, in particular for child protection agencies where he had to turn up on a council estate and take someone's child away.

In the morning Rawlinson rang Ballheimer again: 'On a personal level he was very worried. Yes, he was nervous, but so would you have been had you been there.' Ballheimer and his colleagues wanted to damage the board, and the board would resist that as best as it could. But Rawlinson reassured him that the courtesies of corporate life would be observed. Neither the board nor its advisers wanted the Glazer representatives to come to any physical harm. The club were keen to impress on the Glazers that they would behave in an utterly professional manner. However much they might disagree with their decision, the board would in effect help the Glazers in their mission to vote against it.

Of course none of this contact between the Glazers' advisers and the board leaked out to the fans. Had it done so it would have caused an enormous explosion among the activists. But this demonstration of the bond between the two sets of professionals indicated yet another fascinating aspect of the battle. It was a game being played according to its own special City rules. Each side knew what the other was doing. On the day of the meeting there were to be no surprises, and both were keen to insulate themselves from the passion of the fans.

The AGM was meant to start at 11 a.m. As Rawlinson had suggested, Allen & Overy's Mercedes minibus drew up almost three hours earlier and Rawlinson, Beswitherick and the head of United's own security met them at the main entrance by the side of the megastore. Soon they all went up to the Manchester Suite, where the AGM was to be held.

On match days the suite is used for entertaining and is divided into two dining rooms by closing the door in the middle. But for the AGM this was thrown open, revealing the room to be a huge hall. It is so large that people seated at the back of the hall cannot see the directors seated on the podium at the other end of it, and television screens relay pictures of the action. The room seats around 1,500. Everyone knew the AGM would be full. It was quickly decided that Allen & Overy's lawyers would sit near one of the two exits to avoid having to go through crowds if there was trouble. The nearest exit led down the stairs and out on to a side street where the Mercedes minibus was parked and waiting with its engine running. Allen & Overy's proxy forms were checked and found to be in order, and they were signed in. At one stage there was a mini-crisis when nobody could see Ballheimer and there were fears for his safety. It turned out he had gone to the loo.

Under United's poll system, all voting was done at the end of the meeting. At one end of the Manchester Suite, past the podium occupied by the board, were long tables where the company registrars sat. After the meeting, when all the resolutions had been discussed, the shareholders filed past and dropped their poll cards in the boxes provided. The cards were counted and the result declared some time later. Had the Glazers been treated like any other shareholder then, at the end of the meeting, the Allen & Overy lawyers would have had to follow the crowd out of the room and register their vote. This procedure clearly had its dangers, particularly if Ballheimer and his colleagues were recognised as Glazer's men. So it was agreed that, if the Glazer men kept quiet during the meeting, then United would allow them to use their proxy cards and vote in advance. Before the start of the AGM, Ballheimer and his colleagues dropped their four poll cards totalling 17 million shares into the boxes. Even before the meeting began, before the board had taken their seats on the podium, enough votes had been cast to remove Watkins, Yea and Anson from the plc board and to defeat the motion to buy the shares.

Now the Glazer lawyers could relax and take in the meeting. As soon as it was over, while the crowds gravitated towards the ballot boxes to vote, they could slip down the stairs to safety. The militant fans would have been horrified had they known about it, but United were living up to Rawlinson's promise to be very professional.

But why did the Allen & Overy lawyers not leave after voting? Why did they stay on for a meeting which was now an academic exercise, one which held potential dangers for them if they were identified? The reason was that AGMs can be unpredictable affairs. For all United's professionalism, there could be no guarantee that the board would stick to the agreed script once the meeting began. If the script was not followed, an intervention might be necessary. Ballheimer might have to stand up in the Glazer interests and identify himself. There was another powerful reason for staying. No one knew how the fans would react to what the board was saying. That would be useful ammunition for the Glazers. They might have won the AGM battle but knew they still had the war to win. And, for at least two members of Ballheimer's team, Ed Barnett, a fervent Liverpool fan, and David Johnson, the associate from Manchester, and an equally devoted Preston North End fan, there was the added excitement and thrill of being at a football AGM, and a Manchester United AGM at that.

Around ten o'clock the doors to the Manchester Suite were opened to the public and the fans started trickling in. Some were in suits, most casually dressed. Those in suits congregated near each other, as if for protection, so the Allen & Overy men in their chosen spot were surrounded by men who mostly looked like them.

As the Glazer lawyers observed the meeting, on the floor below the United board, along with its advisers, met in the Platinum Suite as they always did before an AGM. This time, though, they looked and sounded like men who knew their future had been decided. Maurice Watkins, a director of the football club since 1984, a member of the plc board since 1991 and a legal adviser to the club since 1977, now faced the humiliation of being booted off the board he had done so much to create and sustain. Rawlinson, however, was excited when he followed the board up to the Manchester Suite to attend his very first AGM. 'It was theatre, but it was also a very intimidating atmosphere.'

The atmosphere at this AGM was very different, and not only because of the Glazer factor. Ever since United had floated back in 1991 the club's AGMs had been dominated by two men. One was no longer on the board and not present, the other was now dead. Martin Edwards had been the most powerful share-holder of the club, the chief executive of the plc and the chairman of the football club. Sir Roland Smith had been brought to the club as the non-executive chairman of the plc by Edwards himself when United floated and it was felt necessary to have a figure at the head who would inspire confidence in the City.

In their different ways, both men played decisive roles in the making of the modern United. The AGMs demonstrated their contrasting roles. Edwards, the chief executive, was the bête noire of the fans, known derisively by many as the butcher's boy. This was a reference to the fact that his father Louis owned a butcher's business; it was from Louis, United's owner, that Edwards had acquired much of his substantial shareholding. The fans saw Edwards as a money grabber who did not care for the club and had even tried to sell it. Smith, in contrast, although an archetypal City man, was the showman of the AGM, often using it to poke fun at Edwards himself.

Jim White of the *Daily Telegraph*, who is also a fan, paints a riveting picture of those Smith–Edwards AGMs: 'Smith was brilliant. He would make jokes about Martin Edwards and his love of money. I remember him saying, "Martin Edwards is coming up on the train counting his money." This always got a great laugh from the floor. He was very good at turning the audience.'

Now Smith and Edwards had gone. Smith's replacement, Sir Roy Gardner, was a fine City man, but he did not have command of the meeting in the same way as Smith. And the fans had a new hate figure in the Glazers. As he listened to the speeches, Rawlinson was glad that the Allen & Overy partners were sitting unidentified near an exit, 'Because there might well have been some people who might have attacked them physically . . . There were thousands of people very pumped up, very hostile people with big biceps and tattoos, wearing

Manchester United shirts and shouting, "Would the Glazers stand up?" Even one elderly man said, "I'll take my coat off and let's go outside." There was quite a lot of hostility to the Glazer representatives and a lot of speeches were directed at the Glazers.'

Rawlinson felt a lot of sympathy for the harassed chairman. 'Sir Roy had a really heavy cold. He was croaking, poor bloke, so he was under the weather. I felt really sorry for him because it was a big day and a difficult meeting to control.' Some of the fans even mocked Gardner's accent, which in the setting sounded rather posh. He was asked a question by a shareholder and said, 'Sorry, I did not quite catch that.' The shareholder responded, 'If you could understand my accent then maybe you would have understood it. Perhaps you should fuck off back to London, you're just a City fat cat.'

One observer at the meeting, a rugby fan who had limited contact with football, was attending his first AGM: 'There were several occasions when a speaker would say, "Mr Glazer's representatives, we understand they are here, please get up and identify yourselves." Shouts of "Identify yourself, Glazer." Shouts of "If you hate Glazers stand up." That was when my antennae were up. They said it on two or three occasions. I was struck by how extremely hostile they were to the board. They were seen, for whatever reasons, if not condoning the Glazer bid, as at least entertaining it. One director [Maurice Watkins] who had sold shares to the Glazers got a very hard time.'

Watkins' name had been booed when Gardner read the names of the direction seeking re-election. The entire board sat stony faced.

After two hours, with more rousing anti-Glazer speeches, the meeting was finally over and those in the Manchester Suite, having vented their feelings, got up to vote. This was the cue for the Allen & Overy lawyers and Greenan quietly to leave.

As the lawyers flew back to London or to a partners' meeting in Amsterdam, the board was dealing with the Glazer vote. The outside world still did not know the damage the Glazers had inflicted on the board; the registrars were meant to be counting the votes cast and would give the information some time in the afternoon. But as soon as the meeting ended the board knew. After the meeting, according to Rawlinson, they asked David Beswitherick whether the Irish had voted: 'He said the Irish didn't put in their votes so we knew they hadn't voted. The poll card with 20 odd million, the number of their shares, was not there.'

Back in the Platinum Suite the directors and advisers had a hearty meal. On such days United provided a buffet, a cooked lunch, a choice of fish and chips or some beef dish and coffee and mints, outside the main boardroom. They then drafted a statement that would go out with the results, designed to explain to an unsuspecting public why the board had lost, while putting them in the best possible light with the fans. In its statement of 25 October, the board had explained why they did not like the heavy debt burden the Glazers planned to put on the company. This time they would reveal that the Glazer action was retaliation for the board not allowing them to look at the books. The board was presented as working for the good of the club, trying to control a gang of wild children who had not got their way. Rawlinson says: 'We went back to our 25 October announcement that the board had undertaken discussions with the Glazers about the capital structure because we felt the proposed capital structure was not right and therefore terminated discussions. We also said they had continued to press for access to confidential information about the company, and had made it clear that if they were not granted the ability to carry out due diligence, then they were going to vote down the board members.'

In this gloom one thing gave the board comfort. This was that the Glazers' action had been opposed by their own advisers. Indeed, sometime in late afternoon, soon after David Beswitherick brought in the figures of the poll vote, it emerged that both J.P. Morgan and Brunswick had resigned. Allen & Overy, however, had supported the Glazers' move and now in a little-noticed statement, they announced that they still represented the Glazers and had no intention of walking away. Despite this it was reported in many places, including the *Sunday Times*, that Allen & Overy too had resigned. Headlines such as 'US tycoon Malcolm Glazer has been left with no friends or advisers in his bid to take control of the football giant' were testimony to how successfully the law firm had kept its involvement with the Glazers out of the public eye.

The resignations of the merchant banking adviser and the PR team helped the United board spin the story. A defeat was made to look like a victory, and the next day most of the media presented the AGM as a colossal defeat for Glazer. United's spin convinced the press. Jason Nisse in the *Independent* pictured Glazer's hopeless plight:

> He is sitting on shares in Man U that were worth around £210m on Friday night and have cost him about £160m to buy. Without J.P. Morgan, he will find it difficult to bid for Man U. He might be able to find another bank but the chances are pretty slim. Friday's actions marked Mr Glazer out as a 'rogue elephant' and investment banks don't like clients whom they can't control.

Under the headline 'Glazer scores own goal over Man Utd move', the *Financial Times* said, 'Malcolm Glazer's planned takeover of Manchester United appeared to be in tatters on Friday after J.P. Morgan, the investment bank prepared to fund most of the US sports tycoon's planned £700m-plus bid, abruptly resigned. The departure was swiftly followed by the resignation of Brunswick, Mr Glazer's public relations adviser, and came after a turbulent annual shareholders' meeting in Manchester.'

Shareholders United spokesman Oliver Houston claimed: 'This underlines the case against Malcolm Glazer. Apart from the supporters, the board and John Magnier and J.P. McManus, even his own bankers and spin machine are against him now. He has few friends or options but, like a wild animal, Glazer is often most dangerous when he is cornered. We must make sure he is put down once and for all.'

Rawlinson did not share the view that the loss of J.P. Morgan meant the Glazers had lost all hope of getting any advisers to mount a bid but he was consoled that the United board had stopped the Glazer steamroller: 'They didn't have anywhere to go, they had 29 per cent of this company that they had overpaid for, they couldn't sell. They'd have taken a thumping great loss if they'd sold it. They had somehow or another to get control of that company. But they had no Plan B.' However, he also realised that the Glazers hadn't gone away, 'they were like the Terminator, always reforming'. Indeed, even as the press wrote off the Glazers, they were forming their own plans. In little over six weeks they had new backers and a new plan that they were confident would succeed.

But what was it about Manchester United that made it so irresistible to the Americans and other buyers? Let us draw back and look at what has made Manchester United, and how over the years it has successfully reinvented itself.

PART ONE

The New Red Devils:
The Men Who Remade
Manchester United

1

THE HEAVY BURDEN OF GLORY

THE MANCHESTER UNITED inheritance is summed up in one name: Matt Busby. Before he arrived at Old Trafford the club was nothing, after him it was set on a path to glory which others, who have come in his wake, have struggled to emulate.

The way the story is told, there was darkness before Busby came. He said 'Let there be light' and Old Trafford has been bathed in glory ever since. Even in official histories of Manchester United, the period between 1878 and 1945, the year of Busby's arrival, can at times be dismissed in a single paragraph.

But as with all faiths, there are dissenters who say that the light Busby shed on Old Trafford has been tarnished by the greed and avarice of the money men. The dissenters' campaign is to restore the Busby philosophy. They acknowledge that Sir Alex Ferguson has created a halo of his own, but while it may shine almost as bright as Busby's, it will never quite match it. Michael Crick, the first and most persistent critic of Martin Edwards and the money culture he introduced, acknowledges that Ferguson's record is statistically better than Busby's – under Matt Busby United won only eight trophies in twenty-four years. But Crick writes, 'Busby's legacy is much wider, not only in founding the modern Manchester United but also as a pioneer of the post-war game.' For Crick and other critics, Edwards and his family are held to have usurped the Busby legacy and ruined it.

Like all myths, Busby's is only partly true. United had started life in 1878 as Newton Heath Lancashire and Yorkshire Railway Company Cricket and Football Club (known as Newton Heath LYR). The name was changed to Manchester United in 1902 and the club moved to Old Trafford in 1910. Much of its early existence was undistinguished. In the opinion of Eamon Dunphy, a biographer of Busby, the club was a pre-war music hall joke. It had not even been one of the twelve founders of the Football League, although six of the twelve clubs were from Lancashire: Preston North End, Burnley, Accrington, Blackburn Rovers, Bolton Wanderers and Everton.

Even after Newton Heath changed its name to Manchester United, its fortunes did not change much. There were isolated moments of glory: United won the League championship in 1908 and 1911 and the FA Cup in 1909. In between, on Saturday 19 February 1910, the club moved to Old Trafford, a ground whose lush green carpet received rave notices in the press. For the first game against Liverpool there were 50,000 paying customers, while another 5,000 got in without paying. The *Manchester Guardian* reported that such scenes had never before been seen.

But this was fleeting fame. Even as United fans celebrated, they lost the man who had made the success possible. Ernest Mangnall, the manager who brought the trophies, soon moved across the city to Manchester City. The club had exhausted its resources in building Old Trafford – and, worse still, there was a match-fixing scandal.

On Good Friday, 2 April 1915, with United facing relegation, they played Liverpool who were secure in mid table. Two days before the game some players met in Manchester's Dog and Partridge pub and decided that Liverpool would lose the match 2–0. The match, played in driving rain, saw just that result as an apathetic Liverpool allowed United to score two goals. However, fans were incensed and a bookie, smelling a rat, refused to pay. The FA investigated and Jackie Sheldon of Liverpool confessed. Nine players were suspended, including several from United. United's Enoch 'Knocker' West did not have his suspension lifted until 1945, when he was sixty-two.

The inter-war years saw the club relegated three times to the Second Division. In 1934 they missed relegation to the Third only when, against the odds, they unexpectedly won the last match of the season at Millwall. Between the wars the club spent as much time in the Second as the First Division.

In the early 1900s the club had been saved from bankruptcy by J.H. Davies, a rich Manchester businessman who behaved in an autocratic fashion that would be unthinkable today. Responsible for the club's move to Old Trafford, he also changed the name and the colours, but there was no protest. His death in October 1927 plunged United into such a crisis that for a time the very existence of the club seemed in jeopardy.

In the 1930s it appeared that nobody could save United. By November 1930 they had not won a single League point after a run of twelve consecutive defeats, with forty-nine goals conceded since the start of the season. The previous month had seen a revolt by the fans when 3,000 of them met at Hulme Town Hall and voted a motion of no confidence in the board. The meeting also called for fans to boycott the game the following day against FA Cup holders Arsenal. Just 23,000 turned up when 50,000 had been expected, though that may be partly due to the fact that it had been a day of rain in Manchester.

The following year, with United in the Second Division, prospects were if anything grimmer. On Friday 18 December, when Walter Crickmer, the secretary, went to collect the players' wages from the National Provincial Bank in Spring Gardens, he was refused by the bank. The club was in debt to the tune of £30,000, a vast sum in those days. It was then that wealthy local businessman James W. Gibson, a director of a major clothing company, Biggs, Jones & Gibson Ltd, came to the rescue. He paid the players' wages and gave a further £2,000. The existing directors resigned, new shares were issued, a public appeal was made for £20,000 and Albert Hughes, chairman of Manchester City, joined in the efforts to save United. At City's Annual Hot-Pot and Social at the Stock Exchange restaurant, held on 20 January 1932, he urged his guests to do what they could to support United's appeal.

United bounced back into the First Division before being relegated again, but as the Second World War loomed Gibson, the benevolent owner, and Crickmer, the efficient secretary, provided some stability and far-sighted management. In 1938 the Manchester United Junior Athletics Club was set up to produce young players, the forerunner of the famous United nursery.

The war put a stop to football but not to United's misery. On 11 March 1941 the Luftwaffe bombed Old Trafford. United were homeless and forced to play at Maine Road, Manchester City's home. Not only had City dominated football before the war, now they were United's landlords.

However, the light was about to descend. Louis Rocca, a legendary scout and a man with a reputation for turning up players and men – it was he who had found Gibson in 1931 – now sought out a manager. On 15 December 1944 he wrote to Matt Busby, then an instructor in the Army Physical Training Corps. Before the war Busby had played for City, bringing back the FA Cup in 1934 before signing for Liverpool. Rocca, like Busby, was a Catholic and their connection went back a long way, in the letter Rocca described himself as 'your old pal Louis'. By the time he wrote to Busby Rocca had been at United for fifty years, having joined as a tea boy in the 1890s when United was still Newton Heath. He would later claim he suggested the name Manchester United in 1902, which as Eamon Dunphy says would make him the most influential tea boy ever as he was only nineteen then. When he wrote his 'Dear Matt' letter his official title was assistant manager and chief scout.

Rocca had timed his letter brilliantly. Busby was looking for opportunities when the war ended. Liverpool had offered him a coaching job, other clubs north and south of the border were interested. But Rocca, whose letter spoke only of 'a great job if you are willing to take it on', tempted him. In February 1945 Busby, on leave from the army, met Gibson at Cornbrook Cold Storage, one of his companies, a mile from Old Trafford and which had housed United's offices since the war damage to Old Trafford.

On 19 February 1945 Company Sergeant-Major Instructor Matt Busby was made manager of Manchester United. The war would rage on for another three months in Europe, another six in the Far East, but the Busby era had begun and with it the legend of Manchester United.

Much has been written about the Busby era and there is little point duplicating it. Busby was a man of vision who remade British football. He also began the cult of the manager with which we are now so familiar. Before him there had been notable managers – Herbert Chapman, who had led Huddersfield and Arsenal to the championship in the 1930s and whose success made Arsenal the team of that decade, was the most renowned – but the concept of a manager as understood in modern English football was totally unknown. In many clubs the secretary also acted as manager and the team was often selected by the directors. Since 1937 Crickmer had acted as secretary and part-time manager, following the resignation of Scott Duncan, and until 1947, two years into the Busby reign, the first item on the United board agenda was team selection. Busby would leave the meeting after this had been dealt with. Only then would the directors move on to other matters.

But in this, as in many other areas, Busby set about moulding things in his fashion. He was no tactician. When he signed Noel Cantwell and the big Irish defender asked what kind of system he liked playing in defence, Busby was nonplussed. He had bought a good defender, he expected him to play, and Cantwell is not the only player to suggest that Busby was an off-the-cuff man.

Wilf McGuinness, who succeeded Busby as manager, has said this is myth – that Busby talked tactics, had a blackboard with magnetised discs to represent players, and every Friday would go through the opposition individually, pointing out weaknesses and strengths. In all this he was way ahead of most managers of the immediate post-war years, who would refuse to allow their players to practise with the ball during the week on the theory that, starved of the ball, the players would be hungry for it on a Saturday. Danny Blanchflower, who had moved to Bradford from Northern Ireland, would cast envious glances at his brother Jackie who at Old Trafford was allowed to practise with the ball during the week while he was not.

The great contrast between Busby and conventional managers of his era came in the 1948 Cup Final. At half-time Manchester United were 2–1 down to the Blackpool of Stanley Mathews and Stan Mortensen. At half-time the Blackpool manager Joe Smith told his players to 'keep it going' adding, 'Try to get another goal in this half, lads, so I can enjoy my cigar. It being the Cup final, I've treated myself to a reet good 'un.' Busby meanwhile was telling his team how to counteract Mathews and Mortensen, ordering Stan Pearson and Henry Cockburn to get tighter and close down the Blackpool skipper Harry Johnston and Hughie Kelly and for winger Charlie Mitten to drop deeper in order to help full back Johnny Aston cope with Mathews. The result was that United scored three times in the second half, Blackpool did not score another and

United won 4–2, landing Busby the first of his trophies. Managers of that period said little to their players about what to do on the field and Jimmy Greaves recalls that his first manager Ted Drake at Chelsea, who had won Chelsea their first championship in 1955, would not take training, and on match days all he said to players as they went out was 'All the best.'

Busby, however, was not the sort of tactical innovator that one of the other great English managers of the period proved to be. In 1961 Bill Nicholson at Tottenham became the first manager in the twentieth century to win the Double and the following season Tottenham, in their only foray so far in the European Cup, reached the semi-finals. On the way they beat Dukla Prague, Nicholson surprising everyone by playing a sweeper, Tony Marchi. It was an extraordinary innovation from an English coach but typical of Nicholson. Busby's gifts lay in other directions.

Players like Bobby Charlton emphasise that for coaching skills and detailed tactical knowledge they looked to Jimmy Murphy, like Busby a Catholic, whose job it was to coach the reserves. But Busby knew how to get the best out of people and always had the right person for the right job. When in 1950 Rocca died he appointed Joe Armstrong. Helped by Bob Bishop and Bob Harper in Northern Ireland and Billy Behan in Dublin, Armstrong found United a whole host of talented young players whom Busby could groom into stars. Slowly the 'Busby Babes' began to impress the world of football.

United had won the FA Cup in 1948. In 1952 they won the championship, and there were further championship wins in 1956 and 1957. Busby had in effect created two winning teams during his first ten years at Old Trafford. The 1948 team was very experienced, containing as it did pre-war players like Johnny Carey, Jack Rowley and Charlie Mitten, Jimmy Delaney having been signed in 1946 from Celtic for £4,000. By 1954 the Busby Babes in the shape of Roger Byrne, Duncan Edwards and Denis Viollet were coming through.

Busby's leadership was most evident when the debate started about whether English clubs should enter Europe. England may have created the game of football, or more accurately codified the laws of the game, but when it came to international competitions, England, true to its island mentality, had stayed away. Before the Second World War the Football Association had dropped out of FIFA, the organisation formed to run world football, and had not taken part in the first three World Cups. It was only for the fourth tournament, in 1950, that England finally sent a team for the first time. By the mid-1950s English superiority had been badly dented. In 1953 the Hungarians had destroyed the myth of Wembley's invincibility, winning 6–3 in a scintillating display. They repeated the triumph even more emphatically in Budapest the following year, winning 7–1. English football was forced to concede it was not the best in the world.

In 1955 Gabriel Hanot, editor of French sports daily *L'Equipe*, and his colleague Jacques Ferran started a competition where the champions of Europe played each other on a home and away basis to decide the best club side in Europe. The trophy was called the European Cup and Chelsea, champions in 1955, were invited. But the Football League, always resistant to change, stopped Chelsea from taking part.

However, Busby realised that Europe and international competition was where the future lay and the United board decided to participate. Although the League tried to stop United, Busby would not give up and in September 1956, they played their first match against the Belgian champions Anderlecht. With no floodlights at Old Trafford, and with fears that a Wednesday afternoon kick-off would meet from objections from local employers, Busby persuaded City to let them hire Maine Road, which had floodlights. The City chairman did not think this European idea would work, did not expect more than 30,000, and asked for £300 or 15% of the gate. Over 43,000 saw United beat Anderlecht 10–0. The European idea, thanks to Busby, had been born.

For the following match against the German champions Borussia Dortmund 75,598 turned up, again at Maine Road, to see a 3–2 victory. That season United reached the semi-finals before losing to the eventual champions, Real Madrid.

In 1957–58 United were again in Europe and again reached the semi-final, this time beating Red Star Belgrade. What Busby did not know as his brilliant team boarded the return flight to England after the match was that it was the last game they would ever play. On 6 February 1958, the Manchester United team and officials left Belgrade in their chartered aircraft. The 1,500 mile journey could only be completed by a stop-over in Munich. Flying conditions were bad and, as the aircraft tried to take off from Munich airport for a third time after two failed attempts, it hit a house at the end of the runaway and crashed.

It was a disaster that touched the heart of the nation and the world. Twenty-three people were killed, including eight journalists and the flower of Busby's remarkable side: Roger Byrne, David Pegg, Tommy Taylor, Eddie Colman, Mark Jones, Billy Whelan, Geoff Bent. If all these players were wonderfully gifted, then the eighth who died, after fighting desperately for his life for two weeks, was the greatest of them all and, arguably, the greatest English player ever: Duncan Edwards. He was only twenty-one but already an England legend.

Walter Crickmer had also died, while Busby himself was badly injured and given the last rites. But he survived and returned to build another winning side.

Munich changed everything. As Eamon Dunphy wrote in 1992:

Many planes have crashed, costing many more lives since that day almost thirty four years ago. Yet the Munich Disaster lives poignantly in memory. On an afternoon like the one on which President Kennedy was assassinated, a shadow fell across the world, when something was lost never to be replaced. Those who saw them claim this was the greatest team ever to grace the English league. The average age of that Busby side was twenty-one. Mere boys, they had won two successive First Division Championships, one of them by eleven points.

It is interesting to compare the effect of the Manchester United crash with a very similar tragedy suffered by another city and its football club. In 1950 a plane carrying the Torino team hit a mountain side and killed the entire team. They were then the best side in Italy, leading the Italian League, and were awarded the title that year. But while the supporters of Torino still mourn a brilliant team that was so cruelly destroyed, the disaster did not create the nationwide – even worldwide – resonance of Munich. The Italian team did not have the benefit of the global power and reach of the English-language press and media which clearly helped make United's tragedy a world football phenomenon.

Manchester United were a well-known, well-respected club before Munich, but the air crash elevated them on to a different level. The glory had been touched with tragedy, one in which young lives which seemed destined for greatness had been destroyed. The whole nation was drawn to Old Trafford. Like Kennedy's death people, as diverse as Jimmy Saville and the novelist H.E. Bates, remembered precisely where they were when they heard the news. Bates was driving home from London, Saville had been preparing for that night's Manchester Press Ball at the Plaza. It was cancelled and they put the radio in the middle of the floor and tried to follow the news. From now on United became everyone's second team, millions willing them to win for the sake of the boys who had died in Munich. That year in the most dramatic of circumstances the team, managed by Murphy while Busby recovered, reached the FA Cup final before losing, despite the entire nation urging them on.

Just over ten years later, however, Busby was to fulfil his European dream. In 1968 his rebuilt Manchester United team, having won League championships in 1965 and 1967, went on to win the European Cup in a memorable night at Wembley, the first English club to do so.

Yet the Busby legacy is not all dreams and the tragedy of Munich. Busby could be a smart street operator. As a working-class Scottish Catholic he was well aware of sectarian prejudice, having suffered from it in his playing days at Manchester City, and in his life he worked the Manchester Catholic network to his advantage. Great and farsighted as he was as a football manager, he had all the prejudices and failings of a man of his generation and background.

He was also very much part of a system which gave backhanders to parents to persuade young talent to come to United. Under football rules it is illegal to pay schoolboys or their parents to persuade them to sign for a club. But all clubs, tempted by the irresistible prospect of signing the next great star player, at some stage make some such payments – although they all deny it. United under Busby was no exception.

In 1979 Granada's *World in Action* programme found a wealth of evidence that Busby was actively involved in United's scheme of paying for young talent. In a signed affidavit, Johnny Aston, who had been with United for thirty-two years and had succeeded Joe Armstrong as chief scout, described how a young player called Bernard Marshall was signed from Liverpool for £1,000 at a meeting in a small room off the Old Trafford boardroom. Aston, Armstrong, Busby and Murphy were present, the money being paid by either Murphy or Busby. Aston's affidavit said: 'Some of these boys were induced to sign because United offered them or their parents backhand payments. In some cases I was personally involved in obtaining cash from Les Olive, the United club secretary and later handing it to the families of the boys.'

To some extent United were forced to pay because other clubs were doing the same. When it became known United were interested, the size of the backhander increased. According to Aston, a boy's father might be given a scouting role and paid between £3 or £4 a week for a year or two, even if it was well known that he knew nothing about football.

Aston listed many young players and their parents as having received money. In the case of Brian Greenhoff, United knew Leeds were interested and other clubs were willing to pay, but that £500 would swing the deal. Aston, who had paid at least six visits to the Greenhoff home, told Murphy, who told Busby. Then Aston himself spoke to Busby. 'He said "Fair enough" or words like that.'

Aston then went to Les Olive's office and received money in an envelope which Olive took out from a file kept in the drawer of a filing cabinet. Aston drove with his wife to Barnsley. She counted the money in the car and Aston gave it to Greenhoff senior, an unemployed miner. As they were talking they heard young Brian come in and Greenhoff senior hid the envelope under a cushion. Aston never knew whether Brian Greenhoff was aware that his parents had received the money. Aston went on to emphasise that while Busby was against such payments, he was aware of them.

It could be argued that Aston was a disgruntled employee who was bitter about the way he was sacked at Christmas 1972. But the wealth of detail he provided was impressive and, despite being given many opportunities to do so by Granada, neither Olive nor Busby made any efforts to rebut it. Les Olive when contacted by Granada researchers felt that as company secretary he could not discuss confidential company policy with them.

In November 1979 when Granada sought a meeting with Busby he refused to meet with them and there followed correspondence between John Gorna, senior partner in Manchester's King Street of a solicitor's firm of that name, and Granada. In the course of the correspondence, which became quite acrimonious,

Gorna wanted Granada to 'refrain from intruding on the privacy of Sir Matt
Busby'. However, Busby could not avoid the League and, as Graham Kelly, who
was both secretary of the League and then chief executive of the FA, put it, he 'lay
himself at the mercy of the Management Committee, saying he had always done
his best for the game'. The League decided not to pursue the matter.

More than a decade after the Granada programme, Michael Crick and David
Smith wrote *Manchester United: The Betrayal of a Legend*, a book claiming
Busby's legend had been betrayed by the Edwards family. But Crick and Smith
made little of the detailed research on how United recruited schoolboys. Their
one paragraph on the subject reads:

> As other clubs began to copy United, there were stories of boys' parents being
> offered illegal payments to clinch their signatures. Five hundred pounds or
> £1,000 might be handed over in banknotes. Alternatively, the father of a
> promising young player might be employed as a part-time scout, though of
> course he was not expected to do anything for this. But such inducements
> were rarely the deciding factor in joining United. The club's growing prestige
> was more important.

Eamon Dunphy is nearer the mark when he says, 'Year by year Matt Busby had
found himself sucked into this moral quagmire. A few quid in an envelope to
the father of a talented youngster for scouting, no bribe intended.'

The reason why Crick and Smith fail to see this 'moral quagmire' is because
they already have a villain ready at hand, one unearthed by the same Granada
researchers. That villain was the then chairman of Manchester United: Louis
Edwards, father of Martin. Granada's research went beyond payments to schoolboys into Edwards' business practices and the way he had acquired control of the
club. It was a damning programme on which others have built. Supplementing
Granada's evidence with their own research, Crick and Smith depict Louis
Edwards very clearly as the great villain in the Manchester United story. So
detailed and damning is Crick and Smith's book that few others have felt the
need to question it. In the modern history of Manchester United, the Edwards
family have been demonised as the usurpers who stole Busby's heritage.

But as Eamon Dunphy says:

> Louis was no villain. He was a nice man, a classic, 'Billy' in the argot of the
> dressing room . . . most importantly he was not Harold Hardman [who had
> succeeded James Gibson as chairman in the early years of the Busby era].
> Hardman, Busby's chairman, was of the Gibsonian school of directors.
> Straight as a die, bright as a button, tough as they make them. Hardman never
> succumbed to Matt's charm. He respected his manager but expected respect

in return. Hardman unsettled Busby . . . Harold Hardman had been a player and that was a problem in Busby's view. He had an opinion. The worst kind of director was the man who thought he knew. Louis Edwards came along at the right time . . . Louis Edwards did as he was told . . . Louis Edwards tipped the boardroom balance in Matt's favour.

Louis Edwards was descended from Italian silversmiths on his mother's side. He had inherited a family business of food and grocery and, after the war, built it into a formidable one in the meat trade in and around Manchester, supplying meat to local authorities and running meat counters in Woolworth's and Littlewoods stores. In 1962, when the business went public, it had more than eighty retail outlets and a turnover of £5 million.

Edwards, who was known as 'Champagne Louis' for his liking for cigars and champagne, had a family connection with Busby's great friend Louis Rocca (Rocca's cousin having married Edwards' sister). This developed into personal friendship with Busby in 1950 when Tommy Appleby, a leading theatre manager in the north, introduced them.

Louis Edwards was drawn into the Busby circle. It no doubt helped that, like Busby, he was a Catholic. He was on the *Queen Elizabeth* in 1952 when United, having just won the championship, travelled to New York to play Tottenham in an exhibition match. On the trip Edwards entertained, and for the first time came to the notice of the players.

Jackie Blanchflower said that the first time he met Edwards was on this trip. To his knowledge Edwards had never been a prime candidate for the board. Busby fought Hardman all the time, and with all the directors getting old, Busby set about to pick his own. Blanchflower thought Busby was grooming a man called Willie Satinoff, who died in the Munich crash.

The day after the crash, the board met at the home of Alan Gibson, son of James. They had originally gathered to mourn the death of George Whittaker, a United director, who had died the previous Saturday, just before United defeated Arsenal 5–4 in the last game the Busby Babes played in England. (It is said that Whittaker had opposed Edwards' appointment to the board, which was the reason Edwards had missed the trip to Belgrade.) Now the board had to cope with a much greater tragedy. They appointed Les Olive to replace Walter Crickmer and unanimously appointed Louis Edwards as a director.

That date marks the beginning of what is seen, by those who argue that the Edwards family betrayed Busby, as Edwards' villainy. And the way the story is presented, like all good villains Edwards started by being very nice and useful. Soon he was the most active United director, going to all the Munich funerals, including that of Duncan Edwards, attending to the insurance policy claims post-Munich and transfers like that of Denis Law from Torino.

All this was a prelude to a takeover of the club mounted in 1962. Working from the share register, he began approaching United shareholders and buying their shares. Soon after his election he had been given ten shares. Now, four years later, he wanted to increase his shareholding.

Manchester United was a private company. There was no market in the shares, which were held by a diverse collection of people. Many shareholdings had been inherited from people associated with the club in the past and were looked on as being of immense sentimental value but no monetary value whatsoever. Now Louis Edwards came along offering unheard-of money for what had seemed worthless pieces of paper.

Initially, he offered the money via the Conservative councillor Frank Farrington (who according to Crick and Smith was corrupt). Farrington knocked on the unsuspecting shareholders' doors and made them an offer they could not refuse. Soon Edwards decided it would be simpler to write personal letters. By January 1964 he had bought 54 per cent of the club, having paid, Crick and Smith calculate, between £31,000 and £41,000. 'In return for that money he had bought control of one of Britain's wealthiest and most popular clubs.' In December 1964, Edwards became vice-chairman; in June 1965, when Hardman died, he became chairman.

This is the first charge against Edwards, that he bullied shareholders into selling and bought United too cheaply. But did he? The bullying charge seems overdone. He certainly badgered them – one observer close to the scene says that 'Edwards badgered Alan Gibson, who was not in good health, until he sold. There is no doubt he hounded the poor man and it was not pleasant' – but then they held what were in effect worthless shares.

That deal, in September 1963, when Edwards acquired 500 of Gibson's shares, paying £25 each for a total consideration of £12,500, made sure he would be the majority holder. Gibson later sold his last packet of shares to Martin Edwards, which would eventually help him in turn to become the majority owner.

But even if Louis Edwards was hard with Alan Gibson, and exploited what he saw as an opportunity, this hardly amounts to villainy. The larger question is, did he pay too little for United?

In 1964 football clubs were effectively closed companies. The directors who controlled them could decide whether to register a share sale or not. They were also essentially feudal places where a man once in position could not be removed – and it was always a man. Edwards had to employ the methods he used to get the shares because there was no other way. There was nothing remotely illegal or shady in what he did. What is more, all the evidence suggests that he paid the going price, if not a little more. If Edwards paid £41,000 for his 54 per cent of United, then the entire club was valued at about £70,000, standard for a club of United's standing. In 1963 the biggest club in the land was not Manchester United, contrary to what many United supporters may like to believe, but Tottenham. The London club's income was £328,849, with a profit of £125,044, which compared to United's £271,181 with a loss of £51,429. That year Tottenham had became the first British club to win a European title, the Cup Winners' Cup. And Everton were next in size, with a revenue of £313,165 but a profit of only £19,659. That year Everton's shares – there were only 2,500 of them – were valued at about £30 each, giving the club a total valuation of £75,000. This was, notionally, £5,000 more than what United was worth.

The idea that in the early 1960s Edwards saw the amount he had spent as an investment is nonsense. Nobody at that stage thought of football clubs as an investment. The maximum dividend Edwards could earn was £100 a year and television, which has made football into a business, had barely started. In 1964 BBC began broadcasting recorded highlights in *Match of the Day*, then on BBC2. For these highlights BBC paid the Football League £5,000, of which United's share was £50 a year. Edwards would have had to be a genius even to daydream in 1964 that thirty-five years later United's income from television would be £10 million a year.

Even critics like Crick and Smith have to concede, albeit grudgingly, that Edwards started the stadium redevelopment which would see United awarded two World Cup games in 1966 and would ensure that thirty years later Old Trafford was the greatest club stadium in the country. United were the also one of the first club grounds in the country to have executive boxes.

The more serious charge laid against Louis Edwards is that he exploited United for personal gain by holding a rights issue in 1978, through which United raised £1 million. In essence, the charge is that by this time Edwards' meat business was doing very badly. It had started making losses and the Edwards family, which by now owned 74 per cent of United, had at last realised that the club was a business to be exploited. The grand strategy was, say the critics, that football could take over from the declining meat business and keep the Edwards in the luxury they had become accustomed to. The critics were doing a certain amount of post-event revisionism implying that in 1978 the Edwards could have anticipated football could have become a profitable business when this did not seem at all likely then.

The fact is that United desperately needed money. In 1978 the club had made a loss of £132,000. Even more worrying, income, having reached the £2 million mark the previous year, had fallen to £1.77 million.

That year was also crucial for English football. Although in the history of the modern game 1961 is seen as the turning point, the year the maximum wage of £20 a week was abolished, the economics of the game and modern wage inflation for players really started in 1978. That is when the retain and transfer system, challenged by players as long ago as 1963, was finally abolished. Under this system a player whose contract with a club had expired was not free to move. His old club could offer him a new contract at a lower wage and still hold on to his registration, without which the player could not sign for another club.

The 1978 change was dramatic for the English game. As Stefan Szymanski and Tim Kuypers indicate in *Winners and Losers*, the advent of free agency led to an explosion in wages and expenditure over the next five years. It was also to lead to a huge rise in transfer costs; within two years the game had its first £1 million player in Trevor Francis.

The Edwards family knew money would be needed and identified that Manchester United desperately needed more capital. With double-digit inflation and high interest rates, they were not willing to borrow from the bank and burden the club with debt. They felt the best way would be a rights issue, whereby existing shareholders put money into the club. Every United share-holder would be allowed to buy 208 new shares for £1 each.

However, the plan met with opposition from both within and outside the club. Busby, who had gone to meetings as early as 1976 at the merchant bankers Kleinwort Benson, did not like it. Les Olive voiced opposition. And from outside, John Fletcher, a rich businessman and a supporter for forty years, started an action group, launching a court battle to stop it.

The merchant bankers patiently explained that the Edwards family were underwriting the rights issue, itself an indication that no merchant bank would underwrite it, and that this was the cheapest way to put money into the club. Martin Edwards took a lead in making the case for the issue, presenting an affidavit in the court case. He himself had to borrow money to finance his take-up of the rights, which was agreed on 18 December 1978.

The most amazing charge made against the family was that they were financing the rights issue in order to increase the number of shares so they could pay themselves more in dividends. If that was the intention, it did not work out very well. Over the next twelve years up to 1990, the year before Manchester United floated, the club made pre-tax losses in six. Therefore there were no profits to divide.

The rights issue did, however, lead to a chill in relations between the Edwards and Busby families. Louis and Matt had an agreement that both their sons, Martin and Sandy, would join the board. Martin Edwards had done so in 1970, but Sandy Busby had been in the bookmaking business and could not become a board member. Once he had left the business, Busby raised the subject but Louis Edwards proposed that instead his younger son Roger should join. At the next meeting, the board supported Edwards. Eamon Dunphy tells the story of how, after the meeting, Sir Matt and Lady Jean went round to Sandy's house that night to break the news: "'My Mam was sick," Sandy recalls. Sir Matt was too. Sandy told them not to worry he would not be on a Board with people like that.' The Busbys still had the club shop to run, at a rental of £5 per week, Sir Matt remained on the board and eventually became President but he would never be chairman.

The controversy of the rights issue brought Granada's *World in Action* to United's door. As well as payments to schoolboys, the programme, screened in January 1980, dealt with how the Edwards family had bought their way into United. It also showed how, over many years, Edwards had used bribes to win and then maintain his meat contracts. Corruption in local government and provincial business was hardly new, but linked to the man who had bought Manchester United it made the news.

A month after the programme was aired, Louis Edwards suffered a massive heart attack in his bath and died. Martin Edwards has always believed the programme killed him, although Crick and Smith suggest he was overweight and had a history of heart trouble. On Saturday 22 March 1980, just before United played Manchester City at Old Trafford, the board met to elect a new chairman. Alan Gibson proposed Martin Edwards. Busby had been urged by Paddy Crerand and Paddy McGrath to go for the position, but he did not have the votes and Edwards was elected. Busby was elected president, a post that had been vacant since the death of James Gibson in 1951. Two years later he announced he would retire, for 'personal and domestic reasons'. He was now seventy-three and had suffered a cerebral haemorrhage the year before; moreover, Lady Busby was not well.

Edwards was the second youngest chairman in the League after Elton John at Watford, but the events of the last few years, and *World in Action*'s airing of them, had created a millstone round his neck that he was never able to escape.

David Meek, who reported on United for forty years for the *Manchester Evening News*, emphasises that Busby brought in Edwards because he knew that he had no feel for business and saw the need for people of business to be involved. But for the fans, as Jim White says, 'the feeling was that the man of football lost out'. In the eyes of many United fans Martin Edwards was the son of the interloper who had taken over a club that rightfully belonged to Matt.

The man of football was undoubtedly the greater man, and there can be no comparison between the Edwards, father and son, and Busby. But both Edwards and Busby shared one trait; they were in the great post-war United tradition of always being at the right place at the right time, able to see how to exploit the opportunities created by the others.

Busby himself was the best example of this. He is rightly hailed in English football as a great innovator for taking United into Europe. But the truly revolutionary idea belonged to the two French journalists who dreamt it up. Busby's skill lay in seeing what no one else in England could see: that this was a great opportunity, an idea whose time had come.

In the same style, his successors at United have been able to exploit ideas dreamt of by others. This does not diminish what they have achieved. It is in the nature of great ideas that while there must be an inventor, for them to work there must be people who take them up and run with them.

But for United the battle between Busby and Edwards left a sour legacy in the boardroom, among the fans and on the field. Busby's glorious inheritance proved such a heavy burden that his successors could not cope, until Alex Ferguson finally achieved success more than a quarter of a century later.

The way the Busby–Edwards story has been told must be judged against the way the story of English football is nowadays retold. The rise of football to the centre of British life, replacing all other sports and many other forms of entertainment, has spawned its own myths, many of which have distorted the story of football and in particular Manchester United.

Even at the best of times the Manchester United story, made of many complex strands, would be difficult to unravel and explain. It is now, at times, almost impossible because the level of public discourse on football is conducted with such frenzy that almost all rational argument seems useless. The result has been that the picture built of the club and the men who run it at times bears no relation to the truth. For almost the entire Edwards regime Manchester United did not help matters by having wretched public relations. But even with the best PR, they would have found it difficult to escape from the myths that have built up round the club. For they are connected with the wider myths about English football and how it has developed in the 1990s.

The most corrosive of these is that English football, once the people's game, played for fun by lionhearted men and watched by the most radiant souls on earth, has been massively corrupted by money and greed, that men of commerce have taken the game away from the its true owners, the real salt of the earth.

The fact is that English football has always reflected English life. English football has more than its fair share of xenophobic, racist supporters, whose distrust of anything not seen as truly English runs deep. If the money in the game now seems excessive, then what has changed is not that money has come into football – it was always there – but the sheer volume of it and the way it affects individual clubs.

As Professor James Walvin points out in *The People's Game*, even in its halcyon days before and just after the Second World War – when modern myth would have it money had not yet corrupted the game – football was already a well-established business. There was money to be made from football and plenty of it was made. However, it did not go into the football clubs as it does now but to a few commercial people outside it, in particular the pools companies.

As so often in English life, change came slowly and was often forced on the football world. It took defeat by the Hungarians in 1953 to realise that in other European countries, such as Hungary itself, the money made from pools went back into the game (between 1946 and 1953 alone the Hungarian ministry of sport had financed the building of some 60,000 sports stadia). This remains the norm abroad, even in America where local taxes are used – as for instance in the stadium built in Denver for the Colorado Rockies baseball team. But UK governments have never looked kindly on it. The Inland Revenue has never allowed tax breaks for building stadia, as opposed to buying players.

Even after 1953 nothing much changed in the way football was run. In 1966, Len Shipman, then president of the Football League, could airily dismiss the idea that money should be spent on renovating stadia which would encourage women – who had begun to be attracted to football following England's World Cup victory in 1966 – to attend games.

It required the horrific tragedies of the 1985 Bradford fire and Hillsborough to force dramatic changes. Although £200 million of public money has gone to rebuilding English and Scottish stadiums since the Hillsborough disaster, Manchester United, in common with other Premiership clubs, have received £2 million, a drop in the £112 million spent on ground development and other capital spending by United alone since 1991. Clubs can argue with no little conviction that they have had to go down the commercial route to raise the money to rebuild grounds and fund the ever-increasing costs of players. It is against this background that one must judge the commercialism that has undoubtedly come into the game and the charge that Edwards was the monstrous man of commerce, as opposed to Busby, the saintly man of football.

As Martin Edwards has put it, 'Supporters want the best players, they want the best stadium. If you want all these things you must be commercial. Unfortunately in the world you need money to buy players, you need money to expand stadiums, you need money to set up operations . . . By the end of the day things have to be paid for and apart from a dividend, which the club pays to its shareholders and which amounts to about £5 million a year, every other penny that this club makes is ploughed back into the club.'

But even so, United's success on and off the field has led to myths that are quite remarkable. The image presented of United is that it is a pioneer in commercialism. The reality is that the club has been true to its cautious, pragmatic northern roots and has more often followed than led, but having seen the opportunities created by others has often done things better. It was not the first football club to come to the stock market but followed Tottenham's lead. But having learnt from the London club's experience, United avoided the mistakes Tottenham made.

Again, when it comes to marketing, such as shirt sponsorship, others have showed the way. In 1978 Peter Robinson, then chief executive of Liverpool, noticed in a FA circular that the rules about carrying logos on shirts had been relaxed. In a week he did a deal with Hitachi for about £150,000. United's deal with Sharp came much later.

United's rise in the 1990s coincided with a new era. Sky and its money revolutionised televised football, UEFA's Champions League now brings in the sort of money Liverpool could not even dream of in the mid-1980s. Sir Alex Ferguson, after years of failure, timed his success at just the right moment. His first domestic title, in 1993, was also the first season of the Premier League, which was also the first season of the new UEFA Champions League. Martin Edwards had supported the formation of the Premier League but was not the driving force behind it. Edwards himself made more money from football than any previous club chairman, yet for many years, when football clubs had little money, he had to borrow heavily to sustain his investment in United.

This is one topic that provokes the normally placid Edwards. Suggest to him that he inherited Manchester United from his father Louis and he bristles: 'Why do you say inherited? I was on the board and I became chairman when my father died. But my father gave me only 16 per cent of the shares, exactly the same as my brother. I bought the rest which took me to just over 50 per cent.' As he insists, 'I was about £1 million in debt to the bank for years.'

The United story is one of exploiting opportunities created by others, as Matt Busby did so brilliantly with the European Cup. In his own way so did Martin Edwards, although he took several wrong turnings before getting there.

2

A LUCKY ESCAPE FROM
WALTER MITTY

SOMETIME IN LATE 1983, Irving Scholar, then chairman of Tottenham, received a call from Martin Edwards, as a result of which they arranged to have dinner at Harry's bar in London. Edwards had contacted Scholar because he wanted to know more about how Tottenham had floated on the stock market and was wondering whether Manchester United should follow the example. In the mid-1980s football clubs were desperately looking for money, and there was little to be got from television.

Tottenham's need for money had been desperate. Their glory days long gone, the club had run into huge financial problems in the way many English football clubs do: trying to build a new stand. Unlike in Italy, local authorities do not fund grounds in England and the intense tribalism of fans means a Tottenham fan would not dream of sharing a ground with an Arsenal fan in the way fans in Milan, both of AC and Internazionale, share the San Siro.

Scholar, who had made his money in property, won control of Tottenham after the previous board had mismanaged the construction of the West Stand at White Hart Lane. However, once he had done so, Scholar found the problems even worse than he had imagined. The question was, how could Tottenham raise money and wipe off their debts? The fate of Chelsea haunted every club. It was then that the idea came. Why not float on the stock market? No football club had ever floated before, but this seemed the most democratic and fruitful idea. Fans could buy shares, which could be freely traded without feudal Victorian restrictions, and Tottenham would receive enough money to wipe out their debts.

In October 1983 the club made its debut on the Stock Exchange, raising £3.8 million plus another £1.1 million in new shares underwritten by Scholar and to a lesser degree his fellow director Paul Bobroff, who then ran a property company. Initially the share price did well, but it soon fell from the £1 it had been floated at and drifted below the issue price for a long time.

Martin Edwards had first met Scholar during the summer of 1983 when Manchester United and Tottenham travelled to Swaziland to play in a series of friendly matches. But could United follow Tottenham's lead and float on the market? Scholar recalls the dinner with Edwards: 'He listened to what we had done and then said he did not think Manchester United would be able to afford the dividends which would have to be paid if the club was floated.' If flotation was out, what could Edwards do?

Not long after the dinner Edwards was visited by an intermediary who told him that a bid of £10 million was on its way. The bid was from Robert Maxwell, then one of the most controversial businessmen in the land, who after his death was revealed to be a crook. Edwards recalls: 'We arranged a meeting ten days hence. I said, "Look, I don't want any publicity on this. We must keep this quiet." Of course, next day it was all over every single newspaper and I think we know where that came from. Then, of course, we had ten days of hell before we were actually due to meet.'

That hell was a combination of the opposition of some fans and rival bidders wanting to buy the club. Maxwell then owned Oxford United and was not much liked even by his own football fans. The rival bid was led by Peter Raymond, who worked for an American chemicals company.

Having been to see Kleinwort Benson in order to ascertain how much the club might be worth, Edwards and Maurice Watkins arrived at Maxwell House near Liverpool Street. Maxwell's adviser, Roland Smith, who had also advised United on the 1978 rights issue, was present. Edwards and Watkins were under the impression it would be a private lunch with Maxwell, but as Watkins recalls: 'It was like a circus with PR men, advisers. That day the Soviet leader Andropov had died and Maxwell was getting calls from everywhere and always interrupting the lunch, so there were no real discussions.'

In any case, by then Edwards and Watkins had decided that a sale was not on. That seemed the end of this curious saga, but unknown to Edwards, Maxwell secretly acquired shares in United. The way he sold those shares would ultimately have a devastating effect on the club.

Edwards knew that Manchester United as a club was not worth much. It did not make profits and at the end of the 1983–1984 season he had actually valued the whole club as little as £3m. The final match of the season was at Tottenham, the match was drawn 1–1. After the match United expressed interest in signing Steve Archibald, who scored in that match, and Alan Brazil, eventually they signed Brazil. As they journeyed down to London, Edwards discussed matters with Watkins who at the time did not have any shares. Scholar gave them dinner at Harry's Bar and in course of his conversations with Scholar Edwards told him that this brother Roger, who owned 10 per cent of United, wanted to sell and would do the deal for £300,000. Would Scholar buy the shares? Scholar could easily afford it and knew that Manchester United was going cheap, at £3m the club was much cheaper than Tottenham, which had been valued at £10m when it had floated on the stockmarket earlier that season. What stopped Scholar reaching for his cheque book was concern about how Tottenham fans would feel. It would not have violated any football rules, which allowed one owner to hold 10 per cent of another club, and, in any case, Everton and Liverpool had a common shareholder in John Moores, but Scholar would not be comfortable as chairman of Tottenham owning a tenth of their major rival. He turned it down and Watkins and a man called Oscar Goldstein, who was later struck off as an accountant and has since died, bought the shares. Watkins later confessed to Scholar that he was not sure how good an investment it was and whether he would ever get his money back. He could not have known it would make him many millions.

Edwards was still looking at the possibility of flotation and talked to Kleinwort, but soon these discussions were to prove academic. English football was about to enter its most desperate decade.

A few months after the meeting with Maxwell the 1984–85 season began. It was to prove one of the most traumatic in English soccer history. The hooliganism that had been a part of English football for much of the seventies and early eighties – in the seventies Manchester United fans had been among the early pioneers of this new English disease – now took on a more vicious note. That season Millwall fans behaved like a pillaging medieval army when their team played Luton in the FA Cup. They not only rioted on the pitch but in the town, causing damage to houses and cars and wrecking a train. Forty-seven people, including thirty-one policemen, were injured.

The end of the season saw a fire at Bradford in which fixty-six fans died. Then, two weeks later, on 29 May 1985, English violence reached its nadir, just before the start of the European Cup final between Juventus and Liverpool at the Heysel Stadium in Brussels. Heysel was a run-down, antiquated stadium and should probably never have been chosen for such a game, but this in no way excuses what happened. The Liverpool fans were very drunk and security and policing was virtually non-existent.

Following the traditional bout of taunts and insults between the two sets of supporters, Liverpool fans charged into the section containing Juventus fans. Italian fans trying to escape were trapped by an old wall, which collapsed. In the panic, the Italians fell over each other and some were crushed to death. By the time the horrific evening was over, thirty-eight people had died. One more died later in hospital, and six hundred were injured.

The next day English teams were banned from Belgium and a day later the FA took English clubs out of Europe; they did not return until 1990, five years later. To add to the problems, television seemed to give up on football. Indeed, the 1984–85 season had seen a television blackout of the game – almost unthinkable these days.

Then in April 1989 there was an even greater tragedy at Hillsborough. On a bright, warm day with clear skies, 54,000 fans from Liverpool and Nottingham Forest travelled to Sheffield for an FA Cup semi-final. As a result of over-crowding and wretched police management a horrible crush developed, not helped by the fact that the police initially thought fans trying to escape onto the pitch were actually hooligans.

Ninety-six Liverpool fans died, and the report by Lord Justice Taylor blamed the police for 'a blunder of the first magnitude'. Clearly something drastic had to be done if Hillsborough was not to be repeated, and Taylor's final report laid out a blueprint for safe all-seater grounds.

Martin Edwards, like everyone else connected with the game, knew the tragedy of Hillsborough meant English football could never be the same. The recommendation of the Taylor report was to bring in remodelled stadiums, without terracing and the traditional standing. It forced football authorities to accept that fans could not be treated like caged animals.

But where was the money to come from? Initial reports suggested the cost of implementing the Taylor report might come to £1 billion. In fact, by the time all the changes were made the total cost was four times as much. Some of the money came from the Football Trust, while the government helped by cutting the tax levied on football pools. The rest had to be funded by the clubs, with the Premier League clubs facing the heaviest burden.

It was against this background of a game apparently in terminal decline and a desperate need for money that Martin Edwards was to receive a most intriguing phone call.

Just two months after Hillsborough, Edwards took a call from Barry Chaytow, a former chairman of Bolton Wanderers. Would he be interested in meeting a man called Michael Knighton? Edwards knew nothing about him, had never heard of him. But it was agreed Chaytow would bring him over to Old Trafford to have lunch.

Knighton was thirty-seven, a former teacher who had made his money in property and retired: 'Barry Chaytow knew I was looking to buy a football club and I'd targeted one or two. He phoned and said, "You're one of the few men who would be interested." He said he understood Martin was ready to relin-quish his shares. So I made an appointment with Martin and went for lunch.'

As they lunched on that summer's day, Knighton gave Edwards a very brief vision of his view of the game. 'We sat and looked at the Stretford End. Martin's dream was to see the oval finished. He said, "Michael, it'll never be done." I smiled and said, "Martin, I assure you that the Stretford End will be developed in my time. Not only that, I can assure you I have the financial wherewithal and the vision to make it happen." Whether he believed that or not is almost irrelevant.'

Edwards could hardly believe what he was hearing. Two months after

Hillsborough there was an investor who was not only prepared to buy him out but develop the ground. It seemed too good to be true. 'When Michael Knighton approached me the Stretford End needed replacement. It needed £10 million of expenditure. We hadn't got £10 million in the bank. In fact we had debts in the bank. What should I have done? Could I turn round to the supporters and say "I have turned down a deal which would mean the Stretford End is going to be completed for nothing"?'

There was also a huge personal factor in making a deal with Knighton: 'I was in debt. It was more than a million because I'd been carrying that debt for ten years. My house in Cheshire was mortgaged to the bank. Nobody knew quite how things were going to go in those days. Some day I knew I had to become liquid.'

On a Friday evening in July 1989 Edwards flew to Killochan Castle in south-west Scotland to discuss the details of the deal with Knighton. There, at midnight, the two men shook hands on the deal whereby Edwards would sell his stake to Knighton. But even at this stage, after weeks of talking, nobody had mentioned the price. Edwards had not asked and Knighton had not offered. As Knighton explains: 'We'd never mentioned price until the stroke of midnight, when we shook hands. It's a pretty poignant point, because we knew we'd got a deal, whatever the price was going to be. Call it Martin's public school reticence, call it what you will, the English don't like talking about money.'

The price was £10 million for Edwards' 50.2 per cent stake in United. It meant Knighton was paying £20 a share. When the news emerged it would be said Edwards had sold United; in fact he had given Knighton an option to buy his shares, a crucial distinction and one that was lost. The next morning Edwards flew back to Manchester. Now the United board began to learn about the deal. Among its members was one of Edwards' close friends, Mike Edelson.

A Manchester fur trader and a United supporter for thirty years, Edelson had known Edwards since 1971 and joined the United board in August 1982, at the same meeting Busby announced his retirement, Busby having opposed his appointment. When Edelson heard about the Knighton deal he was 'surprised and shocked because I didn't know there was anything brewing. Martin didn't tell us until after the event.' Edelson did not know Knighton but knew Chaytow, with whom he had done business.

Other people were also surprised to hear Edwards was selling to Knighton. Edwards rang Irving Scholar, who says, 'I quickly sensed something was wrong. Michael Knighton was supposed to be in the property business, but I had never heard his name and the property business is a little too small for mysterious strangers with lots of money to appear. I remember asking Martin whether he had proved that the money was available. Martin seemed to get a bit nervous about this and quickly ended the conversation.'

Edwards' nervousness was understandable. He did not quite realise what he had let himself in for. Almost from the beginning there was a touch of the comic opera about the proposed sale. At the press conference announcing the deal, Edwards introduced Knighton as Michael Whetton – the name of the catering manager at Old Trafford.

Worse was to come on 24 August, the opening day of the 1989–90 season. Manchester United were at home to champions Arsenal. Barely had the Old Trafford faithful been able to take in that they were getting a new owner when Knighton was on the pitch wearing the United kit, juggling with the ball and kicking it into the empty net. Knighton had told Edwards the previous day that he wanted to go on the pitch before the game in the United kit. Edelson says, 'Martin told him not to. As directors we don't normally go out until the teams are coming out – about ten to three. Knighton went out on his own before that. I only saw it on the news that night. I heard it obviously, because the ground was abuzz.'

That night Edelson rang Maurice Watkins, who was on holiday in Malta, and said, 'You won't believe what that Michael Knighton did today.' Watkins would have time to savour the Knighton experience when he visited him in his Scottish castle – the only United director to take up the invitation – to find himself in the company of Rod Hull, the man with the Emu, who was also Knighton's guest.

Knighton accepts in retrospect that he did not help matters by juggling with the ball in front of the Stretford End: 'I appreciate you are going to set yourself up as a target. It comes with the territory. You don't just juggle a ball in front of 50,000 people and not accept people are going to sit up and notice, that would be absurd.' He goes on to explain his rationale: 'There was a gap of mistrust between the fans and the board. Martin is a good man, but I don't think he is somebody who understands the media. The media requires special skill. You have to have that charm. There was a huge divide between the boardroom and the terraces in 1989.' Gates at Old Trafford had fallen; against Wimbledon the attendance was 23,368, even against Everton only 26,722 were present. 'There was this tremendous gulf of feeling and empathy. In fact it was incredibly hostile.'

If Knighton thought his ball-juggling act would strike a chord with the fans, it merely raised more risible questions and for one man it solved a puzzling mystery – he was very thankful that the letter he was planning to write had not gone off saving his company half a million pounds. Two weeks earlier Knighton had met Graham Sharpe, head of publicity for William Hill, and asked what odds he would give about Knighton playing in the first team of a First Division club before the end of the season. Knighton told Sharpe he had played for the youth team of a league club but been forced to give up because of injury. His wife was writing a book on dieting and will power and in order to publicise it he wanted to get back to league football. The bet was he would play in a First Division match before the season was out and he would win £500,000. Sharpe checked him out and it looked like a safe bet. But Sharpe wanted to get some publicity out of it and so he proposed that Hill would also offer odds on Knighton not playing. Sharpe was about to confirm all this in writing when he saw the pictures of Knighton's ball juggling on television and realised who the mystery player to be was. Then Knighton rang to say, 'Well, the cat's out of the bag now. I suppose it is too late for the bet.'

'Yes,' replied Sharpe.

'You've had a lucky escape. I can tell you that if you'd taken the bet, I would have got Alex Ferguson to play me as substitute in an end-of-season game.'

The incident was both an instinctive act and part of the essential character of this showman. It marked out the great contrast he would have been as owner.

News of Knighton's bid inspired the newspapers to try and find out who he was. There followed a media frenzy of stories, with intense speculation as to whether he had the money and who his backers were. Knighton did not help matters by at first suggesting he was acting on his own, only for it to turn out that he was backed by two well-known businessmen, Robert Thornton and Stanley Cohen. He says: 'Once we knew we were making progress and a deal could be actually struck, it was at that point that the partners came on.' Thornton was Knighton's next-door neighbour in Scotland. A retired former chairman of Debenhams, he was a highly respected City figure. Knighton would tell Crick and Smith that Thornton in turn had made a private arrangement with Cohen, whom Knighton had not even met at that stage.

Edwards had been told about Thornton's involvement, but the other United directors did not know. They only found out when the *Manchester Evening News* revealed the names of Thornton and Cohen. However, Thornton didn't want the publicity. As the media frenzy grew, he and Cohen withdrew just seven days before Knighton was due to confirm the deal.

A whole host of stories now emerged suggesting that Knighton did not have the money. Knighton has always maintained that the newspapers got it wrong. Here we may be dealing with semantics. When newspapers speculated about whether he had the money, some of them meant it in the very literal sense: did he have it in his back pocket? He didn't. But he had access to finance and could have done the deal. Knighton says: 'The Bank of Scotland had provided a £24 million overdraft which was simply awaiting my signature. I've got faxes urging me to get to their head office in Edinburgh to sign the documentation.' David Murray, owner of Glasgow Rangers and a man Knighton admired, helped Knighton put together the financing deal from the Bank of Scotland. But Knighton did not seem to like the deal and now tried to find other backers. Thus he came into contact with Eddie Shah, who had taken on the print unions and revolutionised British journalism, and Owen Oyston, then a socialist radio owner, who was later to be jailed for rape.

Shah confirmed that his office had contacted Knighton to explore financial opportunities, but being a Tottenham supporter he had no interest in financing United. In response, Knighton sent Shah information about his own finances and copy of a report on Manchester United prepared by his accountants, Robson Rhodes. That decision would prove a big mistake. Confidential information about United was now floating about, some of which might reach the hands of their rivals Manchester City. Moreover, David Murray's involvement meant the extraordinary situation had arisen whereby the chairman of Glasgow Rangers was trying to help sell Manchester United on behalf of a man who did not own it but merely had the option to buy the majority stake.

By this time a group of United directors were determined to stop Knighton. They included Edelson, Bobby Charlton, Nigel Burrows, a businessman who had joined the board in June 1988, and Amer Al Midani. Al Midani was the most crucial member. His father, Mouaffac Al Midani, was said to be one of the richest men in the world, and Al Midani's arrival on the United board was the story of two basketball teams. In 1985 United had had bought the Warrington Vikings basketball club. Midani owned the rival Manchester Giants and a legal battle ensued between him and United. After United lost money on their venture, it was resolved that the two basketball teams were to be merged. About this time Al Midani bought 100,862 shares in United. In 1987 he joined the United board.

A week after Edwards' deal with Knighton this group had met at Edelson's house. They were confused by what Edwards had done and did not know how to react. As Edelson recalls: 'We didn't actually know our rights or duties at that time, so it took us some time to get together and discover what we had to do . . . The meeting at my house wasn't behind [Edwards'] back. He wasn't allowed to be there by company rules.'

Gareth Hayward of CityCorp, one of Knighton's advisers – he had been introduced to them by Thornton – had suggested that the other directors should take advice, and as so often in such a situation they turned to Maurice Watkins. Edelson says: 'Maurice was a commercial lawyer. He was the one who realised that we needed advice on our duties as directors. We approached merchant bankers in the City but they did not want to know . . . They didn't want to act for a football club. Too common; too small; not worth the problem and all the rest.'

Eventually Ansbachers took the group on. Glenn Cooper, who was then at Ansbachers, and was to be one of the main architects of United's stockmarket flotation, recalls how the association began: 'Gareth Hayward, one of the people acting on the Knighton side, felt that it was important that Manchester United ought to be properly represented by a merchant bank and they recommended us. We were brought in specifically to deal with the situation which had arisen as a result of Michael Knighton's involvement in 1989.'

Cooper sympathised with Martin Edwards' predicament: 'I think he's been rather castigated, unfortunately, for entering into that Knighton situation but he wrongly presumed that Knighton had the necessary money and would be able to provide collateral support. Halfway through the process he recognised – there was the wonderful moment in a TV interview where you could see the first look of recognition of his mistake going across Martin's face – that he was dealing with a man of straw. Knighton's real intention was to go off and raise the necessary money, having secured the option. He's a very charming and rather whimsical character in lots of ways. For instance, he's reported to have seen flying saucers. As I say, a rather Walter Mittyish type of character.'

But with Edwards having given Knighton the option, the other directors had to cope with the consequences. Knighton was asserting he had the money to buy United while Edelson, Charlton, Burrows and Al Midani, advised by the canny Watkins and now the man from Ansbachers, sought to stop him exercising his option. One moment in the campaign stands out for Edelson: 'I remember going to Eddie Shah's house to get something he wanted to give us. [This was the copy of the Robson Rhodes report on Manchester United that Knighton had sent Shah.] Bobby came with me. Eddie Shah has three Dobermans and when we got there they came from nowhere. Bobby was very good because he's got dogs and he just stood there. I dived back in the car and wouldn't get out!'

Getting the report was important. It was to be the springboard for a legal action that Edwards now filed on behalf of Manchester United to stop Knighton releasing confidential information. The hearing took place in chambers and the judge granted an interim ruling in Edwards' favour.

It was clear that while Knighton might have the money, the deal could not go ahead. Even if he took control of United most of his fellow directors would leave. But he still had the option to buy Edwards' stake and he could insist on exercising it. Edwards had got United into this, he had to get United out of it. He met Knighton on the evening of 9 October 1989, but this time he did not go alone. He was accompanied by Maurice Watkins to a more humdrum location, the Novotel hotel on the M63, on the outskirts of Manchester. Edwards sees it as his lucky escape. In the modern history of Manchester United it must rank as one of the most important meetings ever held.

Edwards recalls: 'At the meeting he did say he had the money to complete. But we said, "This has gone too far now." From June to October there was incessant press speculation and he'd had a lot of adverse publicity by then. Clearly the supporters didn't want it to happen, so we said, "This isn't going to do any of us any good. We suggest you tear it up the contract and come on the board."'

There followed what Knighton describes as 'a very civilised discussion. I decided to return the contract to Martin.'

Knighton's dream was over and Martin Edwards had had a very lucky escape. The Novotel agreement was ratified on the night of Tuesday 10 October at the Midland Hotel where, with advisers and the other directors present, Knighton gave up his option and in return joined the Manchester United board.

Knighton blames the media and in particular Robert Maxwell for the fiasco: 'Robert Maxwell already had an illegal over 5 per cent stake in a plc, which he should have declared in the accounts. He had tried to buy the company before in 1983–84 and he'd always coveted the great jewel in the crown. He was the existing chairman of Derby County and his son was chairman of Oxford United, and clearly he coveted Manchester United. Through his *Daily Mirror* title in particular and with various journalists – and we all know who they are – he set about creating a media circus, front and back page.'

The media is an easy scapegoat and the dead Maxwell, who no doubt had his own agenda, can be blamed for just about everything. The fact is that it was Knighton's own actions, including the ball-juggling act and, in particular, the way he organised the financing of the deal, that led to the media circus.

When I interviewed him in 1998, Knighton consoled himself with the thought that he was the one who saw how rich the prospects for Manchester United would become, that in business terms he was ten years ahead of his time: 'I had a blueprint to make Manchester United what I believe to be the greatest sporting leisure company . . . This was the greatest brand in the world, which needed to be exploited, not in a pejorative way, but in a positive way to enable the football club to buy any player in the world and to make it profitable.'

Having claimed to predict the future but missed out on the riches, he took pride in the fact that he was a witness to United's transformation: 'I saw that football club achieve six major trophies: FA Cup, FA League Cup, European Cup Winners' Cup, European Super Cup – even the FA Youth Cup. We'd been to Wembley three or four times and we'd just missed out on the championship. But more importantly we'd turned the company around and put in the seeds of all those items in my blueprint. I claim no credit whatever to say it's all down to Michael Knighton, because that falls straight into the hands of those people that just think I'm some kind of raging egomaniac. What I do say is that Old Trafford on that sunny August afternoon was the new horizon and was the catalyst that made everything that happened subsequently happen.'

Edwards, for one, does not share that view. Ask him if the subsequent success of Manchester United is due to the Knighton plan to reinvent Manchester United and he responds: 'I wouldn't have thought anything we'd done since was as a result of Michael Knighton. I think if you speak to any other member of the board they'd say the same thing. Michael is a dreamer. I know he claims he saw the vision. A lot of people saw the vision.'

Yet there is one vision whose memory Knighton will carry and which still consoles him. On the very first day, as he had lunch with Edwards at Old Trafford, he had looked out at the old Stretford End and promised to redevelop it. Now, 'on the very last day, as I left that football club as a director, the JCBs and bulldozers were driving in to pull the Stretford End down to rebuild it'.

There is something of the little boy in the way Knighton tells the story and it is an appropriate conclusion to what must still be the strangest story in the history of Manchester United. It is a story that reflects little credit on Martin Edwards, and he was always to carry the burden of the Knighton fiasco, but it could be described as part of his steep learning curve.

3

THE RINGO STARR OF FOOTBALL
AND HIS MANAGER

PROBABLY NO MAN in English football has had more abuse heaped on him than Martin Edwards. Any assessment of him is, as Carlyle said when writing of Oliver Cromwell, like trying to excavate the real person from underneath the mound of abuse and myths that have been heaped on him over the years.

For many of the fans he is the ultimate Old Trafford hate figure. Some of this is part of his inheritance, Martin the son reaping the fruits of the alleged villainy of his father Louis. Michael Crick and David Smith's book *Manchester United: The Betrayal of a Legend* was published in 1990, following the Knighton deal. It was one of the first books of its kind, and there have been many since – polemical tracts written by committed fans using their undoubted love and passion for the club, backed by what they argued were facts to prove what was wrong with their club and English football. In this case the authors sought to demonstrate that Martin Edwards, developing the ruthless business instincts of his father, destroyed the legend of the club by his desire to make money.

By the time Crick came to write the book he had been a United supporter for almost twenty years, having first seen the team in action in 1970 at the age of twelve as a boy at Manchester Grammar. By the time he published his paperwork edition of *The Boss*, the life of Alex Ferguson in 2003, he estimated that he had seen three-quarters of United's matches during Ferguson's reign, which had then entered its seventeenth year. Before his collaboration with Smith he had written several well-received books, including *The March of Militant* and *Scargill and the Miners*, and in 2002 was to win his second Royal Television Society award, this one for his Panorama Special on Jeffrey Archer.

There can be no denying Crick and Smith's research, yet for all their diligence their predictions of where Edwards was leading the club turned out to be rather wide of the mark. Some of their assumptions are very questionable, and underlying the whole book is a depressing tone of English snobbery.

One of the chapters is entitled 'The Butcher's Boy'. Butchers, bakers and candlestick-makers are the legendary owners of English football clubs, small-town businessmen who flaunt their wealth by owning their local clubs, and the sneer in this chapter and in many parts of the book towards Edwards' family background is unmistakable.

Lest anyone miss it, Crick and Smith rub it in by highlighting Martin Edwards' educational deficiencies. Young Martin at thirteen did so poorly at the Common Entrance exam that he could not go to Stowe, his parents' first choice and a major public school, and was packed off to Cokethorpe, 'a far from distinguished private school of about 200 boys which had just opened in 46 acres of parkland near Witney in Oxfordshire'.

But even here, say Crick and Smith, he did not do well: he finished with six 'O' levels, but only after several sittings. Even then he was not good enough to take 'A' levels. The only option was the family meat business. It is difficult to resist the conclusion that Crick, who went to New College, Oxford and was editor of *Cherwell* and president of the Union, thinks Martin Edwards is not only part of the undeserving rich but not very bright to boot. This point is worth stressing because, a decade later, it had developed into the settled myth that Martin Edwards was where he was, not because he had earned it, but because of chance and luck. It was voiced, albeit in private, even by some of Edwards' colleagues in the Premier League.

Crick and Smith's other major attack on Edwards has also resonated down the years. This is that he was not devoted enough to Manchester United. At school he had played rugby. As a grown man he played rugby on Saturday afternoons for Wilmslow and continued to do so even after he joined the board in 1970. 'Many United fans would give the world to sit regularly in the Old Trafford directors' box. Yet even after Louis Edwards had got his son elected to the United board in March 1970, at the age of twenty-four, Saturdays for Martin Edwards were still devoted to Wilmslow and his "first love", rugby.'

In the eyes of many supporters this is an even greater sin on Edwards' part than his love of money. It is now an accepted part of the creed of English football that only a fan, preferably an anorak fan, can truly own a club, and that anyone else must be suspect. Edwards has always been touchy about suggestions that because he played rugby at school – 'I was at a rugby school. I played rugby, I never played football. I have not touched a rugby ball since 1971' – he does not know enough about football or the history of Manchester United. But he responds: 'I've been supporting Manchester United since 1958 on a regular basis. I came here in 1952 first of all as a seven-year-old. I had six years playing rugby from 1965 to 1971. I have missed very few games since 1971 – that is more than thirty-five years. If I didn't like football, do you think I could really put up with more than thirty years on the board and nearly a quarter of a century running it every day?'

This aspect of the attack on him is the most revealing of what is called 'fans' psychology'. It suggests that a person's loyalty to a football club must be in doubt if he has any other sporting interest. Edwards is part of the generation who grew up as sports lovers before they became fans of individual clubs. While this did not stop them from developing loyalty to particular clubs, it did not mean they could not enjoy other sports. So Edwards played rugby and cricket and still follows cricket avidly. Indeed, two weeks after United won the Champions League in Barcelona, he was at the other Old Trafford to watch perhaps one of the greatest ever one-day cricket matches, the semi-final of the 1999 Cricket World Cup between Australia and South Africa, which ended in a tie. Edwards later described the final heart-stopping moments of the match – as dramatic as United's Champions League victory – with great fervour, and if United's victory meant more to him he also enjoyed the cricket semi-final.

For the modern football fan, following such a wide range of sports is incomprehensible. If having a family who made their money from the meat business and a father who bought his way into United was bad enough, the fact that Edwards played rugby and likes cricket is the ultimate heresy.

In 1990 such one-eyed love for a club was not quite as prevalent as it is today, but for Crick and Smith, writing just after the Knighton fiasco and after nearly two decades of underachievement since Busby retired, it was easy to see Martin Edwards as the alien presence in the United boardroom, ultimately responsible for all its faults. They wrote:

As Alex Ferguson's side grappled with the threat of relegation in the 1989–90 season, media speculation inevitably grew that he would became the sixth manager to be dismissed since Sir Matt Busby. Despite the occasional chants of 'Fergie out', few people associated with United believed that another manager would solve the club's troubles. If change was required, it was at the very top. Even the world's most brilliant manager could not transform Manchester United, so long as the club is run from the chairman's office in the way it has been. United have been dragged into mediocrity by both administrative mismanagement and obsession with money, which has infected the whole club.

Even in 1990 such a conclusion was extreme but from the perspective of the fans, unable to appreciate why United were not winning, perhaps it was understandable. If anyone objected, they pointed to what United had then achieved under Edwards. Ferguson was Edwards' third manager, after Dave Sexton and Ron Atkinson. In the 1988–89 season Ferguson, entering his third year at Old Trafford, had won nothing and United that season finished eleventh, having lost in the third round of the Littlewoods Cup and the sixth round of the FA Cup.

However, the alternatives held up as models for United to follow by the anti-

Edwards brigade exposed the weakness of their argument. Crick and Smith proposed Liverpool and Everton as ideal role models, explaining that the clubs' chairmen, at the time John Smith and Philip Carter, did not get large dividends and salary bonuses, and that everything that was generated went back into the club.

But there was no direct comparison between Smith, Carter and Edwards. Edwards was a majority owner – Smith and Carter did not own their respective clubs. One person, John Moores of Littlewoods, had majority control of Everton and 27 per cent of Liverpool. Carter was an employee of Littlewoods and while Smith had shares in Liverpool, a little above 10 per cent, it was John Moores who called the shots. He had put the managing director of Littlewoods, Eric Sawyer, on the Liverpool board. What is more Tom Williams, the Liverpool Life President and director, held shares as a nominee of John Moores, although this fact did not emerge until after Williams' death.

Through the 1990s this joint ownership of the two Merseyside clubs unravelled. In 1991 David Moores, son of John's brother Cecil, took charge of Liverpool and built up a stake of 58 per cent paying £12m in total. Everton in the last decade and a half has gone through two ownership changes. It was initially sold to Peter Johnson, who also owned Tranmere, despite the fact that League rules prohibited that. By the 2000-01 season, he was forced out, more due to fan pressure rather than anything else, and Everton was sold to the current consortium headed by Bill Kenwright for £40 million, only £20 million more than what Knighton was prepared to pay for Manchester United in 1989.

Nobody can blame Crick and Smith for not predicting the turnaround in United's fortunes, let alone the vast changes that would sweep through English football in the 1990s, but it is remarkable that a book published five years after Bradford and Heysel and a year after Hillsborough did not appear to understand the implications of these tragedies or try to look ahead to the sort of changes they might force on the game.

Yet there was one possible change Crick and Smith did examine, confidently predicting that it would drive fans away and bring disaster. This was the idea of what was called the Super League, led by the then 'big five' of Tottenham, Arsenal, Manchester United, Liverpool and Everton. Fans were opposed to it, Crick and Smith said, and they warned the chairmen planning such a move that if a Super League ever came about it could 'easily kill, or at least seriously maim, the goose that still lays many of their clubs' golden eggs – the supporters who trudge faithfully through the turnstiles'.

Two years after the book was published the Premier League came about, and the television money it attracted through Sky helped pave the way for the football revolution of which Manchester United has been such a beneficiary. Before the Premier League was set up ITV had exclusive rights to League football for which they paid £14m a year. The Premier League auction in the summer of 1992 saw Sky out bid ITV. The original Sky deal is often given erroneously as £304 million. This was a nonsensical figure and a projection of what the new League might earn if all rights including the marketing deals worked. This never happened. In reality what Sky paid was much less, although much more than football had ever got. It paid £35.5 million a year for the next five years. In 1996 the deal was renegotiated for another four years starting from the 1997–98 season. This led to even further increases and it meant by the 2000–01 season Sky was paying £180 million a year. The Sky deal also saw the BBC, which had lost recorded highlights to ITV in 1988, come back into the picture. In 1992 it paid £4.5million a year and by the 2000–01 season it paid £20 million a year.

The deals since then have gone on increasing in magnitude. The deal that will kick off in August 2007 will see Sky and Setanta pay just for live rights a total of £1.706 billion for the next three years with Sky paying £1.314 billion and Setanta £392 million. Given that the deal is now for three years this means each Premier League club will each get £28 million a year, not far short of the £35.5 million the entire Premier League club got back in 1992. The goose, far from being killed, keeps on producing golden eggs.

In such circumstances it is clubs with stability in the boardroom, like Manchester United and Arsenal, who have had the resources to make necessary changes to their grounds and compete successfully in the League. Others with less boardroom security have floundered or fallen so far behind that it may take them years to catch up. Martin Edwards can argue with great conviction that the turnaround in United's fortunes in the 1990s owed a great deal to the fact that he owned the majority holding and provided the necessary stability.

If I have dealt at some length with Crick and Smith's book it is because the picture they painted of Martin Edwards – embellished many times since by other authors – has essentially remained unaltered. This picture is that Edwards was not a very bright man who did not love football, let alone Manchester United; that he was merely in love with money; and that if Manchester United have been successful it was not due to him but in some ways in spite of him.

Or, as Jim White says: 'He is the Ringo Starr of football – the Beatle drummer who inherited the role Pete Best had made and got all the glory when he really did not deserve it. Martin Edwards is the luckiest man. This thing has happened despite him not because of him. He is only interested in making money.'

Not surprisingly, Edwards' friends say this is far from accurate. Glenn Cooper, who helped United to float on the stock market, and who confesses unashamedly that he is a Edwards fan, says: 'I think he's done a phenomenally good job.' His view is that while many factors played a part in making United the greatest club in the world, Martin Edwards had a central role: 'A lot is said about how different Manchester United is, and that it is successful because of some magic touch that gave it this phenomenal support and took it out of the realms of an ordinary football club and into the realms in which it now finds itself.' While Munich gave United recognition and sympathy round the world, 'what is often overlooked is that this club and this business have been very well run indeed for a number of years'.

Cooper even argues that some of the success Alex Ferguson has enjoyed was due to Edwards and the way he operated the management team at United. 'He kept his nerve when the fans wanted Alex Ferguson sacked and one must give him credit for that. In my opinion he was very much more instrumental in the way the player end of the business has gone than anybody outside understands. I think he had a considerable influence over who is bought and sold. Alex Ferguson had a huge influence, but I think [Edwards] was a considerable moderating and thoughtful influence on all of that.'

It is one of the many paradoxes of the way fans judge Martin Edwards that even his biggest critics resent the fact that he has at times tried to sell up and get out. Jim White echoes the view of many supporters who, while chanting 'Edwards out', also deplored his many attempts to sell the club. 'On three occasions he tried to sell United – to Maxwell, to Knighton and to Murdoch. He may have been better off sticking to it.'

Here White stresses one of the many contradictions of a fan's attitude to the owner of a club he supports: 'It is a curious thing about football fans, they are happier with an egotist as owner or chairman rather than someone who just takes the money. Their reasoning is egotists would like the team to be successful. Take Silvio Berlusconi, who owns AC Milan. He has used football as a platform for his ego. Edwards was no Berlusconi, let alone a Roman Abramovich. He is perfectly happy to take the money.'

One reason why Edwards may not have been given the recognition Cooper and his friends think he deserves was his style which, as former commercial director Edward Freedman says, was not quite like that of other chairmen: 'I think Martin was very laid-back, did not panic outwardly or make rash decisions. He was very good at appointing people to do the jobs they do and he didn't interfere with them, which I think is an asset.'

Even White, however reluctantly, is prepared to give Edwards credit for the way he delegated: 'He has got the best person for the jobs. Ferguson is a good example.' And it is Edwards' decision to hire Ferguson, then to keep him when fans were baying for his blood, that has been at the heart of the modern Manchester United.

Ferguson, appointed in November 1986, was Edwards' third manager. He had sacked Dave Sexton, whom he had inherited, in 1981 before hiring Ron Atkinson. Under Atkinson United had won the occasional cup, but the League seemed unattainable. This feeling of despair was heightened during the 1985–86 season when United started with ten wins in a row, looking as if they might overhaul Tottenham's record of eleven in a row at the start of the 1960–61 season. They then stumbled so badly that, long before the end, their title chances were gone and they finished the season fourth.

Then in November 1986 came a humiliating defeat in the League Cup at Southampton. On the plane back the talk turned to replacing Atkinson, which was continued the next day at Old Trafford. The choice had been narrowed down to two options: Terry Venables and Alex Ferguson. Mike Edelson took part in those discussions and he explains: 'Terry Venables wasn't really available because he was at Barcelona. They were still in the European Cup and they wouldn't release him, we thought. We decided it wouldn't be worth considering Terry. Alex was obviously the first option, considering the relative merits of the two. (His success with Aberdeen and the ability to dent the old firm dominance of Celtic and Rangers was an achievement that had impressed many in football and marked him out as an innovative manager who was several cuts above the rest.) The only thing against Alex was no Scottish manager had ever successfully come from Scotland to England. Busby was Scottish but he had never managed in Scotland.'

Earlier that year, during the World Cup in Mexico, Bobby Charlton had talked to Ferguson when he was managing Scotland and said if he wanted to move to England he should think about getting in touch. Two years earlier, in 1984, Ferguson had very nearly moved south, shaking hands on a deal with Irving Scholar to come to Tottenham. They met twice in Paris and everything seemed agreed but then Scholar was told his wife Cathy did not fancy London. Curiously, Ferguson does not mention this in his autobiography and in June 1999, a week after Manchester United won the Champions League, Scholar, waiting by the carousel at Nice airport, saw Ferguson. As they chatted he introduced Scholar to Cathy and Scholar said: 'Ah, you are the woman who stopped him coming to Tottenham.' Cathy Ferguson just looked at Scholar and did not say anything.

Now, in November 1986, Edwards, Watkins, Charlton and Edelson met in the Old Trafford boardroom to discuss how they could approach Ferguson. Watkins had got to know him when Gordon Strachan had joined Manchester United from Aberdeen, but it was Edelson who volunteered to make the call, putting on a phoney Scottish accent and claiming to be Alan Gordon, Strachan's accountant. 'When Alex came on the phone I told him I was a director of Manchester United and asked him if he'd like to speak to Martin Edwards. Martin said, "Would it be possible to have a chat?" and Alex said he'd clear it with his chairman. He had an option in his contract that if a really big club – Rangers, Tottenham, Manchester United – were interested, he was allowed to speak to them. It was all done within hours. We rang him on Wednesday, Maurice and Martin went up on the Thursday and spoke to him, and Ferguson came down on the Friday. By this time Martin had spoken to Atkinson.'

It was not so much the money but the lure of managing Manchester United that brought Ferguson to Old Trafford. But three years later, in 1989, nobody would have blamed Edwards if he had sacked Ferguson. Results on the pitch were so bad that the crowds had turned on Edwards.

One of the most dramatic nights was that of 25 October 1989, when Tottenham beat United 3–0 at Old Trafford in the third round of the League Cup and fans tried to get into the directors' box to assault Edwards. The abuse had reached such a point that he would often vacate the directors' box and watch much of the match from high up in the main stand.

For Ferguson the lowest point was a 5–1 defeat by Manchester City at Maine Road. Had Edwards decided to sack him at that stage, he could easily have turned the abuse around and become something of a hero with fans, saying the chairman had listened to them. But Edwards would not hear of it: 'It was a tough time for us and there was a lot of pressure for us to do something. A lot of supporters and fans don't always realise what's going on in the background at a football club and we knew how hard Alex was working behind the scenes.' That year the club had spent heavily to bring in Mike Phelan, Paul Ince, Gary Pallister, Danny Wallace and Neil Webb. 'The last thing we were going to do was suddenly pull the rug from underneath him.'

Edelson too is emphatic that the board did not discuss sacking Ferguson: 'You have to remember that although the years were very tough, Alex was almost replicating what Matt Busby had done. He knew everybody in the ground – the laundry girls, the waiters, the groundsmen. We were also evolving the more continental style of management, where the manager was less and less in charge of everything because Martin was getting involved more and more. On the commercial side the manager would not have done a transfer. It was getting to the stage where at least they went together. It was moving on to the new pattern.'

Ferguson had restarted the youth policy first launched by James Gibson and Walter Crickmer back in 1938 and developed so brilliantly by Busby. He had also started tackling the drinking culture centred around players such as Paul McGrath and Norman Whiteside, seeking to make the club more professional and the players fitter and more capable of coping with a hard League season. But it is indicative of the deep distrust that developed between some fans and Edwards that even when his faith in Ferguson was completely justified, fans still found it difficult to accept that he did not think of sacking Ferguson. White takes this view: 'Edwards did stick by Ferguson but I believe there has been post-event rationalisation. I know Bobby Charlton says they did not think of sacking him but

I am sure the axe was poised and had Ferguson failed to beat Nottingham Forest in the third round of the FA Cup he would have been sacked.'

As we know, United were not beaten and Ferguson was not sacked. Ferguson went on to win the Cup, the Cup Winners' Cup the next year and the League title in 1993. Soon after the Cup Winners' Cup victory over Barcelona, in 1991, Ferguson was sounded out by an intermediary on whether he would be interested in becoming manager of Real Madrid, an approach he rejected in favour of trying to win the championship. Within two years he had done just that, winning the inaugural Premiership title and beginning a sequence of triumphs. But as the trophies accumulated, the relationship between Edwards and Ferguson soured rather than deepened.

Eric Cantona was a key player in Ferguson's march to glory and the recruitment of Eric Cantona had been a supreme example of the Ferguson–Edwards partnership at work. Ferguson was talking to Edwards one drizzly November afternoon in 1992 about the need for a new, world-class striker. His attempt to buy David Hirst from Sheffield Wednesday had collapsed and he mentioned that it was a pity United had not had the chance to hear about Cantona before he joined Leeds earlier that year. Just then, Bill Fotherby, Leeds' managing director, came on the phone to ask Edwards if United would be willing to sell their full-back, Denis Irwin. Edwards countered by asking Fotherby about players Leeds might want to sell. Ferguson scribbled Cantona's name on a piece of paper and passed it to him, 'Ask him about Cantona.'

Edwards said to Fotherby, 'Any chance of you selling him and we'd be interested. Need to be pretty quick, mind you, because we have the money for a striker and want to do some business now.'

Cantona had already made an impression at Leeds, scoring fourteen goals in thirty-five games – including two hat-tricks – but his tendency towards indiscipline had led to tensions with manager Howard Wilkinson. Fotherby, having consulted Wilkinson, told Edwards that United could have Cantona for a mere £1 million. 'That's an absolute steal,' Ferguson cried, when Edwards broke the news. Edwards evidently thought so, too.

The day the deal was done Freedman had lunch with Martin Edwards at Old Trafford and during the meal Edwards asked, 'If there's any player you could pick in this country at the moment who would it be?'

'You couldn't buy him,' said Freedman.

'Why, who is it then?' asked Edwards.

'Eric Cantona,' replied Freedman.

'How much would you pay?' Edwards asked.

'He must be worth at least four or five million,' said Freedman.

'I can get him for £1.2 million,' said Edwards.

'It can't be true,' said Freedman, thinking Edwards was kidding.

The relationship between Ferguson and Edwards during the Eighties had been so close that in one successful attempt to recruit a player they had what the player described as 'a cloak and dagger meeting'. The player was Jim Leighton, the then Aberdeen goalkeeper. He narrates how he borrowed a friend's car, met Edwards just off the M73 near Cumbernauld, then followed Ferguson's car to the home of one of Ferguson's relatives. The two cars did not stop at the front door, they drove past. Ferguson indicated the house, drove on and returned later. Meanwhile the back door had been left open for Leighton and Edwards to go in. The cloak and dagger was necessary because United was going behind Abderdeen chairman Dick Donald's back. Car telephones, says Leighton, ensured 'the manoeuvre was completed without a hitch'.

In the winter of 1988, Edwards and Ferguson drove to Nottingham Forest's City Ground together with the intention of persuading Brian Clough to sell Stuart Pearce to United. Clough, not keen to see them, pretended he was not in his office, despite the fact his Mercedes was parked outside. They could not find him and it proved a fruitless trip but it demonstrated Edwards and Ferguson were at least forming a working partnership.

It could be argued that in the early years, Edwards and Ferguson were drawn together by their common predicament. Both were beleaguered – Edwards was in debt, did not know how he could raise the money to build the Stretford End, and was troubled by the abuse from the fans. In the summer of 1989, before the Knighton lunch at Old Trafford, Edwards had told Ferguson he had had enough and was planning to sell. A decade later, with Edwards having no money problems and Ferguson fit to rank as one of the great managers of all time, the chemistry between the two men was no longer the same. Success had driven them apart.

It was in the summer of 1995 that relations between Edwards and Ferguson started taking a turn for the worse. Ferguson, dealing with that summer in his autobiography *Managing My Life*, entitles the relevant chapter 'Public Enemy Number One', and it expresses his feeling that the 1994–95 season when United won nothing – apart from the Charity Shield won at the beginning of the season – saw him isolated from the supporters. The transfer of Paul Ince to Inter Milan did not go down well with the fans. Ferguson admits he wanted him to go; he told the board to sell him four days before his views were reinforced by the Cup Final where Ferguson held Ince responsible for Everton's winning goal. But he also maintains that the player wanted to go anyway and had been heard at the Cup Final reception saying he was off to Italy. Ferguson writes, 'Yet, in spite of all that, I was being branded as Public Enemy Number One for driving him away. I was out on my own, with no hint of support from the corridors of Old Trafford, and the people who keep queueing up for jobs as managers of football clubs should consider the vulnerability I felt then.'

The reference to Edwards is clear. But he, in turn, was feeling the pressure of fans who saw the Ince move as a purely commerial deal from an increasingly money conscious United board. Edwards felt he was being targeted when the manager wanted to sell the player anyway. This resulted in a conversation between chairman and manager where Edwards urged Ferguson to think again about selling the player and added Brian Kidd, Ferguson's assistant, did not want the player sold. This further angered Ferguson who wrote in his auto-biography, 'That was a surprise. Brian had never voiced such an opinion to me.'

By the summer of 1998 the relationship between Edwards and Ferguson had sunk a lot lower. Tim Bell was to discover this most dramatically that summer when he suggested to Edwards that Ferguson be told about the Sky bid in advance, and perhaps even given some money to endorse the bid. Bell discovered to his utter amazement that Edwards did not entirely trust his manager. Bell told me:

It was Friday 4 September and it was at the HSBC headquarters in the City. Mark Booth (the American head of Sky) had asked me to go with him. Sitting in front of us were these great gods: Martin Edwards, son of the proprietor, the man who had invented Manchester United, Professor Roland Smith, the great chairman and king of Manchester, Peter Kenyon, deputy chief executive, and the finance director David Gill.

I had gone there with only one objective: to get Alex Ferguson to endorse the Sky bid. Before I went into the meeting I had had a meeting with Mark to try and find out how much he would spend getting Ferguson on side. I said, 'As a matter of interest, how much do you want to offer him?' He said: 'I don't know, two million would probably do it, maybe more, whatever it takes to get him on side.'

We knew that, no matter what the resistance to the bid and to Rupert Murdoch, if Alex Ferguson said, or even half-said, that this was vaguely a good idea, this would completely wrong foot all the opposition. I really wanted to walk in and say, 'What do you think it would cost Ferguson to say yes?' But, with the board there, we couldn't be quite that crude. We had to be slightly subtle. So Booth said, 'Would it be a good idea if we met with Alex Ferguson?''

We suggested that Mark might have dinner with Ferguson, to introduce himself and have a chat. I said we could explore what it would take to get Alex to say what a good idea the bid was. And Martin Edwards looked at me and said, 'What sum are you talking about?' I said, rather crudely, 'You know, a million, £2 million, something like that. A special one-off payment, a golden handshake, whatever.' He said, 'But I've just given him his first warning letter for misbehaviour.'

I said 'What?' He said, 'It's not right, it's very unacceptable, I mean, he's a pain in the arse, he never does what you tell him. When it comes to the second one, then we'll sack him.' I said to him, 'You can't be serious. He's the greatest football manager the world has ever seen. The most popular man the world's ever seen.' He said, 'Christ.' I said, 'Well, maybe you should withdraw the warning, maybe that'll get him to be onside. Tell him, Sky's insisted that you withdraw the warning letter.'

The conversation deteriorated from there. He said. 'No, you can't discuss money with him and you can't trust him with money. I mean, he has no idea what money's worth. He's just out for himself. He doesn't understand that he's an employee of the club and he must abide by the club rules. He's just a bit too big for his boots; that's why I have given him a warning letter.' The other board members just stared. I got the feeling that they had actually agreed with this and it was only when they heard it said out loud that it dawned on them what an utterly stupid idea it was. Ferguson and Edwards had a bad time during the summer. They'd obviously had a huge disagreement about Dwight Yorke and other things as well. [Ferguson had threatened to resign.] I think it was to do with money. I'm not so sure it wasn't also that Edwards wanted him to buy other players and he had failed to do so.

The general attitude of the board to the club was peculiar, Bell says.

The impression you got was that the board had actually created this great institution. They felt they were doing the fans a favour by letting them in and the players a favour by allowing them to play for Manchester United. And the manager had better toe the line; otherwise he wouldn't be the manager any more. I was absolutely amazed. I thought that they would have had a very acute idea of what their assets were worth, how valuable they were and how they should be treated – with some care and caution.

This conversation would have repercussions which threw interesting light on the Edwards-Ferguson relationship. When in December 1999 I revealed these facts, Ferguson, understandably, reacted furiously. There was, I believe, some talk of legal action against Edwards, which came to nothing.

When Ferguson came to write the paperback edition of his book, published in 2000, in the final chapter he discussed what I had written, saying, that there had been:

claims that Martin described me as being useless with money. Bose is usually defined as an investigative journalist but I would have to question the quality of his investigation. Martin wrote to me categorically denying that he had ever spoken to the man about me. The remarks quoted amounted to such blatant nonsense that I had never for one moment believed the chairman could find himself capable of uttering them. For a start, Martin has no knowledge whatsoever of my personal finances so in that area there could be no foundation for comments of any kind. Suggestions that my record with United had shown me to be useless with money would be rather difficult to sustain, considering that Martin's fortunes has swollen by upwards of £120 million over the past ten years as a result of his shareholdings in the club. There was no substance to the story and I can only assume that Bose had been listening to a lot of tittle-tattle which, as I have observed earlier, is always plentiful around a big organisation like ours.

It was just the sort of robust defence one would expect from Ferguson, including questioning my ability to research, but what was interesting was that Edwards had denied something I had never claimed, but not denied the remarks he had made to Bell. He had denied talking to me but I had never claimed Edwards was my source and so this was the classic non-denial denial. Edwards was helped by the way I originally had to write my story. At that time, with the Sky bid having recently been rejected and memories still fresh, Bell, while telling me the story and allowing me to use it, would not be identified as the source. I had to describe him as 'a source present at this meeting'. For this book Bell has allowed me to identify him as the source and given a much fuller version of what happened. My original story created a storm and some journalists worked out who my source was. Charlie Sale, now of the *Daily Mail*, appeared to have done so. He rang Bell and asked: 'Are you going to sue Bose?' Bell was most amused by the idea.

Ferguson, himself, has spoken about the money problem and level of distrust between him and Edwards in his autobiography, *Managing My Life*, which lays bare the true relationship behind the public façade of chairman and manager working together for the good of Manchester United. Ferguson revealed a complex story of strain and unhappiness: 'Conversations with Martin Edwards are usually straightforward and pleasant until you ask him for more money. Then you have a problem.' Through the later half of the 1990s Ferguson's demands for more money and Edwards' refusal to accept them became something of a boardroom serial, each episode more acrimonious than the last.

The seeds of this controversy were sown in 1992. At a board meeting that year, Edwards announced that everyone, including Ferguson, would be allocated 25,000 share options. But Robin Launders, the finance director, would get four times as much: 100,000. Freedman recalls: 'Alex Ferguson was very annoyed that he was getting 25,000 while Launders was getting 100,000. After all, he was the manager. He refused to take the 25,000 offered and so did Ken Merrett, the club secretary, who said all the employees should get the share options.'

In 1993 Ferguson, having won his first title and talking from a position of strength, went to Edwards to ask for a pay rise. He had been very upset to discover he earned a lot less than fellow Scot, George Graham, who with two championships, two Littlewoods Cups and one FA Cup for Arsenal, was at that time the country's highest-paid manager. Graham had told Ferguson how much he earned and Ferguson mentioned that figure to Edwards, hoping to achieve parity. Edwards checked with David Dein, vice chairman of Arsenal, and came back to say the figure was not right. Ferguson was crestfallen, but he did get a new contract.

The next round of this periodic pay battle came at the end of the 1994–95 season, when United looked like repeating their double but won nothing. The 1995 summer, in addition to the departure of Paul Ince, had seen Andrei Kanchelskis and Mark Hughes leave the club. Ferguson was not best pleased to be interrupted on holiday by Edwards and told that Hughes, a player he wanted to keep, had signed for Chelsea due to pension problems which had prevented him from signing a new contract at Old Trafford.

Ferguson returned from holiday to find the *Manchester Evening News* holding a poll asking whether he should be sacked. It was at this point that he went back to Edwards and asked for a pay rise: 'My timing may have been ill-conceived but I still felt seriously aggrieved over having been lumbered with a pay deal that left me trailing so far behind George Graham.'

Edwards could not accept what Ferguson wanted and it was decided that Ferguson would go and see chairman Roland Smith at Roland Smith's Isle of Man home, where Maurice Watkins would also be present. Ferguson was now fifty-four years old and wanted a new six-year deal that would take him to sixty. He was also looking for a role in the club after he retired. As Ferguson showed Graham's contract to Roland Smith and Watkins, Smith counter-attacked by suggesting he might be taking his eye off the ball: 'Some people at Old Trafford think you are not as focused as you have been.' Soon it was clear he would not get a six-year contract – no United manager ever had such a contract, and there could be no role for him, as for Busby, after retirement.

In any case, Smith and Watkins said, the whole debate would have to be delayed until June 1996, when the remuneration committee would meet.

Ferguson admits that he came back from the Isle of Man flattened, confused and worried, although this probably drove him to achieve the second Double in 1995–96, United moving to a higher gear when Eric Cantona returned from suspension in October 1995. However, Ferguson's demands for more money and United's refusal to meet them were very much part of that second Double season. The night before the FA Cup final, when United beat Liverpool in a scrappy match through a Cantona goal, Ferguson had a tremendous row with Watkins about his contract. 'I was absolutely disgusted. It was annoying that they had insisted on leaving the business until the end of the season in the first place and now their words, "We'll look after you" seemed utterly hollow.' Ferguson was so upset that he was thinking of resigning. Indeed, so frustrated was he by his failure to broker a better deal that he threatened not to perform the manager's traditional Cup final role of leading his team out on to the Wembley pitch. Ned Kelly, United's former head of security, remembers the reaction of Edwards before the match began. 'You won't believe this, Ned, but Ferguson telephoned Maurice Watkins at his hotel and told him that unless he got his bonus and pay rise he wouldn't be leading the team out today. He was serious. He told Maurice that *he* could lead the team out.'

What Ferguson did not know was, at this stage, Edwards was thinking whether it was time to let him go. If Ferguson did resign it would be useful to have someone in mind to replace him. England manager Terry Venables was to become free at the end of June after the European Championships and, after a board meeting, Edwards approached Freedman and said they were thinking of Venables. Freedman could barely contain himself: 'What, Terry Venables? You must be mad.' Ferguson, at the same time, was approached by Jimmy Armfield for advice on who should be the next England manager and expressed, according to former FA chief executive Graham Kelly, some interest himself: 'It soon became clear that (Ferguson) was interested in succeeding Terry Venables as England coach.'

Nothing came of either possibility and a week after the Cup final Ferguson's accountant, having negotiated with Smith and Watkins for six hours, hammered out a deal. The directors understood full well, it seemed, the depth of Ferguson's emotional bond to the club, and the fact that he would be unlikely to walk away. They probably played a bit on this. Ferguson was unimpressed: 'The arguing over the figures I had requested went on all day. To be honest it was pathetic.' Having thought of resigning, he accepted the deal but remained unhappy. 'I was not given what I believed I was worth, but nonetheless I had made huge strides in relation to my existing agreement.'

United had seen off the spectre of Terry Venables at Old Trafford but there was a final cycle of pay negotiations that took place just before the team achieved the treble in 1999. Ferguson was on holiday in France during the 1998 World Cup when he learnt that Brian Kidd had been approached by Everton and United were giving him a new contract to keep him. It seemed to him that Kidd always got money whenever an approach came. Enraged, he flew back from holiday to confront Edwards and Smith at his offices in HSBC. At the meeting, much to Ferguson's surprise, Edwards began with a long speech in which, while praising Ferguson, wondered if he had allowed his celebrity status to go to his head. Was he focusing on his job enough? And what about his new-found interest in racing? Ferguson was so enraged he said, 'Do you want me to call it a day?' No, replied both directors hastily. Ferguson was pacified, but it was clear he would have to be given a new contract.

Then came the Sky bid, where Sky with the approval of Edwards and the entire Manchester United board bid £623 million to buy the club and make it part of Rupert Murdoch's media empire. Sky were anxious to keep Ferguson. After the bid stalled, Ferguson made his money demands clear. Edwards discussed possible terms with the board and opened negotiations with Ferguson, but could not reach agreement. He returned to the board only to find that they had amended their previously strict guidelines and were prepared to accede to Ferguson's demands. The whole thing left Edwards unhappy and only helped reinforce Ferguson's image of Martin Edwards as the man who would not loosen the purse strings.

For Edwards' detractors, there came yet more evidence of his Scrooge-like approach to employees. As the 1999–2000 season began there was trouble with a new contract for Roy Keane, who was then in the last year of his old contract and thus entitled to talk to foreign clubs in January 2000. Juventus and Bayern Munich were interested, and he could have left on a free transfer in June 2000. Ferguson had recruited him from Nottingham Forest in 1993, in a sensational last-minute transfer coup after the player had verbally agreed to go to Blackburn. As Keane describes in his autobiography when he told Ferguson he had agreed to go to Blackburn Ferguson told him, 'You've signed nothing. Come over for a chat.' Keane did and allowed Ferguson to change his mind. But when he spoke to the then Blackburn manager Kenny Dalglish, Dalglish nearly burned the telephone lines with his fury: 'Nobody does this to me, nobody does this to Kenny Dalglish. You are a wee bastard and you won't get away with this.'

But now Keane would not agree to a new contract, which would give him nearly £40,000 a week. By then he had become an iconic figure at United, not only the captain and the man who ran the midfield but in a sense the most important player Ferguson had signed since Cantona. With the board dithering over Keane, one tabloid newspaper totted up all of Edwards' income, dividends, salary, proceeds of share sales since United floated in 1991, divided it by the number of days since flotation, and found it came to £50,000 a day.

So, it asked, if Roy Keane was not worth more than £40,000 a week, why was Edwards worth £50,000 a day? Had he really done more for Manchester United?

While Ferguson acknowledges that Edwards treated him well, never interfered in the slightest about the buying or selling of players and supported Ferguson's youth policy, he laments the rise of the plc and suggests it is responsible for the cooling of his relationship with Edwards: 'The chairman and

I have got on well much of the time but in recent years there have been serious strains in the relationship, and always the disharmony has developed over money . . . I appreciate that life at United has changed drastically since the advent of the plc and that Martin Edwards had a difficult job. The new set-up had sadly reduced communication between us. Gone are the days when we maintained a constant, healthy dialogue.'

Ferguson felt he was hamstrung by United's inflexible wage structure, which determined that the top players were paid roughly the same amount – £23,000 a week. While the policy might encourage strong team morale, Ferguson understood that a wage cap would deter world-class players from joining. 'My hands were tied,' he wrote in his autobiography. 'I think the restrictions applied to wages prevented us from being the power in European football that we could have been in the Nineties.'

Edwards was well aware that in this battle between himself and Ferguson only Ferguson could win. Many years ago he told Irving Scholar: 'One thing you should never do is get into an argument with the manager on the back pages. If you do you will lose.' Scholar forgot the advice in 1991, took on Terry Venables, and ended up losing Tottenham. Edwards never made that mistake. But he was so reluctant to enter the public arena that, even after Ferguson had revealed details of his pay talks, Edwards refused to give his side of the story.

A reluctance to engage in any sort of public debate was deeply ingrained in his nature: 'I don't sell myself. I am not interested in PR and having PR people around me saying what a great bloke Martin Edwards is. All I am interested in is doing a job. I do not want any publicity. All I want to do is run a successful business. I feel a sense of hurt about the way my father was treated. I am not impressed by publicity.'

His reluctance to talk publicly went so far as to keep secret stories that might improve his image and convince the fans that he was one of them. The most illuminating concerns the 1999 FA Cup semi-final replay between United and Arsenal, which United won with Ryan Giggs' wonder goal.

Just before Giggs scored, with Arsenal just having missed a penalty and United down to ten men, Edwards could not bear to watch and left the Villa Park directors' box to go downstairs and have a drink and a cigarette. 'I was in a dreadful state. My nerves had gone.' As he was having his drink, the goal went in. 'I did not watch the Ryan Giggs goal.' The state Edwards got into is one a lot of fans would understand, but he was reluctant to talk about it.

He did give a revealing glimpse of this aspect of his personality after United drew 2–2 at Anfield that season, having led 2–0. Liverpool came back through a hotly disputed penalty and Denis Irwin was sent off for kicking the ball away after a free kick had been given against United. That Sunday the late Joe Melling of the *Mail on Sunday* ran an exclusive story on Edwards' less than complimentary remarks about the referee. His comments led to an FA inquiry about whether he had brought the game into disrepute, but he had no regrets: 'It was said from the heart. I am as passionate about Manchester United as anyone. I don't run around taking my shirt off or breaking the law or run round thumping people or running on the pitch. But nobody who knows me well enough can question my loyalty towards the team.'

But if Edwards was reluctant to court publicity, Ferguson was the master of the back page, and his handling of another reporter from Melling's *Mail on Sunday* illustrates this. Bob Cass, who knows Ferguson well, had run a story saying Bryan Robson, who was often injured, was making a comeback in a televised Sunday match. It was the back-page lead but as the television cameras rolled there was no Robson, not even on the bench. Roger Kelly, then sports editor of the *Mail on Sunday*, was not best pleased and told Cass so. Kelly then went off to play golf and as he returned home the telephone rang. The voice said he was Alex Ferguson: Kelly thought it was a joke but it was the real man and he told Kelly that Cass had the right story but Ferguson had made a late change and Cass was not to blame. It showed how Ferguson can control the back-page agenda, something Edwards could never hope to match but what is more did not, unlike some other chairmen, even try.

Indeed, the problem in evaluating the Edwards–Ferguson relationship is that the way it was perceived in the press, particularly the sports pages, did not reflect reality. There, Ferguson is always referred to as the 'boss' of Manchester United when he is in fact an employee – the most important employee, but by no means the only figure. While Ferguson is supreme in his domain, the field of play, this is quite distinct from the rest of the business.

Edwards told me, 'He is not the old-fashioned type of manager. His role is quite sharply defined. Alex would report directly to me as chief executive.' United have gone to considerable lengths to separate Ferguson's role as the man who handles the team from the rest of the business. Unlike many other Premiership managers, Arsene Wenger for instance, Ferguson has no office at Old Trafford. His office, originally at the Cliff, is now at Manchester United's Carrington training ground, where he prepares his players for their tasks on the field.

As for Ferguson's role in achieving such success for United, Edwards was keen to stress that Ferguson has been helped by the structure of the club: 'I don't want to take anything away from the manager – he has done a great job team-wise. But he also benefited from a well-run company at the back of him that took advantage of the team success and that created revenue to allow him to buy the best players. Look at 1998, when we won nothing. I don't believe any other club would have gone out and bought Stam, Blomqvist and Yorke and spent £28 million.'

In the 1998–99 season Edwards was involved in another tussle with

Ferguson, where the spin on the back pages made it seem that he and the plc board were once again failing to help Ferguson. The struggle concerned United's coach, Brian Kidd, who for the third time in less than a year had been approached by another club. On 21 November, Blackburn slumped to the bottom of the League, sacking manager Roy Hodgson and seeking to replace him with Kidd. Before the season began Kidd had asked for permission to speak to Everton and this had nearly led Ferguson to threaten to quit. The issue had been resolved with Kidd getting a new contract that had answered Kidd's moan that Everton had offered more than three times what he was being paid by United. The contract made him the best-paid coach in the country and it was his second pay rise in quick succession, having had a new four-year deal in March 1998 when Manchester City had been sniffing around.

Ferguson did not think Kidd really wanted to go to Everton or even to be manager. He felt Kidd was too insecure, too full of doubts about his own ability to become manager. But Blackburn, desperate to avoid relegation, offered him vast riches, believed to be around £1 million. While United were prepared to offer more, the main problem, as Kenyon told me, was that 'Brian was offered an amount of money he could not afford to turn down. He had a burning desire to be manager, to be number one, and there was no guarantee of that at Old Trafford. He did not ask for [the manager's job] because he knew he would not get it.'

On the afternoon of 2 December (later that day Tottenham would meet Manchester United in the Worthington Cup quarter-final) Kenyon, Edwards and Roland Smith had a meeting at HSBC with Kidd and his adviser. Edwards had said that Kidd would leave Old Trafford over his dead body. But at that meeting it was clear that even such a dramatic gesture from Edwards would not stop Kidd from going to Blackburn. He made it clear he wanted to manage more than he wanted the money, having spent most of his career on the backroom staff.

It was one of those classic football conversations, in the coded language the sport loves: at no stage in the conversation did Kidd say he had spoken to Blackburn. On the way to the game that night, the traffic was heavy and Kidd was becoming anxious about getting to White Hart Lane on time. The driver was asked how far it was. He said it was a mile so Kidd jumped out and ran to the ground. It turned out to be three miles: it was a more than a little breathless and less than composed Kidd who arrived that night at White Hart Lane.

The moment he got to Tottenham, Edwards went to see Ferguson. He told him Kidd was going or, in the curious jargon used by football, that United had given permission to Blackburn to talk to him. United made sure Blackburn compensated them for this permission. Edwards started by asking for £2 million and settled for £750,000.

For all the doubts Ferguson may have had about Kidd's inner resolve, he was less than pleased to see him go. That night Ferguson's mood was really black. Tottenham had beaten United 3–1. League Cup defeats in 1998 were much different from those Ferguson had suffered in 1989. Now United were secretly relieved to be out of the competition. However, Kidd's departure put a different gloss on it. Ferguson came to the post-match press conference, having spoken to Edwards and Kidd. At this stage the press were not aware that Kidd was definitely going. John Dillon of the *Daily Mirror* asked Ferguson whether it was difficult for Kidd to decide between Manchester United and Blackburn, a question that was neither aggressive nor meant to provoke, but Ferguson responded: 'That's a fucking stupid question.'

Such is Ferguson's command of the press that Dillon made no mention of it – indeed, he wrote a piece very complimentary about Ferguson's style of management – and none of the other papers referred to the outburst. Kidd's departure produced an orgy of press comment and Talk Radio even had a full afternoon's phone-in on the effects of Kidd's departure. It was treated as a major blow for Ferguson and Edwards and the board were blamed. Nine months later the truth of the relationship between Kidd and Ferguson was revealed in Ferguson's autobiography.

The media like to see Ferguson as a pop star who performs with his band. Old Trafford may be the theatre of dreams and the players great artists, but this comparison does not quite hold up. A pop group is by definition an anarchic phenomenon, whereas Ferguson is part of an organisation. He is not the master of Old Trafford.

Edwards' relationship with Ferguson was shaped by the lessons he drew from his father's relationship with managers. 'My father got too friendly with Tommy Docherty (who was manager between 1972 and 1977 and had won the FA Cup in 1977 but was sacked shortly afterwards). He used to go to races and things like that with him.' When Docherty had to be sacked over his affair with Mary Brown, the wife of United physio Laurie Brown, it was very difficult for Louis. It was Martin who took the phone call from Docherty telling the Edwards about his affair. He remains bitter that although Busby was allowed to have a mistress in London – he always stayed with her when United travelled south – Docherty was shown no such leniency. Martin watched this at first hand and was determined that he would never repeat his father's mistake by getting too close to the manager or, for that matter, anybody else at United. 'I think I had a very good working relationship with Alex Ferguson. But if you say did we go out socially together, no we didn't.'

Edwards carried this approach through to his operation of the plc. Some of this reflected his desire to get things right, his belief that there should be a distinction between the business of football and football as a sport. So, while

Edwards went to the dressing room, he was never matey with players. He felt, having been involved for more than thirty years, that he knew how people behaved. 'I just believe there are certain things you do and certain things you don't do. You have to divorce yourself a little bit. You can never get carried away in football.' It is this that shaped a philosophy where 'I don't particularly make great friendships with anyone – my finance director, my deputy managing director . . . I don't believe in being bosom pals with them, that does not necessarily work. I have seen it go wrong so many times. I am a businessman. I run a business.'

This aloofness is combined with an essentially cautious nature. Although United were part of the 'big five' who played a leading role in forming the Premier League, Edwards followed the lead of Irving Scholar and David Dein, Arsenal vice chairman. Edelson says: 'It would be fair to say Scholar and Dein played a more prominent role than Martin Edwards in the creation of the Premier League and the television deals before that. That is because of the type of people they are. Martin is more careful, and there's a lot to be said for not being innovative, for joining immediately after the innovators have done their bit. Martin was there, but not initiating the actual steps.'

All this is combined with one other Edwards trait – namely, that he did not ever really fall out with people. Ron Atkinson remains a friend despite the sack. Glenn Cooper will never entertain a bad thought about Edwards, even after United changed merchant bankers from Ansbachers to HSBC. 'I must say I was upset,' Cooper says. 'But did I have a row with Martin? No.'

To dismiss the man who has done all this as a mere butcher's boy, not very bright but with the right genes and fortunate to see everything fall into place, is ridiculous. Edwards is not charismatic, he was not an innovator, but he was more than the Ringo Starr of football. He made mistakes – the Knighton saga was not his best moment – and his personal life has had many less than edifying moments. But over the years he spent at Old Trafford he learnt and can claim great credit for the way Manchester United developed.

There was only one man Edwards became close to at Old Trafford – Maurice Watkins. Edwards acknowledges this but justifies it on the ground that he didn't 'work with Maurice day in, day out'. But Watkins has always occupied a special position at Manchester United, particularly in the Edwards regime. He was the trustee of the shares Edwards held in trust for his children and in the near thirty years he has been involved with United Edwards almost invariably turned to him in moments of crisis or grave importance. Not surprisingly Maurice Watkins was a vital player in the Edwards–Ferguson relationship, a confidant of one and friend of the other.

But then Watkins was much more than a mere non-executive director. In many ways he was something of a super-director. Ever since his involvement with United began in 1977, he had played a pivotal role in almost every major decision affecting the club. Even more than Edwards it was Watkins who acted as the spokesman for the club, and he was often its most prominent public face.

Watkins was in many ways the classic Manchester United supporter. His mother was a teacher and his father a solicitor's clerk, the sort of aspirational middle-class background where Manchester Grammar was the obvious school – his son was head boy there – and where the morning paper was likely to be the *Manchester Guardian* and the evening paper the *Manchester Evening News*.

Like many Lancastrians of his generation he grew up as a sports lover, taking as much interest in cricket as football and playing football himself for Old Mancunians in the Lancashire amateur league, which meant he missed many of the great games at Old Trafford in which George Best played. Watkins still insists that while he is a good supporter he is not a fan – 'It is a useful distinction; if we lose, I can sleep at night.' When Watkins finally joined the board, on the same day as Sir Bobby Charlton, he quite surprised his fellow directors after United had drawn a game by saying: 'The Old Mancunians would have been happy with the result.'

United came into his life professionally, quite unexpectedly, one evening in 1976, when Bill Royle, a fellow partner in Manchester law firm James Chapman & Co., suddenly died at a meeting at the Law Society. That night the Manchester United file was brought round to Watkins' home and he was asked to attend a meeting the next day at Old Trafford.

His first big task came when, following the 1977 Cup final victory, United decided to sack Tommy Docherty. Because Louis Edwards had been close to Docherty, Watkins was summoned to Edwards' home in Alderley Edge to sort out the mess. After that he became, almost invariably, the first port of call when the board ran into problems or had new issues to confront. Not long after the Docherty sacking the board were embroiled in the rights issue. The very morning after John Fletcher started his action seeking to prevent it, Martin Edwards and others filed into Watkins' office to prepare affidavits, on the basis of which Watkins helped the board defeat Fletcher.

Through the 1980s his workload for United increased. In 1984, as United signed Gordon Strachan from Aberdeen, Watkins found himself at three in the morning on the floor of the Intercontinental Hotel in Paris with Dick Donald, the Aberdeen vice-chairman, sorting out the mess Strachan had made of his contract. Strachan had, without telling his Aberdeen manager Alex Ferguson, signed a pre-contract with Cologne. When United came in for him this caused enormous complications. Watkins had to go to UEFA and then FIFA before, in the end, Cologne decided that it was hardly worthwhile pursing a player who did not want to play for them. The whole affair also brought Watkins in close contact with Ferguson and this proved very useful when two years later United returned to Aberdeen to hire Ferguson himself. Ferguson, in his book, goes out of his way to praise Watkins: 'He has consistently earned my respect during my time at the club', and particularly praises the way he got United and Clayton Blackmore out of a very difficult situation when the club were on a tour of Bermuda during the 1986-87 close season. Blackmore had been to a nightclub in Hamilton, Bermuda's capital, and returned to his hotel only to find that a woman had accused him of rape. Late that night police had come to the Elbow Beach Hotel, where United was staying, and taken Blackmore away.

Watkins, informed of the situation, first ascertained that the charge was baseless, with Blackmore maintaining it was a set-up. Watkins quickly realised that he had to prevent Blackmore getting charged. He knew if Blackmore was charged, he would face at least ten months in jail even before the case came up and, after he had prevented any charges being laid, he flew him back to England via Boston to avoid the British press, which by this time had gathered in force in Bermuda.

One of Watkins' most high-profile moments as the voice of reason for United, as the *Manchester Evening News* called him, was when he dealt with fallout from the Eric Cantona kung-fu incident and then the transfer of Andrei Kanchelksis. One was the most high profile case of common assault, the other, involving a transfer of a player from eastern Europe, suggested that lives may be in danger.

Watkins, while present at Selhurst Park, on the night Cantona launched at the Crystal Palace fan, did not actually see the incident, but the moment it happened he went to the dressing-room to be on hand should Cantona be charged with assault. He found Cantona sitting very quietly in the dressing-room, but over the next few weeks as the crisis developed neither Cantona nor the world was silent about this most amazing episode in English football.

United could have got rid of Cantona by selling him to Inter Milan, whose then general manager Paulo Taveggia was at Crystal Palace that night watching Cantona. A few days before, he had rung Edwards inquiring about Cantona, but his approach had been rebuffed. However, if Inter had offered more money Cantona might have gone – as it was, they came back later to buy Paul Ince. United, realising the seriousness of the incident, was torn about retaining Cantona and when, the following night, Watkins met Edwards, Roland Smith and Ferguson at the Edge Hotel in Alderley there was no consensus as to what should be done about Cantona. In the end it was decided that Cantona would be suspended until the end of the season and this was a classic lawyer's decision. United were seen to be doing something and in taking the decision before the FA had acted United felt it would stop the FA doing anything even worse.

However, when things did not work out quite that way, Watkins was involved in damage limitation both on behalf of Cantona, who was being represented by his firm, and United. Watkins, himself, has always seen his involvement in the Cantona affair as the high point of his association with United. There was the moment at the FA hearing when sitting next to Cantona, Watkins heard Cantona, after apologising to the FA, the fans, his team-mates and the club say: 'And I want to apologise to the prostitute who shared my bed last evening.' Graham Kelly, then chief executive, who was in the room, says: 'Maurice turned, his mouth dropped open and he almost fell off his chair.' Gordon McKeag, one of the three-man FA tribunal hearing the Cantona case, misheard and turned to Geoff Thompson, the chairman, and asked, 'What did he say? "He prostrates himself before the FA?"'

'Yes,' said Thompson, eager to get away from the subject.

Later that day, the FA decided that United's suspension was not enough and Cantona should be banned until 30 September. Thompson and McKeag had wanted a longer ban but the third member Ian Stott, persuaded them to limit it to 30 September. Cantona was such a big star that Stott actually wanted his autograph. Thompson told him he could not ask for it, as it would look ridiculous. However throughout the hearing Cantona was doodling away. It turned out to be a sketch of Thompson which Cantona presented to Thompson and Thompson decided to pass on to Stott.

Watkins' most notable moment with Cantona came following the trial. Cantona was originally sent down to serve a prison sentence; Watkins appealed and got him out on bail and then on appeal it was reduced to community service. At the end of it, Watkins decided that there had to be a press conference. Cantona agreed but only if he was allowed to speak. Just before the press conference began, Cantona came to Watkins's hotel room and taking a piece of paper started to write.

He asked Watkins: 'What is the name of the big boat when they catch fish?' Watkins told him it was called a trawler. Then Cantona asked, 'What is the name of the big seabird?' Watkins replied, 'A seagull.'

Having had a Watkins tutorial, Cantona then went to the press conference and uttered his by now immortal lines: 'When seagulls follow the trawler it is because they think sardines will be thrown into the sea.' Watkins, not sure he should allow Cantona to speak, pretended he did not know what Cantona was on about – the exact meaning of his words are still debated on the sports pages – but it had helped bring the whole affair to a close.

In many ways it was his involvement in the Andrei Kanchelskis affair that reveals best how he fits into the modern Manchester United and why, despite the fact that his full-time job is elsewhere, he has so often been at the centre of things at Old Trafford.

Kanchelskis was transferred from the Ukrainian club Shakhtar Donetsk to

United on 24 March 1991. Watkins, along with Edwards and Ferguson, negotiated a deal, which also involved the Norwegian agent Rune Hauge. Watkins' firm James Chapman negotiated the contract and United also paid £35,000 for Hauge's services, a payment which technically broke football's then rules but was common practice in the game, indulged in by all clubs.

However, the Kanchelskis story did not end there. On 23 August 1994, United returned to Old Trafford at one in the morning after a 1–1 draw at Nottingham Forest. Watkins asked Ferguson for a lift to the Four Seasons Hotel where, like many of the United players and officials, he had left his car. As Ferguson was about to leave the car park, Grigory Essaoulenko, a Russian agent who was part of the advisory team around Kanchelskis, stopped Ferguson and said he had a gift for him. Late as the hour was, he told Ferguson he had to give him the gift that night and asked him to come to the Excelsior Hotel near Manchester airport. When Ferguson got there he found a handsomely wrapped box. He threw it in the back of the car and drove home.

There he unwrapped it, expecting it to be a samovar. It turned out to be stuffed with £40,000 of cash.

The next morning he took it back to Old Trafford, where he went to the offices of Ken Merrett, the secretary, and emptied it in front of him. Inevitably, Watkins was the first to be called. He advised that the money should be lodged in the Old Trafford safe and that Ferguson should document what had happened with United's lawyers and his own solicitor.

The money stayed in the safe for a year, when Kanchelskis wanted a move to Everton. Essaoulenko then returned to Old Trafford because the move was proving complicated due to clauses in Kanchelskis' contract which gave him a third of the transfer fee. United had thought this amount would be waived and had done a deal with Everton, then realised the money had to be paid to Kanchelskis. That meant United were not going to get anything like the money they thought they were going to get.

But it gave United the opportunity to talk about the money in the safe. Ferguson told Essaoulenko he could not accept it. It required the intervention of Martin Edwards to persuade the Russian, who claimed it was a thank you to Ferguson, to take it back. Ferguson says he was bemused as to why the Russian should thank him this way, since he had done nothing he would not have ordinarily done. The discussions about the Kanchelskis transfer became so heated that Essaoulenko threatened Edwards with physical harm. When Watkins was asked for his opinion his response was simple: sell the player.

But in order to work out the deal with Everton Watkins had to fly out to Kiev to deal with Shakhtar Donetsk. He had been warned there might be trouble and took with him Ned Kelly, head of United security. In Kiev Watkins was introduced to a man who was described as a lawyer, but who when he left got into a Mercedes with three armed policemen and with a police escort. Some time after, before Kanchelskis had moved to Everton, Shakhtar's president Alexander Bragin was assassinated in a remote-controlled bomb explosion as he walked to his reserved seat at the start of a match. Watkins was relieved to read later that it was not linked to his own negotiations with Shakhtar, but connected with the growing links between the Russian mafia and sport.

What is illuminating about this story is how very differently Watkins and Edwards dealt with it. Watkins, while nervous about the Kiev experience, readily talked about it, whereas Edwards even several years later, could barely bring himself to do so. When I asked him about the death threats from Essaoulenko he said: 'There were veiled threats, definitely. I got threats because they wanted Kanchelskis to move on, I believe . . . I think we have to be very careful what we say . . . I wouldn't want you to play too much on that.'

This difference in attitude, and how they deal with the world, led to the situation that, although Edwards as chief executive of the plc and holding 12 per cent of the shares was the most important man at United, it was Watkins who took the lead in many matters.

The final chapter of the Kanchelskis affair, which came in 1999, also showed the standing Watkins has in the world of football. The story of the £40,000 stashed away in the United safe was first revealed by Ferguson in his autobiography. Nobody knew about it in the outside world, not even the Premier League bungs inquiry. Composed of Rick Parry, then chief executive of the Premier League, Steve Coppell, temporarily out of football then, and Robert Reid, then a QC now a judge, the inquiry spent several years looking into various transfers. About the Kanchelskis affair it concluded, 'There is no evidence that there was any irregularity in any of these payments or that any part of any payment found its way back to anyone at Manchester United.'

Reid and his colleagues were not told about the £40,000. However, after Ferguson decided to talk about it, the FA was forced to investigate. Graham Bean, the bung buster the FA had appointed after the Reid inquiry, went up to the offices of James Chapman and talked to Ferguson and Watkins. He found Ferguson very forthcoming and decided he had no case to answer but that Manchester United should be charged by the FA under Rule 26 for 'improper behaviour and conduct likely to bring the game into disrepute'. But the FA did not agree with him. Watkins had never had any doubts that such a charge would be quite absurd and the FA were not about to take on the best football lawyer in the business.

For all the growing animosity between Edwards and Ferguson, Watkins remains a good friend of both. In February 2002, when Ferguson was to make one of the most important decisions of his career, Watkins was the first person he rang.

4

DROPPING BOBBY AND THE STRUGGLE TO FLOAT

THE RECENT HISTORY of Manchester United could have been vastly different if in 1989 the managers of the Manchester-based Granada Television had listened to one of their executives, Paul Doherty, the son of a former Manchester City player.

Doherty, then head of sport at Granada, had got a tip-off that summer that Manchester United was about to be sold. He took a camera crew down with him to Old Trafford, arriving while Edwards was having lunch with Michael Knighton. He did not know who Knighton was and approached several people on the forecourt to ask, 'Are you the gentleman buying Manchester United?'

He got a dusty answer, but when news of the bid broke he approached his bosses at Granada with a proposal that the television company buy the club. As he watched the struggles with Knighton in amazement, he was further convinced this would be a good deal for Granada. The Premier League, or Super League as it was then called, was a gleam in only a few eyes and television had not begun to pay huge sums of money for football. For Doherty it seemed to make perfect sense that Granada, very much a Manchester company, should buy its local football club. Such links between local business and football were hardly unknown. But although chief executive David Plowright was keen, the rest of the board was not and Doherty's proposal was turned down. United did not even know of the idea.

With the Knighton fiasco now behind them United had to find some other means to get money. Ansbachers, having fought off Knighton, now turned to the issue of what United could do next. Mike Edelson says: 'Once the deal with Knighton was done, when he finished, it was almost as though United was "in play", in Stock Exchange terms, and somebody would come along . . . Ultimately it became obvious that the float was the best way forward.'

It was at this stage that Glenn Cooper became involved. Cooper was a vastly experienced City man, having started in 1963, the year Louis Edwards bought control of Manchester United. He had worked for a whole host of blue-chip City stockbrokers including Grieveson Grant, which would later be taken over by Kleinwort Benson, the firm that had advised Edwards on the rights issue. He also had experience of the North American investment scene. But he had no interest in football and had not really followed the game. Even more than a decade and innumerable visits to the boardroom later, he can find the passion in the United box when the news of the defeat of Manchester City comes through quite bewildering.

His first visit to Old Trafford came sometime in early 1990, where he was asked whether a flotation was possible. 'There was still going to be the need under the new Football Supporters Act, which had not then been passed but was at the report stage, for the whole ground to be seated and covered. This would require a lot of money, including the redevelopment of the Stretford End. So although Michael Knighton had gone away, the important issues which had got him involved hadn't.'

The board members were Knighton, Edwards, Watkins, Al Midani, Edelson, Les Olive, Bobby Charlton and Nigel Burrows. As we have seen, that 1989–90 season had been a dreadful one for Manchester United. Knocked out of the League Cup losing at home to Tottenham 3–0, a succession of League defeats including the awful 5–1 defeat at the hands of Manchester City meant that at one time they faced the prospect of relegation. Only an FA Cup win after a replay kept Alex Ferguson in his job.

Cooper met the board just before United's cup run began. The meeting, he recalls, was in the old, small, windowless boardroom, which is now a suite. As they discussed flotation they went round the table and finally came to Cooper. All the directors looked at him as Edwards asked him: Can we float Manchester United? 'I hesitated for a long time before I gave an answer and then I said just one word, "Just." I was not very confident it would not all be a ghastly mistake.'

Cooper's doubts about flotation were based on how the City had taken to Tottenham, the only other major football club that had floated. (By the time United floated, Millwall were also on the stock market, but they were not in Tottenham's or United's league.) The City and the financial press took a dim view of football clubs on the stock market. Tottenham had been on the stock market since 1983 and by now they were in serious financial trouble. After the problems of the West Stand brought Scholar to Tottenham, the costs of rebuilding the East Stand had now made a bad financial position dire. By 1989 they were casting round for a way to raise money, either through a rights issue or some other means, and not long after Cooper went up to meet the Manchester United board Tottenham were in such a parlous state that Irving Scholar had to borrow £1.1m from Robert Maxwell to pay for the balance of the transfer money owed on Gary Lineker to Barcelona, otherwise Lineker would have had to go back to Barcelona. The disclosure of this loan at the start of the 1990–91 season would trigger a chain of reactions that eventually contributed to the departure of Scholar from Tottenham and the sale of the club the following year to Alan Sugar and Terry Venables.

Cooper says: 'At that stage not many City institutions had invested in Spurs. They shied away from football. There was a very substantial body of opinion that said football clubs should not be on the stock market; that they were fundamentally not capable of being commercial.' During the Knighton saga both Burrows and Al Midani had called for flotation. Edwards, who alone among the directors had experience of being involved in a public company – albeit his father's – was not convinced. 'There was strong support in that board to float. I warned if you float, this will no longer be a private company. You won't be able to do everything you want. You will have to look after shareholders' interest and pay dividends. And although it will give us what we want in building the Stretford End, there will be restraints in the future.'

However, Edwards was well aware that by floating he could finally clear his debts. 'I was not prepared to carry on for the rest of my life being in debt to the bank. We had a situation where I was the majority shareholder, holding 50 per cent, but how could I liquidate my position? The choice was, instead of selling to an individual, to go public.'

Cooper says: 'It wasn't an act of intuitive genius to reach the conclusion that they ought to consider flotation. The question was, could it be done?' He set about trying to find out. 'There was quite a lot to do. First of all we had to create a takeover of the old Manchester United Football Club by a new plc, because the FA has some rather odious rules in the Memorandum of Articles of Association of a football club which aren't accepted on the Stock Exchange. One of them is that you can't pay dividends. The other is that in the event of liquidation any surplus goes to the players' pension funds – things which were perfectly understandable in the context of a private football club but not acceptable to a plc.'

So just as Tottenham had done, an off-the-shelf company was bought and a plc created. The football club, which continued to exist with its own board, became a wholly owned subsidiary of the newly created plc. A company called Voteasset Public Limited, formed on 21 December 1990, was bought and on 25 January 1991 its name was changed to Manchester United plc. The plc's first task was to acquire all the shares of the football club. This was done on 27 February 1991, when the company recommended a share-for-share exchange for the whole of the issued share capital of the club. On 22 March 1991 the exchange was declared unconditional (which meant the conditions attached to the offer had been met or waived and it could not now be withdrawn) and during the period up to 10 May 1991 the company acquired all the club's issued share capital.

In many ways the structural device of creating a new plc was a fairly standard procedure. More problematic was to get the United board and management right so that the company could be taken to the stock market. 'You've got to put a board together which is going to be acceptable in name and in form. That meant a non-executive chairman and a proper finance director and more non-executives than executives on the board.'

With Ansbachers the sponsors of the issue, Cooper was the one-man selection committee. He did not find it easy: 'There was a lot of manoeuvring from the existing board of the football club. None of the directors were appropriate to be non-executive chairman of a public company. I had discussions with Martin and he said I needed Maurice Watkins. He had the legal background and was important and essential to the functioning of Manchester United, so he came on the plc board. Al Midani, who had a substantial stake, came on the board. That left Edelson, Burrows, Knighton, Charlton and Les Olive. Les Olive was not a contender. Knighton was never a contender and I told him so.'

Edelson and Burrows were also very keen to be on the plc board. Cooper could not select them: 'Edelson lobbied me hard, really out of an inexperienced belief that he was important. Charlton was the most grumpy. He threatened to resign at one point if he did not go on the plc board. He realised later that he was much better off sitting where he was on the football club board rather on the plc board. But he didn't feel that at that time.'

The most important decision was that of chairman. Tottenham's troubles were by now well known and Cooper needed a name who would inspire confidence in the City. 'Martin came up with Roland Smith's name after I suggested we needed a non-executive chairman who had some standing in the City. Roland was ideal. The City knew him well, he was a Manchester United supporter, a Mancunian and it was very important that Martin as chief executive and Roland as chairman had confidence in each other. He was an old friend of the Edwards family.'

Cooper's decision not to put Nigel Burrows on the plc proved prescient. At the time of the float Burrows was a director of a company called Independent Financial Group plc, the holding company of IFG Financial Services Ltd. This administered United's staff pension scheme and insurances. Burrows had a 4 per cent share in United through IFG. However, sometime after the float, he ran into trouble with the law. He was jailed and made bankrupt, while his United shares were taken control of by his bank and sold, ending up with the BBC pension fund.

Cooper also had to make sure that the directors sold some of their shares. Edwards sold the biggest chunk, bringing down his stake from just over 50 per cent to 27.8 per cent and making him £6.445 million. Al Midani sold 283,690 on his own and 143,381 held by his company, Philen Establishment, which gave him a total of £1.644 million and left him with 7.1 per cent of the floated company. Watkins sold 175,725, which gave him £676,541 and a stake in United of 2.9 per cent. Edelson and Burrows also sold various chunks.

After years of prospective buyers coming to the doors of Manchester United, the directors now had a ready outlet for the shares. For Edwards this was very sweet. Finally, after many fruitless years and one humiliating experience, he had found the ideal route. The float was going to raise the £7 million necessary to rebuild the Stretford End. He could sell some of his shares, pay off his bank manager, make vast sums of money on a scale no previous director of a football club had ever made, yet still retain control. He had at last squared the circle no previous football club chairman had quite managed.

One of Cooper's major tasks was to find a finance director for the new stock market company. United had been going for very nearly a century but, he says, 'A secretary did the books. There was a whole department but there was no financial director in the sense a public company on the stock market would need.'

Broadbent, recruitment consultants, were appointed as headhunters and some forty people applied, from whom Robin Launders was chosen. He came from Reg Vardy, the car distribution firm in the north: 'I believe Robin had a combination of skills that was very attractive to the board at the time. He was a chartered accountant. He had also qualified as an engineer and that was one of the reasons he was hired for the flotation. They were going into a major construction phase that would lead on to other construction work, so it was even bigger than they thought at the time.'

As fellow United board members were to discover, Launders did not always have the man-management skills that would endear him to his colleagues. However, at this stage in the flotation his arrival marked the final modernisation of Manchester United. It gave the right impression to a City looking for reassurance that Manchester United on the stock market would behave in a responsible manner financially. The plc board now consisted of Smith (chairman), Edwards (chief executive) and Robin Launders (finance director), with Watkins and Al Midani as non-executive directors.

Launders achieved financial respectability partly through an innovation called the Transfer Fee Reserve Account. Its prospectus stated: 'At the discretion of the Directors this reserve may be increased both from profits after taxation arising from Cup success and from transfer fee receipts, and may be used to the extent available, to offset the effect of transfer fee payments on reported profits in any particular year.'

It was pure accounting fiction, created to reassure the City that United would not use up the money they made to splash out on players and that the dividend policy would be maintained. The reserve was never used, but its existence would feed any number of stories over the years of how much Ferguson had in the kitty. In truth the figures in the reserve were purely an accounting entry, never representing hard cash or determining United's ability to deal in the transfer market.

But if getting a board together that would please the City was not easy, Cooper had a torrid time trying to get a stockbroker to handle the issue: 'I was going round the City pulling strings to get myself a broker. I must have seen six or seven brokers. BZW, Kleinwort Benson, firms like that.' Stockbrokers were again influenced by what had happened to Tottenham. Aware that sentiment in the City was against football clubs, they didn't want to be involved. 'Finally I got Smith New Court and I think they were persuaded it was a good idea. It took me about seven weeks to find a broker.'

The next big problem for Cooper was convincing the institutions that it was worth investing in Manchester United. Before they visited Old Trafford they were dubious about investing. But, says Cooper, 'the moment you got an institution up to Old Trafford and they saw and understood the scale and nature of the business, they turned from being dubious to being quite enthusiastic.'

The only City people Cooper did not have to persuade were the financial PRs. 'It showed the PR business was different. Everybody wanted to do it. I think we short-listed six or seven. Brunswick made the best overall presentation, the most convincing.'

Cooper knew Brunswick's founder and main man Alan Parker very well, although the man who handled the account, John Bick, is a committed Tottenham fan. Brunswick's task was not easy: 'You can't change press view, you can only make sure that it is properly informed as it's required to be. It's very difficult because – it's a much more familiar problem now – at the time you had for the first time the crossover between sports journalists and City journalists. The sports journalists were writing for the first time about City matters and the City journalists were writing for the first time about sporting matters.'

For the flotation Cooper valued Manchester United at £42 million, £22 million more than Michael Knighton was prepared to pay two years earlier. 'I valued it the same way I value football businesses today. I took core earnings – that's to say what they received from their forty-odd League games – twenty matches at home, together with two rounds of each Cup (FA and League): the core repeatable earnings, pre-transfer. It included no transfer deals. It included sponsorship, merchandising and other commercial income. At the time I did the core earnings that applied came to £4 million. I then multiplied it by the multiple on the leisure index, which at that time was eleven.' This figure was then discounted to reach £42 million.

Alex Ferguson, having won his first trophy in 1990 after three years at Old Trafford, was now going for his second. In the 1990–91 season English clubs had been re-admitted to Europe after a gap of five years, and United were in the Cup Winners' Cup final. This was always the easiest of the three European competitions to win but they faced Barcelona and it looked tough. Cooper was ready to float in early May 1991 but decided to wait until the end of the final. 'It was my decision, on the basis that if we won the Cup Winners' Cup it might help and it wouldn't hurt if we didn't. We delayed the flotation as a gamble. I think in the event these things are always marginal.'

Ferguson prepared meticulously for the match. He consulted Steve Archibald, who had played for Barcelona, and also relied on a Dutch friend, Tom van Dalen, to make the right arrangements at Rotterdam, where the final was staged. Before the match he presented Johan Cruyff, the Barcelona manager, with a bottle of single malt Scotch, just as he had Real Madrid manager Alfredo Di Stefano eight years earlier when Aberdeen defeated Real in the same competition. Ferguson wanted history to repeat itself and it duly did. United won 2–1 on 15 May 1991, although the second goal by Mark Hughes was probably offside.

Flotation day was fixed for 10 June. This was the day the first dealings in United shares would take place on the stock market. At two that morning Cooper and Edwards were driven down from Manchester to Ansbachers' headquarters in Mitre Square in the City. 'We had the final negotiations in Manchester, the closing and signing documents, underwriting agreements. We left at two in the morning and got to my offices at five, maybe a bit later, and there were press conferences and all of that for much of the day.'

Old Trafford was abuzz with this new dawn, but one man in Old Trafford did not share the excitement. That man was Alex Ferguson. Cooper says: 'I don't think he was particularly interested in the process. He was always around and about but I don't think we had any meetings with him directly. I think he found the process a bit alien.' Ferguson's indifference was shared by most of the fans.

The share issue was divided between an institutional placement and an open offer to the public, who it was hoped would be supporters of the club. Of the 4.675 million shares, 2.077 million were offered to the institutions, and slightly more, 2.597 million, to the public. Cooper says: 'The institutional quota was fully placed and the public offering was the one that was not completely taken up. Contrary to what most people think, football fans or supporters are not great buyers of shares, not even of their own club. The public not taking it all up meant there was about 5 to 6 per cent left with the underwriters.'

Cooper insists the issue was not a flop, but 'As an underwriter we had to swallow the shortfall on public subscription, which we did because that's what we are paid for.' Ansbachers had charged £300,000 for the flotation and were left with some 3 per cent of Manchester United. They decided that it was not worth holding on to the shares.

But in the week following 10 June 1991 it would have required rare courage to hold on to Manchester United shares. The share issue might not have been a flop but in the days after that the price was a disaster. It seemed all the old fears of Tottenham were being revived, if anything in an even more alarming way. And this was because of the actions of that bugbear of Manchester United, the Maxwells.

Crick and Smith, writing in 1989, had doubted that the Maxwells had a holding. But they did. They held 505,000 shares bought years before the float, a 4.25 per cent stake in the new plc. It was a stake that had worried Cooper.

'Prior to the flotation, it must have been in early 1991, I had a conversation with Kevin (one of Robert Maxwell's sons), when I asked him what his intentions were in respect of that holding. He said the Maxwell family was a friend of Manchester United and they intended to hold on to the shares and they would prove to be no embarrassment on the flotation.' In the event Maxwell did precisely the opposite. 'He just banged them out into the after market, having said he wouldn't. Within a day or two.' The price fell straight away. 'If I'd thought he'd be a seller in the after market, I would have tied it up at the time. I'd either have placed them or taken them out during the course of the flotation or obliged him to sign a standstill. That is to agree not to sell. The last thing in the world you want is a loose cannon shareholder in the after market.'

On 10 June 1991 the share price was £3.85. The moment Kevin Maxwell sold, the price dropped like a stone and within a week it was down to £2.60. Having been floated at £42 million, United was suddenly worth £26 million. However, even as the board watched this fall in frustration, a man from Tottenham was on his way to Old Trafford to help United recover its share price and its stock market standing.

5

THE THIRD MAN – THE MAN FROM WHITE HART LANE

IN THE MODERN history of Manchester United many people can lay claim to have turned the club around from one with a vast following but not much money to what is now called a corporate monster. Alex Ferguson and Eric Cantona have both had supremely important roles in shaping the modern Manchester United, but there was a third man: Edward Freedman. And, like all such stories, his association with Old Trafford began unusually. Freedman went to Old Trafford to try to get business for another club, and ended up driving the marketing juggernaut United became in the 1990s.

In June 1992, when Freedman first visited Old Trafford, he was in charge of merchandising at Tottenham, a club which seemed the natural home for him. Educated in London at a grammar school in Hendon, after he left school he went to the Retail College of Distribution in Charing Cross Road. From there he trained in a company which was then called Times Furnishing, now part of the GUS group. 'I thought at the time retailing for clothing needed to be changed. I thought what was needed was a supermarket style of presenting the product. I was probably the first person to bring it to England and we started and built up a chain of shops. This was about 1965. We built up a chain of retail shops and then sold them. Then we started again.'

Growing up in North London in the 1950s, he had been going to White Hart Lane since he was a little boy. However, football support in those days was not quite so intensely tribal as it has since become. One week he would go to Tottenham and another week to Arsenal. His cousin was an Arsenal supporter so they went on alternate weekends. The result was that, as Tottenham were building up their greatest side, the Double team, he saw every home match and quite a few away ones.

Freedman moved into football in the 1980s when he came into contact with Irving Scholar. 'I had a friend, Jan Stoord, who was an accredited football agent in Belgium. He telephoned me just after the Mexico World Cup in 1986. He said that David Pleat [then Tottenham manager] had been looking at one of the players, Nico Claesen, and asked me if I knew Irving. I said I did, which was not quite true. I knew of him, of course, but I didn't know him personally then. I contacted Irving and he said he was interested in the player. There were protracted negotiations and during them Irving had found out quite a lot about me and that my knowledge was in the retail area and in products and producing. He asked me to have a look at the Tottenham shop – and also the products they were selling.'

Impressed with Freedman's approach, Scholar asked him to join the club. His arrival revolutionised Tottenham's marketing and it seemed the partnership would work well. But in the summer of 1991, as a result of other financial pressures, Scholar sold Tottenham and the club was taken over by Alan Sugar, who had made his fortune through the electronics firm Amstrad, and Terry Venables, a former player, who was then the manager of the club.

Venables became chief executive of Tottenham Hotspur plc and brought with him as his financial adviser a man called Eddie Ashby. Freedman soon found that the Venables regime had a rotten core. He could not work with Venables and in particular Ashby, who despite being a bankrupt with a questionable business record had major executive responsibility at Tottenham. By 1993 Venables' relations with Sugar were at breaking point due to his refusal to sack Ashby and other disagreements. In May what had been seen as the dream team dissolved into a bitter court battle as Sugar sacked Venables amid much acrimony. In October 1997 Ashby was jailed for violating bankruptcy laws, while in January 1998 Venables was disqualified for seven years from acting as a company director.

However, in June 1992, Ashby's and Venables' wrongdoings were not known and while Freedman was not happy at Tottenham he had no immediate plans to leave. But his visit to Old Trafford was to dramatically change both United and Freedman's life. He recalls the moment he went up to Old Trafford: 'Martin Edwards had known about me through Irving and what I'd done at Tottenham. At the time Tottenham were turning over more money through merchandise than Manchester United – by a long way, I would say 50 per cent more than Manchester United at the time. I knew the Manchester United shop wasn't doing very well. I had an idea we at Tottenham could sell our expertise to other clubs and show them how to be as successful as Tottenham.'

He went to see Danny McGregor, the commercial manager. As Freedman was making the presentation Martin Edwards came in and listened for a while. Before he had finished Edwards said to him: 'Edward, is it possible for you to come up to my office and have a chat with me before you leave?'

Freedman found that Edwards had been so impressed by what he was saying that he wanted him to come and work full time for United. 'I was shocked because I'd never worked outside London before. At first I said no and he suggested another meeting. I talked it over with my wife and she said, "You're unhappy at Tottenham and even though it will be difficult, I think you should do it."'

Martin Edwards' decision to appoint Freedman was not so spontaneous as this account may make it appear. For almost six months he had been mulling over bringing someone in to do something about United's marketing. It was Peter Kenyon, then chief executive at kit manufacturers Umbro, who had first suggested Freedman's name. In 1990 Umbro were in talks with United with regard to their new kit contract. 'One of the things I talked to Martin Edwards about when we were making the pitch was that the product was not distributed well enough. You could not get it in Scotland and parts of the South-east.'

Some time after that Martin Edwards rang Kenyon and said: 'We've taken on board your views regarding a bigger merchandising set-up.' They'd decided they wanted to look for someone and he asked Kenyon who he would suggest. 'I put forward Edward Freedman. We at Umbro had dealt with Tottenham and I had got to know Freedman.'

Now that Edwards had made his play it did not take long for Freedman to be persuaded that it made sense to leave his beloved Tottenham for United. Life with Venables and Ashby was getting increasingly difficult. It also helped that 'Manchester United was always my second team. It wasn't Liverpool because I thought Manchester United played in a style similar to the way Tottenham played.'

By the time Freedman returned to Old Trafford as an employee it was a year since United had floated. The club had barely gone forward in that time. If anything, by the end of the 1991–92 season many felt that the elusive championship trophy, which United had sought since Busby last won it in 1967, would never come back to Old Trafford. Part of the reason for the depression was the tremendous expectations raised by that season, the last of the old unified Football League. For much of 1991–92 it seemed almost certain Alex Ferguson would end the hunger that had gnawed at United for twenty-five long years. But in the last weeks of the season United stumbled and a moderate Leeds side managed by Howard Wilkinson won the title, much to their own surprise. Edwards was convinced Manchester United were cursed. In the run-up to the season's end United were defeated in a crucial match by Liverpool, Edwards turned in the directors box and said, 'We are never going to win the League.'

Off the field the share price was going nowhere. The price after the Maxwell dump had been flat and United's marketing was underperforming Tottenham, a club which on the field was doing nothing and what is more had serious financial problems off the field. Why?

'There were,' says Freedman, 'a whole host of reasons. One, the retail environment itself at Manchester United was very, very old-fashioned and backward. The store they had was approximately 12,000 square feet and 500 square feet of that was given over to the lottery. The mail order had just one telephone operator. The product range was very poor and old-fashioned. The product quality was very bad.' Freedman encountered enormous cultural problems. United may have had great support, but when it came to marketing they still had to understand how to make their name and their considerable reputation into a product that would sell. 'They did not understand what a brand was, they had never realised they *had* a brand, that Manchester United *was* a brand.'

During the flotation Glenn Cooper had already come across a great deal of internal resistance to change in the way the business was run. 'One of the criticisms that comes out a lot is, "Ee, bah goom, lad, you don't understand. This is about passion, it's not about business." On one occasion in an interview I heard myself responding, "Yes, but have you tried passion in a cold bedroom with an ugly partner?" You can't actually divorce these things. Clubs sustain incredibly long periods of poor performance without it reflecting amongst their supporters or customers.'

The problem, as Martin Edwards saw it, was structural. That was the reason he had recruited Edward Freedman: 'When Edward came marketing was basically the shop. There was no wholesale. We had a video agreement with VCI but that was purely on a royalty basis. In other words they paid us so much for each video they sold. We didn't actually do the videoing ourselves. A lot of our products were licensed out. Apart from what the shop sold – jackets, T-shirts – on a lot of items we got a royalty for what was sold.'

In 1968 the shop had been given to Matt Busby on a 21-year lease and it had been taken on by Sandy, his son. Some time before Freedman joined, the lease had expired and United had given the shop to another businessman to run. When that did not work there was even talk of Tottenham running the United shop. Tottenham, who under Scholar had gone into publishing under the imprint Cockerel Books, had already published a United book, *Red Devils in Europe*, which sold some 2,000 copies. But these talks over the shop had come to nothing.

As Freedman recalls: 'The Busby family were still very affectionate towards Manchester United. The shop's lease was coming to an end anyway. And we quickly opened another shop.' United built a megastore of 5,000 sq ft and a superstore of 2,500 sq ft at Old Trafford, with a third store of 3,000 sq ft open only on match days.

Expanding the stores was only a part of the Freedman marketing revolution. Freedman also, says Martin Edwards, 'started the wholesale, whereby we brought the product in, sorted it and then sold it to other retailers. And he also took the videos back on board ourselves and started the magazine.'

One of the first things Freedman did was stop licensing of products and re-source the whole product range. He also improved the retail environment. He took on good staff who understood marketing and how to portray Manchester

United, not just as a football club but as an environment which would compete in the market with people like Marks & Spencer and give customers what they wanted.

With merchandising becoming a major business, Freedman persuaded United to set up a separate merchandising subsidiary. 'I always believe you have to account in your own right for everything.' He wanted it to run as a separate business. 'Every month we produced management figures and management reports and we knew where we were going profit and loss-wise. That had never happened before either.'

Perhaps his most significant innovation was the launch of the Manchester United magazine, the first time a club had its own individual magazine. Soon after he arrived he surveyed the publications available to the supporters: 'At that particular time the major ones were *Shoot!* and *Match*. They were aiming at a very much younger age group and market. I thought there was just a possibility that if we launched our own publication this could succeed because it would talk to the supporters on a level which I thought they needed to be talked to, not talked down to, but at the correct level. We did a lot of research and some surveys on this.

'I also wasn't very happy with the Manchester United programme at the time. It was pretty bad, produced in-house and was an old traditional thing which was very hard to get changed. It was done by committee, rather than by understanding where the future of publishing lay.'

The obvious answer was United's own magazine, but Freedman did not find it easy to launch. Almost in desperation, he turned to his son James, who had studied classics at Cambridge before going into the film industry. James set up the magazine in the bedroom of his flat in Belsize Park in London with a couple of Apple Macs. 'I worked very closely with a friend of mine who was at Cambridge with me and he had a friend who was writing for *The Guardian* and *The Observer* called Gavin Hills.'

The problem for the Freedmans was to convince the retail trade that it was worth stocking the magazine. In 1992 United was seen as a north-western provincial club, interesting but not a winner with a world-wide appeal. Nevertheless in November 1992 the magazine was launched and the first issue sold 15,000. James Freedman recalls: 'After a few months I put forward a proposal that was more attractive to Manchester United. I had found a much better publishing organisation, a much better repro house, much better journalists and we took the idea back to the board. Within eighteen months it was selling over 100,000 a year and was hugely successful.'

As United started to perform on the field and Freedman was able to market the brand name of Manchester United, the magazine took off. 'The retailers, led by W. H. Smith, liked the magazine which proved a big seller for them and all the major retailers. Soon it was the biggest-selling football monthly in the world, selling about 80 to 90,000 a month.'

In December 1993, six months after the club had won their first League title since 1967, United launched a monthly video magazine, which was to prove enormously successful. This was another proposal made by James Freedman, whose company by then had expanded its work as a contract publishing company for United. The club decided to take video production in-house and at one stage had 2 per cent of the video market in England. In 1995 Freedman's company, Zone, was so successful that, no longer run from his bedroom in Belsize Park, it won the Small Publisher of the Year Award.

In January 1996 United sold the magazine, the publications and the videos to VCI for £6 million for a ten-year deal, with £3.5 million received in advance royalties. But they continued with the retail and wholesale operations Freedman had set up.

Freedman had tapped into a previously unexplored source of support. 'We were doing business overseas by mail order and then the magazine started to open the market up. Someone came from Thailand and said he would like to produce this magazine there. He had seen the magazine and he produced sports magazines and a major daily sports publication. He had written to *every* club in the country, saying that football was becoming very big in Thailand and could he come and see them. The only one to answer his letter was me. I invited him to come and see me and he got on a plane the following week.'

Yet for all Freedman's marketing skills, his innovative idea of the magazine, which was key to driving the Manchester United brand, might never have got off the ground but for the support of Martin Edwards. Having chosen the man for the job, Edwards firmly supported him, a characteristic of his and a sign of a good manager and delegator. 'The major thing was Martin Edwards let me get on with it and he didn't interfere.'

Statistics can often be misleading. But figures comparing Manchester United with Tottenham illustrate how badly United had been underperforming before Freedman arrived and how he succeeded in building up the United brand. In 1991, United's revenue was £17.8 million; by 1997 it was nearly £88 million, for a net profit of £27.5 million. In contrast, over the same period Tottenham having started ahead of Manchester United fell behind and never recovered. Its revenue, £18.7 million in 1991, rose to just £27.8 million by 1997.

Of course by then United were having tremendous success on the field. The League title in 1993 was followed with a Double in 1994, which fuelled Freedman's marketing drive. But, crucially, Freedman had built the mechanism and infrastructure to exploit that success.

Success on the field building up an historic fan base, even relative success after years of under-performance, can translate into higher revenues. For example, in 1991 Newcastle United had not won a domestic trophy since the 1950s. Their revenues were £4.4 million; they spent £2.75 million in wages and made losses of £2.5 million. By 1996, when they were challenging Manchester United for the Premiership title, Newcastle's revenues had increased to £28.9 million. But wages rose to £19.7 million and transfers of £27.6 million meant losses were £23.6 million.

What these figures emphasise is that Newcastle remained a conventional club. Better performances on the field lead to higher income, but as more money is spent on players the club goes into the red. Manchester United from the 1994 season did something very different. They created a virtuous cycle where whatever the temporary setbacks on the field, the club kept growing. From 1994 United started bucking the universal trend where instant success brought instant money and sudden failure led to huge debts. In the 1994–95 season United were chasing trophies on three fronts at one stage but won nothing. However, the marketing machine went rolling on. From the chance business of football United had created something quite permanent.

Freedman's impact is best judged if we compare an average take during a League match in three seasons, 1991–92, 1993–94 and 1994–95.

On a League match day in 1991–92, the last before Freedman arrived at Old Trafford – and a season, it is worth recalling, when United came closest to winning the League since 1967 – the average income was £500,000: season tickets £240,000, gate receipts £160,000, executive boxes £20,000, programmes £30,000, shop £22,000, catering £30,000. In 1993–94 a League match day produced on average a total of £760,000: season tickets £420,000, gate receipts £180,000, executive boxes £20,000, programmes £30,000, shop £44,000, catering £60,000.

By the 1994–95 season a match day produced £900,000: season tickets £500,000, gate receipts £180,000, executive boxes £40,000, programmes £20,000, shop £70,000 and catering £80,000.

Before Freedman came to United there had been a huge gap between reality and hype about the club's financial resources. The huge gates United attracted fed this illusion. While the gates were large the money they brought in was often less than clubs in London like Arsenal and Tottenham, who had smaller stadiums but could charge more money. Martin Edwards had always been sensitive about ticket pricing and even today United are in the bottom half of the ticket price league headed by London clubs such as Chelsea.

While the huge support led to the illusion that United had pots of money, the reality came as a big shock to Alex Ferguson, as he explains in his auto-biography. In the summer of 1987, little more than six months after he became manager, Ferguson went to Edwards and told him he needed to sign eight new players. Ferguson says that to his surprise, Edwards was 'taken aback' by this demand. 'It was hardly cheering to hear the chairman say that the club did not have the resources to finance the purchases I knew were necessary . . . That conversation might have astonished all the outsiders who even back then thought of United as an organisation rich enough to attack the problems with a blitz of cash.'

A crucial part in Freedman's merchandising revolution was played by the arrival at United of Eric Cantona. Edwards sees Cantona's transfer from Leeds as 'the greatest deal in the history of English football. In 1994–95, when after the kung-fu kick he didn't have a full season, it was the only season we didn't win anything. His first season we won the League [1992–93] and we won the Double twice [1993–94 and 1995–96]. His contribution is absolutely enormous. He unlocked the door for us.'

Off the field Freedman made sure that he made the most of the Cantona factor. 'He was on T-shirts, sweat shirts – whatever I could do with him. We did books, a calendar and magazines. I sent someone over to spend a whole weekend with him in France to take photos. With Cantona I made every product possible available. Anything that people wanted, that was possible to justify Cantona. Apart from the normal things I spent £25,000 on a tie.'

By the mid-1990s the marketing drive was going so well that even when Cantona was missing from the field it went on. In 1995, his absence from the game for seven months between January and September, after his kung-fu kick at a Crystal Palace supporter, did not affect the marketing. Nor even in the spring of 1996, when he made known he was going to leave United for good. 'There wasn't any drastic dip in circulation or product selling with Cantona away. The ground was still full every week, so what more we could have done with him there I don't really know, but I don't think we found any really big effect.' Even Cantona's suspension and eventual departure was good publicity. 'It was all over the world and everyone was talking about Manchester United. It was on front covers everywhere.'

Cantona would later be critical of what he saw as over commercialisation at United, which he said had contributed to his departure from Old Trafford. Between 1995–96 Cantona twice thought about quitting United, Ferguson stopping him the first time. However by the end of the 1995–96 season, despite helping United to their fourth Premiership title in five years, he was disillusioned by United's failure to win the European Cup. Cantona would later tell Michael Crick, Ferguson's biographer, that the commercialism that Freedman had brought in was also one of the reasons he left. 'I didn't,' he told Crick, 'play football for business.' United he said, treated him 'like a pair of socks, like a shirt, like a shit. I am not a shit.'

But after his retirement, when he came back to Old Trafford for a benefit match which was meant to raise money for the victims of the Munich air crash

– and also be a farewell to Eric Cantona (Edwards having decided to combine the two) – his own commercial behaviour raised the hackles of those working on behalf of the victims. Jeff Connor in *The Lost Babes*, the story of how Manchester United forgot the victims of Munich, details how the victims and their surviving dependants were unhappy that the testimonial committee had to pay for a Lear jet to ferry Cantona's friends and family from Paris, for their stay at the De Vere Mottram Hall Hotel, which cost £15,869.94, while at the end of the match each of the dependants or divisions of dependant of the Munich air crash received £47,283.89, half of the £90,555.01 Cantona received. The event organisers argued Cantona's presence made the testimonial match such a success.

Not surprisingly Freedman, the ultimate marketer, rejects Cantona's view. 'Over-commercialism has to be looked at carefully. If it's bad over-commercialism and you are giving bad products or bad value, that's another story. But if you are giving good value and giving what the customers want, at the end of the day they are the people who say yes or no and who buy the tickets.'

However, he agrees that there is ground for fans to complain that United have made frequent changes of replica shirts: 'There should only ever be two shirts, a home shirt and an away shirt. The home shirt should be changed every season because the fans don't mind that being changed every year. The away shirt should only be changed every other year. It is changed too many times.'

At times United's proliferation of shirts even led to a revolt from the players. In the 1997 season, while playing away at the Dell against Southampton, United's players wore a grey shirt. With United losing 1–0 at half time the players decided to throw away the grey shirts. 'Alex would have been involved all along when we produced a new shirt . . . He never said he didn't like a shirt. But on this occasion Alex got it into his head that it was responsible for the bad performance. There's a lot of superstition in football, so if the manager can blame anything other than the players for a bad team performance, he will. They had a terrible first half and blamed it on the shirts. They said they couldn't see each other playing in grey shirts.' United played the second half in white and still lost. But the incident, while trivial, highlighted the whole issue about shirts and their marketing.

And another consequence of Freedman's marketing revolution and United's success on the field was that the club everybody loved became one of the most hated in the country, even round the world. If Busby had created a club everyone wanted to cherish, the new United of the 1990s and its success was resented by many. The cry 'Stand up if you hate Manchester United' began to be heard round the country. In 1996 Hunter Davies, the author, journalist and Tottenham fan, made a television documentary castigating United for always looking to make money and losing touch with its supporters.

Apart from criticising United's pursuit of marketing riches, Davies made much of the fact that match days at United showed many of the supporters come from hundreds of miles away, often on long coach trips from the south of England and even overseas, from both Scandinavia and Ireland. Surely, he argued, this was ultimate evidence of the club losing its soul? It was no longer a community-based football club but had instead transformed itself into a money-making machine, attracting mercenaries from all over the world who had no affinity with the club but were drawn to it by its success.

Even before Freedman had started his marketing revolution, in Ireland a movement had started which had turned from love to hate for United. The Irish broadcaster Des Cahill, who presents the breakfast programme on the pop music station of RTE, the Irish broadcasting service, had started ABU, 'Anybody But United'. Cahill, who is himself a West Ham supporter, found his mind filled with anti-United feeling in 1992 when United just lost the First Division title to Leeds. 'The United supporters started crawling out of the woodwork. Ireland has always had a huge United support. Some 4,000 to 5,000 go to Old Trafford from Ireland for every home game and what got me was, why should someone from Cork care so much about what happens to the full back of United?'

Since then, with each United success what had started as a state of mind expanded into an almost evangelical movement delighting in every United defeat. A T-shirt was produced which listed all the clubs, such as York and Galatasaray, which over the years had inflicted humiliating defeats on United. Cahill emphasises that much of this is done tongue in cheek, as part of the celebrated Irish sense of fun. However, he feels strongly that what spoils United is not so much their success on the field but their supporters who, he says exude an air of arrogance and invincibility.

James Freedman says, 'There's an arrogance about Manchester United, unquestionably. There's been some incredibly poor handling of the media. Ferguson doesn't want to be liked. He has always enjoyed playing the under-dog.' At Aberdeen, Ferguson had the perfect excuse. Outside the Old Firm, he was able to rally the players around an idea that everyone was against them. At Manchester United he gained much less sympathy because the club were so successful. 'Then you've got Cantona, someone that fans who do not support Manchester United loved to hate. Keane, Ince – these are also characters that supporters of other clubs do not like.'

Edward Freedman offers another reason why United, once one of the best-loved clubs in the land, is now the most hated: 'In England we don't like success and Manchester United have been remarkably successful. People now haven't grown up with the memory of Munich. If you grew up in the sixties and seventies with the memory of Munich and what Busby did and Duncan

Edwards dying in this great northern tragedy, then obviously you are going to
feel sympathy for the club. Then you've had people like George Best, who was
obviously a massive national hero, together with Denis Law and Bobby
Charlton. All three of them have reason to be loved and are very popular figures.
But even in their heyday United did not have the success they had in the 1990s.'

The on-field success from the mid-1990s and the explosion of media interest
meant that the sports marketing men, of course, could not get enough of
Manchester United. This was to provide Freedman's crowning moment of
glory. In 1996 United, inspired by Cantona, won their second Double. Even as
United were chasing this then unique honour, marketing talk had turned to a
new kit sponsorship deal. Previously the value of such contracts had been
agreed on an ad hoc basis. This time Freedman calculated what the contract was
actually worth. 'We went through how many shirts are sold, how many
tracksuits are sold – how many of whatever product we were involved with was
sold. We worked out how much it cost to produce the kit, how much to buy the
kit and we came up with three scenarios: the worst-case scenario which saw us
get £8 million, the possible scenario which meant we could get £15 million, and
the optimistic scenario where we could get £21 million.'

With United having won the Double twice, Nike were keen to win the kit
contract from Umbro. They contacted Martin Edwards and flew him,
Freedman and Danny McGregor to the States: 'We went to see Niketown and
then on to Portland, where they have their operation. We were there two or
three days. We were wined and dined – goods in the room, all that sort of thing.
We had very hard negotiations and they wouldn't come to the figures I wanted.
It was nowhere near. Five million was the most they would offer.'

Peter Kenyon and Umbro had watched United's trip to Niketown with a
great deal of anxiety. But Freedman relished the situation United were in: 'They
were very keen to discuss with us. I thought these were the best negotiations I'd
ever had in my life, because I felt I'd got them into such a corner.' During the
course of the negotiations Umbro were given Freedman's figures. 'I thought the
following morning they would tear it to shreds and shoot holes all through it.'
In August 1996 United signed a new six-year deal with Umbro. While its value
was never revealed, Umbro had in fact matched Freedman's second scenario,
agreeing to pay £15 million. For Freedman the deal justified everything he had
been doing at United.

But are we making too much of the Freedman merchandising revolution? He
certainly pushed up the turnover at United, but how did this feed through to
the bottom line, the profits? Glenn Cooper accepts that there is much merit in
Freedman's view that when he went to United it wasn't the mega-club that it has
since become. 'In 1990 Manchester United had won very little for a longish time
– apart from a couple of cups – but in the previous sixteen or seventeen years

they hadn't really done a great deal. Then you got the flotation and the resolution of the immediate capital problem; the development of the ground, which began to create more revenue; the development of merchandising. All of that began to flow alongside a more successful team.'

Kenyon sees Freedman's success as part of the wider changes coming to the football industry at that time. Just as the mid-1980s were a grim period for English soccer, the tide had begun to turn in the early 1990s. 'We'd come through the hooliganism of the eighties, had a very successful England in Italia 90 and within three weeks football almost became respectable again. It became a national game. Hooliganism didn't necessarily stop, but it stopped getting reported. There was a real feel-good factor. That coincided not long after with the Premier League being formed and the emergence of football clubs potentially becoming businesses, so there was a lot going on in the industry. As far as Manchester United was concerned two things happened. Sales went up through better distribution and there was success on the field.' According to Kenyon, 'Edward did a job for Manchester United that needed doing at the time.'

Martin Edwards is keenest to caution against excessive glorification of Freedman. As he points out, 'the merchandising side of the business is a big part of our turnover, but it only operates on normal retail or wholesale margins. There's a big cost of sale involved in that. So the actual contribution to our overall profits sometimes gets exaggerated. Whereas sponsorship and TV income almost fall right through to the bottom line.'

In 1997 United declared profits of £27.6 million on ordinary activities before taxation and after net transfer fees of £293,000. The turnover was £87.9 million, to which merchandising contributed £28.7 million. But how much did merchandising contribute to the £27.6 million profit?

Edwards says: 'The actual merchandising element would not be enormous. It is a big turnover, low margin, whereas a lot of the rest of the business, even gate receipts, is big turnover and pretty high margins . . . People talk about Manchester United's merchandising. It's big and it makes a contribution but it's not the be all and end all. The footballing side, the results on the field, getting into European competitions, getting TV deals, getting sponsorship deals – these are more important profit-wise.' Merchandising has accounted for around 30 per cent of United's revenue since the Freedman marketing revolution but with a 12 per cent margin on products it produces only 11 per cent of profits.

Edwards and Kenyon later fell out with Freedman, and they may be seeking to make sure he is not seen as the great marketing Messiah who made United. It could also be argued Edwards is seeking to dim some of the glory that Freedman has claimed, but there is backing from what he says from City analysts.

In November 1996 Julian Easthope, then at UBS Global Research, wrote: 'Gate receipts (which include programme sales) have a gross margin of 90 per cent and are the largest contributor to group profits. It is a high-quality revenue stream, with around 70 per cent received in advance from the sale of season tickets.' The growth in gate receipts during the 1990s was exceptional, with the compound annual rate amounting to 21 per cent, from £6.2 million in 1990 to £41.9 million in 1999.

So if Edwards believes Freedman wasn't the magician who waved the wand at United, then what did? His answer is that while Freedman contributed, the real key was that United was converted into a successful football business where, matching its position as a plc, it began to look after its shareholders and give them the sort of comfort and satisfaction they needed. In this wider context it would, he says, be wrong to see the financial revolution at United as the work of just one man: 'The turning point was when we started to show results, because don't forget we were floating in the aftermath of Tottenham.' Finally investors could see the growth of the company, while promises made at flotation suddenly came to fruition. 'We started to pay a dividend while Tottenham were erratic with the dividend, or didn't pay it at all. One of the things we're proud of is that every dividend since the flotation, every interim, every final, has been increased. They could see that steady increase in the profits and the dividend and suddenly they realized, hang on, this isn't just a football club. This is a serious business.'

Edwards and his board did not find it easy to sell United to the City. 'They didn't believe that a football club could generate profits on a regular basis. They didn't believe that football club directors would be disciplined enough to pay dividends on a regular basis and generally act as proper plc custodians of the business. That doubt was always there. So we've only done it by our results.'

The City slowly took to United but it was only in 1996 that a majority of stock, 60 per cent, was in the hands of City institutions. Edwards says: 'I can't think what the figure was just after the float, but I would suspect it was 20-odd per cent, maybe 30 per cent. Slowly but surely it's crept up, mainly because the institutions took up any of the share sold by the directors.'

Cooper supports Edwards' assessment that turning United round was not just Freedman working his marketing magic: 'It is not a case that United went nowhere until 1992 and then all of a sudden Freedman came and it came together. That is not quite fair. Earnings started to go up on a trend. We made forecasts in the prospectus and these forecasts were met and exceeded in all cases, which is a very good point for a flotation. As you know, a number of flotations of football clubs have happened where that wasn't the case. Then, of course, the TV contract came up for renewal.' The advent of Sky in 1992 was the manifestation of the fact that football is an enormously important driver to the viewing public. 'Everything's changed, because when we floated I think we anticipated revenues of £14 million. By 1998 player wages alone were £22 million. The order of magnitude changed.'

But while Edwards and Cooper are right to emphasise that Freedman on his own did not make the modern United, there can be no denying that his marketing success drove United's efforts to persuade the City to buy its stock.

The most interesting evidence of this came when United presented its preliminary results for 1995. As with all such presentations, there were a number of charts showing how the plc had performed. The most prominent figure highlighted was that turnover had increased by 38 per cent. This was on the back of Freedman's merchandising, which had increased by 65 per cent, from £14.2 million to nearly £23.5 million. Gate receipts may have contributed more to the bottom line profits, but what caught the City was that merchandising sales had grown by £9.25 million.

Six months after these results were issued in April 1996, the City first began to take to Manchester United. There was now an appetite from institutions for shares. On 1 April 1996 Edwards sold 785,000 shares for £2,119,500, his wife Susan sold 350,726 shares for £950,467.46 and the Edwards family trust sold 500,000 shares for £1.35 million, making a total take for the family of £4,419,967.46. Just a year previously Edwards had received £1.5 million from selling part of his stake.

This was a new phenomenon for the back pages. When Tottenham had floated in 1983 nothing like this had happened. Now Edwards could sell part of his holding yet retain control. For the back pages, 'Gold Trafford' and Edwards 'the fat cat Gold Trafford chief' was born.

Soon afterwards came the second Sky television deal, along with a new deal for highlights on BBC. As against the previous five-year deal, due to expire in 1997–98, which brought in £40 million a year to all twenty Premiership clubs – meaning that United in 1996 could at best hope to get £3.3 million from television – the new deal, which was to start in 1997–98, was for four years and would bring in £135 million a year for the Premiership clubs. Add money from other rights such as overseas televison deals and by 1998 United could see its own television income treble to £11.4 million.

As football television deals went the 1992 deal was big, but it was the second deal that was really different. The City recognised that and on the back of it not only Manchester United but football shares in general took off. The period between March 1996 and October 1997 would see fifteen clubs coming to the market. It was the start of the stock market's love affair with football. Although the love affair ended quickly, for a time analysts even spoke of a separate football sector on the market.

By this time United's share price had begun to climb. Having drifted along the bottom, valued at less than 50p at one stage (a share split of three for one in September 1997 means this price is restated after taking the split into account), it had by 1996 moved up to just over £1 and then, following the announcement of the new Sky contract, to nearly £2.

The City's optimism had already started seeping into the outside world. Exactly a month before Easthope issued its report the *People* led its back page with a story of how super-rich Arabs from Abu Dhabi had emerged as major players in the battle for control of United. The *People* had looked at United's share register and discovered that a range of City institutions now held shares in the club, including Abu Dhabi Investment Authority. This was the cue for a story to suggest Arabs were into 'Gold Trafford' and for a photograph of Martin Edwards in Arab headgear. 'The city suits reckon MUFC stands for Money Unlimited Football Club – because they're a licence to print cash.' Five years after United had floated, and within days seen its share price nearly sunk by a broadside volley by Maxwell, the City had finally started taking to United shares.

However, even as this was happening there was change in the air. Martin Edwards was planning to bring in someone whose arrival would ensure that Freedman's departure in the summer of 1997 was as unexpected as his arrival. Like so many things at Old Trafford, it started with a lunch that ended quite unexpectedly.

6

BOARDROOM SHENANIGANS

IN DECEMBER 1996 Peter Kenyon decided to leave Umbro. 'I'd been with them for ten years. As well as being chief executive, I was responsible for all the commercial plans. I'd taken the company through one sale. When I started it was worth £16 million and now it was £600 million.'

In February 1997 Kenyon, on his way to Germany, came to Old Trafford to have lunch with Edwards in the Warwick Suite. 'It was a typical winter's day in February, a non-match day and we had lunch overlooking the pitch. We talked about the business and I told him I was leaving. He asked me what I was doing and I said that I was still evaluating what I was going to do. Then he said, "Why don't you come to Manchester United? We've been looking at the structure of the board. Roland's coming up to seventy. I'm looking to get out of the day-to-day running of the business, but I want to retain a definite interest. So I'm looking for somebody to put in that position. Why don't you join us? We've been looking to come and contact you anyway, so you've presented us with an opportunity for you to come in to spend some time as a deputy and then move up to chief executive."' He was surprised, flattered, even flabbergasted. 'I'd never have dreamed of working for a football club.'

However, Kenyon had been born in Manchester, grew up there and supported United. 'I think, to be fair, Manchester United was the only football club I would work for. Not from a fan's perspective, but as a business and commercial opportunity. There was an immense heritage in the football club and a huge international opportunity.'

Kenyon spoke to me many years before anyone even knew of a Russian called Roman Abramovich, and his attitude would change. But his words reflect the need football executives feel to assert, for the benefit of suspicious supporters, that they are the most loyal of fans.

Edwards did not think bringing in Kenyon would cause any problems but not long after this, just after a United board meeting, he approached Freedman. 'He said, "I need your advice." I thought this was strange because he had never asked for advice before. "I'm thinking of bringing Peter Kenyon. What do you think about it?" I said I wasn't very happy. He said, "Why?" "I don't think we need him or want him," I said. He said, "Would you give it three months and see if you can work together?" I actually said yes.'

Freedman was finding it difficult to reconcile himself to the idea that the man with whom he had negotiated the last Umbro contract was suddenly no longer a client from whom he could squeeze more money for Manchester United, but a colleague. He was prepared to give it a try. But a press release in the programme of the home match against Sheffield Wednesday on 15 March, a match United won 2–0, so incensed Freedman that he decided his position at Manchester United was untenable.

Kenyon recalls: 'Martin and I drafted the press release in conjunction with the finance and PR people. It was a press release saying I'd been appointed and part of it said I was being brought in to develop the merchandising and the brand with my past experience. It was a fairly innocuous statement. But the reference to brand and merchandising is, what I think, upset Edward. He felt that undermined his position in the business and that's the job he was there to do.'

The press release did not directly mention Kenyon was coming in as Edwards' deputy, but it alluded to it. Freedman was not at the Sheffield Wednesday match, but he picked up the programme later. Already unhappy about Kenyon's arrival, it was just too much for him. 'It was a very badly worded press release saying that he was going to look after the merchandising and I wasn't very happy about that. I saw him coming in over me, definitely.' He told the board and Sir Roland Smith he wanted to leave.

Martin Edwards, having decided to bring in Kenyon to groom him as his successor, was clearly bewildered by this turn of events. Freedman recalls: 'He looked at me and said, "You're older than me so how can you be the next chief executive?' I said, "That doesn't make sense. I've got different priorities to you."'

Freedman felt very sore about how he was treated. 'I definitely didn't see the press release, which was a disgrace. They probably didn't think I would go. I was earning a lot of money and Martin believes that money is a very important issue. It was important but not that important. Martin was earning a lot more money than me but I was second largest earner at Manchester United.' Freedman believes others were also unhappy at Kenyon's arrival. 'David Gill (who had joined Manchester United a few months previously as finance director) was shocked when Kenyon came in. Before I left I spoke to Roland Smith. I liked the Professor. Every time I had dealings with him I found him very straightforward and honest. In fact he said when I left that if he had been there full time this would never have happened.'

So did Freedman leave because he thought Kenyon's arrival meant he himself could not now succeed Edwards as chief executive? Kenyon does not think so: 'I was seen as a successor to Martin, not Edward Freedman. So there was never a conflict in that respect.'

However, in keeping with the style that Edwards built up at Manchester United, despite Freedman's anger over the way he was treated there were no scenes, no public rows. Freedman knew he could not row with Edwards: 'He doesn't like confrontation. I went to see him in the morning and said, "I've made my decision. I don't want to stay on." I told him I wanted to leave at the end of August, which is the end of the financial year for Manchester. This would leave everything clean and tidy. They actually gave me a year's pay-off, so I wouldn't go with any other Premier League club during that year, which I honoured and they honoured.'

Officially it was presented as a smooth transition. Kenyon took over as deputy chief executive in May 1997 and Freedman went on working with him until August. He was then replaced by Steve Richards from Allsports, who also had experience with Marks & Spencer. But when two years afterwards Freedman spoke to me, he could not hide his anger at the way he was treated: 'He [Kenyon] never interfered with me but I just didn't see a future for myself . . . Kenyon has been very corporate from what I understand. They have taken "Football Club" off the crest, a very sad thing to do as well. Kenyon, almost as soon as he joined, brought in a design agency to look at the crest and they took "FC" away. Kenyon trained at Courtaulds and then Umbro. He's very easy going but he has no flair, he's very boring and very corporate. He plays very much by the rules.'

Kenyon skirts similar criticism of Freedman: 'Edward is an entrepreneur. Within a certain business development cycle you need entrepreneurs. Then you reach a point where you've got to be a bit more formal. You've got to delegate. You've got to put structures in place. That's where we are today. I think Edward felt that he contributed to the success but that he wasn't treated as a success at Manchester United. That is because Manchester United is the success at Manchester United. Everybody plays a part. You are talking about something that has international reach, that has heritage.'

Kenyon sees Freedman as having done a particular job for United at a particular time. Exactly a year before he left another man who had also done a particular job at a particular time departed the United management. The departure of the two men marked the end of the first phase of United's emergence as the top football club in the world.

That man was Robin Launders. Although his departure was more low key than Freedman's and almost amicable, he was a much more controversial figure in the Manchester United management team. During his five years as finance director he helped create a strong impression that there was tremendous tension in the United boardroom.

Freedman had operated almost like a one-man business within United. Robin Launders' reign as financial controller was very different. As we have seen, Launders was brought in by Glenn Cooper at the time of the float to reassure the City that a safe pair of hands was running Manchester United's finances. But he actually made his mark at Old Trafford not as an accountant but as a civil engineer.

When Launders arrived at Old Trafford there was little thought that he would fulfil such a dual role, but United soon discovered that they had got two for the price of one. The prospectus listing Launders' qualifications had stressed his accounting background, but there was nothing in it about his engineering expertise. Mike Edelson was certainly unaware when Launders came that he was also an expert in construction. 'But he was a civil engineer as well as an accountant. He had two degrees.' For Martin Edwards, Launders' dual role was immensely satisfying. The history of English football was littered with clubs which had gone into ruinous debt when rebuilding their grounds. Here the accountant actually supervised the construction. However, Launders combined this with a style and a personality that always grated. In the process he produced an immense cultural shock for many at Old Trafford.

With the arrival of Launders, for the first time a man with a public company background came to a business which had been a private company where individuals had worked and lived together for years. Although much had been made of Les Olive's opposition to the rights issue in 1978, he was still at Old Trafford in 1991 when United floated. Glenn Cooper presents an interesting picture: 'Launders presents himself extremely well and it isn't difficult for the outside world – given the rather reticent Martin Edwards and a very effusive, very rhetorically able Launders – to form the conclusion that Launders was very much at the heart of Manchester United's success.' Although Cooper wasn't part of the day-to-day workings of Old Trafford, he heard stories that indicated that 'Launders was not much liked and he was not popular at the time he was at United. I wasn't there but I gather he could be rather autocratic and perhaps arrogant.'

There was not much doubt that Launders was a gifted City man but the recollections of Ned Kelly, the club's former head of security, attest to the sense of mistrust that surrounded Launders – arising, it seemed, from a perception within United that he was a creature of the City, more of a money man than a genuine football fan.

In his book *Manchester United: The Untold Story* he has a chapter entitled 'Buggers in the Boardroom', which describes Edwards' paranoia that the board rooms and executive offices were being bugged. Kelly says he was twice asked by by Edwards to carry out searches for bugging 'due to feelings of mistrust resulting from internal wrangling with other Manchester United board members'.

The first search happened in 1990, sometime before Launders came, and related back to 1989, when Michael Knighton had unsuccessfully tried to buy the club. Edwards had become convinced that somebody at Old Trafford was passing information to the press, and although he did not name the former employee whom he suspected he clearly signalled who this person was. After a thorough search of the stadium by Kelly and a team of counter-surveillance experts showed no evidence of bugging, attention switched to the boardroom. Kelly acknowledged that when the room was locked, this was the one place where telephone calls could be made in total privacy. It was decided to plant a bug in the boardroom telephone, and a voice-activated recorder placed nearby. This led to the discovery that the office girl Kelly and his team had suspected of being involved with the former employee had been using the telephone on a regular basis – but for no more sinister purpose than a risqué conversation with a man unknown to either Kelly or Edwards.

The same 'technical search' of the club took place during the 1995–96 season, when Edwards began harbouring similar suspicions. This time, the search was not fruitless, since equipment was uncovered in the attic that indicated Old Trafford had been bugged for some time. Wires from the attic were traced to the ceiling underneath Edwards' office, and in the loft space above Ken Merrett's office – directly beneath that of the chairman – Kelly and his men found a tape recorder and several tapes. Merrett went deathly white when told of the discovery. Kelly writes, 'It was then that Merrett told me he was worried about what might be on the tapes. He confessed he had little time for the finance director Robin Launders. Indeed, Launders was not well liked at the club generally, because as far as most of the old guard were concerned, he was from the City and was viewed as a money man not as a football man.'

It later transpired, says Kelly, that Launders had been in the building the night that the devices were found, and he – in common with most of the other United directors – had the demeanour of one who had been talking out of turn about a fellow director. 'I could tell by Robin's demeanour that he, too, had obviously been talking "out of school" about a fellow director, and was fearful of it all coming back to haunt him.' Fortunately for him and his colleagues, the tapes yielded no conversations of any consequence. The conversations, says Kelly, 'were deemed to be old, and all were completely innocent'.

The whole episode illustrated the tensions in the boardroom, particularly between the old guard and Launders.

Edward Freedman certainly had problems with Launders. 'Robin Launders started to ask questions about what I was doing and how I was doing it. Three or four months after I was there I actually went to Martin and said, "This guy doesn't understand what I'm doing. If you don't get him off my back I'm going. Let me get on with it." Martin got him off my back.'

While Freedman's view is undoubtedly coloured, it is instructive: 'He wasn't a very good man manager. He's one of those people who is difficult. Martin calls him a genius, but I don't know.' After their initial clash Freedman and Launders generally kept out of each other's way. 'We had a board meeting for the separate merchandising division once a month – Martin, Robin and myself. Robin wasn't very commercial and I don't think he understood how the commercial world worked.'

Freedman's view of Launders as a difficult man is shared by many at Old Trafford with the exception of Edelson, who did not like Freedman but was very impressed with Launders: 'You just know when you talk to someone that he's on a higher plane than you are. He could certainly quote various things, the scriptures, the classics, and when he spoke to you it wasn't down to you but always on your level. He knew nothing about football, and he'd admit that he knew nothing about football. But he had a thirst for knowledge.' However, even Edelson concedes that 'some felt he was pushy and argumentative'.

As far as the wider world was concerned, Launders' responsibility was to make sure that the City appreciated that United was not like Tottenham. This was a responsible football club that was run very professionally. The money made would not be frittered away irresponsibly and dividends would be protected. As we have seen, Launders had come up with the idea of a Transfer Fee Reserve to reassure the City that there was a definite pot of money for buying players. Launders' presentations to the City always made much of this reserve account. Presenting the 1995 accounts, he devoted a page to the Transfer Fee Reserve. It had slowly been built up in the early years of flotation, reaching £4 million by 1994. In 1995 a further £4 million had been added to it following United's entry to the Champions League. In 1996 the balance stood at £8 million, equivalent to £12 million before tax.

As Launders' successor David Gill told me some years ago, this was a neat piece of accounting fiction. 'The transfer fee reserve account was something Robin, Martin and Glenn Cooper had devised. If the club made additional profits from participation in cup competitions they would be assigned to the transfer fee reserve. If we weren't as successful and we needed to buy players then the accounting reserve – clearly the cash is irrelevant – which had been built up would be used. At the same time dividends were to be protected. In the City this was seen as a dividend protection policy. But now we just ignore the account. I don't believe in it.'

The fiction of the reserve is illustrated by the fact that since that £4m was added in 1995 there were no further entries in that account despite the many millions United have spent on players. Launders' style was best exemplified in the 1994–95 season when in January 1995, in what was seen as a sensational coup, Manchester United bought Andy Cole from Newcastle.

'The Cole deal', as Martin Edwards recalls, 'started with a conversation with Alex and Kevin Keegan. We'd tried to get Stan Collymore from Forest. Alex had spoken to Frank Clark (then manager of Forest) about him. They were prevaricating. They couldn't quite make up their minds about it. (Ferguson tried to contact Clark but was told he had flu.) So then out of the blue Keegan rang Alex about Gillespie. Alex said, "I don't think I could sell Gillespie. I might do. But what about Cole?" That's how it started.'

It was agreed that United would pay £6m for Cole plus Gillespie, who was a home-grown player but was valued at around a million. This led to the back pages presenting Cole as the first £7m player. At that time it was a British record fee. Unlike in America, English football clubs do not disclose the exact transfer fee and newspapers try to guess what the figure is. But with Manchester United a public company the actual figure had to be disclosed. This showed that in the Manchester United accounts Launders had valued Gillespie not at a million but at £250,000 so the transfer had effectively cost United £6.25m. It was some months after the transfer that this emerged and when it did there was a great commotion.

Terry McDermott, Kevin Keegan's assistant at Newcastle, poured scorn on the idea that Gillespie was worth only £250,000. How can that be? He was valued by Keegan and Ferguson at a million when he was sold by Manchester United and if anything his value since then had gone up to perhaps £2.5m.

I was asked by my paper to speak to Launders to investigate what seemed like a mystery and it was clear Launders was irritated by what he saw as uninformed questions by sports journalists who did not understand figures or how Manchester United reported them. After he had harangued me for sometime about the ignorance of sports journalists I pointed out that like him I had qualified as a chartered accountant, had become a fellow of the English Institute before he had and what is more had been a partner in a major international accounting firm before turning to journalism, a fact which seemed to so impress Launders that he grew very quiet and our conversation ended soon after. It was an illuminating illustration of Launders' style.

Freedman may be overstating it when he says Edwards considered Launders a genius, but he clearly appreciated Launders' work, particularly in relation to the rebuilding of Old Trafford. When I put it to him that Freedman and Cantona made Manchester United, he said, 'Robin Launders thinks he made Manchester United.' But during the crucial years 1994–96, Edwards made sure Launders was well rewarded. In that time Edwards earned roughly 2.5 times what Launders did. In 1994 Edwards' total remuneration, including bonus, benefits and pension contributions was £229,000, Launders' £104,000. In 1995 Edwards' package had risen to £290,000, Launders' to £123,000, and in 1996 Edwards' had increased to £321,000 while Launders was on £152,000.

We have already seen the dramatic consequences for Edwards' relationship with Alex Ferguson of his grant of lucrative share options to Launders in 1992. Two years later a bonus issue of four shares for every one held was announced, and on 26 March 1996 Launders exercised his options, now multiplied to 500,000 shares, at 67.8p when the market price was 282p, making more than £1 million of profit in the process. He would have earned a lot more had he waited a little longer, for the United share price was to rise sharply within three months. But by the time Launders exercised his option he appears to have decided that he did not have much of a future at United.

By the spring of 1996 he had been finance director for six years, he had supervised the rebuilding of Old Trafford including the North Stand, and the only way was up, to become chief executive. Edwards was clearly not going to make way for him. However, there was another northern club keen to make use of him.

Leeds were about to be floated on the market. They were listed in August 1996 with Caspian, a public company, doing a reverse takeover. Chris Akers of Caspian knew Launders and was keen he should become chief executive. Although not everyone at Leeds was keen on Launders (they had heard stories of his Old Trafford style and feared his arrival), he was offered the job by Bill Fotherby. In a sense it was the reverse of the transfer that brought Cantona to United, one where United it seems could not wait to see the back of Launders.

The story goes that Launders went to Edwards and told him that Leeds had made an offer. Edwards, instead of coming up a counter offer to persuade him to stay, is supposed to have said, 'When are you going?'

Cooper doubts if that is how it happened. 'One of the things about Edwards is that he doesn't respond immediately. He's not at all an instinctive person. So I'd be extremely surprised if, whatever he felt, he said that . . . But one result is that whatever tensions there were on the board were ended with the departure of Robin.' Freedman believes that when Launders went to Leeds, if the United board did not exactly dance with joy then 'I don't think the boardroom were *unhappy.*'

Launders resigned on 14 August 1996. He had also been company secretary and two days later Maurice Watkins was appointed to the position, staying until David Beswitherick took over. The search for a finance director to replace Launders took a little longer. The headhunters finally found David Gill, who was well known to Keith Harris, a great friend of Martin Edwards who then worked for HSBC, Manchester United's City advisers.

The contrast with Launders could not have been greater, both physically and in terms of personality. Gill is an enormously tall man who, like many tall men, can belie his physical attributes and be surprisingly gentle and amiable. And, unlike Launders, he neither feels the need to impress people with his knowledge nor is football for him an acquired taste. Gill has been steeped in Manchester United and, what is more, he can claim to be the modern United supporter, the one born outside Manchester but drawn to the club. 'I grew up in Reading. My father was a Plymouth Argyle fan. My brother choose Tottenham, his son is a big Chelsea fan and I chose United.'

Gill joined Manchester United on 7 February 1997. Within days, Kenyon came for lunch with Martin Edwards, starting the chain that was to see the departure of Edward Freedman. A month after Freedman left in August 1997, on 26 September Greg Dyke joined the board as non-executive. Although all these changes at board and management level meant little to the supporters, cumulatively they marked the end of the first phase of Manchester United's existence as a plc and the start of the second phase.

A picture in the 1997 annual report, issued on 16 October, captures this new phase. For the first time United had decided to have pictures in their annual report. Most were to be expected – Ferguson and Kidd holding the trophy, Teddy Sheringham, the new £3.5 million signing from Tottenham, an aerial shot of Old Trafford showing the new North Stand – but the most prominent and eye-catching was of the board of directors taken on the Old Trafford pitch: Roland Smith looking a little stooped, Greg Dyke bringing up the rear with his hands behind his back, Watkins and Gill looking quite jaunty with one hand in their pockets. This was the new plc face of United and the half-smile on Martin Edwards' face said it all.

The opening page of the accounts had gloried in the fact that on 11 May 1997 United had won the Premier League for the fourth time in five seasons. Superimposed on a photograph of David Beckham and the boys running out to a packed Old Trafford were charts showing how well the plc had done, increases in turnover, profits before tax, earnings per share and the dividend per share. The page was entitled 'The Theatre of Dreams'. Edwards had given Old Trafford the title and had every reason to feel that United was now fulfilling his every fantasy.

The success, of course, owed much to Ferguson's remarkable achievements on the field and he had every reason to look back and smile at how critics had scoffed at him. In August 1995 Alan Hansen made his now famous remark on BBC's *Match of the Day*, 'The trick is always to buy when you are strong, so he needs to buy players. You can't win anything with kids.' Yet it was the Ferguson kids – Scholes, Butt, Beckham – who had driven United forward.

If in the early years of flotation, with Freedman and Launders dominant, United had focused on merchandising and getting Old Trafford right, it was now decided to diversify the club in an effort to make it a more rounded organisation. The dominant thinking in football then was that a football club needed to surround itself with a hotel and even have its own television station.

In the summer of 1996, United had come up with the idea of its own television channel and approached Oliver Olbaum, then television adviser to the Premier League. United were looking for television partners and, says Edwards, Olbaum 'came up with the names. We started talking with Granada, with Sky and Flextech. Out of all this came the three-way deal between Sky, Granada and ourselves. TV business is very incestuous. In the end they made a joint approach. We thought the best way to do it was jointly.'

Edwards saw this, the first football channel, not as a channel for screening live Manchester United matches – it would hardly make sense to show these on MUTV, where United would have to give two-thirds of its profit away to Granada and Sky – but 'purely to nourish the supporter base'. Paul Ridley, sports editor of the *Sun*, was recruited as its first head. Without any live or even recorded matches, except for old Premiership ones, programming required dexterity but Ridley used his journalistic skills. He formed an effective partnership with Granada, who recruited most of the staff and found offices in Deansgate near their own. MUTV was launched in September 1998, fortuitously coinciding with the Sky bid. (Interestingly neither Sky nor United tried to control what MUTV said about the bid.) Soon afterwards Ridley decided to return to London and the *Sun*.

United, who like their partners Sky and Granada have two directors, have never disclosed their investment in MUTV. All Edwards would say is: 'We put in money, it was less than our two partners. Not tens of millions, more than a couple of million. It is in the infrastructure, the setting-up cost, quite a big staff.' United did not expect to break even until year three or four and estimated that 300,000 subscribers were needed to do so.

By the time Ridley was ready with MUTV, Manchester United were also involved in hotels, having paid £481,000 for a 25 per cent stake in Extramini, a company set up to invest in the hotel. The 111-bedroom Quality Inn hotel, just down the road from the ground – with prices at £65 to £70 a night – was promoted as providing a grand view of the ground, although not of the playing surface.

United were the second club to have a hotel next to their ground, Chelsea being the first. Edwards was adamant that United were not influenced by Chelsea: 'I think we would have done it anyway. It just made sense. It was a bit of a one-off investment for us and it had the provision that if ever the hotel was sold we would have the first option of buying it.'

The hotel was meant to cater for the fans of United travelling from different parts of the British Isles, or even overseas, to watch the team. 'Lots of Irish and Scandinavians come for match days,' said Edwards. 'They are fairly well off.

They stay the Friday night, maybe take in a show, have dinner somewhere, the next day go to Red Café for lunch, see the game, probably stay the next night and go home on a Sunday. A proper weekend package. Now they can stay in the Manchester United hotel.'

Just as the hotel investment was being made and Ridley launched MUTV, in June 1998 United also acquired a property manager, George Johnson. For Edwards this has always been an important strategy. 'We are huge owners of land in Trafford Park. Apart from Trafford Park Estates we are the biggest owners of land in the area. We always need land and we are always looking to add to facilities on match days. There are match-day car parking needs. When you have 6,000 executive customers, that might mean 4,000 cars plus all the rest of the 55,000, a large majority of whom come by cars and want easy access.'

And in addition to the big property portfolio, their ground and training ground, United are 'also always looking out for houses. The last thing foreign players who come over here want to do is buy a house. When their careers end they may want to go back home. So we need a property portfolio of houses.'

By the summer of 1998 United the plc had taken shape. There was Manchester United UK Merchandising Ltd, run by Steve Richards, Manchester United Catering Ltd, run by Mike Whetton, the man Edwards had confused with Michael Knighton back in 1989, and then in August 1998 came Manchester United International, a new subsidiary set up for the overseas merchandising business. Mike Farnan was managing director although Peter Kenyon, with his international business background, took a special interest in it. It is an area where Edwards had always felt United had barely scratched the surface of the huge potential. 'We had been looking for a while to take United into China and other places abroad. In the Far East, the Middle East and Scandinavia. These are big areas for United.'

Some of these expansion plans started bearing fruit in the month after United won the treble, during the pre-season tour of Australia, China and Hong Kong in the summer of 1999. As United played the Australian national team and teams in Shanghai and Hong Kong, business followed performances on the field and the opening of new shops were announced. They marked the final development of the global Manchester United brand name.

By this time this brand name had excited the interest of one of the world's biggest media groups. In the summer of 1998 as Edwards and the board decided to set up international merchandising, he received a call that was to produce one of the greatest upheavals in the club's history. The caller was eager to go where Granada had not gone ten years earlier: buy Manchester United, lock, stock and barrel. What nobody could have anticipated was how fans, and the world in general, would react to the bid.

PART TWO

Rupert Murdoch, George Best and Bobby Moore – Sky's Tears and Fans' Joy

7

A LUNCH FROM THE CANTEEN

THE 1998–99 SEASON was the greatest in Manchester United's history. The season ended with United winning the Champions League and completing a unique treble: the Premiership, the FA Cup and the European Cup. A little over a month after the triumph over Bayern Munich at the Nou Camp in Barcelona, Alex Ferguson had been knighted. Yet in the midst of these on-field triumphs, off the field the club was tearing itself apart in a battle between the board and the fans over yet another attempt by Martin Edwards to sell the club.

The first moves had begun two months before the season started with a seemingly innocuous phone call. But that call was to prove both misleading and quite historic.

Towards the last week of June 1998 Mark Booth, chief executive of BSkyB, called Martin Edwards suggesting a lunch to talk about pay-per-view television. Edwards wrote down in his gold embossed Manchester United diary: "'Meeting with Mark Booth, Sky TV, Isleworth, re pay-per-view.'"

Edwards did not find it surprising that Booth wanted to talk about pay per view. Sky had run into problems on the subject with the Premier League and United's sympathies were with Sky – and certainly not with the way Peter Leaver, chief executive of the Premier League, had handled the issue.

A pay-per-view option had been part of the first television contract Sky negotiated with the Premier League in 1992. Nothing had been done about it, but as Leaver took over from Rick Parry at the Premier League, Sky suggested that in the 1998–99 season they would like to start pay-per-view. They intended to launch their own digital channels in the autumn of 1998 and saw pay per view as the ideal vehicle to drive their sale. Pay-per-view would do for digital what live Premiership football had done for the main Sky channels since 1992.

In early 1998, Booth and Vic Wakeling, head of Sky Sports, had met Leaver for breakfast at the Lanesborough. There for the first time Leaver heard Sky's plans: 'Their original proposal was that all 320 matches which they did not televise [Sky then showed 60 of 380 Premiership games every season] would be on pay-per-view. There was a meeting of the clubs in March 1998, and they said they wanted a decision by then. I said I don't think it is feasible in that sort of time frame. Then they came back and said they would like just under 120 matches a season on pay-per-view.'

There followed other meetings, but Richard Dunn and Mark Oliver, television advisers to the Premier League, were unimpressed. According to Leaver, 'What troubled us was that there did not appear to be any real research on the sort of audience they might have expected, or when the matches were going to be played. It was just they were going to do it. I did not think it was possible. I spoke to the police and the supporters and it was clear it would not be popular.' Dunn and Oliver said they could not recommend it to the clubs.

At their summer meeting in early June 1998, the Premier League discussed a proposal that from the 1998–99 season four matches be moved from their Saturday slot to Sunday and put on pay-per-view. If the experiment worked then more matches could be added. Manchester United, supported by Aston Villa, were quite keen on the experiment, but the other clubs were not so sure and there was no majority in favour. Sky had offered £15 million, which many chairmen felt was nowhere near enough to disrupt the traditional football Saturday. They publicly advertised their rejection of the pay-per-view experiment as a victory for the fans, saying they were just as fond of the traditions of the game as the fans and that the experiment interfered with the ancient Saturday sanctity of English football.

But the fact remained that several clubs were keen on pay-per-view. United for one had been more than a little miffed by the way Leaver had dealt with the Sky proposal. Despite the rejection, United were convinced that some experiment would come before the end of the season. So on the morning of 1 July 1998, as Edwards flew down with Maurice Watkins to London, the pair mulled over what Booth might now be proposing. How could he get the experiment going again?

United's relationship with Sky had come a long way since June 1992, when Sky had beaten ITV for the right to televise the games of the newly formed Premier League. At that crucial meeting in London's Royal Lancaster Hotel, Edwards and United had voted against Sky and in favour of ITV. For some time after that Edwards had been critical of Sky innovations such as Monday night football. But since then, Sky had worked so closely with the Premier League that not only had United been won over but had formed a particularly close relationship; Sky were even United's partners in MUTV.

Edwards and Watkins were driven to the only building in Sky's Isleworth complex that catches the eye. The elegant design and wide entrance foyer of Athena Court marks a striking contrast with the hangar-like buildings that surround it and the desolate landscape that is the hinterland of Sky's headquarters. A former biscuit factory, it was typical of a Murdoch media operation, somewhere between a factory and an army camp. Like all of

Murdoch's operations it went in for few of the frills indulged in by similar companies. There was nowhere to go to eat or entertain. Food came from the cafeteria, where under strict Murdoch orders no alcoholic drinks were ever served. However, for special guests the cafeteria could prepare more than standard canteen food. On this occasion Booth had asked the caterers to come up with a three-course lunch which was a bit special, more like something to be found in a reasonable restaurant.

Booth had also invited Ian West, another Sky official, to the lunch. He was chairman of MUTV and well known to both Edwards and Watkins. They felt sure that at some stage talk would turn to this new channel, details of which were due to be revealed at the Edinburgh International Television Festival at the end of August. West's involvement was a shrewd move on Booth's part. Neither Edwards nor Watkins knew Booth all that well. An American and not long arrived in England, he had taken over from Sam Chisholm, the previous chief executive, in August 1997. But he was yet to make his mark on the wider world.

Edwards and Watkins were shown into Booth's offices and soon after the pleasantries were over Booth led them to the adjoining boardroom. There lunch had been laid out: a smoked salmon starter and a main course of chicken and rice. As the first drinks were consumed and the four men tucked into smoked salmon, Booth dropped his bombshell.

'Look, Martin,' he said, 'I have got you here under false pretences. When I rang to invite you for this lunch I said I would like to talk about pay-per-view, but I have a bigger agenda which I didn't want to say over the phone.'

Edwards and Watkins looked at each other. The silence was filled by Booth. 'What I really wanted to talk about is Sky buying Manchester United. We have looked at it and we would like to make an offer to buy your company.'

Edwards would later joke with friends that he nearly fell off his chair, but whatever inner turmoil Booth's devastating words produced, outwardly he remained calm. Watkins recalls, 'Probably we dug our forks a bit harder into the potatoes and the chicken, but otherwise we did not react.'

Booth could see that both Edwards and Watkins were taken totally by surprise. A takeover could mean they might have to leave United. He quickly moved to reassure them: 'I can assure you the only way we would like to do it would be on a friendly basis. The great attraction of this deal is the management you have built up at Old Trafford, Martin. It is superb. You have an extraordinary sports franchise and an extraordinary business. That is a key part of what we are proposing. The only way we want to do it is if you are equally enthusiastic, so I would ask you to think about it.'

Sky had often thought of owning a football club in England and even considered buying United. But Sam Chisholm had always rejected it. He had felt the regulators would not allow such a merger. And whenever the subject had come up, he had dismissed it by saying that if he wanted to buy anything in Manchester it would not be its best-known football club but its best-known soap opera, *Coronation Street*.

Booth saw things differently. This was partly a reflection on the very different ways the two men saw Sky and where it should now go, and partly because of the new dangers facing the company.

The biggest of them came from the Office of Fair Trading, which had taken Sky, the Premier League and the BBC to the Restrictive Practices Court alleging that the latest television contract was anti-competitive and against the public interest. The OFT's target was the collective way the Premier League had negotiated these rights on behalf of the twenty clubs. It was argued that such collective power was illegal and that individual clubs should have the right to negotiate their own deals. They also argued that no broadcaster should be given the right to sign exclusive contracts.

Booth had been assured by lawyers that Sky would win the case, but there could be no guarantee. If the court found in the OFT's favour, Sky's hold on English domestic football would be in grave danger.

Booth himself had been thinking about making such an offer since February, when he had asked Kevin Kinsella, the Zimbabwean head of BSkyB's business development unit, to come up with options. As an American Booth had grown up on the idea of media companies owning sports clubs, or franchises as they were called in America. Media ownership of baseball, American football and basketball teams was very common; Murdoch had just bought the Los Angeles Dodgers. However in the UK it was unknown.

Kinsella, recalls Booth, 'drew up a list of clubs Sky could take over. Arsenal and Liverpool were considered but top of his recommendation was Manchester United.' Kinsella argued that should the Restrictive Practices Court declare collective selling illegal, it would benefit top clubs like United who could then use their muscle to get the best television deal. Many continental clubs were already pressing for an end to the collective selling of television rights.

United would provide Sky with a solid UK base around which a competitive soccer package could be built. With its very large fan base, the club was likely to be a major beneficiary of pay-per-view when that was launched. By buying United, not only would Sky have a seat at the domestic football table, but also involvement in a European Super League, plans for which were in the air and which always included Manchester United as the major English representative.

The European dimension was crucial. Sky then had no European football rights, the major ones were all owned by ITV. But if Sky bought United, just as Murdoch's purchase of 20th Century-Fox in the USA had helped him influence movie negotiations, they could shape the development of European Super League to their advantage.

For the next hour and a half, Booth outlined the broad philosophical idea of Sky buying United. He did not tell Edwards how much he might pay, and Edwards did not ask. Booth was very keen to keep this as a conceptual meeting. He wanted to see how Edwards would react, he had to get to know the man and see if he could work with him. The time to work out a price would come later.

Edwards and Watkins emerged into the sunshine not knowing what to say or do. This, as we know, was not the first time someone had come knocking at Edwards' door wanting to buy the club. However, this was something much bigger and very different.

When Edwards had agreed to sell to Michael Knighton he had done the deal and then told the board. But then United was a private company and Edwards owned more than 50 per cent. Now it was a public one with City institutions owning more than 60 per cent. The board would have to consider it, but not yet. What Booth had proposed was so revolutionary that Edwards felt he could not take it to the board yet. However, there was one man who had to know about it straight away.

Before he left the lunch Edwards had told Booth that he would like to talk to one man, and Booth understood. Now Edwards and Watkins jumped into a car and drove across London to Upper Thames Street to see that man.

For Sir Roland Smith, Booth's approach could not have been better timed. He felt United was in need of a business doctor and the offer seemed designed to exploit United's vulnerability and provide Smith with an answer he had been seeking for some time.

Kinsella may have felt United was a great buy, but just then United felt more than a little nervous about the future. The season that had ended had been dreadfully barren. Since the start of the 1990s, when Alex Ferguson had won his first FA Cup, United had rarely gone through a season without adding to the trophy collection at Old Trafford. Only once before, in 1995, when they had lost the talismanic Eric Cantona, had they finished a season with nothing. But while that season had been just as bleak, the failure to win anything in 1998 seemed more worrying. In 1995 United had lost the championship by a point to Blackburn and the FA Cup to Everton by a single goal. Neither club seemed capable of challenging United's dominance.

However, in 1998 the challenger seemed on a different level. Arsenal, who had started the year twelve points adrift, had come from behind splendidly. United, who had appeared impregnable at the turn of the year, had won nothing, while Arsenal had done the Double. They were a big club, well funded and well run, with an astute manager in Arsene Wenger, and had the potential to match United. United had so badly lost their way after March that they were dumped out of the cup by Barnsley and went out of the Champions League to Monaco. Football supporters, even at boardroom level, always live with fear and the dread of future failure. Smith in particular was haunted by the thought that United's golden run may have come to an end.

There was also another fear. Would United's barren 1998 be followed by a stock-market collapse? On 8 June the FT All Share Index had reached a peak of 2868 but by 23 June it had fallen to 2708. Although it recovered, within days of Booth's approach the markets started a decline which by mid-August would see the index to fall to 2539. (Between 30 June and 30 September 1998 the FTSE 100 index fell by 13.2 per cent, from 5832.5 to 5064.4.)

Everywhere Smith looked there seemed to be economic disasters looming. Russia was in crisis, Asian 'tiger economies', once seen as showing the way to the West, were now on the brink of collapse. There were fears that the UK would soon be in recession. But the greatest worry was about the US. For six years since Bill Clinton had come to power the United States had enjoyed unprecedented growth and prosperity and Wall Street had soared. But now there was talk of that growth slowing and of Alan Greenspan, the head of the US Federal Reserve, the central bank, putting up interest rates. The sudden demise of a hedge firm based in Connecticut, Long Term Credit Management, had shaken the stability of the markets and history books were consulted to look up if all this meant another Wall Street crash.

To add to the fears there was growing talk of Clinton being impeached. Clinton would soon be forced to testify before a grand jury about his affair with Monica Lewinsky and nobody could predict how the markets might react if he was forced out of office. So, that summer day, Edwards, Smith and Watkins wondered if the economic winds of change blowing against United might not make merging with the biggest and most entrepreneurial media company in the world the best option.

Smith's office was opposite that of Keith Harris, chief executive of HSBC's investment banking arm. Edwards, in the strictest confidence, informed Harris of Booth's approach. Harris had long been Edwards' confidant and had been a Manchester United fan even longer. Brought up in Manchester, his father took him to Stockport County on Friday nights and United on Saturday and he still recalled his first match just before Munich against Ipswich at home.

The Harris and Edwards families had old ties. Keith's father knew Louis Edwards and had done business with him, he was in the confectionery business and manufactured pickles which he supplied to the butcher shops owned by Louis Edwards. Their sons had renewed this business relationship more than thirty years later when, following United's float, Glenn Cooper took a group of City investors to Old Trafford. Although the match Harris watched, a 0–0 draw with Liverpool, was less than enthralling, what made his day was that he had lunch in the boardroom with Sir Matt Busby. For a United fan this was like meeting the creator. The friendship with Edwards that was formed as a result of this visit blossomed and Edwards found that he had much in common with Harris. Like him Harris was a man with wide sporting interests, avidly following Lancashire cricket during the summer. Edwards had other links with HSBC and also knew Rupert Faure Walker, managing director of corporate finance, through his family's meat distribution business in Manchester.

Harris had been the conduit for an approach made to United by video and publishing company VCI in the summer of 1996. VCI were looking to expand. Euro 96 was about to happen and football was fashionable, but the share price showed that the market did not value clubs highly. Although United were about to win the Double, the share price had been around £1.50 for a long time. It seemed this might be a good time to buy the club.

On 11 May 1996 United beat Liverpool 1–0 in the FA Cup final to become the first team to do the Double twice. However, the share price moved hardly a jot. The following Monday Harris took VCI chief executive Steve Ayers to Old Trafford to see Edwards, where Ayers presented his proposal for a takeover with VCI looking to pay about £2 a share.

Edwards listened intently to them, promising to consider their proposal. But before Edwards or the board could do so events intervened. Soon after this the Premier League met for its summer meeting in a hotel near Coventry and Sky beat off rivals organised by Lord Hollick's United News and Media Group and a consortium organised by Kelvin MacKenzie and Michael Green's Carlton for the Premier League contract.

For this new contract Sky was prepared to pay £670 million for the rights to televise sixty live games for four years. It was undreamt-of riches and the share price, unmoved by Ferguson's achievements on the field, took off. VCI's approach was sunk; it did not even turn into a formal offer.

However, Edwards had now begun to worry that others might start thinking of buying United. What if they made an unfriendly approach? He turned to Harris and wondered if HSBC might be willing to act as United's merchant bankers. Harris was keen, although his colleagues in corporate finance were not convinced: 'They said, what will United bring? I could see their point. United were not going to take over companies, which generates work for corporate finance. But I said, you watch, there will be a bid for United.'

In return for their appointment, it was agreed that HSBC would prepare a defence document for United, working out a strategy for coping with anyone else who might want to buy the club. While Harris had secured the business, Rupert Faure Walker and David Blake, a director of corporate finance, would be in day-to-day charge. Harris and his two colleagues had a bet about who might bid for United. 'David said Sky, Rupert said Granada and I agreed with Rupert.'

Edwards was well aware that United needed to spend money to buy players.

One reason for the barren season had been their failure to find a replacement for Roy Keane, the captain and influential midfielder, whose injury early in 1998 had played a major part in United's decline. Ferguson had already drawn up a shopping list. United had bought one player on that list – Jaap Stam, the Dutch defender, for £10 million – but there were others including Dwight Yorke and Patrick Kluivert. Then there was the cost of increasing the capacity at Old Trafford, which would mean an investment of upwards of £30 million.

Costs were always going up. Players' wages were rising inexorably, and even as Booth was making his approach, Edwards had to deal with another wage rise. Everton's approach for Brian Kidd forced United to make him the best paid No. 2 in English football.

Edwards was not gullible enough to believe that letting Sky buy United would mean millions for his club. However, it would mean being part of a much bigger organisation with vast resources that could come in handy should times get tough. There was also the personal consideration. If Sky could be persuaded to pay 215p then Edwards's 14 per cent would bring in just under £80 million. Ever since United had floated on the stock market Edwards had been selling shares; in the process he had made millions but also retained control, a fact that made other Premier League chairmen extremely envious of him. Now he could sell his entire stake but still run United for Sky.

The next day Edwards called Booth and told him that he had spoken to Roland Smith and a couple of other people. And while he was not yet sure whether the bid made sense or not, he was prepared to discuss it further.

For Edwards there was one problem. On 3 July the United plc board was due to have a whole-day meeting at Old Trafford to discuss strategy. The idea was to review the bleak season that had just gone and discuss where the club was going as the millennium approached.

The board could hardly discuss future strategy without being told of Booth's approach but Edwards felt it was too early to share this information. He was very keen to keep it in a tight circle – himself, Smith, Watkins and Harris – until it had developed into something like a firm offer. He decided that while the board would meet, the strategy session would be cancelled.

The board met as planned on the morning of 6 July. Most members were present including Greg Dyke, who was then also chairman of Pearson Television. Dyke, although born in west London, had been a United supporter since childhood. He had been invited onto the board by Edwards in September 1997 to provide television expertise and it seemed a shrewd appointment. He had held various positions in ITV; as head of ITV Sport he had lost the rights to televise football for the new Premier League to Chisholm. It was Dyke who had complained about the deal to the Office of Fair Trading.

Now, on 6 July, the directors found a rather strange United board meeting, although the strangeness struck them only afterwards. The next meeting was not due until 8 August and by then Edwards hoped things would have progressed enough for him to tell the board. Two other people at Old Trafford knew nothing about the approach from Booth: Peter Kenyon and David Gill. Both these men, in particular Kenyon, were heavily involved in another secret negotiation. Edwards felt it was best they work on this extremely sensitive project and not be dragged into a possible takeover by Sky. Edwards says: 'We advised the board, the non-executives and Peter and David at the appropriate moment, once we realised how serious it was.' It was revealing of the way Edwards worked as chief executive of a plc.

Meanwhile, something potentially just as explosive was opening up for Manchester United. It might mean that by the time the season began, United might not even be playing in the Premier League and the face of European football could be changed for ever.

8

A DRINK IN THE BASEMENT BAR

THE DAY AFTER Edwards and Watkins went to see Booth, Kenyon and Gill arrived in another part of town. On 2 July they had a meeting not far from where Edwards had briefed Sir Roland Smith on Booth's offer, at the offices of the highly paid City lawyers Slaughter & May.

In early May, at the invitation of Pelé, Kenyon had visited Brazil. Partly through Bobby Charlton, United had long been associated with Pelé and Kenyon himself, in his previous job at Umbro, had had a very warm relationship with the great Brazilian going back ten years.

The relationship was so intimate that when in April 1998 United opened their museum in Old Trafford's North Stand, it was decided to bring Pelé over to Manchester to inaugurate it. He arrived on 10 April and spent a weekend in the city opening the museum and talking about his own plans for Brazil. Kenyon recalls: 'Pelé, who was then the Brazilian sports minister, was very involved in the restructuring of Brazilian football. When he came to Manchester he asked if I would go over and do a conference in Sao Paulo on the implications of what was being introduced as the Pelé Law, which was meant to help restructure the game there.'

One evening during the conference, which took place on 12 and 13 May, Kenyon was having an early drink with Watkins – inevitably present when United discussed any issue of importance – and Cooper in the low-ceilinged bar of the Intercontinental Hotel. The three were approached by two Italians and a Swede. The Italians, Andrea Locatelli and Paolo Taveggia, were known to Kenyon; the Swede, he was later to discover, was Peter Ecelund.

Cooper recalls: 'Peter Ecelund, who I later learnt was a Swedish gentlemen and got to know quite well, introduced himself to the rest of us and immediately went into this pitch about a European Super League. I must say my initial reaction was rather sniffy and British. It raised my hackles that here we were sitting in the middle of a bar, not a discreet environment at all, and we were talking about this quite revolutionary plan. If you have world-shattering news then a bar in the basement of the Intercontinental in Sao Paulo is not the place to discuss it.'

Ecelund, recalls Kenyon, said 'There was a document they'd like us to have a look at. It was a new concept for a European football competition and it would derive significant revenues and give ownership back to the clubs. They'd done an awful lot of work on it. They gave us a booklet, which we took away and packed in our bags as we left Brazil for the UK.'

After Ecelund had gone Cooper looked at the document and concluded, 'It seemed to be thoughtfully put together and quite clever.' The proposal was for a midweek league of twenty-four or thirty-two teams whose membership would partly be determined by merit and partly by status, such as previous record in Europe and the size of the club. The most radical part of the plan was that a group of founder members would enjoy permanent membership of the league because of their size and wealth.

Ecelund, Locatelli and Taveggia were partners in a company called Media Partners. Kenyon knew the Italians quite well, in particular Taveggia, a former Italian Foreign Office official. He had been at Crystal Palace on the night in January 1995 when Eric Cantona had attacked a Palace supporter. Taveggia, who was then general manager of Inter Milan, had come over to try and buy Cantona and in the aftermath of the incident came quite close to returning to Milan with him.

Some months later, after the world learnt of the plans for a European Super League, there would be intense speculation about Media Partners. Who was the Mr Big behind these men, the virtually unknown boys from the Milan tennis club as they were derisively dubbed by some at UEFA? Not all of them were from Milan but seven members of their management team were Italians. Their president, Rodolfo Hecht Lucari, was an AC Milan supporter, while Locatelli had played for AC Milan. This connection, and the fact that Hecht and Taveggia had worked for Silvio Berlusconi, the former Italian Prime Minister and owner of AC Milan, led to intense speculation that they were really front men for Berlusconi. Media Partners refuted this, saying that while many of their partners had worked for Berlusconi they were the sole owners of their company, one with a good track record in sports rights having put together football's first pay-per-view contract for Italian television. What they shared with Berlusconi was the vision that that one day there would be a European Super League bringing together the best clubs in Europe and producing the sort of money not available in the current UEFA competitions.

Two days after the meeting, as Kenyon, Watkins and Cooper flew back to the UK, Patrick Harverson, then working for the *Financial Times*, first broke the story of Media Partners and its plans. Harverson had been put on to the story at the prompting of Adriano Galliani, general manager of Berlusconi's AC Milan. Before Harverson wrote his story he checked with Martin Edwards, who assured him that United had not been approached. At this stage, of course,

Edwards was not even aware of Media Partners. In any case, neither Kenyon nor Watkins had any reason to believe that this proposal was any different to umpteen others that float across the desks of United and other top clubs. Unlike Kenyon, Watkins had not even taken the material Ecelund had given them. The case the OFT had brought against the Premier League, Sky and BBC had reached what lawyers call the discovery stage, when everything relevant has to be disclosed to the other side. Watkins was a witness and might have been required to yield up documents regarding Media Partners.

However, a few days after their return, the initial scepticism of Kenyon and United about the project gave way to guarded enthusiasm. Kenyon says: 'It was intriguing from two points of view. First and foremost, the quality of the advisers that had been involved with the project. It was obvious from the outset that this wasn't something that had been put together the week before. There'd been significant research done on competition formats, TV revenues, club ownership and rights.'

Kenyon was now seeing increasing evidence of the enormous potential of this project, a potential that was underlined two weeks after his return from Brazil when Real Madrid won the Champions League for the first time since 1966. United had won the European Cup only once, in 1968, and Real's victory after thirty years merely made the hunger for the ultimate goal all the greater at Old Trafford. But as the fans yearned for the glory, the money men asked: if United won, what would it mean in hard cash?

UEFA made much of the fact that Real would now bank some £8.5 million, while United as beaten quarter-finalists had received £5.37 million. Media Partners' figures not only promised each club four times as much money but made much of the fact that UEFA gave the clubs a raw deal. Only 55 per cent of UEFA's total income of £155 million came back to the clubs. UEFA themselves kept nearly £30 million and Team Marketing, the company that did the deals for UEFA, took nearly 12.5 per cent of the gross take. Media Partners' plans promised a complete break from all this. To top it all, they promised that the European Super League would be owned by the top clubs themselves, not UEFA.

Outside the boardrooms and conference chambers the World Cup in France riveted the world of football, and it was in Paris that a little-noticed decision was taken which further spurred Media Partners and the top clubs. For the 1998–99 season AC Milan, four times winners of the Champions League, had failed to qualify for Europe. This was the second year the club was out of Europe and as Hecht had told Harverson, 'It's a tragedy. The question is how do you deal with that? I think sport in Europe is ready to be privatised.'

Milan had proposed to UEFA that in such situations clubs like themselves with an established pedigree in Europe should be given a wild card, in much the same way that tennis players get for major tournaments. The UEFA executive discussed this proposal at their meeting in Paris on 25 June, during the World Cup, and decided that football was not tennis. Media Partners made much of UEFA's decision, emphasising that in their proposal the original founding clubs who formed part of the Super League would be guaranteed to remain part of it irrespective of form.

By late June United were drawn into the net. After some informal discussions, Media Partners called their first formal meeting at the offices of Slaughter & May on 2 July. United decided that not only would Kenyon go to the meeting but so would David Gill.

They arrived to find an interesting collection of clubs: the two Milan clubs, AC and Inter, Juventus, Ajax from Holland, Marseille and Paris St Germain from France and Borussia Dortmund from Germany. But nobody from Spain and just one other English club: Arsenal. The English club was presented by chief exeutive Ken Friar and major shareholder Danny Fizsman; it later emerged that David Dein felt unable to attend due to his close links with UEFA and his doubts about the project.

The first meeting was followed by another one on 14 July which saw Franz Beckenbauer and Karl-Heinz Rummenigge representing Bayern Munich. Rick Parry, chief executive of Liverpool, was also there, the only meeting Liverpool attended in a setting that clearly made them distinctly uncomfortable. Soon other clubs joined in, including Galatasaray from Turkey. Arsenal, despite the fact that the project opened a boardroom split between Dein and the rest, did not miss a meeting and were as involved as United.

Once involved, United began to take a very active part. They quickly saw ways in which Media Partners' plans could be improved. Kenyon, Gill, and increasingly Watkins, contributing his sharp legal mind to the issues, began to play a major part in shaping the plans.

Gill was soon part of a finance sub-committee. Again, he was impressed with the quality of the people who came to the meetings, in particular Sibel Erkman of Galatasaray, a female Turkish lawyer with an excellent command of the English language, Guy d'Arbonneau from Olympique Marseille and representatives of AC Milan and Bayern Munich. He was equally impressed by the fact that Media Partners had spent some two years working on this project and had invested a lot of their own money in developing the concept. Hiring lawyers Slaughter & May was not cheap and they had done a lot of work researching competition law and meeting Karel van Miert, then the European Union's competition commissioner.

The American bankers J.P. Morgan were willing to finance the project for the first three seasons to the tune of £2 billion, a sum they planned to recover through the sale of television rights. This was a name that some years later would have specific echoes for United. However, as Gill and his subcommittee probed into the financing, they discovered the first flaws in the plans. If the television income did not match what Media Partners were offering the clubs, how would J.P. Morgan get their money back? Would the clubs have to pay money back to J.P. Morgan? Gill says: 'In essence it was sold to the clubs on the basis that there would be no recourse to the clubs if income did not match expectations. But when we reviewed the documentation it was not as clear as that. Reality was that when we saw the documentation there was recourse.'

The fact was there was a hole in the financing and Media Partners were well aware of that. Even before they began their formal meetings with the clubs, they had begun to look for ways to raise money and turned to a contact they had found through United. Sometime in June, just before meetings with the clubs started in earnest, Peter Ecelund rang Glenn Cooper and the two men met for lunch. Cooper by now was no longer feeling quite as sniffy about the way Ecelund had introduced the whole thing back in the Sao Paulo bar.

The lunch with Ecelund led to further meetings and in June Cooper, having concluded that there was no current connection with Berlusconi, flew to Milan to meet Hecht and the other Media Partners men. United by now were becoming quite enthusiastic about the idea. Gill had no doubts regarding the advantages. 'It was a very sensible, well thought out project . . . It would certainly have been of benefit to us. From our perspective clearly playing in Europe was important to us. Our wages are mainly fixed. You have to look at ways to maximise revenue.'

At this stage, in mid-July, Media Partners and the clubs had successfully kept their involvement secret. All this changed though, due to two journalists in Hamburg. On Monday 13 July Bodo Mueller, in charge of sports at the nationwide Sunday paper *Bild am Sonntag*, and his colleague Helmut Uhl, were trying to contact two Bayern Munich officials, manager Uli Hoeness and vice-president Karl-Heinz Rummenigge, about a routine matter. But Hoeness's secretary, normally so helpful, appeared to be extremely nervous and told Mueller that there was no way he could speak to Hoeness until the following Monday. He mentioned this to Uhl, who looked at him and said, 'Funny, that is exactly how Rummenigge's secretary reacted. Why should two secretaries react so nervously to a routine inquiry to talk to their bosses?'

The next day, says Mueller, 'I got a call from a contact telling him that Rummenigge and Hoeness were in London having secret talks with top European clubs about what we in Germany call the Wild League.' This was the meeting on 14 July, when Bayern attended for the first time. Through the offices of Springer News in London, Mueller contacted Colin Gibson, sports editor at the *Sunday Telegraph*. 'Some hours later Gibson, who I have never met, rang and he was very excited. He must have spoken to someone, maybe Liverpool. He said, "Do you know, Bodo, we are writing football history."'

Gibson, a former football correspondent of the *Daily Telegraph*, had indeed made calls to Liverpool, Manchester United and Peter Leaver. 'Peter Leaver went ballistic and dropped the phone. United refused to comment and when I rang Liverpool there was a long pause, then the person said, "There is nothing I can say."' That person was Rick Parry, an old friend.

Gibson worked in close collaboration with Muller, who faxed his story to the *Telegraph* on Friday while Gibson did the same. The *Telegraph*'s story was written by Steve Curry, the veteran soccer reporter. Under his byline, with an exclusive tag, the story described how United were having secret talks with Europe's other leading clubs. They were discussing a sixteen-club league with midweek matches and no promotion or relegation, which would involve playing as many as nineteen European matches in a season.

Mueller's story was more detailed and less England-centred. He detailed the two groups into which the sixteen clubs might be split. In the first would be Juventus, Milan, Barcelona, Liverpool, Paris St Germain, Ajax, Borussia Dortmund and Roma or Glasgow Rangers; in the second Real, Inter Milan, Manchester United, Bayern, Monaco, Antwerp, Arsenal and Sporting or Benfica.

United were totally unprepared for the story breaking. They had agreed a confidentiality clause in their discussions with Media Partners and few people outside the boardroom knew about the group. On the Sunday morning of 19 July, other newspapers tried to follow the *Sunday Telegraph* story and rang Ken Ramsden, the assistant secretary, who also handled press relations. Naturally he denied it, saying: 'There is no truth in this at all. It is pure speculation. We are getting fed up with stories linking us with a European Super League.' Over the previous two years Ramsden had often been asked questions about such speculation. Now, without checking with Watkins or Kenyon, he felt safe to issue the same denial.

United were stuck with that denial, and the whole episode revealed a tremendous lacuna in their press relations. As assistant secretary, Ramsden was a good public relations man for a football club. However this was a corporate story. United's failure to have an in-house public relations man who could deal with such stories meant that a blanket denial had been issued which clearly could not be sustained. Worse for United, as the story developed, the confidentiality agreement with Media Partners meant they could do nothing to correct the first fatal impression Ramsden had created. This made United easy meat for the tabloids, led by the *Daily Mail*.

On 1 August, by which time the *Sunday Telegraph* had had two weeks of exclusives, The *Mail* devoted its back page and two other inside pages to denouncing United. Kenyon was portrayed as 'The man with soccer's future in his hands'. Using a quote from Watkins, who had refused to confirm whether United were involved in talks, the *Mail* thundered, 'So the country's highest profile club continues to leave its supporters, shareholders and Premiership rivals in the dark with a stoic refusal to deny its clear involvement in the rebel league plotting.'

The *Mail*, without acknowledging that it was the *Sunday Telegraph* which had broken the story, led its back page on 6 August with 'Guilty as Sin: Those Superleague plotters Manchester United and Arsenal own up after Sportsmail campaign'. The reason for the excitement was another comment by Maurice Watkins, who was described as trying to repair the damage of previous misleading comments by saying, 'The club considers it has a responsibility to examine the proposal for a new European competition for the benefit of supporters, shareholders and football generally.'

Media Partners' plan was to make more money for the top European clubs; this was what had attracted those top clubs to their discussions. Yet in order to curry favour with the fans they now wanted to strike a populist pose and stress how this would generate more money for the grassroots. Kenyon realised quickly enough the confusion at the heart of the project: 'probably one of the biggest issues they got wrong was the PR strategy'. Kenyon believes it was not Media Partners' sole intention that three or four League clubs would get more money, although that would doubtless be the case. It was also intended that substantial funds would go back to football at the grassroots. 'None of the clubs wanted the Scottish model. We didn't want to play Aston Villa or Arsenal four times. It doesn't work. It's not in anybody's interest to limit it that way. Our prime consideration is the domestic League and we wanted to help the domestic League. We would like fewer clubs in the domestic League, to be honest, but we'd like a stronger European competition.'

In order to get round fans, who by this stage were denouncing the plans around Europe, Media Partners hired MORI to poll opinion and reported that after a survey of 1,061 fans in 159 sampling points across Britain, 70 per cent favoured replacing the UEFA competitions with a midweek European league. However, such surveys always depend on how the questions are framed. For this survey, fans were asked whether they would like to see more English clubs in Europe, more games on free TV, more money for amateur and youth football, no conflicts between club games and national leagues and cups. Only after listing such virtues was the question put: Do you approve of the Super League or not? The surprise was that only 70 per cent approved.

However important public opinion was, it was UEFA that would make or break Media Partners. A Super League clearly meant going against UEFA, yet Media Partners kept insisting that they wanted to work with them. Kenyon had always understood this: 'Whilst the model that Media Partners constructed showed that it would generate the monies for the Super League outside UEFA, from day one every club that had the initial conversation with Media Partners said UEFA has to be involved in this project. We all said UEFA must run this competition.'

Media Partners made much of the fact that the clubs would own the Super League, but a competition owned by the clubs raised questions about the part, if any, UEFA would play. The more Gill talked with Media Partners the more he seemed to sense an uncertainty at the heart of the project. 'At some of the meetings they stressed UEFA could get involved but the way they were approaching the project tended to suggest to us that it was unlikely . . . They should have said UEFA is part of our set-up as a regulator from the beginning.'

Privately Media Partners had sought to put out feelers to UEFA. Sometime in the middle of August Peter Ecelund and a colleague went to see Lennart Johansson, UEFA president, at his holiday home near Stockholm. Says Gerhard Aigner, the then German-Swiss UEFA general secretary, 'They said they had an interesting proposal. Lennart was unaware what it was about. Lennart said speak to the general secretary. So they rang me up.' By this time not only had several clubs told Aigner what was happening, but Aigner and his colleagues had begun shuttle diplomacy to the various capitals of Europe to make sure the organisation that had been built up over four decades did not vanish with a puff from Media Partners.

UEFA knew that their most important task was to establish a dialogue with the clubs. For years the big clubs had moaned that they could never talk directly to UEFA, they always had to go via their national associations. The national association in any country is generally dominated by the amateur side of the game, while the clubs are professional. It riled the clubs that they brought the money that sustained the amateur side yet they had no direct voice at UEFA.

By the weekend of 15 August Aigner had started a whirlwind tour of major European football capitals to lobby the clubs. That weekend he met Real Madrid and then saw officials of Benfica. Markus Studer, his deputy, went to see Ajax in Amsterdam. On Tuesday 18 August, both Aigner and Studer flew to Manchester to meet United, Liverpool and Arsenal.

The meeting was arranged at a conference room at Watkins' law firm James Chapman & Co. in the centre of Manchester. Watkins, Kenyon, Peter Robinson and Rick Parry came from Liverpool and Ken Friar and Danny Fiszman from Arsenal. Aigner's message was simple: stick with UEFA. We are ready to change, completely revolutionise the European competitions if necessary and it will bring you more money.

Aigner was willing to consider a Champions League where the top five European countries, including England, could have as many as four teams each

– double the existing allocation – a much larger qualifying competition so the champions of Eastern Europe and other European minnows would be eliminated early, a merger of UEFA and Cup Winners' Cup into one competition and even the ultimate heresy, perhaps a wild-card system as desired by AC Milan. Most importantly, there would be a bigger share-out of television money with some games on satellite television to generate more money.

Guido Tognoni, then a UEFA official, even went on to talk publicly about the heresy that Aigner had mentioned to Watkins and co. in Manchester. UEFA would still insist that a club could enter only on merit but it might be prepared to look at the definition of sporting merit. 'This could mean entry into European competitions on the basis of the last five years' record and not just last season.' UEFA was coming close to what Milan had proposed. Despite United's deep involvement with Media Partners, Watkins, Kenyon and Gill listened with great interest and gave the impression that they could work with UEFA.

By this time, however, United relations with Peter Leaver, never the best, had been further strained. Leaver had had a number of clashes with United ever since he had taken over as chief executive of the Premier League in the summer of 1997 but the Media Partners situation was the most explosive. At the end of July he sent a letter to the three clubs, warning them that if they were planning to sign with Media Partners they would face consequences including expulsion from the Premier League.

The letter incensed United. They felt a letter like that, coming with no warning beforehand, was as Kenyon says outrageous, 'and to send it to one of the founder members of the Premier League is ridiculous, particularly in light of the OFT enquiry'. United felt they were being put in the dock and this became most evident when the Premier League met.

Leaver had agreed that Media Partners, instead of having secret meetings with clubs, would make a formal presentation to all twenty Premiership clubs. The meeting was fixed for 3 September. It was to prove a crucial day both for Media Partners and for Manchester United.

Leaver also arranged for Gerhard Aigner to make a formal presentation on behalf of UEFA. UEFA had never before spoken in such a fashion to any gathering of clubs anywhere in Europe. Media Partners had so shaken UEFA up that the very survival of the organisation and its competitions was at stake. Manchester United and other clubs had to be wooed and Aigner came in a very conciliatory mood.

Leaver had so organised the day that Media Partners were to make their presentation followed by Aigner. Media Partners' plans had changed considerably since they first met Kenyon and co. Now their Super League would have thirty-six teams in three divisions of twelve each. Four English clubs would be involved, three of them Manchester United, Liverpool and Arsenal, as part of the group of eighteen founder members who would be guaranteed qualification for the first three years. Eighteen others would be selected on their performance in the previous season, one of them English.

In addition there would be a ProCup, a knockout tournament of ninety-six teams including six English teams. In other words half the Premier League could play in Europe. And the money was more than any English club had ever earned in Europe. The Super League would give the four English clubs a total of £43 million a year, the ProCup would give the six English clubs £28 million a year.

But the presentation began to run into problems. Not all the clubs were convinced of the financial basis of the figures. When Keith Wiseman, then chairman of the FA, asked, 'When did you approach the FA of England?' they answered, 'Never.' Media Partners had been branded as rebels.

In the discussions that followed the two presentations United soon found themselves on the defensive. This was the first time the clubs had met since the Media Partners story broke and many of them made it clear that they saw the way United had acted as indefensible. Although Arsenal had been just as active with Media Partners, it was United who took much of the heat. Ken Bates, who always felt that everything should be done through the League, was one of the most vocal and clashed with Watkins, suggesting that if United did not want to be part of the Premier League they could piss off.

Watkins and United's argument was that they were committed to the Premier League, but Media Partners was a project they had to look at. In any case what they did in Europe was no concern of the Premier League, they were a public company and had to consider projects that were interesting. Leaver was determined to make sure that there was no more such freelance activity by United or any of the clubs and went round the table asking clubs to promise that if there was to be contact, it must be through the Premier League.

When he reached United, Watkins and Kenyon looked at Martin Edwards. To their horror he agreed that all future contact would indeed be through Leaver. Watkins and Kenyon knew this decision had put United in a very difficult situation and as soon as the clubs broke for lunch there was a hurried confab. As Kenyon recalls, 'We had already committed to two things: to have a meeting with Media Partners and I was due to go to a meeting with Karel van Miert on the Monday.'

Watkins offered to repair the damage caused by Edwards' pledge. He had a private word with Leaver before the afternoon session, and it was agreed that he and Kenyon would meet Leaver the next day.

When they came the next morning Watkins told Leaver, 'Martin made a bit of a cock-up yesterday. He should never have said all future contact will be through the Premier League. You see, Peter has a meeting with Karel van Miert on Monday and there is a meeting of the clubs at Slaughter & May on Tuesday.'

The previous day's meeting represented a triumph for Leaver and he was not about to relinquish it. But he offered United a compromise: they could continue meeting Media Partners, provided they did so as representatives of the Premier League. So Kenyon could meet Karel van Miert on behalf of the Premier League and report back.

As Kenyon and Watkins left Leaver they felt angry and unhappy. However, no sooner had they stepped on to the pavement outside the Premier League offices than the mobile phone rang. It was Gill.

'Where are you?'

'We're outside the Premier League.'

'Well, what are you doing there? You are supposed to be at HSBC, we are waiting here for you.'

'Right, we're on our way.'

Within hours Kenyon was to learn that he could not have attended the meeting with Karel van Miert, irrespective of whether he wore his United or Premier League hat. A much bigger issue had intervened.

9

KEEPING THE SECRET

THROUGH JULY 1998, as Kenyon, Gill and Watkins busied themselves with Media Partners, Martin Edwards kept his counsel about his takeover talks with Mark Booth and Sky. He spoke only to Watkins, Roland Smith and Keith Harris.

Sky was not the only company sniffing round United. Frank Lowe was another old Manchester boy and United fan who had done well. He had sold his advertising company Lowe Howard Spink to Interpac, a large multinational, American-controlled company, and appears to have had some thoughts that Interpac could buy United. It seems that Lowe spoke to Edwards as a preliminary to a bid, though nothing materialised. But the approach convinced Edwards that more than one multinational was looking to bid for his club. If so, who should he go with? Sometime in early July he rang Booth and told him, 'We are definitely interested. We should spend more time together to see that it makes sense for us.'

Soon after his initial discussions with Edwards, Booth turned to Martin Stewart, his thirty-five-year-old chief finance officer, to work out the money that would be required. Unlike Booth, Stewart knew and loved football. He was a lapsed Tottenham supporter and had a sharp and instant appreciation of how big and complicated a task Booth had taken on. Booth's decision had come as no surprise to Stewart. There had been talk in the corridors of Isleworth about buying Manchester United for some two years before Kevin Kinsella's proposal.

On the evening of 28 July Stewart and Kinsella drove to the Royal Lancaster Hotel to meet Maurice Watkins. It was little over ten days since news of United's involvement with Media Partners had been revealed in the media and both Watkins and Stewart were paranoid about any plans for Sky buying United leaking to the press.

So instead of meeting in the first-floor lounge of the Royal Lancaster, they sat in Watkins' room to discuss Sky's plans. Both Stewart and Watkins knew this was a very preliminary discussion, but what Stewart wanted to know was the ball-park figure Sky would have to pay. How much, he asked, did United expect Sky to pay for the club?

Watkins pulled out a piece of hotel stationery, did some sums on it and said 290p, which was 130p more than the price at which United's shares had closed that evening on the London stock market. If Booth's offer to buy United in July had shocked Edwards and Watkins, that price took Stewart's breath away. United would be valued at nearly £750 million, far beyond anything Sky was prepared to pay.

On the drive back that night to his home in West London, Stewart could not hide his amazement. The next morning he went back to Isleworth and told Booth that if United were serious about asking for 290p then Sky should forget about the whole thing. When United were finally sold in 2005, the price paid by the Glazers was 10p more than the price Watkins had so hurriedly conjured up, but in the summer of 1998 the price seemed astounding. Nobody had ever conceived of a football club being worth so much. However, surprised as he was, Stewart instinctively felt that this was just an opening gambit.

Booth had told Stewart and Deanna Bates, Sky's legal counsel, to put a team together for the bid. He now asked Stewart to choose his banker for the deal. Stewart turned to Goldman Sachs. Booth had already mentioned to John Thornton what he was proposing to do. Thornton, chief operating officer at Goldman Sachs and a member of the executive that managed their global operation, had been a director of BSkyB since 1994. Goldmans had intimate links with Rupert Murdoch and had been advising Sky on football for some time. Whatever price BSkyB eventually paid, the deal would have to be recommended by Goldmans. Booth planned to borrow some £623 million for the deal, hoping to refund 50 per cent with equity. Companies like Sky do not carry great huge cash banks. They borrow at or below commercial rates, funding their investments through such borrowings. The component parts of the transaction were to be the responsibility of Goldman Sachs.

It was not Thornton who became intimately involved but Richard Campbell-Breeden, managing director of Goldmans' investment banking division. Campbell-Breeden was an old United fan, having lived in Manchester from the age of four until thirteen, and had first seen them in the 1974 season when they had been relegated to the old Second Division.

Campbell-Breeden was well aware of the contradictions produced by modern football. A close friend says: 'His father is also a very enthusiastic Manchester United fan but is part of the generation that refuses to pay to watch football on TV. He is part of the generation who watched football for free on television. So whenever there is a match on Sky he comes round to Richard's house.'

Soon after Booth approved Kinsella's plans Goldmans, in the style of such City takeovers, gave the project a code name: Moore and Best. The M of Manchester United became Moore, the B of BSkyB became Best. Best's selection was understandable given his place in the heart of United fans, but that of Moore can only be explained as a desire to involve the one English captain to lift the World Cup. The code names were meant to ensure that even if some of the paperwork fell into the wrong hands nobody would know the identity of the two companies. However, as often happens, security was not always watertight. Occasionally letters would be addressed to Moore plc, Busby Way, Old Trafford, Manchester, which would not have taken a genius to work out.

As takeovers went, this was pretty small fry. At best Sky would be paying around £600 million, the sort of takeover that ordinarily excites little interest at the merchant bank. But this was not a standard takeover. Apart from the emotive factors involved, valuing a football club was not what merchant bankers normally did. Goldmans had to start from scratch.

By the end of July they had worked out a range which would give Booth enough room to negotiate with Edwards. The range was between 210p and 225p per share, about 40p more than United's market price at the time. If Sky paid 225p, Goldmans' upper limit, United would be worth £570 million, not a significant takeover in City terms but one which would make United the most expensive football club in the world.

The United board was due to meet at Old Trafford on Thursday 6 August. In the early evening of 4 August, Edwards and Watkins met Mark Booth, Ian West, Mark Kinsella and Martin Stewart for a formal meeting in a conference room at the Royal Lancaster Hotel. United had booked the suite and such was the paranoia about secrecy that when a waiter walked in with coffee, everyone froze and the hubbub of conversation ceased instantly. On the table were papers marked Sky and Manchester United and the immediate fear was the waiter might see them and sense something was going on. But the waiter, unnerved by the total silence that greeted him, stopped in mid-stride. Then someone said, 'Oh coffee, fine, fine, just leave it there,' and the waiter almost dropped it on the nearest table and hurried out of the room not sure whether he had come to the wrong room.

Had the waiter managed to eavesdrop, then what he would have heard is Sky insisting that they needed to get some reality into the discussion about the price: 290p was just not realistic. United were arguing that the higher price was justified on the grounds that the Super League could happen. But neither Booth nor Stewart thought this was realistic, and even if it happened it would not bring in the money United thought it might.

The 290p was soon knocked out as utopian and it was agreed that a realistic price would be around 200p. Sky's starting price was 190p, which was 30% above what the United share price was then. Sky knew it would have to go a bit north of 200p, but it wanted to make sure that it would be just a little over 200p rather than going over the 250p mark.

Edwards and Watkins soon accepted the logic of this and as the talks developed Sky got the distinct impression that Edwards, who had already consulted Keith Harris informally, was much the more pragmatic one, with Watkins trying to drive a hard bargain. He was trying to get as much as possible. However, by the end of the evening, both Edwards and Watkins had realised that if they wanted the deal, much as Sky wanted United, there was a limit to what it would pay for the club.

By the time the meeting ended an agreement had been struck and after some negotiation it was decided that the price would be 217.5p. Happy with the result, Edwards and Booth went off for a meal at a Thai restaurant to further develop what both felt was a very good personal chemistry. Edwards assured Booth he would go to the board and recommend the offer. Edwards also agreed to sell his own 14 per cent stake to Sky, an irrevocable undertaking, at that price. Meanwhile Martin Stewart, Ian West and Kevin Kinsella took Watkins to the bar of the Royal Lancaster.

Booth drove away from the Royal Lancaster feeling not a little pleased with himself and confident the deal was now done. However, later that evening when Booth rang Campbell-Breeden at home and told him the news, Campbell-Breeden's response surprised him 'This is ridiculous. He takes it to the board. The board appoints advisers and they do due diligence. Then they come back and say whether they can recommend it. That's the point where they will try and screw us for some more.'

Campbell-Breeden was to prove prophetic; the auction for United had just begun.

The United board met on the morning of 6 August. An hour before the meeting Sky, having formalised the offer, had faxed it to Old Trafford. All the United directors were present. Kenyon had just come back from holiday in Sicily, Gill was about to go away for two weeks to Kos. The three non-executive directors, Watkins, Dyke and Amer Al Midani, who had missed the July meeting, were also present. Apart from Edwards, Roland Smith and Watkins, all of them had come to the meeting unaware of the momentous announcement awaiting them. This was meant to be a routine pre-season board meeting, three days before the Charity Shield. The strategy discussion that had been adjourned in July was still on the agenda and some of the directors hoped there would be time to think of plans for the future.

As everyone settled down, Roland Smith said that before he turned to the agenda he had something to say. Sky had made a bid for United, offering to pay 217.5p in cash and shares and 212p if it was cash only. Martin Edwards told the board that not only had he negotiated the price with Sky and recommended it, he had done a personal deal with Booth to sell Sky his shares. Smith made it clear he was in favour of the deal.

David Gill could not contain his surprise, even though he knew that as a public company United could be taken over. 'My initial thoughts were why do we need to tie up with someone? What is Sky going to bring to the party? What are they going to add?'

Dyke echoed Gill's sentiments and felt more work needed to done. Why was it necessary to sell to Sky or anybody else? And if there had to be sale, how much was United worth? Clearly there was the need to commission specialists to examine the subject. Dyke, of course, was an old foe of Murdoch and Sky. He had no faith in Murdoch. Back in 1992 he had turned down an approach from Sam Chisholm to bid jointly with Sky and ITV for the Premier League rights. Now, while totally unconvinced United should sell to Sky, he concentrated on the price. United should be worth much, much more.

Kenyon was, perhaps, the least surprised. 'I was supportive of the bid. I was not agnostic. I always thought a bid would come from a media company if only because of what has happened. Media companies are after content. Sports bodies are content and if you look at the American model what happens over there happens here sooner or later.'

Soon, what Campbell-Breeden had told Booth the previous night came to pass. United were not going to say the quick yes that Booth had hoped for. It was decided to employ HSBC and Spectrum, a firm of media consultants recommended by Dyke. Spectrum would be asked to do an analysis of the business and what the contribution of television would add up to, HSBC to analyse what the takeover would mean financially and what the price should be. In mid afternoon Edwards rang Booth and told him that United had decided to involve HSBC. Only after HSBC had looked at the bid would the United board be able to respond to the offer.

So far Rupert Murdoch had played little or no part in the discussions, although Booth had discussed the offer with him and a couple of other board members including BSkyB chairman Jerome Seydoux. But now it was decided to brief Murdoch. Later that Thursday Murdoch, on his boat somewhere off Sardinia, was told how the United board had reacted to the offer. Murdoch was to get a first-hand report in the second week of August when Booth took a few days off and joined him. 'His reaction was if we could make the deal and it made sense then it was fine. We also discussed the reaction to the bid and the Murdoch factor. We felt it would be a hot topic and, like everybody else, we were conscious of it.'

By this time Booth had also decided that it was time to widen the circle of people who knew. On 10 August, four days after the United board meeting, he summoned Tim Allan, former deputy to Alistair Campbell, Tony Blair's press officer at 10 Downing Street, who had joined Sky in June of that year. Allan, a keen sports fan who plays cricket and was a member of the No. 10 football team, was taken aback. He recognised it would be a huge story with massive repercussions.

Booth also rang Tim Bell, the media guru who had made his name by advising Margaret Thatcher and was a long-time adviser to both Rupert Murdoch and Sky. He was on holiday on a boat off Sardinia. Bell didn't become fully involved until he came back from holiday a couple of weeks later. 'I then got involved in conversations internally with Tim and Mark. It was a very small group of people who knew about it – Tim Allan, Vic Wakeling, Elizabeth Murdoch, Martin Stewart, Deanna Bates, and Mark, of course.'

Yet, small as this group was, it is interesting to note that compared to Sky, United played it much more secretively. Nobody apart from the plc board were told, not even the members of the football board, including Bobby Charlton. Booth had told his PR advisers but Edwards did not tell John Bick, his financial PR. And at this stage he had absolutely no intention of bringing Alex Ferguson into the loop.

Nor at this stage did United tell HSBC, its merchant bankers, who the bidders were. Gill had rung Rupert Faure Walker and on 10 August Faure Walker, accompanied by David Blake, travelled up to Manchester to meet Gill and Edwards. They were told that United had had an approach and wanted HSBC to prepare a valuation of Manchester United and determine at what price, says Faure Walker, 'we felt an offer could be accepted'.

On the way back from Manchester Faure Walker and Blake talked about their bet as to whether Sky or Granada would bid and how Blake was sure it was Sky. Blake was a United fan, having been to university there. He had stood on the Stretford End, followed Tommy Docherty's team and taken to the club not long after Campbell-Breeden and many of the supporters who would soon see both of them as mortal enemies. It is one of the many ironies of the United story that the merchant bankers doing the United–Sky deal and the fans who would fight them had all been attracted to the same United team Docherty had built up, a man whose name is still chanted by the fans at Old Trafford.

Over the next two weeks, while Gill was glued to his mobile phone in Kos, HSBC prepared their report. Faure Walker and Blake went up to Old Trafford on 23 August. This time they met Edwards, Gill and Roland Smith. HSBC had come up with a valuation but both Faure Walker and Blake were impatient to know what they were offering. They asked to be told and Roland Smith now informed them it was Sky, that the price was 217.5p and that there might be another bidder. (The identity of this bidder was never disclosed.)

The implication of Sky's offer of 217.5p in cash was that it was as far as they were prepared to go. United shares were trading at around 160p and the Sky offer was a 40 per cent premium on the market price. Normally a 30 to 40 per cent premium on the market price is an offer which a merchant banker will support. As Faure Walker confesses, 'it was giving us some difficulty, that figure of 217.5p. We had some contact with Goldmans at that stage. Goldmans were very keen to get on with things. I think they got in touch with us very shortly after the tenth of August but very little happened until about the end of August.'

Goldmans were getting fed up with how slowly things were going. What they did not know was that Sky's offer was causing enormous waves of anguish and disquiet on the Old Trafford board. Greg Dyke had not shaken off his reservations about the deal and sometime during this period he spoke to Mark Booth. Booth was not surprised to hear that Dyke felt the price was too low, but what considerably surprised him was that Dyke told him the deal would not go through. It would face competition arguments. All his legal advice from Herbert Smiths and his own in-house lawyers had been that though the deal might be referred to the Monopolies and Mergers Commission, in the end there would be no problem. United were in football, Sky were in television – surely there could be no conflicting competition grounds.

No, argued Dyke, those who say that do not know how television works. Here was a monopoly supplier of television sports buying the biggest football club in the country, if not the world. It would raise competition arguments.

The United board was due to meet on Friday 28 August. On 25 August Edwards came down to London and met Booth at the Royal Lancaster Hotel. Harris also came along. The three met in the first-floor tea room just outside the carvery. As far as the deal was concerned Edwards exuded confidence. The share price was 157p, Sky was offering 217.5p, what more could anybody ask?

Edwards and Harris then went off to dinner at the Nobo restaurant in the Metropole Hotel. The City was still in deep gloom. August had been a month of misery on the stock market and while United looked like they would qualify for the Champions League proper – they had taken a 2–0 lead over LKS Lodz in the first leg of their qualifying match – Arsenal had thumped them 3–0 in the Charity Shield. It did little to lift the gloom that had descended on Old Trafford after Arsenal had done the Double the previous season. An alliance with Sky now looked even more appealing.

The same day Faure Walker had met Campbell-Breeden to discuss the details. On 26 August Campbell-Breeden wrote to him confirming that Sky's 217.5p offer was a cash and share alternative.

On Friday 28 August the United board met again at Old Trafford. Faure Walker told Gill and Dyke that they had a duty to shareholders to accept the price and recommend it to shareholders. Neither Gill nor in particular Dyke was truly convinced, but by the end of the meeting the board agreed that United would accept. This was the best they could get.

However, there was one thing they could do to improve the offer. Sky's offer of a mixture of cash and shares meant that every United shareholder accepting the offer would get 109p in cash and 108.5p in Sky shares, or could opt either for more cash or more shares. They could not have it all in cash. But what if they did not want to own Sky shares? Many small shareholders had bought United shares merely because they were fans and did not care for the stock market. For them an all-cash alternative might be more tempting.

By now it was nearly two months since Edwards' lunch with Booth and very near four weeks since a much wider circle of people, numbering nearly a couple of hundred, had known about the bid. There were fears that it might leak. Indeed, over the August bank holiday weekend the *Guardian*, which had picked up some City rumours about a bid, had suggested Sky were about to buy – Tottenham. And within days, another reporter picked up the scent. On bank holiday Saturday Tim Allan was at the Edinburgh Television Festival. It was a time of some activity for both Sky and Manchester United. Elisabeth Murdoch, Rupert Murdoch's daughter, was speaking at the festival and Paul Ridley, managing director of MUTV, was also in Edinburgh to talk about the new television channel. Allan was approached by Christine Harper of Bloomberg News Services, an agency that specialises in business news.

'News is coming through that you are buying Manchester United?' asked Harper.

Allan, still learning his job as press officer, was not sure if he could lie brazenly. He tried to hedge. 'Spurs last week, Manchester United now.' He shrugged his shoulders as if to say, what next?

'So you are not buying?'

'Look, we can't run around issuing denials every time there is a silly rumour about a football club,' replied Allan, trying hard not to give any hint how close Harper was to the truth.

Allan felt that under lobby terms Harper had the story, but she took it as denial and did not run it. Bloomberg, being an American company, seeks to verify its stories by many sources, many more than a comparable British news organisation would require. A week later a British news organisation would show the Americans how with less rigorous checking but a better nose for stories it could lead the way where American reporters feared to tread.

There was a Manchester United exclusive in the *Sun* that Saturday, headlined 'Orgy Video Shame of £12m Yorke'. The exclusive story by Andrew Parker explained how 'Soccer star Dwight Yorke made a shameful secret video of a drunken orgy at his home.' This was, of course, a classic tabloid story and it meant the real secret was safe. However, fears that the story might leak had by now begun to haunt the merchant bankers. On Sky's behalf Tim Bell was planning how to deal with leaks if they came. 'My view was, if it leaked we should put the whole story out straight away . . . Our fear was that Manchester United would leak it into the market place to get the price up . . .'

But by Friday 4 September the story had not leaked. It seemed it only required the details to be worked out before the deal was done and could go public. That day, Campbell-Breeden wrote to Faure Walker saying Sky were now prepared to provide a full cash alternative and this meant all the United board's requests had been met. But now a new City adviser, or rather an old United adviser, came on the scene and threatened to change everything. It was the turn of United's brokers, Merrill Lynch.

Curiously, at this stage Merrill Lynch had not yet been involved. It was only after the 26 August board meeting that Gill had briefed them and on that Friday they produced a preliminary assessment. In stark contrast to what HSBC were saying, Merrill Lynch made it very clear that they thought 217.5p was too low a price.

This was the signal Greg Dyke needed. Immediately he phoned Roland Smith at his HSBC offices and told him that the board decision would have to be changed as Merrill Lynch had produced new information. That day Gill and the main players on the United board – Edwards, Watkins, Kenyon – were due to meet at HSBC with Roland Smith, Faure Walker and Blake. Gill agreed with Dyke and it was clear that Kenyon and Watkins must consider this new information. It was this that had prompted Gill's call to them, catching them on the mobile phone, outside the offices of the Premier League, wondering why they were not at HSBC.

Soon all the principal United board members barring Dyke, who remained at his offices at Pearson Television near Tottenham Court Road, were at HSBC. But how could they persuade Sky to offer more? The mood seemed to be that United would now reject the deal until Sky improved its offer.

Things were not quite as pessimistic as they seemed. Edwards was constantly speaking to Booth and had made it clear that if Sky were prepared to push the price up to 225p or 226p then he might swing the board behind him.

If this was not quite what Booth wanted to hear, his advisers reacted with fury. Goldmans, fed up with the delay, were becoming increasingly angry about what they saw as the constant demand for more money from United's directors. Booth had another problem. He knew that if the price went up beyond 225p he would have to clear it with Rupert Murdoch.

He decided to call Murdoch on his yacht, in the presence of Campbell-Breeden and Martin Stewart. After Booth had informed him of what United wanted, Murdoch said, 'It's your deal, Mark. Do you want to do it?'

'Yeah,' said Booth.

'Fine,' responded Murdoch, and then, in that mock-humble pose he can adopt so successfully, added, 'I am just a board member.'

Booth was confident that, despite the haggling over the price, the deal would go through. It was decided that Sky would offer 226p and Booth called a board meeting of BSkyB for Tuesday 8 September, the first time it would meet to consider the deal. He spoke to Bell and it was agreed that he would travel to Manchester on the evening of Sunday 6 September to meet Alex Ferguson for the first time.

Ferguson fascinated Sky. They knew that to help sell the deal to the fans it would be essential to have him and Bobby Charlton on board. Before Booth made the offer to buy United the feeling in Sky was that the Edwards–Ferguson partnership was a strong one with mutual respect and understanding. The first inkling that this might not be so had come in the third week of August. Edwards and Kenyon came to Sky and had lunch with Booth and Allan to discuss how they would handle the media when the story broke. Conversation turned to Ferguson and Edwards made it clear he did not appreciate his manager's political leanings. 'He has got very close to New Labour and to No. 10. He is very friendly with Alistair Campbell. He is a socialist, you know. Very strange. And all this friendship with New Labour and Campbell I do not understand.'

Booth and Allan listened with some wonder, for Edwards was clearly unaware of Allan's links with No. 10 or the fact that he still saw Campbell as one of his great friends. At that stage Edwards' view of Ferguson's socialism seemed to be the sort of view rich football chairmen may have of their employees. It would assume more significance two weeks later as Bell prepared to manage the publicity when the deal was announced and get Ferguson on board. 'Clearly my view was, at the very least, we must make sure he didn't come out and say he was opposed to it and was leaving the club.' It was finally decided that Edwards was to ring Ferguson on the Sunday morning.

Sky's request for a meeting with Ferguson had come at a bad time. On top of all that had gone between the two men, Edwards felt particularly aggrieved about what he saw as Ferguson's behaviour over a couple of transfers. With the purchase of Dwight Yorke from Aston Villa for £12.5 million United had spent over £28 million on three players and the board was told Ferguson would have to sell a surplus striker. Ole Gunnar Solskjaer was the obvious choice.

Tottenham came in for him and Edwards discussed a deal. When Alan Sugar sent a fax offering £5.5 million he signed and returned it. Now Tottenham had to agree terms with the player. This is when Ferguson stepped in.

David Pleat, Tottenham's director of football, was acting on the deal for Tottenham. He told me, 'The boy went to see Alex. He told him you are still in my plans. I still rate you. Alex says to him you don't have to go, we are not under financial pressure. The boy's wife was about to start a course at Manchester University. Solskjaer being a nice boy says I'd stay here.' Ferguson quickly began to play Solskjaer in his team, and although he never commanded a regular place, he often came on very effectively as substitute – never more so than when scoring against Bayern Munich in injury time to win United the Champions League.

But it was the final straw in Edwards' relationship with a manager he had recruited and supported in his lean days. Chairmen of football clubs know that when it comes to back-page manipulation they can never compete with their managers. Now that he faced the biggest deal of his career, Edwards did not want to see Ferguson ruin it.

Despite the way Edwards had reacted to the idea of recruiting Ferguson (Bell's plans to inform Bobby Charlton also did not work), the meeting that Friday between Bell and the United board went well. Bell left HSBC confident the deal was going through. Booth, who by now had sent out notices of the board meeting and knew it contained representatives from many other broadcasters, made it clear that any board member who felt he might have a conflict of interest should not attend.

The United board were not quite as confident that the deal was in the bag, but clearly a decision would be made the following week. Everybody was relieved that the news had not leaked. The PR men relaxed, confident they had control of the publicity agenda, and Richard Campbell-Breeden went off for a weekend to Sweden.

The English sporting world had enough to worry about that weekend. That Saturday evening England were in Stockholm, playing the first match of the qualifying campaign for Euro 2000 against Sweden. England had bowed out of the World Cup against Argentina feeling distinctly unlucky. David Beckham, sent off against Argentina, was missing and although England took an early lead the Swedes bounced back. By the time Campbell-Breeden's plane touched down in Stockholm England were well beaten. As he landed he switched his mobile phone back on. Almost instantly it rang. It was Mark Sorrell, whose father is the head of the giant media company WPP. Mark's message for Campbell-Breeden was so disturbing that he spent most of the dinner holding conference calls on his mobile with Booth, Bell, Allan and other Sky advisers.

The message was that the cover had been blown. It would be in a Sunday paper the following morning.

10

THE LEAK

MARK SORRELL'S CALL to Campbell-Breeden was one of many whizzing between Manchester United, BSkyB and their advisers on that Saturday evening. It reflected the utter panic that had gripped them as they realised that their secret had been rumbled.

The man who had finally nailed the story and was prepared to go where Christine Harper couldn't was Neil Bennett. On Thursday 4 September, just as Merrill Lynch were looking at the Sky bid, Bennett, City editor of the *Sunday Telegraph*, took a call. 'The call said that BSkyB was planning to bid for United. The caller knew what they were talking about. In the past this contact had given me some good stories and some bum steers. This was a good one.'

On that Thursday evening Bennett called the paper's editor, Dominic Lawson, at his home. 'Dominic was superb. It is difficult in newspapers when you have a great story not to talk but he did not talk. We were worried that if we widened the circle of people who knew and it leaked then BSkyB and United would have to issue a statement to the Stock Exchange. So we had to keep it very tight until the markets closed on Friday evening, when Dominic told Chris Andersen, then executive editor and Mathew d'Ancona, then deputy editor.'

Lawson and Bennett also decided to make sure very few people within the *Telegraph* knew about the story. So, says Bennett, 'one writer was told to write a feature about Manchester United, the history and the background of the club, but wasn't told why we wanted such a story'. Colin Gibson was told about the story at Saturday lunchtime and at the same time Bennett took his deputy, Mary Fagan, to a pub and told her about it. He then returned to the office and told the rest of the City staff, who had spent most of that Saturday morning wondering why Bennett was behaving so furtively.

However, Bennett still had a problem. It was now about 4 p.m. and he needed one more check call to make sure his contact's information was correct. 'I couldn't go to print without some confirmation of the story. The obvious thing would be to ring either United or BSkyB. But if I rang BSkyB and they knew I had the story then they could release it to the Murdoch papers and my exclusive control of it would be lost. I got hold of someone who knew somebody who called back and said the story was broadly correct.'

Bennett, understandably, will not say who he rang. In fact he rang Pearson Television. Bennett knew that even a no comment from Greg Dyke would confirm the story.

The head of PR at Pearson contacted Dyke at his country home in Hampshire and asked, 'I suppose you want me to deny it as complete rubbish?'

'No,' said Dyke, 'you'd better not do that. I don't think you'd better get back to them at all.'

Dyke then phoned Gill and Mark Booth, telling them that this 'thing', as he called it, was out and that Neil Bennett of the *Sunday Telegraph* would be running the story the next day. Gill immediately rang Edwards, Faure Walker and David Blake.

Faure Walker was in his garden at home in Essex. 'It was about 4.30. Suddenly I heard three people had telephoned me. My children came up to see me and straight away I knew there was a leak. When you suddenly get three calls like that within ten minutes you know there's a leak.' The three people who tried to call him were of course Edwards, Gill and Blake. 'They had heard that the *Telegraph* was inquiring into the details and nobody at Manchester United had spoken to them.'

As Faure Walker was clearing out his garden, Keith Harris was with Roland Smith at Lord's to see their beloved Lancashire play in the NatWest final against Derbyshire. It was a filthy day, rain preventing play until 4.30 p.m. The only consolation was that Lancashire won in a canter by nine wickets. Just as play was about to start Smith got a call on his mobile. 'Roland and I went outside the box in the Mound Stand at Lord's at the back of the stand and we discussed the fact that the next day's *Sunday Telegraph* would have the story.' But since the *Sunday Telegraph* had not contacted Manchester United there was nothing for United to do.

Tim Bell recalls: 'I got a phone call from the *Mail on Sunday* who said, "We understand the *Sunday Telegraph*'s got a big story and is boxing out the second edition. They're putting a spoof story in the first edition, printing the second edition late and putting that big story on the front page of the second edition. The *Express* have heard the same thing." So I thought to myself, "Well, this has got to be IT."'

Bell rang his colleague, David Beck, the managing director of Bell's financial PR, who knows Neil Bennett very well. 'I said to David, "Ring Neil Bennett and find out what he's got. Just plead with him to give us a clue."'

Meanwhile Tim Allan was also trying to find out what the *Sunday Telegraph* had. He had sent a fax to Beck. Although neither Manchester United nor BSkyB were named, the fax failed to arrive and Allan was paranoid it had landed on some news desk. Then at 4.30 Mark Booth rang to tell him of his conversation with Dyke. Allan recalls: 'My immediate reaction was Greg Dyke had leaked the story on the basis that the person who is contacted about the leak is the source of the leak.'

Allan drove up to Booth's house in Belgravia. He rang the *Sunday Telegraph* news desk pretending he was responding to a call from them about Sky, but they did not fall for that. He then rang for Tom Baldwin, a political journalist he knew well. (Baldwin was later to move to *The Times* and is credited with close ties to New Labour). The call was taken by Baldwin's deputy Graham Wilson, who said, 'I'll go and find out, I'll call you back in two minutes.' To this day Allan has not heard from him again. Allan was now convinced that the *Sunday Telegraph* had the story.

How much information did Bennett have? 'From limited information you can develop a lot.' The information he did have was quite crucial. He knew BSkyB were prepared to pay 225p, valuing United at £575 million. The fact that his informant had rung on Thursday, about the day Merrill's involvement began to move the price up from 217.5p, indicates Bennett's source was very well informed. Bennett also pictured Roland Smith as the architect of the deal and particularly for securing the price of 225p. If he was premature in saying Booth had already secured Granada's backing – at this stage Granada did not even know about the bid – it was a remarkably accurate story.

Even now Booth could have thrown a spanner in Bennett's carefully laid plans. But, says Bennett, 'To Mark Booth's credit he did not tell the *Sunday Times* or the *News of the World*. They did not get it until midnight when our second edition hit the streets.'

Before midnight every editor in Fleet Street knew something was happening at the *Telegraph*. Bennett says: 'News that we had something began to be suspected because we had ordered extra copies for Manchester and the circulation people who gossip put the word around that we had something special going. This alerted the other papers and when our man went at about ten o'clock to King's Cross he saw a huge knot of journalists waiting for the first edition of the *Sunday Telegraph*.'

As the other papers finally learnt what the exclusive was, panic broke out in their newsrooms. One sports journalist rang up Paul Ridley and asked him for Martin Edwards' home telephone number. Joe Melling rang Trevor East, deputy to Vic Wakeling at Sky. John Jay, City editor of the *Sunday Times*, was hauled out of bed at 1 a.m. to write a special edition just before he was due to go on holiday. Jay spoke at length to Allan, not best pleased that one part of the Murdoch empire did not know what the other was doing.

It was one of the most horrible nights Allan had endured. Among the calls he had to make was one to the *News of the World* to placate Murdoch's best-selling paper in this country as best he could. The *News of the World* tried to make the best of it for its final edition and, true to style, even put an exclusive on its story.

One Sky source says that while Booth did not tell the Murdoch papers, Murdoch, not best pleased his papers were being scooped on their own story, did so himself late on that Saturday night to rectify matters. 'The story appeared in the *News of the World* and the *Sunday Times* before the *Sunday Telegraph* was on the bookstalls, or before the ordinary punter could have got a copy of it. So it seems quite clear to me that somebody in News Corp or News International gave the story to the *News of the World* and the *Sunday Times* . . . I think it was Rupert who rang, or possibly Les Hinton, the chairman of News International. Probably Hinton did it on the back of a phone call with Rupert.'

The *Sunday Telegraph* knew this would happen. Lucy Goodwin, their PR person, worked through the night to make sure radio and television knew that, even if other papers copied Bennett and Gibson's story and tried to claim it, it was recognised as a *Telegraph* scoop. BBC Radio 4 led its eight o'clock news on Sunday morning saying the *Sunday Telegraph* had reported the bid and Bennett fulfilled a lifetime's ambition by going on *Breakfast with Frost*.

Like all good journalists Bennett accepts that 'it was a bit of a luck getting the story'. But the moment his contact had rung on that Thursday he had immediately sensed it was a big story, 'although even I did not realise it was quite as big as it turned out'. Bennett's surprise about the dimensions of the story was shared by Mark Booth. 'Saturday surprised me. That is when I realised the emotion of it. Then on Sunday I saw the papers come out and after that there were no more surprises. I knew this was a very big story.'

11

THE STORM BREAKS

THE *SUNDAY TELEGRAPH* story had put the deal in jeopardy. 'It was an unwelcome moment with the deal a couple of days away,' says Booth. 'What it meant was that we had lost control.' Booth by now had also been warned that the deal might not go through. 'When Greg Dyke rang me on Saturday he told me the bid would not be allowed through on competition grounds. I said nonsense and we had a bet that if he was right I would buy him lunch, if I was right he would buy me lunch.'

What particularly concerned Booth was that now the bid was in the public domain, 'you have the risk of a new entrant coming in'. Granada had figured large in Booth's thoughts. There were part owners of BSkyB and had a member on the board. The other question nagging him was, as a result of the publicity what was the price the United board would now want for their club?

Campbell-Breeden briefed John Thornton from Sweden and sometime on Saturday night Thornton had rung Faure Walker at home. After they discussed the leak the conversation moved to what the United board might now do. Faure Walker told Thornton that 'I believed the board would reject 217.5p, that it wasn't enough. So the seeds were sown. Until then Sky had said 217.5p was the maximum. I couldn't say that the board had rejected it. All I could say was that I believed, and that I would recommend, that the board would reject it.'

Of course Edwards had been telling Booth the same thing since Friday and Thornton knew about the conversations. But his chat with Faure Walker reinforced the impression that, the bid having leaked, Sky would have to pay a lot more if they wanted to get United.

The Sunday morning saw a series of telephone calls between United directors and Faure Walker and Blake. It was decided to have an impromptu United board meeting via a telephone conference call. As often happens in such situations, the United board decided to gather at Maurice Watkins' home. Two people were not present – Peter Kenyon was travelling back from Germany and Amer Al Midani was in Spain.

The leak had transformed the mood of the board. They quickly saw how they could use the *Telegraph* story to their own advantage. Faure Walker says: 'When the newspaper article appeared, one rapidly realised that if terms couldn't be agreed, then Manchester United could put out a statement which would basically say that they had had a number of constructive and friendly talks with Sky, but that Sky hadn't made a proposal which they, Manchester United, felt they could recommend to their shareholders.'

Campbell-Breeden is convinced the leak was part of HSBC's strategy but Faure Walker argues that United had nothing to gain from leaking it and also, 'lots of information was given about the bid and the negotiations which, frankly, Manchester United were not aware of.'

For an hour on Sunday the United board discussed these and other issues. It was agreed that they would unanimously decline the offer of 217.5p. Faure Walker now rang Richard Campbell-Breeden 'to tell him we had decided we would reject the offer'. Everyone knew the rejection did not mean the deal was dead, only that United wanted more money. Publicly the club had to respond to the mounting media interest and by four o'clock Ken Ramsden had confirmed they were in talks with a third party.

Sky were still in a state of shock, worsened by the fact that their PR men were firmly held on a leash by the bankers and the lawyers. Bell, Allan and the others were feeling very frustrated at their inability to tell their side of the story. Bell had driven to Isleworth early on Sunday morning from his country home in Sussex. 'Tim Allan and I and David Beck sat after four o'clock in the room with a loudspeaker phone and a merchant banker watching us, vetting what we were saying. We weren't able to use the case we had for making a bid for Manchester United.'

Tim Allan felt particularly frustrated. He had spent some time on Saturday night fruitlessly trying to prise out from the editor of *Breakfast with Frost* who he might have on his programme. Frost spoke to Tony Banks, then sports minister, on the telephone; Banks made it clear he was opposed to the bid.

On Sunday morning Allan rang Alastair Campbell, a great friend of Alex Ferguson. Campbell was instinctively against the bid. When Allan told Peter Mandelson, who had just taken over at the Department of Trade and Industry, Mandelson's first reaction was, 'Oh my God, what have you done now?' He knew that if the bid went through it would soon land on his desk and he would have to decide whether to refer it to the Monopolies and Mergers Commission. Mandelson's friendship with Elisabeth Murdoch was well known and questions would certainly be asked as to whether he was sufficiently detached from the Murdochs to take a view.

The bankers and lawyers were telling Sky that whatever happened Mandelson could not possibly block the bid on competition grounds, and they were determined to control Sky's press reactions. At this stage on Sunday afternoon, with the stock market not yet officially told, they would only allow

Allan to issue the barest minimum statement. The press team felt it was useless merely to say that Sky was in talks with Manchester United which might or might not lead to an offer.

Allan did talk to Roland Watson, then deputy political editor of *The Times*, and after much badgering he gave one little titbit to the *Sun* that if the takeover went ahead season ticket prices at Old Trafford would be frozen. Faure Walker may have felt that the leak had put United on the front foot in the negotiations with Sky but as far as the wider public were concerned, both United and Sky were firmly on the defensive. And in a sense there had been an army in waiting for just such a day to rise and march.

That army had begun to form several years previously and had originally come together on a very different issue. On 15 April 1995 the Independent Manchester United Supporters Association was set up. The catalyst for this had been an attempt by United to get people to sit down during matches. This added to the growing feeling among some fans that the United board did not care about genuine supporters and was only interested in making money.

The whole thing boiled over on 22 March 1995, when Arsenal came to visit Old Trafford. Despite United's 3–0 victory, fans were not appeased. With stewards constantly asking them to sit down, some of them decided to form an organisation which would channel their views. It was a fraught time for United fans, one of great tension and heartache. Their hero Eric Cantona had been banned from football for the rest of the season and faced a possible jail sentence for his kung-fu kick at a Crystal Palace supporter. If love and reverence for Cantona was a common bond linking these fans, then so was an elemental, almost visceral hatred of the United board and, in particular, Martin Edwards.

A number of supporters had been meeting for some time at the Gorse Hill pub on Chester Road near the Stretford End to discuss setting up a group that would reflect supporters' views. Known as the Dirty Dozen, they included Peter Boyle, Richard Kurt and one man who soon came to be seen as the principal voice of the group, Andy Walsh.

Walsh, an information technology consultant, was well versed in organising protest movements. He had been active in Militant and chaired the Greater Manchester Poll Tax Federation, his opposition to which saw him jailed for fourteen days in Congleton. Boyle had also been jailed in Walsall for his opposition to the poll tax,. They knew how to organise and appreciated how important it was to get the media right. It was decided to hold an initial meeting somewhere grander than the Gorse Hill to gauge reactions. The Free Trade Hall in Manchester, site of the Peterloo massacre, was chosen. Three hundred people turned up and it was decided to set up a formal organisation called the Independent Manchester United Supporters Association, which inevitably became known as IMUSA.

The inaugural meeting was held at Lancashire Cricket Club, between 500 and 600 people attending to elect officials with Boyle, Kurt and Walsh in charge. By September 1997 IMUSA, says Walsh, was established in the minds of Manchester United fans.

Walsh and his colleagues were watching the stock market, trying to follow rumours of a possible bid for the club. In early January 1998 the organisation was put on what Walsh calls a 'professional footing' with specific tasks given to members. The most important of these tasks was media work. People were trained in issuing press releases, how to handle journalists' questions. With increasing demands from the media, Walsh started taking colleagues along when he gave interviews to show how the press should be handled. 'We were establishing ourselves,' he says, 'as the first port of call.'

The world called on Sunday 6 September when at 6.15 a.m. Walsh was woken by the Press Association and asked to comment on the *Sunday Telegraph* story. 'I gave a holding reply and, since we are a democratic body with elected officers, I began to contact my elected officials.' By ten that morning Walsh had gone to the ground, as had many United supporters. The feeling was mixed. Many were bemused, some indifferent and a small minority opposed. Walsh and IMUSA's task was to make sure that the voice of opposition came through loud and clear. By midday, with some 200 supporters gathered outside Old Trafford, Walsh and his colleagues had spoken to the press. While Sky's PR advisers silently fumed, IMUSA made sure their message of opposition to the bid was heard round the world.

It was clear there had to be a campaign. If IMUSA was already organised and ready to strike at the board, then the announcement of the deal led to the birth of another equally potent army.

Michael Crick had spent the summer preparing a proposal to write a book on Rupert Murdoch. The deal was announced just as he finished, so he was well versed in Murdoch lore. He had already written well-researched and well-received books on Jeffrey Archer and Michael Heseltine. Interestingly, one of his first books had been on Militant, researching and exposing Walsh's former colleagues. However, on that Sunday morning such political differences did not matter. As far as United and their views on Martin Edwards and the board were concerned, they were of like mind. Back in 1990 Crick and Smith's book *Manchester United: The Betrayal of a Legend* had excoriated Edwards, describing the United board as 'Businessmen who put profits above all else.' For Crick as for Walsh, news of Sky's bid was ultimate proof that all Edwards cared for was money.

On that Sunday Crick got a call from the *Evening Standard* to write about the bid. He used the platform provided to denounce the bid and, of course, Edwards' greed and drive for more and more money. On Monday he returned to *Newsnight* after a sabbatical researching the Murdoch book and offered to do a piece on the bid. He discovered that the United board were meeting at the offices of HSBC and got shots of them through a window.

Richard Hytmer, who runs the advertising agency Publicist, was one of the millions who saw Crick on *Newsnight*. Hytmer was an old school friend from Manchester Grammar. Both Crick and Hytmer held shares in United and it was quickly decided to set up an organisation of shareholders opposed to the deal. Hytmer came up with the name Shareholders United Against Murdoch. SUAM had joined IMUSA in the battle to stop the bid.

Both IMUSA and SUAM took a major strategic decision that was to prove crucial. From the beginning they decided that they would present this as a Murdoch deal. As we have seen, at this stage Rupert Murdoch had played little or no personal part in the deal, but Mark Booth was an unknown and it would be difficult to generate any passion against him. Nor would it be easy to present Sky as the devil. Murdoch was already evil incarnate, known and hated. By focusing on Murdoch both Crick and Walsh could easily plug into the non-Murdoch press.

If United were behind in the publicity battle, then within the Premier League the initial reaction to the deal was also quite hostile. On Sunday morning Andrew Neil, who then did a morning show on Radio Five Live, had called Peter Leaver to get his reaction.

Leaver recalls, 'My reaction was I don't know very much about it. My view was they are big boys; they are on the Stock Exchange. If you have shares quoted on the stock market then you can have a bid and I could see no reason why BSkyB could not acquire Manchester United. But I could also see there could be competition issues. There could be all sorts of problems in television negotiations.' He then phoned all the clubs, most of whom were hostile. Rick Parry's view was that United should be expelled from the League, and Ken Bates felt similarly. Blackburn said they should be thrown out if the deal went ahead.

As it happens, at that time David Dein and Arsenal were in talks with Carlton about a possible involvement at the Highbury club and Alan Sugar had been mulling over an offer from English National Investment Company for Tottenham of £70 million. Unsurprisingly, Dein and Sugar were more circumspect. Leaver urged the clubs to 'just calm down and play it a bit more cautiously. There was no real Premier League view on this and although there was talk of holding a Premier League meeting, there was no real drive to hold one.'

12

THE DONE DEAL?

ON TUESDAY 8 September 1998, the Manchester United board decided it wanted to go to bed with BSkyB, a decision that later that night prompted Howard Davies, then head of the Securities and Financial Authority, and a passionate Manchester City fan, to say in some exultation: 'I am so glad it is happening. I have hated Manchester United all my life. Manchester United was born in Munich and will die with Murdoch.' Yet Monday had begun with the board still not sure they could accept the Sky offer. They were meeting later that day essentially to ratify the telephone conversation of the executive the previous day, rejecting Sky's offer.

Martin Edwards knew that in fact this would be very far from the end of the story. He knew he would again have to go back to Booth for more money. While he did not like being the supplicant, he nevertheless remained convinced that the deal was a good one for the club and could see no other way of carrying the board, and in particular Greg Dyke. Both Edwards and Roland Smith had spoken to Booth and told him that if Sky were prepared to go up to 230p then they felt sure they could get the board, or rather Dyke, to agree.

By mid-morning on Monday most of the board members – barring Al Midani, who could not be there but was in touch by telephone – were on their way to London, Peter Kenyon having long abandoned his plan to go to Brussels to meet Karel van Miert in the company of Media Partners.

Edwards took the train to London, only to find on arrival at Euston that he was faced by a swarm of media microphones, tape recorders and cameras. From the fringes of the crowd gathered round him, he could hear cries of 'Judas' from some supporters. A picture of him looking hunted and besieged made the front pages of the next day's papers. But he had faced such attacks so often before that he was inured to them. His greater concern was to make sure the board was united as they discussed the Sky bid.

Just as the meeting started, at 5.30 p.m., a messenger came in to say that there was a call for Roland Smith and Rupert Faure Walker. It was Mark Booth. 'They knew the board meeting was about to start and, rather than have the meeting reject their proposal, they decided to increase their bid. They initially increased their bid to 230p in shares and 220p in cash. We had a conversation on this new offer and the long and the short of it was that we said no, that couldn't be recommended. Then they increased it to 230p in cash as well. So both the shares and the cash would be the same value.'

Faure Walker, Smith and Edwards went back to the Tower Room and Faure Walker informed the board of Sky's new offer. As he spoke he glanced at his watch. It was six o'clock, with luck it should be over in good time for dinner. But that was not taking into account Greg Dyke.

Dyke had come to the meeting having pondered his position long and hard. Although the *Sunday Telegraph* had not named him, it had clearly identified him as the one dissident director on the United board. It seemed that there were two perspectives on the bid. It may be right for the shareholders, but did that make it right for the club? The way IMUSA and SUAM were developing their case, these were presented as mutually contradictory positions. The interests of the club, they argued, were not the same as those of the shareholders. Dyke was not convinced the gap was unbridgeable. He would rather there had been no bid, but given that there was one then a good deal for a shareholder might also be good for the club.

What he needed was his own legal advice. What was his fiduciary responsibility towards shareholders? Some time on that Monday he had rung a lawyer from Slaughter & May whom he had met through the takeover of London Weekend Television. The advice was that if he felt the price offered by Sky reached the range where it had to be put to shareholders, then he had a duty to approve it.

As discussions started on whether 230p was an acceptable price, Dyke seemed happy with it. But at that Monday's board meeting Merrill Lynch's report was available for the first time. They had spoken to some of the major institutional shareholders, who had indicated they thought United was worth more. Merrill had worked out a range: in their opinion, the very least Sky should pay for Manchester United was 240p.

On 28 August Faure Walker had told Dyke and Gill that it was their duty as directors to accept a price of 217.5p. Now Sky had gone up to 230p and Faure Walker was even more convinced this was the right price. As Dyke used Merrill Lynch to argue against 230p, Faure Walker and David Blake pulled out what they thought was their trump card: a note that Merrill, as Manchester United's brokers, had prepared on 2 September, two days before they were called in to value the club. At that stage Merrill did not know about the bid and had recommended United to their clients as a long-term buy. The price was 157p and they felt that if within twelve months the price went up to 185p that would be a reasonable objective.

It was with some relish that HSBC flourished this note from United's own brokers. Before Sky had come in, on the basis of the 1997 figures, Merrill calculated that United's price/earnings ratio (the share price divided by its income) was 21.2. From the 1998 figures Merrill worked out a price/earnings ratio of 41.3, prepared on the basis of a United share price of 157p. The price of 240p, which Merrill now said was the bottom of their range, would give United an incredible price/earnings ratio of 60.

Dyke retorted by speaking of future earnings, particularly from television and pay-per-view. The argument was a classic one. Faure Walker and Blake were making the standard merchant banking position: given United's current share price and likely future earnings, 230p was more than Sky should be paying and United should grab it. Dyke was seeing it in terms of television rights and what he, as a expert in this field, felt might be their growth potential.

In buying United Sky were getting Manchester United's television rights in perpetuity. In little over a decade Dyke had seen the amazing rise in the television value of soccer. Between 1988 and 1998 football's yearly income from television had gone from £5 million a year to £160 million a year. Who could say what the next couple of years, let alone the next decade, might bring? Against such tremendous growth, could 230p be the right price? Dyke was more than ever convinced that Sky were getting United very cheap.

Fair enough, said Faure Walker and Blake. The projections of future television income were very alluring. When HSBC were asked to carry out valuation work on United at the beginning of August it still seemed possible there could be a breakaway Super League. But look, they said, at what had happened the previous Thursday when Media Partners made its presentation to the Premier League. The meeting had decided that no club in the Premier League would be allowed to continue discussions about the European Super League. United were not even allowed to continue talking to Media Partners.

Faure Walker tried to sketch out the scenario whereby the club might be worth a lot more. 'If you assume the European Super League happens, you assume a complete breakdown of negotiating rights over television. In other words a free-for-all, so that Manchester United gets the lion's share of that. You also assume pay TV comes in and that the High Street on Saturday afternoons in the UK is deserted, because everybody's at home paying £6 a throw to watch pay-TV Premier League every Saturday of the year. You assume all that – then you can come to valuations of £700 to £800 million for Manchester United. That's in four years' time. You can come to these figures but I think, to be realistic, that won't happen.'

It is interesting to look back on these discussions and reflect that only six years down the line, and without pay-per-view taking hold so dramatically that nobody went to watch Saturday afternoon Premiership soccer, the Glazers would end up paying just under £800 million for the club.

Dyke, unconvinced by Faure Walker and HSBC, had set about making his own inquiries. He went into a separate room and started calling the various people at Merrill Lynch who had made the valuations. He wanted to know how they had worked out the figures. By now most of them had left Merrill's office in the City. Some of them he found in their homes, others he had to drag out from their hotel rooms where they were on business. Dyke spent a good part of the evening trying to get City backing for his view that at 230p Manchester United was a steal for Sky.

He returned to the Tower Room to say that having spoken to Merrill at some length he could not accept 230p. The very minimum was 240p.

Until this point Edwards had kept his cool. But now he lost his temper and shouted, 'Greg, if we lose this deal because of you then I shall sue you.' The remark was uncharacteristic and showed the tremendous strain Edwards was under. Dyke's eyes lit up. Looking across at Edwards he said, 'That's a good one for the book, eh Martin?' With that Dyke laughed in that full-throated, mischievous way of his. But nobody joined in. The Tower Room was tense. Across the Thames the lights were shining brightly on the South Bank and the old London County Council headquarters. It was well past dinner time, there were only sandwiches to eat and the unanimous agreement that Roland Smith was so keen to reach seemed nowhere in sight.

By half past one in the morning the board were no nearer agreement. It was decided to adjourn until the next morning.

On Tuesday morning the board met again, this time in the Thames Room. But this was a replay of the Tower Room: another room with little HSBC notepads, pencils, mineral water and sandwiches and with Dyke again refusing to agree to 230p. The discussions had been going on for very nearly twenty-four hours and there seemed no conclusion to the battle.

Dyke, having got back home well past 2 a.m. on Tuesday morning, was up at six and living, as his partner said, on adrenalin. During the course of the day his resolve was to be further strengthened when he heard what took place at Sky's own board meeting.

Before their board gathered in Isleworth at 2.30 that Tuesday afternoon, Sky sent a fax saying that unless 230p was agreed by five o'clock, the deal was off. Unlike the weary, bleary-eyed Manchester United board at the Thames Room, the Sky board was full of spirit as the directors walked into a room down the corridor from Mark Booth's office. This was the first time they had met to discuss the deal. Many board members had only learnt about it when they received their papers the previous day.

Originally Booth had not expected Rupert Murdoch to attend the meeting. But he was in London for Sir David English's funeral and came along. Everyone was there apart from David DeVoe, Arthur Siskind and Sam Chisholm, who was in the south of France. Graham Parrott of Granada had excused himself on the grounds that there might be a conflict of interest, should Granada decide to make their own bid.

After Booth made his presentation, there was some discussion as to whether this was indeed the right deal. Not the idea of buying a football club, but whether Manchester United was the right club. At 230p Sky was paying £600 million for United, a billion dollars. That, some directors felt, was a lot of money.

Dennis Stevenson, chairman of Pearson and Dyke's ultimate, if nominal, boss, wondered if it would not be a better idea for Sky to buy, say, Wimbledon and then spend hundreds of millions of pounds building up the team. Or why didn't they buy Arsenal or Tottenham? The real centre of population was not Manchester but London. This led to quite a lively discussion between Stevenson and Thornton, with others joining in.

Booth and Campbell-Breeden pointed out that they were dealing with football, which was not like any other business. You could not buy fans. Fans create the value of the club because fans pay for the merchandising and create the demand for TV. However much money you spend on a football club you can't necessarily create a club bigger than Manchester United. Blackburn was the classic example. Jack Walker's money might buy a championship, as it had done in 1995, but it could not create a club that could truly rival Manchester United.

In explaining why Sky was not going for Arsenal both Booth and Campbell-Breeden stressed that there were problems at Highbury. Its capacity was only 38,000 compared with United's then capacity of 55,000. Even if Arsenal moved to a bigger stadium – the talk then was having a new one at King's Cross – that would be at least five years away and by no means certain. After some discussion it was agreed that United was the right choice. It was a great deal and Booth should go ahead and do it.

The meeting had been going for some time when a secretary walked in to say there was a phone call for Booth from Martin Edwards and Roland Smith. Campbell-Breeden suggested they had better take the call as United were having their board meeting as well and it could be important.

Booth, Thornton and Campbell-Breeden went down the corridor to Booth's office. Edwards came on the phone and said to Booth, 'I am sorry, Mark, but I can't do it. I can't deliver. It's Greg Dyke. Would you prepared to do it without the full board because everybody else had recommended it?'

'No,' said Booth.

'Well, if you want the entire board then I can only get them if you are prepared to go to 240p.'

There was a pause.

'I'll have to think about it,' said Booth.

The trio went back to the boardroom and Booth told the board, 'Edwards is telling us it is 240p.'

The silence that greeted the announcement was quickly followed by howls of protest. This is like being salami sliced, said one member. They had been told they had a deal at 217.5p, then last Friday before the leak it was 225p, then it inched up to 226p, on the basis of which board papers were prepared at the weekend. On Monday it was 230p, now on Tuesday it was 240p. And Rupert Murdoch was not best pleased that it was Dyke who was manning the roadblock. He is an old enemy of Sky, warned Murdoch. He fought against us for the Premier League rights, then tried to take us to court, and now he had complained against the Sky deal to the OFT, which had triggered the case in the Restrictive Practices Court and in many ways the bid for Manchester United.

Finally Murdoch looked at Booth and said, 'Mark, it is up to you. I am sure the board will support you. What is your recommendation?'

'This is ridiculous,' said Booth. 'If we say yes at 240p they will come back asking for £3. At 240p it is beginning not to make sense.'

For Booth the ball had moved about far too much since he had tea with Edwards in August. However, he liked Edwards and had a lot of sympathy for his position. Booth, Murdoch, Stewart, Campbell-Breeden and Thornton went into Booth's office. Booth called Edwards and asked for Roland Smith. Murdoch spoke to Smith politely but firmly. 'I want to know why you think your club is worth so much, Sir Roland.' Smith launched into his well-rehearsed spiel about United's global brand, its achievements as a football club, the size of its fan base and their fantastic loyalty to United.

Murdoch was initially not much impressed and made it clear that he did not want to pay more than the 230p that had been offered. That was the price everybody bar Dyke was prepared to accept, so why not cast Dyke aside? 'We don't care. We'll do the deal at 230p and let Dyke vote against you. Let there be a director who doesn't agree with you.' But for Smith, the issue of the unanimity of the board was crucial. He answered, 'I'm not prepared to do this deal unless there is unanimity. The only price I can get unanimity is 240p.'

In the Sky boardroom the debate continued. Then one News Corp director pointed out that 240p 'means paying £623 million for Manchester United . . . But we are ready to approve the deal at 230p, and that is another 10p, only another £26 million. We are agreed, are we not, that this a good deal? So I say let's go and do it.'

Now as Booth, Murdoch and the others were about to leave Booth's office to get back to the boardroom and say it was a deal, a call came which was, perhaps, the most extraordinary of this extraordinary day. It was from Edwards for Booth and it related to the fax Sky had sent to United earlier in the day. Booth, in trying to help his friend Martin prevent Dyke blocking the deal had, says Booth, 'sent a letter to Manchester United saying that we would be prepared to accept a less than unanimous recommendation. We didn't want one person to knock over the deal. It was that simple.'

The director it was meant to isolate was Dyke. However, as can so often happen, the letter had a devastating side effect on somebody else that nobody could have anticipated and hardly anyone in Sky had even given much thought to. The letter had mentioned the names of the directors whose approval would satisfy Sky. The way Sky saw it, if the directors who had significant shares, Edwards, Watkins, and Al Midani – between them, they had 17 per cent – voted in favour, then Sky could go to the City and say the major shareholders supported the deal. Dyke had a few shares. His name was missing from the fax, so was that of those who had share options but hardly any shares.

Sky had picked up that Gill was not very enthusiastic, Bell had reported back from his Friday encounter how hostile he was. But Gill was not uppermost in Sky's mind when they wrote the letter. Booth says, 'We did not know Gill was not in favour of it.' But because unlike Edwards, Watkins and Al Midani, he was not a major shareholder they omitted his name as they did of Kenyon.

Sky thought the letter was of no great significance, it was meant to help Edwards. However as the letter came over the HSBC fax machines all hell broke loose in the Thames Room. The Manchester United board read the letter and were in uproar. As one United insider says, 'Everybody went nuts. The letter showed us they knew what was happening in our board meetings. You get a letter which says we will take all these votes without yours. You are vulnerable. You need protection. We had to protect David and negotiate a deal for him. In any case a few other persons were negotiating their own positions. Maurice was negotiating from the beginning to end. The board said we need to protect Gill.'

It was agreed that Roland Smith would phone Booth, and now with the clock well past five o'clock, which was the deadline imposed by Sky for an answer, the call came. Roland Smith told Booth that Gill could not vote for the offer unless he was sure that he would be protected and would not be out on his ear if Sky took over. According to one Sky insider this caused a great deal of annoyance not least to Booth. He told Roland Smith, 'Get Gill on the phone, right now. I want to hear from his own lips that he won't vote for it unless he gets this.'

Gill came on the phone. He was put on the speaker phone and Rupert Murdoch and others in Booth's office heard Gill say, 'I want this change in my service contract. I have just started the job and moved my family up here and want this increase in my service contract.' As he did so John Thornton whispered to Booth, 'Ask him will he not vote for Sky if he doesn't get a new contract?' Booth did and Gill said, 'Yes. I will not vote for this unless I get an increase in my personal contract.'

Booth recalls, 'I had a conversation with Martin and he asked me to speak to David. And I did. David felt a bit insecure.'

The United boardroom source is adamant that Gill had no part in this but Roland Smith negotiated the new service contract. A source there says: 'Did Gill ring Sky? Gill did not ring them. Roland Smith rang them on behalf of the board and did the deal. We also instructed Martin to get Sky to withdraw the letter, he spoke to Booth and the letter was withdrawn.' The discrepancies in recollection are not as significant as they seem. Roland Smith did make the call but Gill did speak to Booth.

Whatever the minutiae of this, the fact is that when the offer document was issued this showed that Gill did get a deal which ensured he would continue to work for Manchester United after the merger and if anytime before 30 June 2000 his contract was terminated he would be paid 200% of the aggregate of his current salary, the average of his bonuses for each of the two financial years preceding and the value of his benefits excluding share options. The offer document also had details of the arrangement Watkins had negotiated, to continue as non-executive director for another three years after the take-over at his current remuneration.

Meanwhile, in his office, Booth instructed Stewart and Deanna Bates to tell the board the deal was done. Sky was going ahead with the takeover.

However, Sky were no longer prepared to accept Faure Walker's word, or for that matter the word of anybody from United. The feeling against the United board was now running quite high at Isleworth. One Sky source says, 'We were feeling pretty pissed off. For most people their word is their bond. For these people it was not the case. We didn't trust them. They had agreed so many times before. We now said we wanted all the directors to send us a written fax to Sky saying they would recommend a deal at 240p.' Campbell-Breedon rang Faure Walker and dictated to him what Sky wanted them to sign.

But long before Sky received the written confirmation, Murdoch had decided that the deal was done. The moment the conversations in Booth's room had finished, he returned to the boardroom, finished some non-bid board business and announced that he was going to take Concorde back to New York. As he prepared to leave he calmly said, 'I want this story in my newspapers. The *Telegraph* got it the first time, I want to make sure my papers get it tomorrow. I'll call the editors from the car on my way to the airport.'

Nothing revealed more clearly Murdoch's classic journalistic instincts – or was more calculated to alarm the board members, and particularly the bankers and lawyers. They pleaded with him not to do that. The United board had not yet agreed to the price and the deal was very far from done. But Murdoch, as they soon realised, ignored their advice. Sometime during the drive between Isleworth and Terminal 4 he rang his editors.

The Sky and United boards now made their way to the offices of Freshfields, United's legal advisers. There all the United directors, barring Al Midani, signed their undertakings.

It was only now that Edwards felt able to tell Alex Ferguson. He rang the manager on his mobile phone as he was on his way to a home match against Port Vale. Bobby Charlton, away in Thailand where he was helping England's bid for the 2006 World Cup, learnt about it first from the radio and immediately rang Edwards. While the timing of these calls was forced on Edwards by the way the story broke and he could do little about the leak, Sky were not best pleased with the fact that Ferguson and Charlton had not been informed earlier.

Tim Bell says: 'Ferguson was all right. He wasn't great, but he was all right. They spoke to Bobby Charlton, who was in Thailand, and he was furious that he hadn't known about it. They both were important to the bid. We had said all along they would be. We had no intention of these people not knowing about it before it was announced.'

Two days later ITV screened a long-planned documentary about Ferguson, who granted interviews in advance of the programme to various newspapers. In the *Times* he kept his feelings about the bid close to himself: 'I am just trying to do my job. I know the fans are concerned, I understand that. The supporters are very important to this club, they have this incredible loyalty. But we can't know how it will pan out and affect everyone. We will have just have to wait and see how things develop.'

However a day earlier, interviewed by the *Sun*, Ferguson was presented as more upbeat, praising Sky for the fantastic job it had done. The *Sun* may have talked up the praise, but it indicated how cleverly Ferguson played the media, even two different papers owned by the same man.

If Greg Dyke stood out as the dissident in the United boardroom, there is just a hint that one or two other United directors may have been ambivalent. As Dyke signed the undertaking at Freshfields, Watkins came up to him and said, 'We might have stopped that if you had stuck out a bit longer.'

'Who is the we, Maurice?' asked an astonished Dyke. 'Where were you?'

At Freshfields the due diligence to check through the various contracts and make sure Sky was not taking on a company which had any hidden traps still had to be completed. Normally in a deal this can take days; this time it had to be done in a night. At this stage no announcement had been made and as far as the world officially knew no deal had yet been struck. But pressure to make sure all the housekeeping was finished by the morning increased at round 11 p.m. when someone bought the first edition of the *Sun*. The front page read, 'It's a deal ... Sky buys Man Utd for £625 million.' Its editorial commented, 'The deal is done. BSkyB is buying Manchester United. And football is the winner – from top to bottom.'

Murdoch had briefed the *Sun* well, speaking personally to David Yelland, then editor of the *Sun*. After the deal was done there had been further briefings from Allan. The *Sun* had all the important details, apart from the right price.

If the *Sun* glowed about the deal, just as predictably the rest of the press could see little merit in it. The *Mirror* led the way with a front-page headline: 'SOLD TO THE RED DEVIL'. Underneath was a picture of Murdoch painted red with horns sticking out from each side of his head and another two over each ear. The back-page target was equally familiar. 'Traitor', it screamed above a photograph of Edwards. 'Martin Edwards is facing a massive Old Trafford revolt after he last night caved in to Rupert Murdoch's millions.'

The *Mirror*'s reaction, being the main rival to the *Sun*, was understandable, but the rest of the non-Murdoch press took a similar line. Despite all the efforts of Sky and United, the deal was pictured as one personally directed and controlled by Murdoch. Reports of his phone call to Roland Smith soon appeared, strengthening the perception that Murdoch had played a leading role in the bid.

Privately, however, even papers presenting it as the hour of the Red Devil were saying a very different thing. On the Monday Piers Morgan, editor of the *Mirror*, had personally rung Tim Bell and Tim Allan to 'tell us that he thought the deal was fabulous. It was a great deal and brilliant for Manchester United; brilliant for football; brilliant for us . . . Most of the press who attacked it rang us up to say they didn't really mean it. They were just doing it because that's what you do. You attack Murdoch.'

There had been some debate as to whether Mark Booth should be present at the press conference called to explain the deal. Booth himself was not keen, preferring Allan or Vic Wakeling to do it. But with Edwards representing United it was clear Booth had to be there. The plan was to have a London press conference at 11 a.m., aimed mainly at the City, then to fly up to Manchester and hold another at Old Trafford, aimed mainly at the fans. That evening United were at home to newly promoted Charlton. On Wednesday morning, Faure Walker arrived at the press conference and saw all the TV cameras. He turned to Maurice Watkins and said, 'I've never seen fifteen different TV cameras like this covering one transaction before.' Watkins looked at him with a face which suggested he had not lived with Manchester United as long as Watkins had done and said: 'When Cantona resigned there was double the TV and media interest compared to Manchester United being sold.'

But if United coped with the publicity – even the negative publicity – Booth and Sky, the men from the media, could not quite manage it. To add to their agony, their moment of humiliation came just as they thought their ordeal was over. Booth had prepared meticulously for the press conference, leaving Freshfields at midnight to go over the questions and answers Tim Allan had prepared.

He knew the London conference would have a heavy City influence and afterwards he and his team flew to Manchester. Sky had rented a plane from City airport. Booth, Campbell-Breedon and Allan were on board, with Edwards, Kenyon, Gill and Watkins getting a lift home. David Blake from HSBC also came along. As they boarded, the party discussed how on Monday, when Edwards arrived in London from Manchester, he had had to push and shove his way through journalists and photographers to get to his car. Edwards looked out across the tarmac and said, 'If this plane goes down there will be a lot of happy fans.' The laughter this produced relieved some of the tension and by the time Booth arrived in Manchester he was feeling quite relaxed.

The press conference seemed to be going well. He had answered nearly all the questions. There had been many other interviews with radio and television journalists. The day was nearly done. Time for two more questions, said Edwards, and a woman put up her hand. Looking at Booth, she asked, 'Mr Booth, who plays left-back for Manchester United?'

Booth had worked out a plan to deal with football questions. He had never seen Manchester United play. Football to him meant American football. It had been agreed that if there was a football question, Vic Wakeling would answer it. So as the woman asked the question Booth said, 'I'll pass on that. The football side and naming of players is not my area of expertise.' He turned to Wakeling. Thinking the question was who would play left-back that night against Charlton, Wakeling said, 'The only person who can name the team is Alex Ferguson.' He was keen to emphasise that Sky would not interfere with Ferguson. But it backfired.

The press conference dissolved into laughter. Even Booth joined in. But from a PR point of view it was a disaster, as well as a godsend for the *Mirror*. The next day's front page had a picture of Booth looking like a cuddly but clueless executive under a headline:

'Who plays left back for Manchester United?

'Answer: Pass. Football is not my area of expertise.'

Booth's faux pas set the pattern for publicity on the deal. Bell and Allan had planned all sorts of ways they could publicise it – leaflets to fans, pledge cards and a mail shot to all Manchester United supporters on the first day of the announcement to explain why Sky was buying their club. There was to be a jointly signed letter from Mark Booth and Martin Edwards. Sky also wanted to take ads in the local newspapers putting its point of view. But the takeover panel ruled out most of these plans.

When Bell and Allan fretted about the fact that opponents of the bid were free to publicise their cause, the lawyers and bankers who through Sunday and Monday had prevented them from presenting their case to the press reassured them that all the publicity the opponents of the bid were getting would make no difference. Both Sky's lawyers Herbert Smith and United's lawyers Freshfields were confident that even if the bid was refereed to the Monopolies and Mergers Commission there were no competition grounds on which the bid could be blocked. The anti-Murdoch press and supporters might win the media battle, but Sky would win the war and carry off Manchester United.

But the anti-Murdoch supporters were just getting their act together. On the morning of the Charlton match, as United and Sky were holding their press conference in London, IMUSA gave a press conference in the Stretford Trades and Labour Club, attended by some seventy journalists. It had called for demonstrations at the Charlton match. Some fans during the match indeed shouted 'Stand up if you hate Murdoch.' A banner was unfurled at the Stretford End which read 'Sold Out. No Surrender to the Plc.' As Charlton scored the first goal of the match after thirty-two minutes, chants of 'There's only one greedy bastard', a chant reserved in the past for Alan Shearer, were hurled at Martin Edwards. But then, as Dwight Yorke showed how well he had integrated with the team and United won 4–1, all the boardroom talk vanished. The *Independent* noted that no mass demonstration outside the club had taken place.

But the dissenters had not given up, although at this stage they were short of money and yet to properly organise themselves. Just after the Charlton match Walsh was interviewed on *Newsnight*. Like Crick's programme, this triggered a response. Walsh received a call from Roger Taylor, drummer of Queen. His son was a United fan, he had written an anti-Murdoch song. He wanted, he said, to support ordinary people standing up to Murdoch and he was ready to finance the costs of hiring Bridgewater Hall for a public meeting.

By this time Walsh had also been called by Yasmin Walljee of the law firm Lowell White Durrant. Since the Sky bid was more than £70 million, under the law the OFT was required to deal with it. Lowell White Durrant did a lot of pro bono legal work and were keen to help IMUSA prepare a submission on behalf of the dissenters. They could not do pro bono work for the shareholders, since potentially they had money. But IMUSA, an organisation that depended on donations, was different.

On Wednesday 16 September, Manchester United were playing Barcelona in the first group match of the Champions League, having qualified for the competition proper through victories over the Polish champions LKS Lodz. IMUSA decided that on Tuesday night, when fans and journalists would be gathering for the match, it would hold a meeting at Bridgewater Hall. Between 500 and 600 turned up. Walsh and his colleagues were keen that the meeting should convey that this was more than a sectarian Manchester United gathering and asked Jimmy Wagg, a sports presenter for a local BBC radio, but more significantly a Manchester City fan, to chair the meeting.

It was not just an IMUSA meeting. Michael Crick, who was also an IMUSA member, was invited to talk about what shareholders among the fans could do to stop Murdoch, Walsh would speak for what he calls the 'raggy-arsed supporters' and Jim White, now of the *Daily Telegraph*, would do the comic knockabout turn, sending up Murdoch and the board. Crick's involvement meant Bridgewater Hall became in effect a joint meeting of IMUSA and SUAM, although at that stage the organisation had barely been born.

White says: 'Before the public meeting there was a private meeting between Andy Walsh, myself, Michael Crick and a few others from IMUSA. All of us decided to stay focused and concentrate on the first attainable objective, which was to get a referral to the Monopolies and Mergers Commission. Basically it was decided that Michael would go for the middle class and Andy would go for the grass roots, although it was not quite put in those terms. Andy organised the fans who went on the David Mellor style phone-in. The strategy was to work the system. We decided to focus on Rupert Murdoch. At every point we mentioned it was a bid by Rupert Murdoch. We spoke about the *Sun*'s comments following Hillsborough.' (The *Sun* had angered Liverpool fans by suggesting that drunken Liverpool supporters had contributed to the Hillsborough tragedy.)

The Bridgewater meeting, however, did not get much publicity. While the Barcelona game the following evening also saw some shouts of 'Stand up if you hate Murdoch', the antis never gained any great momentum. In one of their most pulsating displays, United took a 2–0 lead and with memories fresh of the humiliations Barcelona had inflicted on them in recent seasons, few fans were worried about who owned the club.

The next morning I travelled back to London with Michael Crick. He readily confessed that much of what he had said in *Manchester United: The Betrayal of a Legend*, written just after the Knighton bid failed, had been proved wrong in almost all aspects. In the decade since then, United, far from being eclipsed by Liverpool, as Crick had written, had won so many honours, including the two Doubles, that it was Liverpool fans who felt they had been betrayed.

I asked Crick what he saw as his aims. 'My plan is to make sure that at least 10 per cent of the shareholders do not accept Sky's offer. If they do not get 90 per cent of acceptances then Sky will under the law have to preserve the separate identity of Manchester United. They will have to publish separate accounts, hold annual general meetings and we will still be able to make our views known. If they get more than 90 per cent then Manchester United will be absorbed in Murdoch's vast empire and our independence will be completely lost, even the nuisance value.'

13

THE REVENGE OF THE
RAGGY-ARSED FANS

ONCE SKY'S BID for United was announced, one question was asked repeatedly on phone-ins and other media outlets: Will United now buy Ronaldo? The idea that Sky would buy United and the very next day Ronaldo, who then played for Inter Milan, would jet in from Milan to Manchester, was simplistic in the extreme. But in the eyes of many fans that was how the bid was seen. And if United fans asked the question in hope, fans from other teams were fearful that the answer would be yes, confirming their dread that a United owned by Sky would rule the world.

The United board did not see it that way. Martin Edwards had always looked with horror at the way other clubs spent most of their income on players' wages. Not for him the ways of Blackburn, spending 98 per cent of their turnover on wages. United in contrast never spent more than a third; in 1998 it was 31 per cent, two percentage points lower than Barnsley in their only ever season in the Premier League. Such a tight spending limit irked Alex Ferguson, who saw it as the plc holding back spending on players. It was all the more galling given that United's Italian rivals, the likes of Inter and AC Milan, on average spent more than 50 per cent of their income on wages. When it came to buying players United allowed the Italians to dominate the international transfer market.

This meant that there was a dichotomy between the way United were perceived in the City and how they came over to their fans. In the autumn and winter of 1998 those opposed to the Sky bid exploited this dichotomy as a populist weapon to make sure that the bid did not go through.

On 5 October 1998 Sky published its offer document to buy United with a joint letter from Booth and Edwards. Crick got to work immediately. It was a classic piece of mischief-making which got him enormous publicity, although in the end it made no difference. The document issued to United shareholders listed the various options open to them. They could either accept all shares, all cash or a mixture of shares and cash.

But what if they did not want to accept at all? This is never mentioned in any such document. In this respect, City bid documents are no different to mail shots by supermarkets or mail order firms. When they make an offer, they do not say that you are free to reject the offer; this is always assumed. However Crick, with a keen eye for the populist angle, saw an opportunity to embarrass Sky and United, and set about trying to exploit it in some style.

A hotline had been set up to help shareholders. Pretending to be Peter Munday, from 12 Keyside, Macclesfield, Cheshire, he rang and asked, 'I'm very confused about the document you've sent out.'

The woman answering the phones responded with a laugh, 'Yes, quite a few people are.'

Crick, as Munday, went through the choices. The woman on the hotline admitted that the fourth option, that of not taking up the offer, had been missed out and that the document was 'sort of mumbo jumbo'. She also admitted that a lot of United shareholders were confused and had been ringing up and asking the same question.

Crick immediately made the transcript available and took the matter up with the Panel on Takeovers and Mergers, set up in 1968 to issue and administer the City Code on Takeovers and Mergers. Crick and his SUAM colleagues had a two-hour meeting with the Panel, making clear their feeling that by not specifying that the offer could be rejected, the document was misleading and Sky and United should be forced to withdraw it. Mark Curtis for the Panel pointed out that all offer documents were similarly worded; this only strengthened Crick's belief that the Takeover Panel and the City were out of touch with ordinary punters. 'The Takeover Panel is a lot of wankers, a racket run for City people, and we proved that.'

United and Sky dismissed Crick's comments, but he had the PR victory he sought. In his campaign to make sure at least 10 per cent of shareholders rejected the bid, such PR victories were crucial.

Walsh and his IMUSA colleagues had meanwhile begun intensive consultations with Walljee and the lawyers at Lovell White Durrant. Their first objective was to make sure that the OFT, which was looking at the bid, would be made aware of the feelings of those who were opposed. The OFT was due to report to Peter Mandelson, who would decide whether the bid should be referred to the Monopolies and Mergers Commission.

IMUSA was working to a deadline. Under the Fair Trading Act of 1973, the OFT had to report to Mandelson by 19 October, although it could ask for another two weeks to deliver its report. Walsh sought out people far and wide who could help his cause: clubs in Mexico, France and other countries where media owners had bought football clubs. He found a man in Berkshire who worked for AT&T, who did not agree with Walsh, but knew Murdoch and did not like what he did. He provided information on how Murdoch operated in the area of media ownership. Walsh says he sought to discuss issues with United but was turned down. But he and a colleague had a meeting with Chris Haynes, head of press at Sky Sports, and Vic Wakeling in a Manchester bar.

Walljee can barely contain her admiration for Walsh and IMUSA: 'In three weeks they produced the most amazing lobbying process going.' Walsh lobbied all the football organisations including the Task Force set up by Tony Banks, then sports minister, and headed by former Conservative politician David Mellor. They already had an ally there: Adam Brown, who was also on the executive of the Football Supporters Association.

The FA had had misgivings almost from the start. Its chairman Keith Wiseman made it clear that it did not support the bid, as did the Football League and many other football bodies. The crucial question was, what would the Labour government say. It was here that Crick and Walsh concentrated their efforts. Crick says: 'Tony Lloyd [then minister of state in the Foreign Office] was the most serious United fan in the government and he said it was difficult to do anything. However, he advised us to work with Terry Lewis, MP for Eccles. He is a United supporter and a member of IMUSA. An early day motion opposing the bid was organised and 150 MPs signed it. We knew Alistair Campbell [a fervent Burnley supporter] was on our side. Stephen Byers was also fairly sympathetic. Labour councillors lobbied him at the Labour Party conference in October and he said he couldn't get involved as he was in the government. But as he walked away he gave them the thumbs-up sign.'

Both Walsh and Crick were well aware that Tony Blair's government was the most pro-football that there has probably ever been in this country. It saw football as a useful populist weapon to curry favour with the public. In such a government many MPs and ministers made sure their own football affiliations were well known; opposing the United bid, more so as it meant a strike against Murdoch, was very popular.

On 12 October, just before they made their submission to the OFT, Walsh and IMUSA met Tony Banks in London at the Ministry of Culture, Media and Sport. They gave him the two papers they were presenting to the OFT: one on public interest, the other on competition. On Sunday the story broke. Banks was supporting football in its battle with the OFT and planned to introduce legislation should the verdict go against the game.

However, one minister who had no interest in sport, let alone football, was Peter Mandelson, and he was the one who would decide whether the bid would be referred to the MMC. All eyes focused on Mandelson, and there were suggestions that he stay away from the process because of his friendship with Elisabeth Murdoch. However, he could not decide on his own. As in all such situations, other government departments like Banks's sports ministry and the Treasury had to be consulted.

The Treasury is the most important department in the British state. At that time, at the right hand of Gordon Brown, the Chancellor, sat Charlie Whelan, Brown's spin doctor but also a fervent Tottenham supporter and a man who had little liking for Murdoch. Whelan was determined to make sure the bid was referred and that the Treasury made the strongest possible recommendation in that respect.

By now, thanks to the efforts of Walsh and IMUSA, the OFT had such a deluge of responses, far in excess of anything it would get in a normal takeover, that it asked for a fifteen-day extension of the deadline to 2 November. On 27 October IMUSA lobbied Parliament, ensuring if nothing else that public pressure was kept on. Two days later, on Thursday 29 October, Mandelson announced that he had accepted the advice of Sir John Bridgeman, Director-General of the OFT, and referred the bid to the MMC. Bridgeman had advised that the takeover 'raises competition issues in respect of the broadcasting of premium English football, and may have implications more generally for competition in the broadcasting market'. There were also public interest concerns. The MMC was given until 12 March 1999 to report.

Fans claimed great credit for the OFT's decision and the received history of the bid's failure is that fans' protests were the primary cause. In fact, John Bridgeman reveals that the moment the bid was made, the OFT was sure it ran foul of competition law. The OFT had just emerged from a lengthy investigation into the market power of Sky concerned by its monopoly on pay-per-view television and encryption technology. Bridgeman says, 'The reason Sky were growing was that they were providing a product no one else could provide. I conducted my investigation and basically said that, in my view, they were treading the very delicate line of being close to abusing their dominant market position.'

It had been indicated very clearly to the United directors, Bridgeman discloses, that the passage of any Sky deal would be far from an easy ride, although this did not mean the bid would be stopped. 'It was likely to be an agreed merger between the parties. It was quite likely that the owners of Manchester United would start cashing in too.'

Bridgeman ultimately came to the conclusion that the Sky deal would have a restrictive effect both for Premier League football and for pay-per-view television. Bridgeman and his officials had a number of discussions with the officials of the DTI, some of whom were not sure if the bid really violated any competition, or even should be referred at all. Bridgeman denies he was placed under any direct pressure from the Department for Trade and Industry not to refer and, while the fans' opposition was interesting, it was not crucial to his decision. It was, as it turned out, just the icing on the cake. The OFT would have come to its decision to refer irrespective of what the fans did.

Sky and United were not worried about the referral. They had been advised by their lawyers and other professional advisers that there was no way the MMC could stop the bid. United and Sky had some of the best lawyers around, and they, according to Booth, 'said it would go through. We had unimpeachable advice from everybody without exception.' David Gill shared Booth's certainty: 'We all expected a referral and then to get clearance. The advice we received from our highly paid lawyers was that it should get through.' This, as can be seen now, was quite contrary to how the OFT was thinking.

Three weeks after the referral, on 19 November, United held their annual general meeting in the Manchester Suite of the North Stand. Leading up to the AGM United had announced that they had submitted a planning application to extend the stadium so that it could now seat 67,400; it would cost £30 million and United were seeking shareholders' permission for it. At any other time such an expansion, making Old Trafford the largest football ground in the land apart from Wembley, would have taken all the headlines and delighted the fans. Now there was only one issue they were interested in: the Sky bid.

Roger Brierley, an actor from Manchester who lived in London's Maida Vale, had bought shares when United had floated in 1991. The 100 shares, for which he paid £364, had since lost a third of their value but he did not much care as he had bought the shares to have them on his wall. He had never liked the Edwards family, and in particular Louis. He felt no single individual should own the club, his preferred ownership being a trust with Granada and Co-op holding shares. When the Sky bid was announced he had written to the *Guardian*; then, reading Crick in the *Standard* and seeing him on *Newsnight* he had rung him and teamed up with him in SUAM. 'I was the Jack Lemmon to his Walter Matthau. I was trying to implement Michael's thoughts.'

In seven years as a shareholder he had never been to an AGM but now he helped marshal small shareholders so well that some 1,100 turned up. Roland Smith opened the meeting by looking round at the packed hall and asking, 'I wonder why so many people are here,' producing one of the few laughs in that fraught, bitter atmosphere. After that, as the *Mail* reported, he acted virtually like a stand-up comedian, which helped him cope with the hecklers and prevent the meeting from descending into anarchy.

Even before the meeting Edwards was aware he would be in for a rough time. Activity on the share register suggested several people had bought shares just to be there. The AGM inevitably turned into a fierce denunciation of Edwards, one shareholder referring to the fact that he had thrice tried to sell United to Knighton, Maxwell and now Murdoch: 'Martin Edwards, I hope you get to heaven when your time is up. Surely, though, it's three strikes and you're out. Go Martin Edwards, go.'

Edwards and the board had the votes. They carried the day and all the resolutions they wanted were passed. Edwards, in one of his rare interviews, gave a spirited defence of the Sky takeover on Radio Five Live. He was confident that despite the fact that Crick and Walsh had made all the noise, the silent majority, as he put it, were still with him. However, Crick and Walsh and their allies had scored another public relations victory. There might only have been a few of them opposing the bid but they were succeeding in giving the impression they spoke for the many.

In contrast, a deafening silence came from Alex Ferguson. After the bid became public knowledge Edwards had spoken to him and tried to get him to support it. Edwards says: 'Alex chose not to come out for the bid for whatever reason. I spoke to him more than once. I suspect Alex would have liked the bid to go ahead because he thinks it would have given more resources. You will have to ask him and he probably would not answer it anyway. He has political leanings and he may have felt this is not the thing to get involved in politically.' Mark Booth, too, spoke to Ferguson but could not get him to commit himself in favour of the bid.

The brief but pointed comments Ferguson makes in his autobiography are perhaps the clearest indication of his feelings: 'Many, but by no means all, bitterly disapproved of the plans for a takeover of Manchester United by BSkyB but government intervention has killed the proposals, so the dispute is academic now. My own feeling is that the club is too important as a sporting institution, too much of a rarity, to be put up for sale.'

In their campaign Crick and Walsh made clever use of Ferguson. In one of the brochures produced by SUAM, the opening page quoted Ferguson in bold red as saying, 'We are United to the core'. SUAM commented: 'So when Alex Ferguson says, "We are United to the core", remember so are we and so are you. Show your support for the club as we know it and help to stop this takeover before it makes us into the club we don't know.' The implication was clear: the bid would transform the club in a way Alex Ferguson would not approve.

By this time the MMC were well into their investigations. Crick and Walsh, having tasted victory at the OFT, now moved to try their luck at the MMC. Walsh had lost his friendly pro bono lawyers, who returned to their more lucrative, if not quite so exciting, legal work. And at the MMC the paths of IMUSA and SUAM diverged, if only in terms of presentation. SUAM had gone along with IMUSA's OFT submission, but to the MMC they made their own.

Until now everyone had assumed that the only reason the MMC could possibly block the bid was in the public interest, but Crick had found lawyers who were willing to argue that there might be a competition angle. In that sense, unknown to themselves, they were echoing the view many in John Bridgeman's team at the OFT held.

Crick brought in an academic lawyer who was also a big United fan, as well as another lawyer, expert in competition law in the City. Just before Christmas a third lawyer was brought on board. Not only was Peter Crowther not a United supporter – he followed Leeds – he was not even a qualified solicitor. He was a consultant to a medium-sized firm called Rosenblatt, but had an academic background, holding a PhD in law. Crowther was an old friend of Richard Hytmer.

As Crick and SUAM prepared to try and persuade the MMC, the panel were completing their site visits to Sky and United. On 17 November they visited BSkyB and were given a presentation about the broadcaster. Twelve days later they made their trip to Old Trafford. United thought they had done a good job of showing the panel what match days were about, but there was no way of knowing what impact this would have. 'The chairman, Dr Morris,' says Gill, 'was very even handed and straight faced but gave no indication which way he was thinking.'

If United and Sky were the principal players at the hearings, apart from IMUSA and SUAM many others either appeared before the MMC to give their views or wrote to them. They ranged from broadcasters and those directly involved in football to local authorities and Members of Parliament. Some 300 individuals also wrote to the MMC.

At the 11 December hearing in Manchester's Piccadilly Hotel, the MMC heard not only from IMUSA but also the Professional Footballers' Association and Football Supporters' Association. Walsh had taken a delegation of twelve and was nervous in what was for them an unusual experience. They had been allocated ninety minutes and Walsh joked at the start that he hoped it would not have to go to extra time or penalty shoot-outs. In the event they were there for three hours. Walsh emerged greatly satisfied that the MMC had given them a good and patient hearing.

Four days later, on the morning of 15 December, at their Carey Street headquarters, the MMC held their first hearing with Sky. The atmosphere was very different to that in the Piccadilly Hotel. Sky had taken a full team including Booth, Martin Stewart, Mike Darcey, economist and planner Michael Rhodes, lawyer Ian West and Elisabeth Murdoch, in addition to lawyers from Herbert Smith. There was no laughter, no jokes and, according to one Sky source, within the first ten minutes they knew this was going to be a very tough meeting. 'They were just so hostile. The meeting was totally out of control. Questions were coming from all directions, from all the panel members. The chairman did not have control. And every time we answered a question we could see they were not believing us.'

After an hour and a half there was a break for coffee. By then the Sky team was convinced it was going badly. But Booth was not too concerned. This was a first meeting, MMC was marking definitions – the power of Sky, the markets in which it operated – and Booth had been assured by his professional advisers not to be alarmed.

Two days after meeting Sky, on the afternoon of 17 December the MMC had

its first session with the United board. United had made their submission via
the lawyers on the day the players travelled to Barcelona. For the hearing United
took their strongest team – Edwards, Watkins, Gill, Kenyon and Roland Smith.
The questions were tough. Smith, the only one among them with City
experience, tried to keep everyone's spirits up. At the coffee break he said, 'We
have had a good first half but I hope we don't follow our usual practice this year
of having a poor second half.'

At the end of this first meeting United and Sky compared notes. They agreed
they were, as one insider put it, 'getting killed' by the MMC. But this was a first
hearing. The advisers, and in particular the lawyers, reassured them that this
was how the MMC operated. There was nothing to worry about – there was no
way the bid could be stopped.

Just a week after the first MMC hearing with United, on 23 December, Peter
Mandelson was forced to resign from the Cabinet. The *Guardian* revealed that
he had borrowed money from Geoffrey Robinson, the Paymaster General and
a fellow minister, to finance the purchase of a house in Notting Hill, a loan he
had not disclosed to his Cabinet colleagues. Mandelson had done nothing
illegal but it was considered bad form and after resisting media pressure for a
few days he went. He was replaced by Stephen Byers.

Jim White, who never thought the campaign to stop the bid would be
successful, is convinced that 'We would have been defeated if Mandelson had
not gone.' We cannot be sure. Mandelson will not talk, nor will the MMC reveal
its inner workings. But as the MMC resumed its hearing after Christmas it
became clear that its position had, if anything, hardened.

On 14 January the MMC had their second sessions with Sky and United, Sky
in the morning and United in the evening. The second meeting with United was
meant to go into the nitty-gritty of the bid. Like the first, it proved highly
emotive. 'It was,' says Kenyon, 'the first time the majority of us had been to an
MMC hearing. The questioning was not hostile but it was certainly probing.' At
the first meeting, the questioning had been tougher than they had anticipated.
'The second meeting we thought had gone extremely well.'

But if United tried to put on a brave face on the meetings, Sky knew after 14
January that their cause was doomed. The meeting was better controlled, Morris
as chairman asked all the questions, they were not being fired at from all sides.
But the questions were, as far as Sky was concerned, just amazing – something
that might have been scripted by Michael Crick or Andy Walsh. One of the first
was: 'It has been put to us that if you take over Manchester United, the first thing
you will do is buy Ronaldo and this will distort the football market.'

No sooner had Sky explained that this was ridiculous – that it was buying
United because it was a good business, that Sky intended United's existing
management to carry on and that Alex Ferguson should make such decisions –

than the second amazing question came: 'It has been put to us that if your digital roll-out is in need of more cash you will sell David Beckham to raise cash.'

Sky protested that it was absurd to think that way. However highly valued Beckham was, selling him and getting say, £25 million, would hardly make a dent in a digital business costing several hundred million. A Sky source says: 'By that stage we knew there was no rationality to that process. There were also questions about changing the name of the team and moving it. It was very obvious that two panel members were so hostile to us they simply didn't believe us. Their whole facial expression and body language said that.'

Booth emerged from the second session convinced the bid was in trouble, the most obvious stumbling-block being the way television rights were voted on. There was no veto, argued Sky. As owners of Manchester United they would have one vote out of twenty. 'You have nineteen self-interested clubs out there. We were prepared to have them not vote on the television rights. When that kind of discussion did not seem to be going very well I was pretty sure we had problems. I did not feel they were giving us the benefit of the doubt.'

The session was particularly telling for Booth. He could sense that every time the MMC looked at him they did not see a cuddly American but the figure of the demonised Rupert Murdoch, the red devil who was going to gobble up this unique British institution. Walsh and Crick's strategy had paid off. In one of his SUAM leaflets, Crick had listed every possible Murdoch misdemeanour he could find, including the fact that there were arrest warrants for him in India for something one of his television channels had shown. As Booth and his Sky colleagues sat at the MMC hearing thinking they were representing a major public company, the MMC saw only Murdoch in front of them.

Until now, Sky had tended to shrug off the many outside voices telling the MMC they must reject the bid. These ranged from Labour and Conservative MPs to Manchester City Council and Portsmouth Trades Council, let alone the 300-odd individuals who wrote to the MMC opposing it. However, the response of the Premier League was critical. Sky wanted to make sure it did not join the growing opposition lobby.

The MMC had asked the Premier League for its views. Initial talk among many clubs of expelling United had come to nothing, and Peter Leaver decided that since there was no collective view he would make a personal response. The League had not taken a view on the bid or even discussed it. Six clubs, Arsenal, Aston Villa, Leeds, Newcastle, Southampton and Tottenham, had made their own submissions supporting the bid, but these were overwhelmed by the weight of opposition. Leaver was not aware that these clubs had supported the bid and only learnt about their submissions when he read the MMC report.

His view was that if the Premier League won its case against the OFT and collective selling of TV rights was still allowed, then the merger would have adverse effects and would require some safeguards. If the OFT case went against the Premier League, 'the adverse effects would be marked'.

Leaver's submission infuriated Manchester United and marked another low point in their relationship. Booth sought out Leaver, aware of how incensed United were with his views on the takeover, and suggested they meet. The lunch took place at Harry's bar just before Leaver went to the MMC. Booth says: 'He told us categorically he did not have problems with Sky and its proposed takeover of Manchester United. But clearly at the MMC hearing, he was saying something different which was not very helpful. All I can tell you is most of the Premier League clubs I talked to thought it was a very good thing.'

Leaver says he did not tell the MMC anything different to what he told Booth and Wakeling. The MMC were very interested in finding out how television negotiations worked. As for his views about the bid, he was making his own personal points as a man of football and a QC. In company law the takeover presented no problem. But in terms of football, there could be problems.

Whether a ringing endorsement of the bid by Leaver would have made any difference is impossible to say. The dice appear to have been already heavily loaded, and were to be further tilted on 26 January 1999 when SUAM and Crick made their presentation.

Crick was extremely nervous about the hearing. Adam Brown of the Football Supporters Association had returned from his hearing saying he had been given a rough time. Crick decided to have a dress rehearsal in Crowther's offices. Far from encouraging him, the rehearsal made him even more depressed. Crowther, too, felt it had gone badly. 'It was nerve wracking.' Crick felt 'so awful, I was terrified about how it would go.'

However, the next morning at the MMC, the hearing, which lasted about an hour and a half, was very different. Crowther says, 'the hearings went better than expected. I knew the MMC is very reluctant to block a merger outright. But what struck me was a throwaway line when we said you can't trust Murdoch, there can be no safeguards, just look at his record. That was picked up immediately. I was pleasantly surprised and they asked us to draft a submission on precise undertakings.' The MMC's response to Murdoch was the first inkling Crick had it might go their way. 'I was surprised they were interested in that. I thought we have a chance here.'

At Sky the gloom was now universal. On 11 February, they had a third meeting with the MMC, who repeatedly questioned what would happen in any television negotiations if Sky took over. Booth wrote offering guarantees. 'At this point I was very pessimistic. I thought there was a very small probability of a favourable outcome.'

On Friday 12 March, the MMC presented its report to Stephen Byers. The next day on the *Mirror*'s back pages Harry Harris had an 'exclusive' story saying the bid had been allowed through. A similar story, but not quite so certain, was on the front page of the *Guardian* under the by-line of Martin Thorpe, their soccer writer and a news reporter. Over at the *Daily Telegraph*'s City offices Alistair Osbourne, who had excellent MMC contacts, had been working on the story for weeks. He finally pieced together that the deal was stopped.

The moment Booth read the *Telegraph* he was convinced his worst fears had come true. 'I told Jeremy and Rupert and a couple of other board members it was very unlikely it would go through.'

On 9 April Stephen Byers announced he had blocked the bid. In the light of the MMC's recommendations there was nothing else he could have done. He did not have to read far to discover what the MMC had decided. Just over two pages at the start of the 254-page report said it all: the bid had to be blocked, there were no guarantees that could possibly make it acceptable and there were not only public interest grounds but competition grounds for stopping the takeover.

Not long afterwards Booth had gone, moving on to work on internet projects for Murdoch, having turned down an offer to join Bill Gates. He maintained that his strategy of not just buying Martin Edwards' stake instead of launching a full-scale bid was right. 'I thought it would be cleaner to have a bid.'

Within months this was exactly what Granada, and Sky itself, were doing. Granada bought a 9.9 per cent stake in Liverpool, valuing the club at £200 million, gaining a seat on the board and the right to do all the club's marketing. Sky, having been allowed to retain its 11 per cent stake in United, then paid £13.3 million for 9.9 per cent in Leeds and was soon talking to Aston Villa. For a time Sky bought stakes in other clubs up to the permitted 9.9 per cent limit, and it seemed that the bid for United had led to media companies owning chunks of football clubs. Once again Sky could claim to be at the forefront of a revolution. But it proved a short-lived one. Before the decade was over media companies, including Sky, began to withdraw from football clubs, none of them making significant gains on their investment. Sky may have reinvented itself by showing live football, but its experiment of owning football clubs was not a success.

Unlike Sky, United were not expecting to be rejected. As the news was announced, Gill was with Sir Roland Smith in the offices of their PR consultant John Bick in London, while Edwards and Kenyon were at Old Trafford.

Kenyon, like Booth, could not understand why the MMC came to their decision. 'We didn't believe there was ever any competition ground, right from the start. That was the legal advice.' He felt that it had become a matter of the public interest. 'Public interest is difficult to define. It was a very soft rationale for taking it out.'

But did that not mean it was fan power that in the end converted the MMC? 'I don't believe the thing was turned down because of fan power. If you talk to supporter groups, people on the terraces, a huge amount of fans individually were in favour. As demonstrated, be it IMUSA or Michael Crick, they mobilised a small but extremely vocal group of people.'

Edwards held to his belief that there was a silent majority to be mobilised, but clearly the United board failed to do so. Jim White, like Crick, readily concedes that the majority of United fans 'did not give a toss'. But as Crick and his friends celebrated with a party at Roger Brierley's house, the MMC decision was seen as a great victory for fan power. They could proclaim, in the words of White, that 'It was the most sophisticated football campaign that there has ever been.'

While this was true, the moment of victory, as so often, bore the seeds of future peril. It made the fans, and in particular the fans who had driven this campaign, believe they were invincible. They came to think they, and they alone, had won this great victory over Murdoch. Belief in fan power can be intoxicating. But it was to prove fatal seven years later, when another predator came calling.

By the time the MMC had rejected the bid, United's season was reaching a remarkable climax. Brian Kidd, the man seen as vital to the Ferguson machine, had gone to Blackburn in mid-season. Two days before the MMC report was published, on 7 April, United could only draw with Juventus in the first leg of the Champions League semi-final at Old Trafford, and that due to a goal in injury time by Ryan Giggs. Juventus had outplayed United for an hour and United had never beaten an Italian team in Italy, but unless they won in Turin they could not progress. The comment of the Juventus general manager that United's marketing was better than that of Juventus – who were looking to own their own stadium to rectify matters – seemed to sum up the new United for many fans: great at selling itself, not so good at winning on the field against Europe's best.

At that stage it looked as if United might end up as in 1998, with nothing to show for the season. They faced Arsenal in the Cup semi-final and Arsenal were also the team to beat for the League. The first match in the semi-final was drawn, but in the replay United turned their season on its head. A goal behind to a Bergkamp special, United were down to ten men. Then Bergkamp missed a penalty and Giggs scored a wonder goal. As we have seen, Edwards was unable to watch and took shelter in the Villa Park directors' bar. Giggs' goal meant United were on course for the Double.

The treble became a possibility a week later. In a pulsating match at Turin, United were 2–0 down to Juventus in eleven minutes but came back to win 3–2. They were now in their first Champions League final since 1968, facing Bayern Munich.

After the Turin result there were a few stutters – away draws to Leeds,

Liverpool and Blackburn – but otherwise United seemed to have an awesome momentum. On Sunday 16 May, Tottenham came to Old Trafford with United needing to win to make sure Arsenal did not retain their title. After twenty-five minutes they went behind to an unlikely goal by Les Ferdinand but again they roared back and won 2–1. It was their fifth Premier League title in seven years, but the first to be won at Old Trafford. A week later they overran a poor Newcastle side in the FA Cup final to complete their third Double in five years.

Only the treble remained. On Wednesday 26 May at Barcelona's Nou Camp, on what would have been Matt Busby's ninetieth birthday, United took on Bayern Munich.

The omens did not look good. In Barcelona United were without their captain and crucial midfielder Roy Keane and also another key player, Paul Scholes. After six minutes they had gone behind to a free kick from Bayern's Mario Basler. Bayern had then hit the United post, and followed that by rattling the bar. With two minutes to go and Bayern leading 1–0, their fans and players were celebrating. Lennart Johannson, president of UEFA, was asked by his officials to go down to the touchline ready to present the cup to the Germans. He consoled Bobby Charlton, who had scored the night United first won the Cup at Wembley in 1968, before taking the lift to make the long journey down to the touchline. But when he emerged and looked up at the electronic scoreboard he was puzzled. It read Bayern Munich 1 Manchester United 2. Johansson thought there had been an electrical failure. While he was in the lift, cocooned from the tumult of the drama taking place a few yards away, first Sheringham had equalised and then Solskjaer had scored the winner. Johansson would later joke, 'I very nearly became the first UEFA president to present the cup to the losers.'

United could join in the laughter. They knew how close they had been to the precipice and how they had miraculously wrought their reinvention that night. A reinvention that was in keeping with the history of a club which throughout the post-war years has shown a remarkable capacity to bounce back.

It was an important result for United and England. For the first time since 1984 an English team had won the premier European club trophy, and for the first time since 1985 and Heysel an English club had got to the final. United in 1968 had been the first English club to win the European Cup, now they were the first to complete a unique treble.

But within a week of this epic triumph United were faced with an unprecedented challenge. The night they won at Juventus, a decision was taken in faraway Tel Aviv, at a meeting of the UEFA executive committee, that the champions of Europe would take part in a pet project of Sepp Blatter, president of FIFA – a world club championship between the leading club sides in the world. It would be an eight-team tournament to be played in January 2000.

UEFA expected those teams to come from a country which had a winter break. Since Germany had such a break and England did not, it was expected that whatever happened in Barcelona, Bayern Munich would go.

Nobody in England paid any attention to the decision. They were more concerned about how many tickets United fans would get for the final. The initial noises were that if United won they would not go. Minds in England only began to focus some time after United won. The FA suddenly realised what it all meant.

England had put in a bid to stage the 2006 World Cup, along with Germany, South Africa, Brazil and Morocco. In fact England stood no chance and should never have entered the contest, since the previous FA chairman had made a gentlemen's agreement to withdraw in favour of Germany. Seven of the eight UEFA votes, out of an electorate of twenty-four, were therefore guaranteed for Germany. But the FA, arguing they had seen no minutes of such an agreement, carried on. The campaign was going nowhere – the fight was between Germany and South Africa – but the campaign leaders were still optimistic, at least publicly.

Playing catch-up in a hopeless race, the FA built up a ridiculous argument that if United did not play, England would lose three vital votes in the election for 2006. Moreover, if United's place was taken by Bayern Munich, it would mean more brownie points for Germany. Germany was already representing Europe, replacing world champions France in the Confederations Cup – another of Blatter's pet projects – to be played in Mexico between 24 July and 4 August 1999.

Blatter had made it clear he was very keen that United, as the champions of Europe, should be in Brazil. The FA and the 2006 bid committee were convinced that in order to keep Blatter and his executive sweet, United should take part. But it would mean disrupting both the FA Cup and the Premier League programme.

The tournament would see two groups of four, the winner of each group playing in a grand final in Rio. A team from Brazil would be invited as host, along with one from each confederation. Real Madrid, as winners of the previous season's Toyota Cup, the match between the champion clubs of Europe and South America, were also invited. Including travelling time, the whole event would take up to two weeks. For Bayern it would have come in their winter break. But for United two weeks off in January would mean something would have to give in the English domestic calendar. United were worried about fixture congestion and the fact that in defending their Champions League trophy they would have to play seventeen matches to get to the final. They had made it clear that they did not much care for this new Blatter project.

A meeting was called for 10 June at FA headquarters. Kenyon and Roland Smith represented United. David Davies, the FA's international director, and

FA and Premier League officials were present. So too was Tony Banks, who had decided to assert his ministerial authority by trying to persuade United to play in Brazil.

At the meeting United were told that for England's sake they must reconsider their decision not to go. If they went, they would have to rearrange two Premiership fixtures and, if they got that far, the fourth round of the FA Cup and the semi-final of the Worthington Cup. Banks decided to apply further pressure. Immediately after the meeting he wrote to Sir Roland Smith:

A refusal could have serious ramifications for England's 2006 World Cup bid. I have been personally informed by three FIFA executive members, all of whom had previously committed themselves to England's cause, that they will not vote for us in the event of Manchester United's non-appearance. I can appreciate how unfair it is to put such a burden upon you but it is clearly in the national interest for your club to compete in the FIFA championships.

Banks went on to say that while the government had no powers to instruct the FA, he would make it clear 'that in the event of Manchester United agreeing to compete, we would expect the most sympathetic consideration being given to easing the inevitable fixture problems'. The letter was copied to No. 10 and to Chris Smith, Secretary of State for Culture, Media and Sport.

Banks had crisscrossed the globe many times to try and secure the 2006 World Cup for England, lobbying the twenty-four members of the executive committee of FIFA who were to decide on the bid. On the morning of Thursday 17 June, he flew back from his latest overseas mission to meet Edwards, Kenyon and Davies at the Hilton hotel near Heathrow. For two hours various ways were discussed of easing the fixture problem.

The semi-final of the Worthington Cup was the least of United's headaches, for they had long since seen the competition as one to be used to field essentially reserve sides. However, the FA Cup and the Premiership were different. Could United field weakened teams? Could the season be extended? Could there be a bye into the fourth or even a later round of the FA Cup? Although in recent seasons the Premiership programme has always ended on the same day, there is no rule saying it must. But none of these options seemed feasible and all of them would increase the number of matches United would have to play. Towards the end of the meeting Edwards came up a radical plan. He proposed that United be given the right to withdraw from the FA Cup. This was a sensational request. Davies thought it was unlikely the FA would allow United to withdraw, but he promised to look into it.

Over the next few days Banks, Davies and officials from the 2006 campaign discussed plans. United's withdrawal from the FA Cup would have implications for AXA, the sponsors. Banks and Davies summoned AXA to a meeting at the House of Commons. As far as Banks and the 2006 campaign were concerned, time was pressing. On 5 July FIFA were holding an extraordinary congress in Los Angeles. Banks wanted a decision before that.

On the evening of 26 June, with the FA gathered in Chester for its annual summer meeting, Banks rang Davies to say he needed a decision. An emergency meeting of the FA executive was held on Sunday morning at eight o'clock. Davies asked the meeting to approve giving Manchester United an exemption from the FA Cup for the 1999–2000 season and after a two-hour discussion they decided to allow United to withdraw.

Publicly, the FA presented this as a decision that United had to take and insisted that there was no pressure on United from the FA. Tony Banks, when asked in the House of Commons to justify the FA's decision, said that if United did not go to Brazil 'significant damage would be inflicted on England's chances of hosting the World Cup in 2006'. However, he did not say there was any government pressure on United and presented it as a decision the club must take.

On Wednesday 30 June United announced they had accepted the FA's invitation and would play in Brazil. A public storm broke out, the *Mirror* leading a campaign to get United back into the Cup. For weeks the FA and government, much to United's anger, clung to the line that they had exerted no pressure on United to go to Brazil. But the fact that Banks had copied to No. 10 the letter he wrote to Sir Roland Smith convinced United that the request had the authority of the highest in the land.

When I revealed the Banks letter in the *Daily Telegraph* it exploded the myth that Banks and the government did not put any pressure on the club to go to Brazil. When I asked Banks about it, he admitted that he had told Manchester United about the threat from FIFA members but said, 'I was told to my face by three members of FIFA. No, I will not name them but I am not making it up. What was I supposed to do with this information? Keep this to myself? What would you have said then if it had come out?' Asked if this did not mean the government put pressure on Manchester United, Banks still insisted there had been none, 'There was no pressure. When you are doing something like this you are all under pressure. There was government pressure on Manchester United, but there was pressure on all of us, there was the pressure of events. The idea that we can pressurise Manchester United is grotesque.'

For Martin Edwards it was yet another case of United not being understood. They had been asked to do it for England, to carry on the legacy left behind by Matt Busby. The modern United of Alex Ferguson was to carry England's flag to the new frontier. Yet Edwards' critics claimed the real reason they were going to Brazil was for the money and the fact that it would enhance the global brand name. The fact was that United did not know how much the tournament would bring. Television rights had not even been sold when they gave in to the FA and Banks's pressure.

In the end nobody gained from the venture. Blatter's dream of a regular World Club Championship has never taken off. United were abysmal on the field. England were ignominiously beaten in the 2006 World Cup campaigning, being eliminated in the second round with only two votes. In some ways it was Edwards who, by proposing the withdrawal from the FA Cup, had made the trip possible, who suffered the most. Edwards had always had immense problems in his personal life. This concerned what Ned Kelly in his book *Manchester United: The Untold Story* calls his 'peeping-tom activities'. They were, he says, well known within the club. In his book Kelly describes an incident when Kelly, then at the SAS, had invited Edwards to present medals at Hereford where the SAS is based. 'The only sour note during an otherwise perfect day occurred when Martin Edwards was spotted following a soldier's wife into the ladies' "toilet"'. Kelly managed that affair, calming down the woman's husband, and later came to work for United. There he says he was aware of more such incidents including ones at Old Trafford and White Hart Lane. In December 2002 this would lead to a police caution under the Public Order Act for Edwards, when there was an allegation of misdemeanour in the women's toilet at Mottram Hall Hotel in Cheshire. Kelly was eventually to confront Edwards one night over a drink in a club in Manchester over all these incidents (this was before the Mottram Hall incident) but Edwards indignantly asked, 'Name me one instance' and when Kelly offered 'nearly a dozen episodes', he refused to accept them and stormed out of the bar.

In Brazil in January 2000 there was Maria Elves, a lady of the night. According to Kelly she had an 'agent' who had negotiated a fee for her silence where her clients were concerned and says Kelly, 'Absolute discretion had been guaranteed for US $250,000. I laughed when I heard about the situation and told Martin I had deep reservations regarding the young lady's integrity, believing she would sell her story to the press anyway. My doubts were not heeded by the chairman and he paid the price both financially, and personally. After he had paid Maria for services rendered, the press also paid her handsomely for her story, and the tabloids loved every salacious minute of it. He protested his innocence on television, 'I did not have sex with that woman' and in the newspapers but there were few who believed his story. There was outrage at the allegations, and calls for his resignation but, as always, he hung on.'

However, with Edwards looking to retire from the day-to-day running of the club and replace Roland Smith as chairman of the plc the Brazilian publicity did not help and would come to haunt him. In many ways Edwards would be the biggest casualty of Manchester United's ill-fated Brazilian venture.

PART THREE

Irish Eyes Are Not Smiling

14

THE IRISH ARE COMING

ON 8 JULY 1999 the *Daily Telegraph* published an exclusive article by Paul Hayward, then their chief sports writer. Headlined 'Gambling group swoop to buy a stake in United', it said:

> Martin Edwards, the Manchester United chairman, is believed to have agreed a substantial sale of shares in the club to a group of investors who revolve around Joe Lewis, the Bahamas-based billionaire, John Magnier, a racehorse owner and J.P. McManus, a legend of the Cheltenham Festival betting ring and tormentor of bookmakers.
>
> The deal falls far short of giving the new group a controlling interest in the European champions, but does offer them a significant stake in the world's most financially powerful club. Edwards owns approximately 28.5 million of United's 260 million shares and was known to be looking for new bidders when the Monopolies Commission blocked an attempt by Rupert Murdoch's BSkyB to buy United for £623 million.

As the article went on to explain, Lewis was the power behind the English National Investment Company (ENIC, a listed company that invested in sports, entertainment and media and gaming organisations) and had close links with Magnier, McManus and Dermot Desmond, the prime mover in the creation of London's City Airport and a director of Celtic. ENIC had been searching for a large stake in English football for several years – their attempt the previous season to buy Tottenham Hotspur from Alan Sugar had faded when Sugar's asking price was deemed to be too high. But ENIC already owned a controlling stake in four European clubs – Vicenza in Italy's Serie A, AEK Athens, Sparta Prague and Basle in Switzerland – and they had a 25 per cent stake in Glasgow Rangers. This brought them into conflict with UEFA, who were worried about the implications of having more than one club owned by the same company competing in European competitions.

As Hayward pointed out, 'The contrast between BSkyB and the Lewis-

Magnier-McManus group could hardly be more pronounced. McManus, who owns the champion hurdler, Istabraq, is a fearless punter, betting in five- and six-figure sums. Magnier is one of the most powerful owners and breeders in Ireland. The chances are that they will have to pay a high premium for a stake in United...'

Hayward had been put on to the story by the paper's racing correspondent, and former *Times* lobby journalist Richard Evans. Evans, a journalist with excellent racing contacts, recalls:

> It happened at the Newmarket meeting in July. Racing contacts told me that the big Irish boys were sniffing round Manchester United. I rang David Welch (then the paper's sports editor) and he gave the story to Paul. Magnier was in Newmarket and later that day I went up to him and asked him if he was looking to buy into United. He played an immaculate forward defensive stroke saying, "You'll have to ask J.P. McManus." That was not a denial and it told me all I needed to know.

The Irish interest in United seemed to neatly complement Ferguson's own growing interest in horse racing. By now this interest, something common to many footballers, had developed into much more than the mere placing of a bet. Ferguson's ownership aspirations had first been ignited two years earlier, during Gold Cup day at the 1997 National Hunt Festival at Cheltenham. He and his wife Cathy had been invited to the Ladbroke box by the company's head of public relations, Mike Dillon, who was also a United fan. As Dillon would later tell Martin Hannan, author of *Rock of Gibraltar*, at the end of that day's meeting Ferguson turned to Cathy and asked, 'Why don't we buy a horse?' The suggestion made Cathy Ferguson fear her husband would end up 'owning Newmarket'.

With Dillon acting as his unofficial race manager, Ferguson was quickly introduced to the great and good in racing. He became a major shareholder of the Right Angle Club. Charles Gordon-Watson bought horses for the club and one of them, Ninety Degrees, provided Ferguson with a winner at Yarmouth on the day he went to Buckingham Palace to be knighted. At Cheltenham in 1997 Ferguson had first been introduced to John Magnier by Dillon, although it was only in 1999 that they met at a racing meeting and spoke at length. Magnier, once described by the *Racing Post* as the 'most powerful individual in racing', had like Ferguson in football made his way up the racing world. Steeped in the traditions of Irish stud farming, he joined the Coolmore stud as manager in 1974 and was to make it one of the pre-eminent breeders of thoroughbred horses. In the early 1990s he bought Coolmore from Robert Sangster, who was widely considered to be one of the most successful breeders in British horse racing. When Ferguson and Magnier got talking they found they had much in common. As Hannan says, 'they found that they shared a distaste for the Establishment in racing'.

By this time there had been born the horse that was to cause bitterness between the two men, casting such a deep shadow over the club and in a way shaping its future. Rock of Gibraltar, sired by Danehill and foaled on 8 March 1999, was trained by Aidan O'Brien, one of Ireland best trainers of race horses who had already produced several champions. Soon Magnier had taken the horse into his Coolmore ownership. He was reputed to have paid £100,000 each to Rock of Gibraltar's breeders.

For United fans news of this Irish interest in United could not have been sweeter. They saw in it the chance finally to right the dreadful wrong that had taken place the last time United had won Europe's greatest club trophy. Back in 1968 Sir Matt Busby's European Cup final triumph had led to his move upstairs to the boardroom, but the move had backfired. On the field there were problems with Busby's managerial successors, off it he had little power as the Edwards family, already established in the boardroom, consolidated their position. Busby eventually retired and the butcher and his son took over the club. Now it seemed that with Irish help, Alex Ferguson could succeed where Busby had failed and become boss of the entire club.

Ferguson has never commented, but according to Andy Walsh, 'People who were close to Ferguson say the Irish were talking about getting involved in football. Ferguson said to them that if they were going to invest in anybody, they should invest in Manchester United. He encouraged them to invest in Manchester United.'

The question of the Irish buying into Manchester United had been raised when, in the summer of 1999, Edwards was invited to dinner with them. This had come through Brian Mann, a South African, who had organised Manchester United's tours to his home country and knew golfers like Ernie Ells. He played golf with Dermot Desmond, who was present along with Magnier and McManus. The dinner was more of a convivial evening, not a hard session looking at Manchester United's accounts. The Irish were keen to buy but as far as Edwards was concerned the price they were prepared to pay was not enough.

Edwards had his own dream. This was becoming chairman of the plc. Smith was due to retire in March 2000 and Edwards set that as the date when he would himself give up being chief executive of the club and become plc chairman. However, in order to do so he had to substantially reduce his 12 per cent stake in the club. The City would not look favourably on a chairman of a plc who was also the largest single shareholder.

In October 1999, just a day after United announced its 1999 results, Edwards sold 7.5 per cent of his take for a cool £41 million, valuing each United share at

221p. This meant that including money received at the float, he had made just under £79 million from share sales since 1991.

The sale meant that for the first time since Louis Edwards had taken over the club, an Edwards was no longer the club's major shareholder; BSkyB with 11 per cent now occupied that role. The share sale revived talk of money-mad Martin Edwards. To make £79 million from an investment of £600,000 was not bad. And he still had 6.5 per cent of the club, which at the 1999 share price was worth another £30 million. Given that old Louis had paid between £31,000 and £41,000 for his 54 per cent controlling interest, the Edwards family had done very well out of United. The consolation for fans who longed to see the back of Edwards was that the sale showed he was on his way out.

A few months later, in December 1999, the Irish bought their first shares in Manchester United. Magnier and McManus had considered investing in several football teams. Before making the investment the Irish got their advisers to look carefully at United. They examined balance sheets and cash flows, and liked what they saw. Once worth £1 billion, now it was valued at around £250 million. It had a stadium seating 65,000 which was always full and it had 50 million supporters worldwide. It was trading at a huge discount to its asset value. Shares had been over £4, now they were available at £1.20 – the initial price the Irish paid. United looked too good an investment to miss. As far as the Irish were concerned, there was no link with Ferguson. They were merely looking at the market value of the club.

A special investment vehicle, a shelf company named Cubic, was set up for investing in United and registered in the Virgin Islands. Because United was a public company, there were many obligations that investors had to meet. But despite the fact that they thought United was a good investment, in this first purchase the Irish merely dipped their toe. At this stage the purchase was so small that it did not have to be declared to the Stock Exchange and thus did not become public.

Magnier and McManus were not the only ones who invested. I am told that Michael Tabor, a rich man in his own right also involved in racing, and who had been interested in buying West Ham and did joint deals with his Irish friends, was also persuaded by his Irish friends to buy a small chunk of Manchester United.

Apart from the sale of his shares, October was a busy month for Edwards, as it was for the United board. Greg Dyke had become Director-General of the BBC and could not remain a director of Manchester United. On 1 October 1999, five days before the results came out, he resigned.

This meant that the only man who could be described as a truly independent non-executive had left the board. United desperately wanted not only to replace him but to find directors who matched the City's increasingly prescriptive rules about the sort of person who could be classified as a true non-executive director of a plc. Under the City's rules of corporate behaviour the United board looked increasingly out of date and out of place. The other major non-executives were Maurice Watkins, who had been there for more than ten years and was involved in a great deal of legal work for the club, and Amer Al Midani, who had also been there for a decade and had been a major shareholder. Even before Dyke's departure the search had started. Heidrick Struggles, a firm of headhunters, which advertised itself as the leader in executive search, had been appointed back in the summer of 1999 to find suitable new non-executive directors.

By the time Dyke left they were ready with a shortlist. During October and November 1999 Edwards, Watkins and Smith, who formed the three-man nominations committee, spent days interviewing the various candidates. The idea was that two truly independent non-executive directors would be appointed in addition to Watkins and Al Midani. But for the first time since United had become a plc a serious problem arose about the choice of directors. The nominations committee could not agree who should be appointed.

An Old Trafford insider described the candidates to me: 'They were Ian Much [then chief executive of De La Rue] who was a fan, very relaxed, very keen on the team. The nominations committee considered the risk of appointing somebody so clearly a fan. Phil Yea [senior executive of Investcorp] had the financial pedigree but no interest in football. It was his wife who was the fan. The third one was Roy Gardner [chief executive of Centrica]. We were looking for two directors. And the problem arose when it became clear that Martin Edwards did not like Gardner. Why? Martin does not like small men, Gardner is short. He also looked like a bruiser.'

The panel had dinner with Gardner at a restaurant off Sloane Street in London. But for all the wine and good food, and Gardner's sense of humour, Edwards remained impervious to his charms and adamantly opposed appointing him.

The insider says, 'Because the three could not agree they decided to have not two but three non-executives. Gardner only got on because of Watkins.' Perhaps Edwards' objection was not just to Gardner's height but because he feared Gardner might succeed Roland Smith as chairman, depriving him of the prize he himself sought.

The non-executive directors would be paid £25,000 a year, plus travelling expenses. Gardner did not go on trips, although he and the others attended London matches. Much, the real fan, liked travelling with the team and became chairman of the remuneration committee. Yea, the man with no interest in football, became chairman of the audit committee.

One man who would have loved to join the board was Keith Harris. He had been interviewed by the headhunters during the initial selection process but did not make the shortlist. One insider told me, 'Keith wanted to join the board but the feeling was that he was not known for being involved in a structured company. His expertise was as a deal maker and we were looking for someone along the traditional executive lines. The feeling also was Keith might want to run the show and upset the existing executive officers of the company.'

It was during the interviews with the headhunters that the first indications emerged that Edwards might not realise his dream of succeeding Roland Smith as chairman. Harris, thinking the job was Edwards' for the asking, was surprised to be asked by the headhunters if he would like the job.

The question of whether Edwards should succeed Smith was being intensely debated. Gill and Roland Smith had taken soundings in the City and among United's institutional shareholders. The City does not like chief executives moving on to become chairmen. They are not considered independent enough and there was also the issue of Edwards's rather large shareholding. The feeling was that the institutions would not object to Edwards achieving his last remaining ambition. If Edwards was relieved to hear that, he was soon dismayed to learn that the three non-executive directors he had chosen had been discussing whether he should have the top job. One of them, Much, approached Edwards and told him that Gardner, Yea and Much had held discussions and decided it would not be a good thing for Edwards to take over.

A friend of Edwards told me, 'What happened was the three non-executive directors actually got together and approached Martin and said they felt it would be better if a new face came in. Much came to see Martin and said they had been having a discussion. They felt that there would be resistance. Martin's view was the last thing he wanted was to be a contentious choice. Martin had always had trouble with the supporters and he realised he would not be a unanimous choice as chairman. All three non-executives must have felt they had an opportunity to become chairman. Martin dropped out of the race and did not even put his name forward.'

Had Edwards forced a vote he might still have won. Watkins would have supported him and also Kenyon and Gill, but for Martin the thought of becoming chairman on a contested election, the headlines it might generate, the prospect of chairing AGMs without the support of Roland and facing the hostility of fans, was not something he could contemplate.

Edwards consoled himself with the thought that Roland Smith still wanted to be chief executive and proudly showed a letter Smith had written some time back saying how he saw Martin taking over from him. But that was in the past. Now, with three non-executives on the board, anyone of whom could be his successor, Smith was changing his mind. He was also contemplating delaying retirement beyond 2000. While in theory any one of Yea, Much and Gardner could have been in line, soon it became clear that Gardner was the chosen one. Smith played a big part in the decision influenced by Gardner's stewardship of

Centrica. One insider who knew Smith well and spoke to him on United issues every day told me that Smith saw Gardner as his successor from sometime in 2000: 'By then Gardner was effectively the chairman elect.'

But if Edwards could not open the door marked 'chairman of plc' he realised he could not keep the door marked 'chief executive' shut in the face of Peter Kenyon. By June 2000 Edwards decided that while he could not move upstairs he could not keep Kenyon hanging around. He told friends he was finding it difficult to come to terms with the increasing use of new technology and at the summer meeting of the Premier League he told some of his fellow chairmen that he had decided to end his day-to-day running of United. The plc board met on 30 June and it was decided that an announcement would be made to the Stock Exchange in a couple of weeks' time.

On the morning of 17 July Manchester United informed the Stock Exchange that Edwards would relinquish his job as chief executive on 1 August. While he would remain chairman of the football club, this would now be a non-executive role although he would still be going to Premier League meetings to represent the club. Edwards was well aware Gill was not happy that Kenyon was being made chief executive, Gill made no secret of it and he decided that Gill should become deputy chief executive, while remaining financial director.

The appointment masked what insiders knew was a problem. David Bick says, 'When they appointed Peter there were two candidates, one was Peter and the other was David Gill. I don't think there's any doubt that although it seemed almost inevitable that Peter would become chief executive, nevertheless David was very disappointed. But I think David and Peter quickly came to an understanding once the appointment had been made.' As another insider put it to me, 'David's nose was put out of joint by Peter taking over as chief executive.'

Unlike Edward Freedman, Gill did not walk out. He had settled his family in Manchester, he loved the club and he accepted the situation. Over the years he was given new titles including managing director. The join did not show, but insiders at Old Trafford knew what the score was.

If these off-the-field events prefigured what was to come, on the field the United story in 1999–2000 was also a preview of the future. The season made the fans realise that their fears had not been laid to rest by the Nou Camp triumph. Their hope had been that United would reign not only in England but also in Europe. But while they were supreme in England, when it came to Europe – or for that matter anywhere outside England – it was a familiar story.

In the Premiership United had walked away with the title, their sixth in eight seasons, winning it by a record eighteen points. But against that had to be set their failures abroad. Some of the defeats did not mean much. They had gone to Monte Carlo to play in the Super Cup in August 1999, an occasion to mark the beginning of a new European season which saw the winners of the

Champions League meet the winners of the UEFA Cup – on this occasion Lazio. The Italians, managed by Sven-Goran Eriksson, beat United 1–0 but Ferguson, aware the match counted for nothing and that there were important Premier League fixtures ahead, deliberately fielded a weakened side.

The match was more significant for the behaviour of the two sets of fans. As Salas scored the Italian winner, a couple of swastikas were waved by the Italian fans, and every time Andy Cole, the only black player on the field, touched the ball, the Italians section booed and hissed, indicating the racism and fascism always bubbling beneath the surface was still very much alive. A banner draped in the Italian section also summed up the mood of their fans.

It read:

> *Noi siamo qui per la Supercuppa Europea*
> *Voi sul priate dura con diorrea*
>
> We are here for the Super Cup
> You are on the hard road to diarrhoea.

In the '70s United fans had been the instigators of hooliganism, laced with racism, that had plagued English football for two decades but now they refused to rise to provocation that might have been too much for a previous generation of United fans. Instead they treated Lazio like country cousins who, after their own hard struggle were just beginning to experience the heady delights of Europe, a delight that did not last long after this Super Cup triumph.

More worrying was the campaign to defend their Champions League trophy. United lost their European crown to Real Madrid at the quarter-final stage. Sandwiched in between had been the disastrous Brazilian trip at the beginning of 2000. However, in characteristic style they made the best of turning disaster abroad into triumph at home. The Brazilian adventure provided a month's rest from the rigours of the Premiership, United's very own midwinter break in the sun. They returned refreshed and their subsequent form was awesome, proving that at their best they were still without equal in England.

One of Alex Ferguson's most persistent problems that season was finding a goalkeeper to replace Peter Schmeichel. He bought the Italian Massimo Taibi, who in four games let in eleven goals, some of them so ludicrous – one a gentle shot that went between his legs – that he earned the title 'the blind Venetian'. Taibi's successor, the Australian Mark Bosnich, earned Ferguson's praise for his performance in the Intercontinental Cup against Argentine side Palmeiras, a triumph that Ferguson rated very highly and was the first by a British side since Celtic had won the competition back in 1967. But Bosnich too did not prove a long-term replacement for the Dane. It was to be years before Ferguson found one.

Just as worrying were problems within the Ferguson football family, in particular one of the kids with whom he had fashioned his great triumphs. That kid, now a married man, was David Beckham.

Beckham in his young life had already learned how to reinvent himself. Just a year earlier he had returned from the 1998 World Cup in France as the most reviled man in England, held responsible for England's defeat after his sending-off in the Argentina game for kicking out at Diego Simeone. The tabloids dubbed him 'the idiot' and compared him with the ten heroes who had battled so valiantly in that match. At the beginning of the 1998–99 season, when Manchester United started their campaign at West Ham, there were plans to boo and heckle his every touch. But he had survived, prospering so well that by the time he again met his nemesis Simeone, Beckham had long been forgiven. His crowning moment came in August 1999 on a balmy night in the Sporting Club of Monte Carlo, where UEFA held the gala dinner to launch the start of the 1999–2000 European season. Beckham went up to the podium not once but twice to receive honours from the revered names of European soccer. The awards that night reflected United's great triumph in the Nou Camp. Jaap Stam, United's Dutch defender, received the award for best defender in Europe, ahead of Bayern's Lothar Matthäus – who had barely been able to accept his loser's medal in Barcelona – and Lilian Thuram from Parma, who had been at the heart of France's World Cup-winning team in 1998. Alex Ferguson received the award for Best Coach of the Year ahead of Valery Lobanovksy, coach of Dynamo Kyiv, who had come so close to winning the Champions League, and Alberto Malesani, coach of Parma, who had guided his team to the UEFA Cup.

Beckham's first award was as best midfielder ahead of Stefan Effenberg, the man who had run the game for Bayern in Barcelona until the final minutes. The award was presented by Michel Platini, one of only three men to be thrice voted European Footballer of the Year. He then went up again to receive the title of Most Valuable Player of the Year ahead of Zinedine Zidane, who had led France to their World Cup triumph but had been bested by United in the epic Champions League semi-final against Juventus.

By his side was his new wife Victoria 'Posh Spice' Adams. The most sought-after couple in England, their wedding had been the society event of the year with *Hello!* magazine paying £1 million for the wedding photographs.

But the development of the kid who Ferguson had nurtured since the age of fourteen had not gone down well with the Scotsman. In the summer of 1998, during Beckham's darkest days, he had publicly supported the player, even taking England manager Glenn Hoddle to task for the way he had handled him. Now it was different. He did not like the fact that Beckham's agent, Tony Stephens, also looked after Alan Shearer, the player who had rejected United for Blackburn. When Stephens asked Martin Edwards whether Beckham could take two extra days for his honeymoon before returning for pre-season training, Ferguson bristled and insisted he come back with the rest of the squad – not even qualifying for the four days off that those on World Cup duty had been given. Victoria Beckham would later report that when Beckham protested it was not possible to have a honeymoon in less than a week, Ferguson said, 'That's your problem, David. I don't give a shit.'

There was clearly a huge divide. According to Victoria, Ferguson had barely spoken to her in the four years she had known her husband. She felt his attitude towards the honeymoon was 'vindictive' and 'unforgivable'.

Matters were to become much more public during the 1999–2000 season. In February 2000 Beckham missed a day's training, saying his son Brooklyn was ill. But that evening his wife was seen at a London Fashion Week event. Ferguson dropped him for the match that followed against Leeds, then challenging United for the title, and fined him two weeks' wages – the maximum that can be imposed on a player by a club. The money – £50,000 – was trivial to Beckham, but the injury to his pride was considerable. In his autobiography, *Managing My Life*, Ferguson justified his action on the grounds that he had to make sure no man was bigger than Manchester United: 'I had to imagine how they would feel if David could adjust the schedule to suit himself ... David worsened the problems between us when we met up on Saturday by making me lose my temper badly, something I hadn't done for years.'

Banning Beckham had no impact on United on the field; they won the match and soon the title. But the picture of Beckham, watching from the stands, told the story of the growing divide between Ferguson and his most celebrated player.

The autumn of 1999 was to see another event that would have a crucial impact on both Ferguson and Manchester United. The story is what the Irish call a bit of a 'craic', a yarn, but one so curious that even now it seems quite extraordinary. That year's Gimcrack Stakes at York was won easily by Mull of Kintyre, a horse owned by Sue Magnier. After the race the owner of the winning horse has the duty of making a speech at the annual Gimcrack Dinner. Sue Magnier never spoke in public. Her husband John, although a member of the Irish Senate, also hated public speaking, and prompted by Mike Dillon had what seemed a brilliant idea: to get Ferguson to make the speech on his behalf. But, says Martin Hannan, when this was suggested informally to someone at York he 'was snootily dismissive of the whole idea and made a remark to the effect that he didn't need to hear from the son of a Scottish shipyard worker'.

Magnier was outraged. He decided that a horse owned by Ferguson must run in the Gimcrack, so if it won nobody could deny his friend the right to speak. Thus were sown the seeds that led to Ferguson's involvement with Rock of Gibraltar, although it would take another three years before the story exploded.

15

EDWARDS LOSES, FERGUSON WINS

FANS AND MEDIA alike saw the arrival of Peter Kenyon as chief executive of Manchester United as a big boost for Alex Ferguson. The demon Edwards, who had held back their beloved manager, had gone. In the style of the classic football club owner, Edwards had always had an employer/employee relationship with Ferguson. Ferguson called Edwards chairman, Edwards always referred to Ferguson as the manager. The strain in their relationship was now well known. With Kenyon it was going to be different. But on Kenyon's big day, the very day the appointment was announced to the world, Ferguson stole his thunder.

That day the media were dominated by an interview Ferguson had given to the *Sun* about his future at United. He had wanted to stay on, he said, but as he had not heard from Edwards he had decided to make other arrangements. Known for playing mind games with other football managers, Ferguson was doing the same with his own directors. As a result Kenyon's appointment was quite overshadowed. Kenyon was not best pleased.

David Bick is certain that Ferguson 'must have known that the principal event that day was Peter's appointment. It was slightly stealing Peter's thunder, I have to say. At the time it looked a deliberate attempt to upstage the new chief executive. The following morning Peter went to Carrington to have it out with Ferguson. According to Peter, Ferguson apologised and said something like that wouldn't happen again. I think in reality what happened subsequently was that Ferguson played the press exactly the way he wanted to.' Ferguson, says Bick, ignored 'the way the relationship should be between senior employee and chief executive. I never felt that Peter had any authority over him. The only person that I felt had any proper board–manager relationship with Ferguson was Sir Roland.'

If Kenyon could not control Ferguson – but then, who could? – he was determined from the beginning to make one fundamental change to the way the plc and the club worked. This was in the matter of how United communicated to the world. He had been thinking of this for over a year now, ever since the Sky bid was rejected by the Monopolies and Mergers Commission.

The rejection of the bid had underlined how isolated the Manchester United board was, not just in terms of the fans but the wider community. Everybody had come out against the bid, even Manchester City Council. I spoke to Kenyon on 14 May 1999, soon after the MMC decision. A year before he took over as chief executive, he was already very aware of the gap between what United felt they were doing and how it was perceived. He argued that while in public perception United's role in society appeared to have diminished since the days of Busby, 'The reality is it has not diminished. We have been reluctant to tell the story . . . What we give back to the Manchester community is a huge amount. We don't have a relationship problem with the city council. We are major promoters of Manchester, a major tourist attraction, a major attraction for people coming to the city. When you look at our various activities across Greater Manchester and its boroughs then we have contributed huge amounts of time, money and exposure.'

He contrasted United's approach with that of Manchester City. 'The difference is they tell people what they do. Every time they do something they tell people.' But he was determined to improve the situation. 'We are very conscious about it and we intend to do something about it. I think what Manchester United hasn't done enough is to talk to people about what its real plans are or what its real objectives are, what we are doing in the community, what we are doing for football in general.'

This was one issue on which Kenyon and the board were in agreement with the fans who had successfully helped block Sky. As Roger Brierley had admitted, luxuriating in the victory over Edwards and the board, 'The Manchester United PR was absolutely dreadful.' Kenyon told me: 'The only communication that has come from the chairman or the board is through the City. It's a consequence of being a plc. And in all the soccer aspects of Manchester United being a football club the board is sidelined. There has to be a change in presentation. There isn't a successful business or club that does not look for its fans or supporters.' United, he said, 'is an enormous organisation with supporters in the four corners of the world. We cannot afford to neglect the local community but neither can we ignore the people in Hong Kong. What we are looking for is more rounded communication. That is what is important.'

Ever since United's flotation they had employed Brunswick, an external financial PR firm, to deal with the City. John Bick, one of the account team at Brunswick, had become close to the United board. When Bick joined Financial Dynamics, another PR firm, in 1996, Manchester United moved their account there. This brought in Bick's older brother David, who had joined the firm in 1995. The two brothers present a great contrast – David is very feisty, John much quieter. As it happened neither were United supporters. David followed in the family tradition, supporting West Ham, John supported Tottenham.

In 1998 David set up a new firm called Holborn. John joined in 1999 and when he did so United again followed. John would deal with day-to-day account issues, either with Kenyon as chief executive or David Gill as managing director, while David developed a separate relationship with Roland Smith. The Bicks' contact was just to advise them on issues relating to the stock market, usually when the half-yearly or yearly results were presented. Occasionally David Bick would get involved in day-to-day business – he handled the press when Kenyon was made chief executive – but generally John dealt with Kenyon and Gill and David dealt with Smith.

Kenyon decided that United must have its own in-house, full-time group PR. Given that United was a business worth nearly £1 billion this was very logical. But Kenyon's first attempt resulted in a mighty embarrassment.

The headhunters had shortlisted two candidates: lawyer Alison Ryan and Patrick Harverson, the financial journalist who now specialised in writing about sport for the *Financial Times*. Harverson, alerted to the job by John Bick over lunch before being approached by Kenyon and the headhunters, was the ideal candidate.

With a father in the armed forces Harverson's upbringing reflected the imperial spread of the British military. Born in Cyprus, he had spent his formative years first in Singapore and later all over Britain. But since the age of seven he had followed United. His earliest memory was of trying to follow a Bobby Charlton coaching book on football as he spent endless hours kicking the ball against a garage wall with his left foot. He grew up, like all United fans of his generation, worshipping Best, Law and Charlton, and red was his favourite colour.

Harverson went up to Old Trafford, where he was interviewed by Kenyon, Edwards and Ferguson. The job was presented as much more than one handling the football media – it would cover the financial press, marketing, public affairs, shareholders, the FA, supporters and the wider football community. The interview went well and Ferguson's presence was significant. According to Crick, in the past Ferguson had opposed the appointment of a full-time PR man. In 1997 he had said the media was a 'monster', too egotistical, all-demanding, and such an appointment would only feed its appetite. However, now Ferguson was very engaging, seemingly happy with the idea of having such a PR person, and responded very incisively to Harverson's questions about how he saw the tabloids. The interview took place just before Harverson went to the 2000 Sydney Olympics and he clearly wanted the job.

David Bick says: 'When it got to a shortlist of two, Alison Ryan and Paddy Harverson, Peter asked us our thoughts on it and we said, "Our choice is Paddy." We knew him well, we knew what he felt about Manchester United, we knew of his ability to communicate with people. Our advice was it should be Paddy.'

But, according to Bick, 'Peter said, "I'm going to go for Alison Ryan because she's got the more rounded CV; she's got political experience, she was a local councillor in Manchester, she used to be an adviser to Tony Blair.'" So it was Alison Ryan who was appointed. In her thirties, a barrister, well connected and clearly a Manchester United supporter, on paper Ryan looked good.

At this point IMUSA and Andy Walsh became involved in the story. Edwards' departure had been seen as a major opportunity for the club to establish a relationship with the fans. 'We were very cautious about Kenyon,' Walsh recalled, 'but I saw an opportunity that if there was somebody new in that position then there was a chance for a new page in the relationship. So, I wrote to him. And he invited me over for a chat. I spoke to him on my own and then did an interview with him for the *Red Issue* fanzine.'

Walsh watched with interest as Ryan was paraded: 'They had her photographed at Old Trafford, she been to the fans' forum meeting. She hadn't formally taken over but she was obviously getting her feet under the table.' Then he started getting calls: 'There was a question mark over a charity that she was involved in, question marks over her political career. And when her name was announced, people who I'd known in Manchester for many years that pre-date my involvement with IMUSA, political contacts I had in the Manchester Labour Party, came forward and said, "Hello, you've pulled a right dodgy one with Alison Ryan. She's not known as Alice in Wonderland for nothing. She's a bit of a female Walter Mitty." So I started asking questions with various people and we uncovered a trail of deceit and – not quite lies, but she was very good at expanding the truth. I contacted the Bar Association and found that there was a disciplinary against her. I then contacted Peter Kenyon and gave him all the information as to what had actually happened.' Kenyon told Walsh, 'We're in a meeting now to discuss this matter.'

Alison Ryan's impressive CV, it turned out, was not quite genuine. As Bick says: 'Within days it started to cut up rough. There was all sorts of mud being thrown about this woman. Peter rang me to say that he was hearing a lot of bad things about her and could we check it out. I said, "Peter, surely your headhunter has done that" and he said "I want you to check all the things that the headhunters won't necessarily have checked on the CV."' When checks were run, there seemed to be 'bad blood' about Ryan. But, said Bick to Kenyon, 'I still can't give you a commanding reason as to why she should not start the job that you've now contractually signed with her.'

Bick now contacted the Bar Council himself. Their communications officer told him, 'We disbarred her a year ago on eight counts of dishonesty. Fraudulent representation in her past career.' He reported back to Kenyon with a heavy heart: 'I could hear his chin drop at the other end of the line.' Kenyon contacted Ryan and told her, 'You will no longer be required to start your job.' It subsequently emerged, says Bick, that Ryan's mother 'feared this was going to happen sooner or later. She'd been lying about her past.'

The Bar Council Disciplinary Tribunal, which considered the Ryan case on 12 March 1999, could not have been more devastating about the lies Ryan told. She was charged with nine offences, eight of them described as 'dishonest or otherwise discreditable to a barrister', the ninth charge related to her failure to deal with the complaints against her promptly after the Bar Council had asked for her comments. The charges of dishonesty included claiming a first-class history degree from Cambridge University and that she had passed the Common Professional Examination in law at Manchester Metropolitan University with Distinction. She had also supplied a forged document which said the Tribunal 'purported to be a reference from Gordon Hennell to Brick Court Chambers in support of her application for pupillage. The document was false in that (a) Gordon Hennell had not made it in the form in which it was supplied and that (b) Gordon Hennell was not a lecturer at the Manchester Metropolitan University.'

To make the case against her even more damning the tribunal's judgement also described how Ryan had failed to respond promptly to the complaints and then asked for adjournment as she was doing charity work in Cuba and undergoing treatment at the Maudsley Hospital in London. The judgement continues, 'The Tribunal concluded that, after due consideration, that there never had been any indication that Ms Ryan would confront the substance of the charges, that she has not taken advantage of the offer of pro bono legal representation by experienced leading Counsel, had not produced any sufficient medical evidence to lead the Tribunal to conclude that she was not capable of dealing with the charges, she had seen fit to go to Cuba for work during the week of the Tribunal Hearing and that her intention was to delay the hearing for no good cause.' The only surprise in all this was that given the sub-Treasurer of the Inner Temple had published the Tribunal findings and sentence on 6 May 1999, more than a year before Ryan was appointed to the Manchester United job, the headhunters, Howgate Sable, had somehow not been aware of it.

It was after Bick had told Kenyon the grim facts that he said to Bick, 'What about Paddy? Will he still take the job?'

Bick had no doubts. He told Kenyon, 'Peter, it's his passion.'

Indeed, when Bick rang Harverson in Sydney, where he was covering the Olympics, Harverson could not say yes quickly enough. By December 2000 he was installed. He was soon part of the executive management group that, operating outside the board of directors, met every Monday morning and ran the club on a day-to-day basis. Besides Kenyon, Gill and Harverson, the group included marketing manager Peter Draper and club secretary Ken Merrett. Its remit was everything from financial and commercial matters to the budget and deals that were in the offing. It discussed all matters necessary for the functioning of Old Trafford and the club; it did not discuss football matters or transfers. And Harverson did not deal on a day-to-day basis with Ferguson's fiefdom at Carrington. Denis Law's daughter handled matters such as pre-match interviews and press conferences at the training ground.

Harverson soon established a good working relationship with Ferguson, the football man. Bick provides a wonderful insight of the first time he took Harverson to meet Ferguson at Carrington, and the football man met the man acting as PR for the plc.

I attended one meeting with him at Carrington. This was when Paddy Harverson was appointed. Peter decided that Paddy needed to meet him. We met in Ferguson's office, a large, modern office, with a chair at his desk but with no chair on the other side of the desk. The point about no chair in front of his desk meant that players knew that any player summoned in there knows he wasn't going to be sitting down. There was an area over to one side with a sofa and the four of us had a meeting in that sofa bit of the room. Ferguson is demonstrably tough, he's intelligent. He came across as sort of agreeable, very pleasant, strong willed. The one thing you came away with, the one lasting impression was his focus on money. The meeting lasted an hour and the vast majority of the period he talked about money in one form or another. I got the impression he has a huge predilection with money.

The ill-fated appointment of Alison Ryan meant the Kenyon regime had not begun well. 'Peter handled all this badly,' says Bick. 'What was hurtful from Peter's point of the view was that he'd made exactly the right decision to appoint a director of communications and I don't think anyone was particularly opposed to that. But it didn't help having to persuade people to hire one and having the first attempt to do so end up in that way.'

It is possible that Kenyon had never wanted Ryan but had been forced to accept her by his fellow board members. Andy Walsh believes Kenyon was relieved to appoint Harverson, who was always his first choice, and that the board had forced him to appoint Ryan. Who on the board pushed for Ryan – whether it might have been Roland Smith, impressed with her political connections – we cannot say.

Had this happened in Edwards' time the fans would have delighted in pointing out the incompetence of management. The headhunters had failed to check out what Walsh calls 'an airhead', something Walsh had done in twenty-four hours. But Walsh and IMUSA were now trying to get in on the inside track. Walsh had spoken to Kenyon on his mobile. 'This was a very different kind of relationship than any supporter had had with Martin Edwards.' It was a relationship they were keen to build on.

From the disaster of the Ryan affair came an important breakthrough for IMUSA: 'With Kenyon that obviously established our reputation as serious people to deal with. IMUSA weren't just raggy-arsed fans, we were serious about how the club should be run and we were willing to co-operate. After discussions with IMUSA, we continued, or agreed to continue to have open dialogue with Peter Kenyon over any number of matters.' Issues such as potential crowd trouble in Europe and standing at Old Trafford were discussed. 'I said instead of the club going out and cracking a few heads – which was happening, the security firm was just going out and pushing people around – we needed something different. There needs to be a dialogue taking place and it needs to be seen. So I invited Peter Kenyon to come with me into that part of the ground where the problem was at its worst. In West Stand, tier two. And, to his credit he did, first time any executive had ever done it.'

Walsh had made a similar invitation to Martin Edwards a few years previously: 'He said no and I was told by someone else internally that he was frightened for his life if he went into the stands. I said it's a chicken and egg situation, if he goes into the stands, nobody's going to attack him; this is all about him showing that he understands the concerns of the supporters.' Kenyon joined Walsh in the stand and at half-time Walsh introduced him to several supporters. 'He discussed issues with people and from there we were able to build a relationship with the board in terms of how to deal with the problem. The problem was certainly diminished and became less of an issue and the board then agreed to other requests, which included creating what is called a singing area. We created a better atmosphere.'

David Bick also persuaded Roland Smith that there should be contact with Shareholders United, as the shareholders' group formed to defeat Sky was now called. Bick says: 'I think Peter was of a mind to widen the debate and consultation out a bit. I persuaded Roland that they should be treated like any other institutional shareholders' block and that, come the results, they should get the same post results briefings on the figures that every other individual institution gets.' Briefings took place in Bick's office, and at the second such meeting Michael Crick, still an important part of Shareholders United, proposed that the club's AGM be televised: 'Michael said one of the things they wanted was for the AGM to be televised so that a wider audience could see it. Before any of the board could say anything, quick as flash I said "What, Michael, and turn it into the Michael Crick show?" You could see the other United shareholders could barely keep from laughing. The Manchester United boys on the board were stony faced and Crick went red.'

Kenyon could claim other successes in the field of marketing, his speciality. On 29 September, just before the disastrous appointment of Ryan, news had leaked out of a thirteen-year kit deal with Nike worth £300 million, double the amount received by the Brazilian national team. It turned out to be a £302.9 million deal, described as a 'strategic alliance between two global brands' but Nike had retained the option to terminate it on 31 July 2008. Nike was to form a wholly owned subsidiary to control the global licensing, merchandising and retail operations, with the club and Nike appointing half each of the directors of this company but Nike alone appointing the chairman, who would have a casting vote. In the press announcements confirming the deal the club boasted that it had around 6 million fans in the UK and an estimated 30 to 40 million worldwide. There was speculation that Umbro, United's then kit sponsor, might consider legal action regarding the Nike deal, but that came to nothing. On 3 November 2000 the deal was confirmed.

This clearly helped reassure the City about United, sentiment having grown restive after the club announced a 25 per cent drop in pre-tax profits from £22.4 million to £16.8 million in the year to 31 July 2000. The reasons given were United's absence from the FA Cup and the breaking of their strict wage structure. Wage costs increased by £5.6 million, with Roy Keane having negotiated a new contract at £52,000 per week from December 1999, and Fabien Barthez, whom Ferguson had brought in to solve his goalkeeping problem, on £45,000. The drop in profits had had an impact on directors' salaries, which had all gone down. Martin Edwards' salary was down £23,000 to £639,000 including bonuses for the year ending 31 July, David Gill's down £31,000 to £290,000, Kenyon's down £2,000 to £371,000.

During Edwards' tenure players' wages – and the wages of Ferguson, much to his fury – had been kept on a tight rein. But Kenyon had clearly decided to loosen it. That season there would be much talk of players demanding increased wages; everyone apart from Barthez and Keane was on around £20,000 a week. There would be many a media story that Beckham was rumoured to want £100,000 a week – even he was still only on £20,000 – but he was not the only player negotiating for an increase. Jaap Stam's seven-year contract was said to contain a clause that at the end of the season his weekly salary would rise from £30,000 to £50,000 as part of the club's new wage system. Andy Cole was said to have doubled his wages and Ryan Giggs was also renegotiating. In April Giggs signed a new five-year deal said to be worth £38,500 a week, excluding bonuses. United were moving to what was called a tiered wage structure, whereby players' wages were based on profits and the perceived worth of the individual player to the club.

The effect was evident when in April 2001 the half-year results to January emerged. This showed that while pre-tax profits were £17 million, up from £11.8 million, there had been a £1.9 million increase in players' wages. Nevertheless, at 35 per cent of turnover the figure was well below the 58 per cent average for the Premiership and Gill made it clear United would keep the proportion at under 40 per cent.

On 6 February 2001 United had announced that they had done a joint-marketing deal with the New York Yankees. Whether this was brought about by United's escalating wage bill is debatable, but it was one of the most curious stories of the season. The whole board of the club, including Sir Bobby Charlton, flew out to New York. It was presented as a bid to develop a worldwide United brand, especially in America. As Kenyon and United saw it, this was all about marketing – no equity, no investment, financial or otherwise. It was knowledge share and the club hoped to benefit in three areas: understanding of media markets, sponsorship and merchandising. Kenyon spoke of overseeing the opening of megastores across the world.

This was almost Paddy Harverson's first big PR exercise. He stressed that it was not a question of selling Manchester United replica shirts in Manhattan or Yankee shirts in Manchester. Both brands were strong enough on their own. It was about how the two sporting institutions could learn from each other about marketing in the global marketplace.

But for the British media this was a world-changing deal. What is more, for them to write the story a number had to be attached to it. The *Sun* saw it as a billion-pound deal, the *Mirror* went even higher, claiming four billion.

The next day there was bedlam when the stock market opened. United's share price had been limping for much of that season. Just a month earlier, at the end of the year the share price had fallen to 225p – having been 412p a year earlier – quite close to its twelve-month low of 190p. Now on this February morning the share price went up 25 per cent in fifteen minutes, reacting to the overnight announcement from New York. Bick says: 'The Stock Exchange got on to the company, demanding a statement in half an hour, if not quicker. And we had to because of the movement of the share price.' Some in the market believed the deal was indeed worth £1 billion. 'It appeared in every paper bar the *FT*. I think the Stock Exchange would not have reacted to the *Sun* or the *Daily Mirror* saying it was a four-billion-pound deal. They did react to the back pages of the qualities saying it was a one-billion-pound deal. They don't necessarily draw a distinction between the sports pages and the business pages of these papers.' A statement was issued and the price went straight back down again. 'Luckily there had been very little trading in shares. Manchester United weren't going to put it out as a Stock Exchange announcement because primarily it was just a marketing tie-up. It wasn't even a deal. It did not earn any money nor was it meant to.' After that Bick told United that for safety's sake, in future every announcement should be put through the Stock Exchange.

Kenyon and United clearly felt they had a lot to learn from the New York Yankees who had done their own TV deal, in particular about sponsorship. The association did open an American window for United: they found more American partners and also toured the USA in the summer of 2001. But the tie-up foundered because of a change in management at the Yankees. The man who had brokered the deal for the Americans was gone within twelve months.

However, the hype served one man's purpose very well. Although he was not involved in the deal, nor did he go to New York with the rest of the Manchester United board, he announced his own plans just as the news was beginning to emerge. That man was Sir Roland Smith, who chose the *Financial Times* to announce that he was to defer his retirement for another year, until March 2002. The announcement was totally obscured in the New York-generated hysteria. The board, said the paper, was keen for him to stay on and it was likely his replacement would come from one of the new non-executive directors, Gardner, Much or Yea.

A year later, after he had retired and Gardner had taken over, Glenn Cooper had lunch with Smith at his HSBC offices. Smith, says Cooper, tried to explain why he did not want Edwards to succeed him. 'He thought that Martin should be out of it. He was not persuasive. The fact is Roland stayed on two years longer than he should have. He failed to hand over the reins to the obvious and popular candidate. Cooper believes that Edwards would have been able to avert many of United's later problems. 'He would not have allowed the Irish situation to develop. He would have had them inside the tent.'

However, if Roland Smith did not want to go, Ferguson throughout the season kept repeating that he would retire at the end of the 2001–02 season, when his contract expired and he would be sixty. Curiously, at the time of the New York Yankees deal United were making desperate attempts to repair Ferguson's relationship with the press, in particular the *Daily Mail*. In January 2001 Colin Gibson had returned from Australia to become the paper's new sports editor: 'I found the *Daily Mail* had no working relationship with Manchester United. There was no access to press conferences. Our correspondent was Ken Lawrence. The traditional football reporter, the Manchester reporter, was not allowed into the press conferences.'

The *Mail* was banned, but freelancers were not and were selling their stories from Ferguson's press conferences to the paper. Nor could Ferguson ban the *Mail* from Champions League press conferences, which were controlled by UEFA. 'But at the Champions League press conference, when the *Daily Mail* man asked a question Sir Alex would say "Next question" and move on. We knew there was a situation.' Gibson's priority was to repair the relationship. 'That was what Manchester United was very keen on at every level.' A meeting was arranged with Paddy Harverson on a very wet and miserable February morning, Gibson drove to Old Trafford to meet Harverson. 'The intention was Alex would join us. But he didn't.'

Even by Ferguson's standards it was a long time to hold a grudge against a paper. The season had already shown how he could punish media he felt had treated him badly. In the autumn of 2000 Ferguson had taken grave exception to a profile of him in the BBC *Match of the Day* magazine, which was edited by a Manchester United supporter. It was not surprising Ferguson took grave exception to how he was portrayed – 'bully, cheat, backstabber' – and he got Watkins to sue. He decided to boycott the BBC and in particular *Match of the Day*, and also to deny the highlights show access to Manchester United players, despite the fact that the magazine had no connection with the television programme. In the end the BBC, recognising that this article was harming their coverage of football, decided to settle. They paid £10,000 to a cancer trust named after Ferguson's mother and printed an apology.

Ferguson's quarrel with the *Daily Mail* went back a lot longer, four years in fact, to August 1997. Ferguson had taken exception to an article by Alan Fraser about Ferguson's supposed dealings with Rune Hauge. It portrayed him as a friend of Hauge, saying he had played bridge with the agent and drunk whisky – both of which were untrue, as Ferguson does not play bridge or drink whisky. Gibson now asked what United wanted in order to settle and was told: 'You have offered no explanation, no corroboration of the story. We need an apology and that will suffice.'

Next morning at Manchester airport Gibson bumped into Bobby Charlton and Martin Edwards, who were on their way to New York, for the launch of the deal with the New York Yankees. 'We had a chat about it. I said, this is the situation, let us try and repair the damage. It is important that the biggest-selling middle-market newspaper in the country has a relationship with the biggest-selling football club in the country. Maybe we will never be the best of friends. We think there is room for criticism and we will obviously be there to criticise. But I do think we do need to have a working relationship.' Maurice Watkins became involved and reconciliation seemed close. 'Then in the *Evening Standard* there was a piece by David Mellor which Sir Alex felt defamed him. Suddenly the reconciliation we were heading towards collapsed. This was mid-2001. The *Standard* was seen as part of Associated Newspapers which owns the *Daily Mail* so we were held party to it.'

The ensuing standoff lasted the rest of the year. It was eventually resolved a year later in March 2002, when the case Ferguson filed against the *Evening Standard* reached court and he won, being awarded damages and costs estimated at around £10,000.

To an extent the very structure of the British media makes life complicated. Britain is the only country which has dedicated Sunday papers which are totally separate from the daily papers. This means football managers have to hold two press conferences on the Friday before the weekend matches, one for the dailies, one for the Sundays. (This also happens after the Saturday matches, as these are reported both by the Sundays and the dailies on Monday.) A Friday briefing meant for a Sunday paper can often be presented in a very misleading light. This was brought home in December 2003, on the day Rio Ferdinand was banned for missing a drug test. The hearing was held on a Friday with the decision to ban him reached late on Friday night. Long before this Ferguson had given his week-end briefing, at which he was asked about Ferdinand. He had no way of knowing what the decision was and was commenting on a hypothetical situation. But when the Sunday tabloids reported the press conference they presented Ferguson's comments as if he had spoken after the ban had been imposed.

In December 2001 Harverson did a deal whereby Ferguson became a bit like a US President, who often grants media access to a pool of reporters selected from the White House Press Corps who then relay the quotes back to everyone else. Ferguson's pool consisted of Bill Thornton of the *Daily Star* and Bob Cass of the *Mail on Sunday* who then passed Ferguson's comments to their respective daily and Sunday colleagues. Manchester United saw it as a way of cutting down time. But this broke down when comments made to Cass suggested Ferguson might be changing his mind about retiring in May 2002. For Ferguson all this was what Andrew Neil had called scoop by interpretation. As one Manchester United insider says:

> The problem was Alex would say something or the players would say something and it would be spun into a massive story. I remember when Roy Keane was injured and he had made David Beckham captain in the interim. There had been a report in midweek completely out of the blue saying Alex [would] keep David as captain because he was better suited to the image of the club. A reporter in the Friday briefing asked, 'We want to ask you about you keeping David Beckham as captain.' Alex said, 'I am not going into that.' Two of the papers interpreted those words, i.e his decision not to say Roy is staying as captain, as a sign that David was. So they splashed on 'Becks to be captain', which was as completely absurd, a classic example of scoop by interpretation. Another example of taking words and spinning them to suit the story.

Ferguson himself could always work the back pages extremely skilfully for his own purposes and in May 2001, well before that settlement with the *Mail*, and when Ferguson was still not on talking terms with the *Mail*, he found the paper very useful in his own battle with the United board. Ferguson's Manchester solicitor Kevin Jaquiss, who had been at school with Michael Crick, rang him and told him that the board had been talking for months about a post-retirement ambassadorial role but had made derisory offers. Interestingly, despite the fact that his long standing lawyer was the Abderdeen-based solicitor Les Delgrano, Jaquiss had been recruited back in 1998, when BSkyB bid for Manchester United, as a specialist corporate lawyer who could advise Ferguson on his rights as an employee in the event of a bid. Now Jaquiss asked his old school chum's help in broadcasting the story of his difficulties with the board, but warned it must not carry Ferguson's fingerprints. Crick placed the article with the *Mail*, feeling that given the strained relationship nobody would link Ferguson with the leak. Ferguson followed it up on MUTV, saying he did not see a roving ambassadorial role for him at the club when he retired. 'When my contract is finished I will leave United for good.'

Ferguson's comments became a huge story, which erupted on the morning of the last match of the season at White Hart Lane. United lost 3–1, although since they had already won the Premiership ten points ahead of Arsenal it did not matter. The previous month they had gone out 3–1 on aggregate to Bayern Munich in the quarter-final of the Champions League, emphasising again that for all their domestic success they just could not repeat their 1999 triumph in Europe. But the fans were happy to savour Ferguson's fourteenth major trophy in his fifteen years at the club. Provoked by the media stories, they decided to display their love for Ferguson. For thirty-one minutes the United fans gathered in the away section sang 'Every single one of us loves Alex Ferguson' to the tune of 'Down by the Riverside'.

Ferguson's post-retirement role was, of course, a subject of much debate at Old Trafford. There were rival voices in the boardroom about what to do with him. Martin Edwards was worried that having Ferguson around might revisit the saga of Matt Busby, whose continued presence after retirement cast such a shadow over successive managers. According to Michael Crick, Ferguson suspected Edwards of wanting to bring in David O'Leary as manager with Brian Kidd as his assistant (the two were then together at Leeds). Harverson and Peter Draper wrote memos saying why Ferguson should get a good role.

The papers by Draper and Harverson laid out Ferguson's value to United as an inspirational figure within the history of the club. There was a strong view that great sporting organisations should have living links with their past and those living should be celebrated and used to keep the magic alive. Both Draper and Harverson were very keen to make a strong case for paying however large a figure was felt to be necessary.

Ferguson got a five-year post-retirement contract worth £7.5 million in total, and his pay for his final season was increased to £3 million a year, £60,000 a week. Edwards was horrified. At the plc meeting approving the deal he voiced his objections, wondering what value he would bring; would he be wheeled out at a Manchester United store in the Far East? But Edwards was in a minority. The board enthusiastically supported the package. Edwards was being increasingly marginalised at United. He had been aghast when United paid £28 million for Veron. Why did they need another midfielder when they had Beckham, Keane, Giggs, Scholes, Butt – surely they could not play all five? And so much money plus a £5 million annual salary for an Argentinean was ridiculous, all the more given that players from South America did not always settle in this country. Edwards was so upset he went to Roland Smith and complained, alleging Kenyon was destroying everything Edwards and Smith had built up: tight budgeting, no big money purchases, paying relatively low salaries. Smith said, 'Martin, I supported you to the hilt when you were chief executive. This is Peter's first year, I have to support him.'

By now Edwards was also selling the last of his shares. But with Magnier and McManus major shareholders he did not want to sell to them and when Joe Stephens, a Manchester stockbroker, rang to say Harry Dobson, the Scottish businessman, was interested Edwards took up the offer. Dobson had known the two Irishmen for twenty years but his investment was unrelated and, as he later said, he benefited from Edwards' feelings: 'Martin Edwards wanted to sell his shares and I think that he didn't want to sell to the two Irishmen. So being Scottish I must have been okay.' For Dobson this was pure investment.

Crick is right when he says the board's deal with Ferguson marked the end of Martin Edwards 'as a major force in Manchester United politics'.

What is more, his Irish friends were now buying shares so seriously that their purchases had to be announced on the Stock Exchange. United's share price had been dropping; in April it touched a low of 175p (compared to the 2000 figure of 393p). Magnier and McManus closely monitored this and on 18 July it was announced that Cubic had become the second largest shareholders in United, increasing their share from 2.9 per cent to 6.77 per cent. BSkyB were still the largest stakeholders at 9.99 per cent. Until now Cubic had not had to disclose their holding as it was below 2.99 per cent, and even the *Financial Times* conceded their intentions had not yet been revealed. What could be said for certain was that they were very rich and friends of Ferguson. The news emerged not long after Ferguson's threat to walk out, increasing speculation that the Irish were coming with the intention of one day taking over and installing their friend as the top man both in football and in the boardroom.

In truth the Irish had no such far-reaching plans, but Magnier still wanted his friend to give the Gimcrack speech. In the spring of 2000 there had been a very curious story involving a horse called Juniper which apparently changed hands several times. According to documents filed at Horse Racing Ireland's registration department, on 11 April 2000 the $1.5 million yearling was registered under the joint ownership of Sue Magnier and Michael Tabor. But on 22 August 2000, the day before the Gimcrack Stakes, Ferguson was shown as the owner. On 11 September he was no longer registered as owner, but his name was restored on 15 September. This time he had a longer run as owner, until 9 March 2001 when his name was removed again. However he was shown as owner once more on 13 June 2001. His name was finally taken off the register on 7 August 2002. According to racing experts such changes of ownership are by no means uncommon, the colours a horse wears being a flag of convenience rather than denoting true ownership. Juniper ran in the Gimcrack under Ferguson's colours, but came third. Ferguson could not yet give his speech.

But with Mike Dillon always prompting him to find a horse for Ferguson, Magnier kept searching. In the summer of 2001 such a horse finally emerged. On 1 July, a few weeks before Cubic bought more shares in Manchester United, Rock of Gibraltar won the Anheuser Busch Railway Stakes, a Group 3 race for two-year-olds at the Curragh. The race was not of great significance but with Aidan O'Brien having two runners in this race – Hawk Wing was the other – he showed which one he preferred. Michel Kinane rode Rock, which started as favourite. The winning owner's name was given as Mrs Sue Magnier.

Three months later, on 17 October, the first formal meeting was held between the Irish as investors in Manchester United and board members. The board were said to be worried about how close Ferguson was to the Irish. In the summer, after United had returned from their pre-season tour to Malaysia, Bangkok and Hong Kong, Ferguson had rung Magnier to congratulate him on the success of his horse Galileo. Magnier was said to have told him, 'Don't be out late, Alex. You're working for me now.' The fans, or at least those who claimed to speak on their behalf, could not have been more delighted. Some of them even saw the Irish themselves as fans of the club. Oliver Houston, spokesman of Shareholders United, commented, 'We are pleased to see United fans buying stakes in the club, rather than faceless City institutions.'

On 17 October United were playing Deportivo La Coruña in the group stage of the Champions League, a match they lost, despite taking the lead, due to two costly blunders for a 3–2 home defeat. The board also made blunders in handling the Irish that day. The two principals, Magnier and McManus, had not come to Old Trafford, they never did. Instead it was their two advisers, Eddie Irvin and John Power, who made their first visit to the Theatre of Dreams. Also at the meeting was Denis Brosnan of the Kerry Group, an important Irish businessmen who did business with Magnier and McManus. They were met by Sir Roland Smith and other members of the United board including Peter Kenyon and David Gill.

They met in the boardroom and it turned out to be a very curious occasion. The Irish had come as the second biggest shareholders in United, after BSkyB. But they were not treated with anything like the respect they deserved or their position would have warranted. The Irish gained the impression that they were being at best tolerated. At one stage of the meeting Smith said that at board meetings of the Bank of England there was no time to read the *Racing Post*. For him Irwin and Power were just representatives of a bunch of Irish horse traders. Smith behaved very haughtily, as if he had no time for such people and could not understand why they were investing in United. The one person who impressed them was Kenyon, who made a presentation about the Nike deal and his vision of United's future.

Normally on a match day directors and their guests dine in style in tables reserved for them behind the directors' box, each director having his own dining table. But the Irish were offered no food, let alone dinner, not even tickets for the directors' box. This is almost the minimum hospitality offered to guests of the board. At the end of the meeting the Irishmen had to go outside to the main concourse for pasties and pies, like any other spectator. They were given tickets for the match, which they had offered to pay for, but Gill said these were complimentary.

The seats were in that part of the ground between the Manchester United supporters and the Deportivo supporters. The Deportivo supporters had a huge drum which they kept banging throughout the match, a noise that increased as their team won and the Irish wondered why they were given these seats. Was this a warning to them from the United board?

Ferguson having announced his retirement, there was some discussion at Old Trafford between the Irish and the United board about plans to replace their most important and valuable employee. Smith and the others gave reassurances that the board had the matter in hand and would soon be looking for a candidate, hoping to finish the process soon after the start of 2002. Ferguson was retiring to spend more time with his horses and reconstruct his lifestyle. Manchester United seemed ready to face the future without him.

16

A CHAMPION HORSE AND A
WANDERING SWEDE

IN OCTOBER 2000 England were looking for a new manager to replace Kevin Keegan, whose sudden resignation following defeat at the hands of Germany had thrown the national team into chaos. Adam Crozier, then chief executive of the Football Association, rang Sir Alex Ferguson. Crozier got on well with his fellow Scot. 'I knew Alex well. I was a favourite. I am a Scot. Alex could never have been more helpful to me.'

Crozier wanted to talk of management in general, ask Ferguson who he thought was a good or bad manager. He made it absolutely clear that the conversation was not an attempt to lure Ferguson into becoming England manager. Crozier knew Ferguson had ruled that out; as Crozier says, 'He was too proud a Scot and did not see himself managing England. He was always quite upfront about that.' But as the best manager in the British game, it obviously made sense to get advice from him on how to set about establishing a proper England coaching structure.

The meeting was fixed for the afternoon of 18 October, just before United were due to play PSV Eindhoven in the Champions League. A couple of hours after speaking to Ferguson, Crozier received a call from Peter Kenyon. Kenyon had heard about the proposed meeting and wanted to sit in. Crozier says, 'He was clearly paranoid we were going to try and steal Alex, even though we must have said twenty times that we weren't. He clearly did not believe us.'

Three hours before kick-off against PSV Crozier met Ferguson and Kenyon at Old Trafford. 'I actually had a dual purpose although nobody knew it at the time. I went to pick Alex's brain about getting the right manager but also to get his agreement to let us have Steve McClaren, his assistant, as part of the new coaching team.' Crozier put forward the idea that in the short term, while a manager was being sought, a mentor could be put in place with two or three coaches underneath instead of a single heir apparent. At one point Bryan Robson had understudied Terry Venables, and the speculation that Robson was going to be the next England manager had put too much pressure on him. 'We wanted two or three good young coaches to learn what it is like to manage England. Kenyon was paranoid that we were trying to steal Alex, whereas Alex twigged very early on that we were trying to get Alex's support to let us have Steve McClaren.'

Crozier asked Ferguson if he would support the FA in persuading McClaren to come and be one of those coaches. 'It was Alex who swung that with the Manchester board. I think Kenyon at first was probably slightly against it. Alex was incredibly helpful in helping secure Steve as one of the coaches to work under an England manager.'

Ferguson was so helpful that the support team for the Under-21 side, initially consisting of McClaren, Peter Taylor from Leicester and Sammy Lee from Liverpool, was in place before Sven-Göran Eriksson was appointed later in the year. Ferguson also pointed his fellow Scot in the direction of the Swede for the top job. 'Having found out as much as I could about potential targets, and having listened to what expert witnesses like Alex had to say, I became absolutely convinced that Sven was our man after that first week.'

Seventeen months later, in February 2002, Ferguson was having to cope with the near certainty that Eriksson would be coming to Old Trafford in the summer as the next manager of Manchester United. With that realisation Ferguson was to perform a dramatic about-turn whose acceptance by the United board would have a lasting impact on the club.

Until that February there was little indication Ferguson was about to take such a step. Towards the end of 2001 he had told Bob Cass that while his mind was made up on retiring, 'the club are looking for my successor but when the thing comes, nearer the time, who knows what will happen?' Angered by the way the story was spun to suggest that he might have changed his mind and now intended to stay, on New Year's Eve he had told Glen Gibbons of the *Scotsman*, 'I'm going all right. That's been settled for some time now.'

The 2000–01 season had certainly begun as if it was a valedictory one. On 28 August United sold Jaap Stam to Lazio for £15.3 million. The club claimed that this was a fairly routine transfer. There had been an offer for the player in the summer, the offer was not pursued, there were doubts about the player's fitness, in particular his performance after return from injury, and he had made a poor start to the season. So when the offer from Lazio was renewed he was sold. However, as it later emerged the club had been looking to sell Stam for some time. Furthermore, Ferguson's son Jason was involved in the deal as an agent, and his involvement would haunt the club for some time to come. What was more, the sale came a week after Stam's book *Head to Head* was sensationally serialised in the *Daily Mirror*, where he described how Ferguson had tapped him up when he was at PSV and also advised players to dive for penalties. The club vehemently denied that the book had anything to do with the transfer, but public perception was different.

United's poor start had also seen Roy Keane renew his criticisms of United.

It was no novelty for Keane to make such criticisms. The previous season, in November 2000, he had been critical of United's supporters: 'Some people come here and I don't think they can spell football, let alone understand it. They have a few drinks and probably their prawn sandwiches and don't realise what is going on out on the pitch.' The following month he had continued his attack on United supporters, explaining that his criticism was against most of the crowd, not just the executive fans.

But now in the autumn of 2001 he was criticising his fellow players. He claimed United's slump in form had come about because the older, established players were not pulling their weight. Indeed, when United came to Tottenham on 29 September, having lost to Deportivo La Coruña in Europe four days earlier, Fleet Street's finest gathered at White Hart Lane to write obituaries for Ferguson. They seemed to have all the material they needed when Tottenham went 3–0 up by half-time.

Then, in statistically the greatest comeback in United history, they scored five without reply in the second half. They won 5–3 and it could have been more. Ferguson called it the best away victory of his entire reign. But even this remarkable victory did little to dispel the feeling that the players were aware they were playing for a manager who was not only going but seemed to have lost his touch. This was illustrated by Ferguson's purchase of Juan Sebastian Veron, at £28 million United's costliest player. In order to fit him into the side changes were made to the team formation which did not seem to work.

In November, following defeat at Liverpool, *The Times* headlined its report 'The day Ferguson's empire began to crumble' and wondered if it was 'a season too far, a fight too many for the ageing heavyweight'. After United lost 1–0 at home to West Ham on 8 December, they were ninth in the table and eleven points behind Liverpool. There were echoes of Ferguson's dark past, in particular 1989.

However, just then it seems that Ferguson decided he need not retire at all. He had turned sixty on New Year's Eve, a check-up showed he was in good health, his wife and family wondered if he really wanted to give up and he decided to change his mind. Or at least this was the version United, and initially Ferguson, put out when in February 2002 the news emerged. But this is far from the complete picture.

New Year's Eve 2001 was clearly a busy time for Ferguson. Having told Glen Gibbons he was quitting, he also rang Paolo di Canio, then at West Ham and a player he had always admired, to wish him a happy new year but really to indicate his desire to bring him to United. It was what Michael Crick calls a 'mild form of tapping', except that in this case Dwight Yorke's refusal to move to Middlesbrough meant the plan could not be achieved. But if Ferguson had decided on New Year's Eve to change his mind, why did he then wait so long to intervene that, had he left it a day later, Manchester United would have met the FA and set in motion the formal steps to secure the services of Eriksson?

The only explanation is that in the intervening month Ferguson heard what United were planning and felt outraged that the magnificent edifice he had built would be handed on a platter to a man he despised. He may have guided Crozier towards Eriksson back in 2000, but his real feelings towards Eriksson were revealed in February 2003. In an interview with *The Times* Ferguson first admitted that he knew Eriksson was coming. 'I think they'd done the deal all right. I am sure it was Eriksson . . . I think they'd shaken hands. They couldn't put anything on paper because he was still England manager.'

He went on to give his views about the man:

I think Eriksson would have been a nice, easy choice for them. He doesn't change anything. He sails along and nobody falls out with him. He comes out and he says, 'In the first half we were very good, second half we were not so good. I am very pleased with the result.' I think he'd have been all right for United – the acceptable face. Carlos Queiroz [Ferguson's no. 2] knows him because he [Eriksson] was at Benfica and Carlos was from Lisbon. Carlos says what he did well was that he never fell out with anyone. He was best pals with the President and the press liked him. I think he does that. The press makes a suggestion and he seems to follow it.

Manchester United have never publicly discussed this. The closest anyone at United has come to saying anything in print was in the paperback edition of Crick's biography of Ferguson, where he quoted Martin Edwards as saying, 'It was very, very close indeed. Terms had actually been agreed.' It was Crick's hardback edition in the summer of 2002 that first indicated that there had been contact with Eriksson; this was denied by United and the FA, although Edwards was not then identified by name. My research has shown that Manchester United were indeed on the point of appointing Eriksson – in fact on their way to London – when a call came from Ferguson on Watkins' mobile phone asking him to come urgently to Carrington. United had spent nearly a year reacting to Ferguson's decision to retire. Now it all had to be binned.

Ferguson's decision to retire was something that had been concerning Kenyon from the moment he took over. He saw a successor to Ferguson as one of his top priorities. In January 2001 he had said at a soccer conference in Cannes that unlike the post-Busby disaster, this time United would get it right. There had been various meetings with Ferguson to make sure he really wanted to retire. Kenyon says Ferguson made it clear he saw this as a lifestyle change: 'He had been at the top of the game for many years. I think he recognised that he hadn't done anything else other than football. He was now starting to get heavily involved in racing, which he saw as his life after football. He owned Rock of Gibraltar. He mentioned that. Racing was clearly becoming a bigger part of his life and something that he consciously felt would offer him that alternative.'

Once Kenyon had satisfied himself Ferguson was going, he drew up a shortlist. It included the usual suspects such a job would attract: a couple of big Italians, Marcello Lippi and Fabio Capello, Martin O'Neill, Eriksson and Steve McClaren, who was still assistant manager at Old Trafford at that time.

The Italians suffered from the fact that their English was not very good. And there was another foreigner already working in England who could speak English well, who wanted to return to club football after a spell as England manager and was close to Beckham. The shortlist was pruned down to one man. Kenyon will not say who the person was. But it can now be definitely stated that it was Eriksson. He was felt not to be confrontational, a man who had been successful at all levels, a very nice guy with a pleasant manner who would have fitted in at all levels of Manchester United.

The club handled their contacts with Eriksson with great skill. Kenyon the great marketer had identified him, Watkins the man of law and many secrets contacted him. Not for Watkins the sort of indiscreet publicity that two years later would attend Eriksson's contacts with Chelsea.

Watkins, a past master at conducting negotiations that required tact and discretion, met Eriksson at a secret location in London, an obscure hotel. While nothing was signed by the last week of January 2002, it was now a question of Eriksson going to see his employers, the FA, and telling them he wanted to leave. Watkins, with his knowledge of contract law, was aware that legally it was first an employee/employer question; the employee should inform his employer. Eriksson would have told the FA that he would, of course, see England through the finals of the 2002 World Cup before taking over at Manchester United.

United also decided to contact the Football Association formally. They arranged a meeting, although they did not tell the FA its purpose. They planned to tell them that they were going to approach Eriksson. It was the sort of thing that goes on in football all the time, and the whole thing was conducted in such a fashion as to ensure that United and Eriksson could refute all criticism. Not for Manchester United embarrassing photographs like those of Eriksson going to Roman Abramovich's London flat.

Within the FA the matter was not entirely a secret. Crozier, having brought Eriksson in and at that time busy promoting Team England, had become quite close to Watkins during the season over the handling of a strike threatened by players at the prompting of the PFA. He would joke with Watkins, 'Keep your hands off our man.' Crozier told me: 'They never approached the FA with a view to talking to us about Sven.' This is technically true, since they had not told the FA what the meeting was about. 'Do I think behind the scenes that they talked to Sven? Yes, I think they did. As I now understand it, I think there were a few conversations between Sven and them about what would happen after the World Cup. I don't think there was ever any question of not leading England to the World Cup. I don't think Sven had decided he wanted to pursue it. But then at the time Ferguson decided to change his mind and stay.'

Kenyon says: 'It got to the point whereby we were going to approach the intended candidate [i.e. the FA] on the Monday morning. Maurice and I were travelling down on the Sunday in order to sort the matter out. The whole thing was planned with a view to making an official approach before we got into negotiations. We were ready to travel down to London when Maurice got a call.'

Ferguson's call to Watkins on his mobile was very urgent. He said, 'Can you come to Carrington to see me, I have to see you urgently.'

The call could not have come at a more inconvenient time. It was a busy day for the lawyer, but Ferguson was insistent. Watkins had no idea what was on Ferguson's mind but clearly it was important. Ferguson told him he had been thinking about his retirement and spoken to the family. He was fit, having had a recent medical. Cathy did not like the idea of him hanging about the house. He had decided to change his mind and now wanted a new contract to take him beyond 2002.

Ferguson's about-turn completely threw Watkins. As he had done so often before, Ferguson had pulled the rug from under United's feet.

Watkins rang Kenyon to tell him that Ferguson had changed his mind. There followed a debate between the pair. Kenyon got hold of Roland Smith and they decided to try and postpone their meeting with the FA. Soon other board members were involved. One board insider at United says: 'There was a big debate on the board. David Gill was very much part of this debate and his view was mixed. He was not the most vociferous for Ferguson staying. Kenyon and Watkins on balance were more for making sure Ferguson stayed. Edwards was not part of the debate but took part unofficially. He was critical of Ferguson and probably would have had him hung, drawn and quartered. To him he remained an employee, no more.'

But the voices on the board inclined to say 'Thanks Alex, but no thanks' were quickly silenced. The decision was that he should stay and what a relief it was that Britain's most successful manager would carry on. However, despite this public endorsement it was not easy to sort out a contract. That debate was much lengthier and grew quite acrimonious. The insider says: 'He wanted a longer contract and more money, something in the region of around £4 million.' Hard work was involved before a two-year contract with a one-year option was agreed. 'He wanted longer, four years.' Ferguson's lawyer at Paul & Williamson in Aberdeen became involved. 'The negotiations got very acrimonious at one point with tense meetings between United and Ferguson's Aberdeen-based lawyer. His sons Jason and Mark, who worked at Goldman Sachs, also got involved in the contract negotiations. 'Jason Ferguson came to see Kenyon and then finally there was the intervention of his other son Mark, which led to further meetings before it was sorted out.'

Ferguson's salary had risen from £60,000 to £70,000 a week, just over £3.6 million a year. This was still less than the £100,000 a week that Roy Keane agreed a few weeks later, after he had made noises suggesting he might move abroad, and what Beckham also agreed after protracted negotiations. At the end of it all Ferguson declared that, once his contract expired in 2005, he had 'no intention of staying at the club in any capacity whatsoever'.

David Bick, who as external financial PR adviser followed the events closely, says: 'They should have said sorry, you've made your mind up. Having accepted that he was going to go, they should have stuck to it. But when he changed his mind they fell into line with that. It was clear Ferguson had a massive grip over them rather than the other way around. I definitely got the impression about his retirement that he'd got himself angry about something. It sounded like toys being thrown out the pram, but nobody said really whether it was a genuine retirement or a fit of pique or anger. When he changed his mind, such was his influence that they just went along with it.'

The United board knew this could be presented to the fans as a great victory, and so it was. But both the board and the fans must have wondered if they had done the right thing. United finished the 2001–02 season without a trophy for the first time since 1998. They also lost the semi-final of the Champions League, having failed to utilise home advantage to Bayer Leverkusen by only drawing 2–2.

This was a bitter pill for Ferguson to swallow. Not only had United again failed in Europe but for much of the season the Champions League final had been held up as his ultimate farewell. It would be staged at the rebuilt Hampden Park, where back in 1960 one of the most magical of European Cup finals had taken place, Real Madrid beating Eintracht Frankfurt 7–3. Like many Scotsmen of his generation, Ferguson had been in the crowd. Now he could lead his team out to try and win it as his farewell to football. What could provide a better ending? Or so the speculation went until the match with the Germans.

One of the reasons Ferguson had given for staying on was that there were now 'people at the club on the same wavelength as me. They want what I want.' He had cited the signing of Veron the previous summer, which he felt may have been 'the best thing the club has ever done in that it told other people and the supporters that we're prepared to try to become the best club in the world'. Veron's performances suggested Ferguson was being rather fanciful, but in the summer of 2001 the Kenyon regime's decision to back him with money and sign Ruud van Nistelrooy indicated that this was only the start of a massive team rebuilding. Veron's signing had taken United's player purchases to a new, very un-Edwards like peak. The summer of 2002 saw another peak when Rio Ferdinand was signed from Leeds.

Ferguson had identified that defence had been the problem. United had conceded forty-five League goals, the leakiest their defence had been for eleven years. He needed a centre-half. Ferguson had long admired Ferdinand and was, of course, a close friend of his agent Pini Zahavi. Leeds were in desperate financial trouble – soon they would be in financial meltdown – and badly needed money to keep the bankers at bay. But their chairman Peter Ridsdale would only sell if he had a headline £30 million figure. So Kenyon agreed to pay £26 million, with a further £3.1 million conditional on United's performances in the Premiership and the Champions League.

The Ferdinand deal cast other shadows. There were further accusations that Ferguson had tapped up the player and also that he had prevented Steve McClaren taking over as Leeds manager, as he felt that in that position McClaren would not allow Ferdinand to leave for United. Like the Stam deal, Ferdinand's transfer would be looked at very critically by the Irish when they began to examine in detail how Manchester United conducted its purchase and sale of players.

The season had finished so badly that Ferguson gave the impression he would rather be anywhere than on a football field. Towards the end of the season he had abused journalists at a press conference, repeatedly swearing at them and finally calling them 'fucking idiots'. In contrast, racing seemed blissful.

True, the Manchester United Racing Club that Ferguson had launched in 1999 had proved a dreadful failure. Started as part of his testimonial, the plan was for 2,000 United followers to pay £235 each, enough to acquire half a dozen horses racing in the club's colours. When the club was wound up in 2001 it had 800 members and the horses had won only two of their twenty-seven races, collecting just £16,000 in prize money.

However, Rock of Gibraltar was a totally different story and his success was taking Ferguson to areas where he had never ventured before. At the end of the previous year John Magnier had fulfilled his ambition to have Ferguson make the Gimcrack speech, the Rock having won the Gimcrack Stakes in August 2001. In a witty speech he compared the Rock favourably with his thorough-breds at Old Trafford, Veron and Beckham. In October of that year the Rock won his first Group 1 race, the Grand Criterium at Longchamp. Over the course of the next few months he won six other Group 1 races, including the English and Irish 2,000 Guineas. He was the racehorse of the 2002 season, winning ten of his thirteen races, and was compared to Mill Reef, who back in 1972 had achieved the same feat.

The Rock had won £1,269,800 in prize money. As the *Racing Post* put it, the horse was 'the talk of the pubs and clubs. He transcended racing into household namedom. People with little or no interest in horse racing switched on their tellies to see how Sir Alex's horse would get on.' The Rock's stud value had risen with every race and by the end of the flat racing season had reached astronomic values. The media was now full of stories of how Ferguson, having paid a mere £120,000 for his half share of this wonder horse, was sitting on a goldmine. What Ferguson's team could not do on the football field, his horse was doing on the race track, which made his decision to stay on as manager all the more inexplicable. Such was the Rock's influence that in 2003 Ferguson was included in the *Sunday Times* Rich List. Magnier and McManus, of course, had long been on the Irish Rich List and there seemed now to be parity.

But did Ferguson ever pay anything for his half share in the Rock, or indeed have a half share at all? He never mentioned the amount. It was what his friends and people close to him are supposed to have said he paid, although one paper reported that he had paid £173,000. In October 2001 Martin Hannan asked in an interview if he was sure about his deal with Magnier for the Rock. Ferguson paused for an instant, and then looking at Hannan as if he was daft said, 'It's all sorted out.' The following year he wrote a first-person piece in the *Observer* where he declared he had bought the horse a couple of months 'before it won the Gimcrack Stakes'. However, Hannan's research undermines this claim. Hannan argues: 'The plain fact is that Ferguson did not pay a penny for his "share" of Rock of Gibraltar . . . in plain English, no money or any binding contracts about ownership had changed hands.'

What had happened was that at some point there had been a conversation between Magnier and Ferguson. Magnier would later testify in papers filed in a Dublin court that he had offered Ferguson 5 per cent of the Rock's winnings during his career and one nomination a year when he went to stud, which at the time the offer was made would have brought between £10,000 to £20,000 for another two decades. Ferguson's recollection of the conversation was that he was offered 50 per cent of the horse, no strings attached. How the misunderstanding arose has never been explained, but Mike Dillon, who was said to be witness, was prepared to testify in favour of Magnier and the final settlement seemed to reflect what Magnier was saying.

All that was in the future. For the moment the impression that Ferguson owned half the Rock was maintained, Magnier doing nothing to correct it. When the Rock retired, Coolmore issued a one-line statement: 'Rock of Gibraltar will stand the 2003 season alongside his sire Danehill at Coolmore.' It was Ferguson as owner who made the fulsome statement to PA Sport: 'As a relative newcomer into ownership, I cannot adequately express the pleasure I have derived from the association with such a great horse . . . I look forward to the future with keen anticipation and I have every confidence that he will transmit his amazing talent and courage to his offspring.'

But even before the horse had been retired to stud, all this talk of the riches the Rock would bring Ferguson clearly began to concern Coolmore. In late October 2002 a source close to Coolmore rang Charles Methven, then editor of the 'Peterborough' column in the *Daily Telegraph*, and suggested he look into the ownership of the Rock. The result was this lead story in the 'Peterborough' column of 2 November 2002:

> Sir Alex Ferguson's foray into racehorse ownership has been the stuff of dreams – his first purchase, Rock of Gibraltar, won seven consecutive Group One races – but will the canny Scotsman ever really cash in on his prized asset? Fergie owns a 50 per cent stake in 'the Rock', entitling him to half its £1.2 million career earnings. But the real cash cow, so to speak, will be the horse's breeding rights – estimated at a whopping £50 million. Rumours circulating in racing circles have it that they are secretly retained by John Magnier, the Irish bloodstock baron whose wife Sue owns the remaining share in the horse. 'The amount Fergie stands to make from the Rock's stud value is almost as much, if not more, than he has ever earned from Manchester United,' says one racing source. 'But no one knows whether he has a share. Magnier's whole operation is opaque and they're suspiciously hazy on this detail.'

The article received little attention in the rest of the media. However, it would not have gone unnoticed by Sir Alex. A few weeks later, just before Christmas 2002, Coolmore received a letter from Ferguson asking about stud fees for the Rock. Coolmore were bemused by the letter and wondered if it was a Christmas joke. There was much scratching of heads. Stud fees to Ferguson? What stud fees? Even if they were payable, such stud fees would only be due several months after the mare was found to be in foal and the date set for the Rock was 1 October 2003. At that stage the Rock had not even covered his first mare.

Coolmore's bewilderment would not last long. It would turn to dismay and anger as soon it became clear what Ferguson was demanding. This story would not emerge in public for several months and when it did Manchester United's very future seemed to be in jeopardy.

Six months earlier in New York, another event had taken place which would have an even more dramatic effect on Manchester United. A middle-aged, slightly balding man had walked into the offices of a law firm to discuss investing in European football.

The man was Avram Glazer, son of Malcolm Glazer. At that time the Glazers were unknown in the UK but fairly well established in the US as successful, if at times ruthless businessmen, holding real estate assets through the First Allied Corporation, a company wholly owned by the Glazers. It also controlled Zapata Corporation, which in turn had controlling stakes in a marine protein products company and a company supplying automotive airbags, fabric and cushions. But above all the Glazers owned Tampa Bay Buccaneers. This had been a struggling NFL team which they had taken over in 1995 and made it not only into a successful business but a team that won the Superbowl in January 2003.

Avram led the initiative into this new field of what they called soccer as the eldest of Malcolm's six children, five of whom were sons. Soon, as the Glazers got more interested in Manchester United, Joel, seven years younger than Avram, became more prominent. Supporting him would be Bryan, three years younger than Avram, who was also the driving force behind the commercial success of the Glazers at Tampa Bay. But all that was in the future.

Avram had come to the Avenue of America offices of Allen & Overy to see Andrew Ballheimer, who was then based in New York. The contact for Allen & Overy had come through one of the partners in the office, a big NFL fan, who was a friend of Bill Pascell, owner of the New York Giants.

At this meeting Avram Glazer, known as Avi, made no mention of investing in Manchester United; nor, it seems, had the Glazers even thought about it. The Glazers were looking to invest in European soccer in general, feeling they could do in Europe what they had already done in Tampa with the Bucks, as the team was popularly known. Their aim was to export a model of sports management which they had perfected in Tampa and which they thought was unique. But from now on the ambitions of the Glazer brothers and the fallout from Rock of Gibraltar and his stud fees would march together to produce perhaps the most cataclysmic events in Manchester United's history.

17

2003 – UNITED'S ANNUS HORRIBILIS

MANCHESTER UNITED'S FANS, like fans of all football clubs, remember some years with pride and some with great sorrow. In the history of the club the year 1958 can never be forgotten and if any fan is inclined to do so, the clock outside Old Trafford, stopped at the moment the plane crashed at Munich, is there to remind them. Other years, like 1968, when the club finally achieved Busby's great European dream, and 1999 when it repeated the feat and also won the treble, stimulate more joyous memories.

2003 was a year to remember in sorrow rather than joy. On the field of play, 2003 was the sort of normal season Ferguson had inspired the fans to expect ever since he had won his first Premiership title in 1992–93. It marked Ferguson's eighth Premiership title, the ninth in eleven years, but underneath the surface were bubbling away some of the club's worst moments. For a time that year there were real fears that a dispute between its most important employee and its most important shareholder might tear the club apart. These, and other events, were to cast a deep shadow that would finally pave the way for the takeover of the club by the Glazers.

United had begun the 2002–03 season dismally. They were eighth in the Premier League at the end of August, ninth by mid-September. Then, after their defeat at Middlesbrough on Boxing Day 2002, they did not lose a single League match for the rest of the season and won the title five points ahead of Arsenal. But glories on the field masked struggles off it and the problems that were haunting the manager.

Ferguson's future earnings from Rock of Gibraltar were now much discussed publicly and even provoked priestly wrath in Ireland, where Father Sean Healy protested that Ferguson would make millions in stud fees from the Rock but not pay a single penny in Irish tax. He was quoted in the *Mirror* as saying, 'That horse will make a ten million euro profit a year and he will get half of that, but Ferguson will not pay a cent of that in Ireland. I believe five million euros is a bit too much to go untaxed. Even a modest levy would bring money into the Exchequer and still leave him with an enormous amount of money in his pocket.'

Ferguson had written to the Irish just before Christmas. In February 2003 there were the first calls to Coolmore and, following that, calls to Weatherbys Ireland, the racing civil service that holds the country's stud book. The first call to Coolmore received the same puzzled response as had the first letter: what money is he talking about? Weatherbys, when asked about Rock of Gibraltar's ownership, confirmed Ferguson's worst fears. Its registered owner was the Rock of Gibraltar Syndicate and Ferguson's name did not appear. Hannan says that 'sometime in the second week of February 2003, i.e. during the week ending Friday 14 February, Ferguson was told once and for all by John Magnier that he was not getting half of the income'.

Did this, perhaps, destabilise Ferguson's emotional balance? Of course he was famous for his hair-dryer treatment of players, but it is hard not to wonder if it was his anger about Rock of Gibraltar that led him to commit an act that weekend which created a deep and permanent rift with David Beckham.

On Saturday 15 February, at home to Arsenal in the FA Cup, United lost 2–0. When the players returned to the dressing room Ferguson shut the door, hung up his jacket and launched into Beckham, blaming him for the second goal. Beckham denied it was his fault and they got into a shouting match. Beckham, feeling bullied and put upon, swore at Ferguson. In his autobiography, *My Side*, ghosted by Tom Watt, Beckham describes what happened next:

> The boss took a step or two towards me from the other side of the room. There was a boot on the floor. He swung his leg and kicked it. At me? At the wall? It could have gone anywhere, he was that angry now. I felt a sting just over my left eye where the boot had hit me. I put one hand up to it and found myself wiping the blood away off my eyebrow. I went for the gaffer. I don't know if I've ever lost control like that in my life before. A couple of the lads stood up. I was grabbed by Giggsy first, then by Gary and Ruud van Nistelrooy. Suddenly it was like some mad gangster movie, with them holding me back as I tried to get to the gaffer. He stepped back, I think quite shocked at what had happened. Probably a minute at most was how long the rage lasted. I calmed down and went through to the treatment room.

Victoria Beckham was outraged and wanted to sort it out then and there with Ferguson, but her husband dissuaded her. The story of the incident soon got out. The Manchester United press staff, as is customary after a home match, were waiting outside the dressing room until Ferguson had finished his post-match talk before going in to arrange interviews. They picked up some of the vibes. Dressing-room strife was not unknown but this was different. They could see the grey faces in the dressing room and the mood suggested something very unusual had happened. Players were soon swapping stories up and down the country. It seems Fabien Barthez told Thierry Henry, his French team-mate at Arsenal, in terms of 'You will not believe what happened after the match'. The *Sun* soon heard and word reached Paddy Harverson. He checked the facts, confirmed they were reporting the truth and that Ferguson had apologised to Beckham. Internally United tried to treat the incident as an accident, but they could do nothing to lessen its dramatic impact. 'Fergie Decks Becks' was one of the great sports stories of the year and won journalist Neil Custis an award.

Other incidents in the dressing room indicate that Ferguson was unusually on edge. He had not been getting on with Beckham for quite some time. There had been various incidents involving the player, including one during the previous FA Cup match when United had beaten West Ham 6–1. At half-time Ferguson had a go at Beckham. At full-time he had run into Sandra Beckham, David's mother. She knew the problems her son was having with Ferguson and raised the subject with the manager. Ferguson told her, 'Do you know, Sandra, the trouble with David is that everybody sucks up to him.'

The exchange further infuriated Beckham. At twenty-seven he felt he was still being treated as the callow youth who had come to Old Trafford, one who needed his mother to intervene with the boss.

All this badly damaged Ferguson's relationship with Beckham and began to raise questions as to how long the player could continue at the club. Even back in the summer of 2000, Ferguson had contemplated life at Old Trafford without Beckham. As Michael Crick has revealed, when Luis Figo was at Barcelona Ferguson had made an audacious attempt to sign him, offering Beckham in exchange. That came to nothing and Figo joined Real Madrid later that summer. In 2003 it was to be different. And although the Rock's stud fees and Beckham's future at Manchester United were not connected, over the next few months both would inflict continuing damage on the club.

Curiously, the two situations had one thing in common. When United came to sell Beckham the club insisted it had nothing to do with his falling out with Ferguson or the boot incident, but was purely a good football deal. Similarly, as the Irish fell out with Ferguson and increased their pressure on the board, they insisted that the row over the horse had nothing to do with their relationship with the board and was a totally separate matter, a matter of corporate governance.

In March 2003 Ferguson finally ended his long-running dispute with the *Mail*, which was now nearly six years old. The *Mail* had offered an apology which, says Colin Gibson, 'Watkins accepted on behalf of Alex. Then, after Ferguson and the *Standard* had gone to court, where the *Evening Standard* lost and Ferguson was awarded a small sum as part of the settlement, there was an interview with Alex in the *Mail* which had to be done by me.'

They met in the first week of April 2003, a Wednesday. Gibson continues,

'One of the things he was very concerned about was that he wanted to protect his family. He felt people outside had an agenda against him and his family, particularly Jason. Jason, he said, had been unfairly criticised by several organisations. While he came over as extremely relaxed, he wasn't the same Alex Ferguson I had known ten years before. He was a changed man. He was more distant, more remote compared to the Fergie I knew.' Gibson had, of course, been away from England since 1999. 'What struck me was that by 2003 the Ferguson I knew had changed from being the open and engaging person he had been with the media into one more suspicious and distant.'

The whole saga had also made Gibson realise the power Ferguson now held over the board. Gibson had spent all of 2002 chipping away at United about the exclusion of the *Daily Mail*, an exclusion which included being banned from United's overseas trips. He spoke to Edwards and other board members and they said they would try and bring Ferguson round, but nothing happened. Gibson got the definite impression that the board was running scared of Ferguson. 'One phrase was uttered to me by a senior executive, "You know what Alex is like, he is Alex, there is nothing you can do about it." Also, having just changed his mind about whether to quit or not over the Eriksson situation, they did not want to upset him.'

One critical factor in all this was that Roland Smith had gone, having retired as chairman in March 2002. By the time Gibson met up with Ferguson in the great reconciliation with the *Daily Mail* it was nearly a year since Smith had stepped down, having made sure Martin Edwards would not succeed him.

The whole operation had been executed by Smith, the master of chairing plcs, with considerable skill. There had been no vote in the board and no need for one. Smith had made sure that everyone accepted that Edwards just could not become chairman and the only alternative was Roy Gardner.

Edwards remained on the board until 29 November 2002. Announcing his departure, Manchester United also confirmed that the following May he would give up his chairmanship of the football club. His departure was accompanied by the familiar stories of Edwards' private life. The Sunday before the announcement the *News of the World* had alleged that there had been liaisons with call girls at a Champions League draw in Geneva. The publicist Max Clifford, who had been offered more stories about Edwards's private life, commented, 'This sort of negative publicity for the chairman of Manchester United couldn't be allowed to continue.' Most newspapers, while accepting Edwards' role at the making of the modern Manchester United, concluded that his lifestyle made his continued presence at board level impossible.

The ending of Manchester United's association with a man who had been at the club since 1970 merited just three lines in Gardner's chairman's statement for the annual report of 2003, a polite note of thanks and goodbye. As it happens Smith himself was dead almost exactly a year after Edwards left the plc board, on 20 November 2003, having suffered from cancer for some months.

For most United fans who followed the team day in and day out the change meant little, but in terms of how the board operated and its relationship with Ferguson it was crucial. It was well known that Smith had had good relations with Ferguson, on whom he had conferred an honorary degree as Chancellor of Manchester Metropolitan University. When Ferguson had fallen out with Edwards over money it was Smith, helped by Ferguson's old friend Watkins, who came to the rescue. Ferguson respected and admired Smith. Gardner was a totally new face and brought a new style to the job.

David Bick, who worked closely with Smith, sums up the differences: 'Most non-executive chairmen, in a sense, come once a month to the board meeting and there are a few phone calls with the chief executive. Roland was on the phone to Martin, Peter, David, Maurice and me, separately, every morning. He had his cuttings faxed to his London flat in Marylebone by 7 a.m. He'd seen and read the press cuttings before anybody did and if there was anything untoward in them he was on the phone to us. He would certainly ring the other board directors every morning without fail, so he'd speak to everybody.'

In effect, nothing would happen at Manchester United without Smith being consulted and his agreement being sought. 'You wouldn't do anything, whether it be the transfer of a major player, the manager's new contract, a dispute with the manager over bringing in a new player. Whether it was Kenyon or Martin or David, nobody would contemplate moving a muscle without consulting Sir Roland. There was a huge difference between Roland as chairman of Manchester United plc and any other chairman. I would say Roland demonstrated why you can't be a conventional non-executive chairman at Manchester United. He must have spent at least half a day every day starting at 7.30 in the morning on Manchester United business. In that sense he was much more of an executive chairman than a non-executive one.' As Bick points out, Smith had vast experience as a director or chairman of major companies: the Bank of England, British Aerospace, House of Fraser. In addition, says Bick, 'He and his wife were hugely passionate about Manchester United.'

Despite his close relationship with the Edwards family, and although appointed by Martin Edwards as plc chairman, he had made himself independent of Edwards. 'The fact was that despite Roland's historic connections to the Edwards family, he was a very independent person and Roland based his judgement on this. Roland was not a man you trifled with. That was partly due to his reputation, partly to do with his judgement, and I think partly because he seemed to be the only one who had any real authority over Ferguson.'

Gardner brought a very different style. He gave the impression of being rather prickly, even a touch arrogant, reflecting his background in the electrical industry in the UK. He had spent much of his early career in GEC and Marconi and then in 1994 became finance director of British Gas. In 1997 when Centrica was demerged from British Gas he became the chief executive of Centrica. Nobody could doubt his ability as a manager but even his friends said he was not an outgoing person. Once one got to know him he could be very warm, but he was not an easy person to get to know. There was a barrier around him. When he took the job, journalists who covered his industry insisted he could not possibly do his Manchester United job and be a success as chief executive of Centrica. But he was eager to become Manchester United chairman, tremendously enthusiastic, and radiated incredible confidence. However, his style of working was very different to that of Smith. He may have loved Manchester United no less than Smith – perhaps more – but as chairman of the plc he behaved very differently, more as a conventional chairman of a plc behaves. His main point of contact was his chief executive. Not for him Smith's daily contact with other board members, let alone that he should try to be the sort of avuncular figure Smith had become to the fans or the man Ferguson knew he could turn to in any dispute with the board.

It may not have helped that early on in his chairmanship Gardner did attempt to stamp his particular style on the club, with disastrous results. Roland Smith had been careful to make sure Ferguson was not involved in any plc business. So unlike other football club plcs, Ferguson did not attend United's annual general meeting.

But the previous November Gardner, presiding over his first AGM as chairman, was very keen for Ferguson to attend and take questions from the shareholder fans. Not everyone at Old Trafford was sold on the idea and Gardner had to work hard to convince quite a few of the management team. One insider told me: 'Roy persuaded Ferguson to come along. We had never done it because we always wanted to ensure that it was a business meeting. Roy thought it was good idea because Alex was in charge of the most important, valuable assets of the business and was in charge of the most important and strategic direction of the business. There was a logic in that. But some of us felt there was a risk. It would lead to a precedent and an expectation that this would be done every year. It would change the nature of the meeting from a business meeting. Most people attending the AGM were fan shareholders rather than City shareholders. It would turn into a fans' forum, which is fine but not what the AGM is about. There was a media risk that a story would emerge that was controversial.'

They were persuaded, but it did not work. Ferguson was very sensitive about Juan Sebastian Veron. A few days earlier the former United player Stuart Pearson had criticised Ferguson on MUTV about the purchase of Veron and Laurent Blanc, urging him to sell them. Ferguson had got so upset that he refused to speak to the in-house television channel for seven days. Now, at the AGM, a man named Peter Brody stood up and said to him, 'This season you've come out wearing Rock of Gibraltar's blinkers. You need to go back to the stable and have a clear-out with the biggest carthorse of them all – Juan Sebastian Veron.'

Ferguson visibly reddened and replied, 'I am not even responding to that.' Then he said of Brody, 'He's an idiot.'

The Old Trafford insider, who was sitting not far from Ferguson when he made those comments, says: 'He won a big round of applause. Veron was not working out but you don't call him a carthorse. I've been with Alex to fan meetings and he has been great. He did not like the tone. This was a particularly disrespectful, rude question or statement. The whole tone of the meeting was not that of a football meeting. It was an uncomfortable mix between business and football. That is why we all felt it did not work. I don't think Alex liked that sort of thing.'

Gardner had behaved rather like a fan in wanting Ferguson there. After the debacle of November 2002 the experiment was never repeated. Peter Kenyon for one had not thought it was a good idea, but had reluctantly agreed. Was there more to this Gardner–Kenyon disagreement? Did Kenyon, perhaps, not want Gardner to take over from Smith? Insiders gained the clear impression that this was the case. Bick says, 'It was quite clear to me that Peter wasn't keen on it.'

By March 2003 both David and John Bick were out of Manchester United as Gardner made further changes. Bick recalls, 'Because, essentially, the account went to Finsbury who also looked after Roy Gardner's interest in Centrica, Gardner must have made that decision. The arrival of Gardner clearly made a difference.'

It was also time for change on other, more significant fronts, most notably David Beckham. On 23 April 2003 Manchester United played Real Madrid in the quarter-finals of the Champions League. The first leg at the Bernabeu saw Madrid give United a masterclass, beating them 3–1 with some of the greatest football seen in Europe for many a year. This was the Madrid galacticos at their best. As Beckham ran out with his United team-mates on that night, his mother, sitting in one corner of the ground on the first tier with the visiting United fans, felt a cold twinge run down her spine. She sensed that her son would one day run out not as a visiting player but in his own right for Real Madrid.

For the return leg Ferguson, who had already dropped Beckham from League matches, started him on the bench. When he told Beckham of his plans on the afternoon of the match the player shook his head and walked away. Ferguson called after him, not in rage but quietly. 'David. Come back here. Don't walk away from me.' But Beckham kept walking, as he put it in *My Side*, 'As if there was anything that needed to be said.'

Beckham says, 'For the first time in my life I wondered if playing somewhere else might be better than playing here.' He rang his agent Tony Stephens, who expressed surprise he had been dropped.

Ferguson started with his 'carthorse', Veron. Beckham came on with half an hour to go and United 3–2 down on the night, 6–3 on aggregate. Beckham scored with a free kick to make it 3–3, then scored another to make it 4–3 on the night. But he missed with a second free kick and Madrid won 6–5 on aggregate. During the match, Madrid players had run alongside him asking to swap shirts at full time and a grinning Roberto Carlos had said, 'Are you coming to play for us?'

After the match Beckham swapped shirts with the Madrid players and lingered to return the applause of the crowd. The gesture was closely scrutinised. To many people it meant Beckham was signalling his intention of joining Madrid and thanking the crowd as a final farewell gesture. Beckham insists that was not the case, the gesture was meant to say the exact opposite. Having received no applause when he came on, but a tremendous ovation at the end of the match, he was indicating his commitment and loyalty to the club. He says that it was the manager's actions before and during the match that convinced him Ferguson did not want him at the club any longer.

After Beckham got home, he sat down to watch the match again and closely studied Ferguson's reactions. When Beckham missed the goal that would have given him a hat-trick and made it 6–6 on aggregate, 'His face in the seconds after I'd missed that second free kick made me feel like a door had just been slammed in my face.' Beckham had grown up and Ferguson 'didn't seem to like what I had become'. Less than two months later Beckham was a Madrid player.

It must be said that this is Beckham's version of the story. The chapter of his autobiography in which his version is presented is entitled 'United Born and Bred', the previous chapter 'About Loyalty'. This is Beckham trying to argue that he did not want to leave United and was forced to do so because Ferguson and the club wanted him to go. Virginia Blackburn, clearly in the Beckham camp, would even write a book on the transfer. She called it *The Great Betrayal*, a title that requires no elaboration on its viewpoint.

But Beckham's sale was not quite that simple. There is a Manchester United version of it, in which Barcelona also became involved. This version, as told to me by an insider, is as follows: 'David Beckham was sold because he was not going to sign a new contract. And if he was not going to sign a new contract we either sold him or watched him go on a free transfer. We knew his advisers had been making discreet inquiries on the Continent about the interest in David Beckham at some point in the next two years. We knew his advisers had a plan for him where he would play on the Continent for part of his career.' That was entirely understandable as part of a career plan.

'His previous contract had taken the best part of eighteen months to negotiate. So we were not going to go through eighteen months of fannying about only to find he was six months away from a free transfer. It would have been absolutely negligent to allow it go on. We would have been roasted alive by everyone including the fans. We talked to him about a new contract. It was obvious from all the mood music, all the word on the street from his advisers that they were not going to sign a new contract. There was an actual offer on the table which was not picked up.' Beckham's contract was until the summer of 2005. Under Bosman rules, if he had not agreed a new deal by January 2005 he could have negotiated with any other club in Europe without that club having to pay United a fee.

The insider continues: 'There are only three or four big Italian or Spanish clubs as possible buyers. There was an interest from Madrid but we did not want it to be a single deal. We did not want to happen to us what had happened to Ronaldo and Inter when Ronaldo moved to Madrid, where there was no one else in the market. So we encouraged Barcelona's interest to the extent they made a conditional offer that enabled us to do a better deal with Madrid. We got £25 million which, looking back, was a very good price for a player. We had him for fourteen years, from a fourteen-year-old to twenty-eight or twenty-nine. It was just the right thing for him to move on. At the same time he had issues with Alex and Alex had issues with him. Manchester United operated as a ruthlessly run business. At such times it is not about personality, it is about what is right for the club.'

The key player in all this for United was Peter Kenyon. Looking back at the whole Beckham affair he told me that as far as relations between Ferguson and Beckham were concerned 'The tension had been building for some time.'

Because of Posh?

'Yes, I think team performance, not being happy with the progression of the team. This was also the time that Roy [Keane] preached one of his sermons about how everybody is more interested now in Rolex than we are in winning and not proud of the competitive urge. Typical Roy geeing things up. Then there was Alex's growing sense of frustration of David spending more time on outside of football activities. And then the whole boot incident got blown up out of all proportion and was played up by David in terms of being a major disaster.'

As far as Ferguson's role in the transfer and whether he pushed for it, Kenyon says: 'No, it was a question, again, of what we did throughout the seasons with these things. As you come to the end of a season you're more and more discussing the future. He and I would discuss our team targets, and in the context of that he said "If we got the right money I would let him go." I think he genuinely felt that we had seen the best of him as a player. The external activities were affecting issues and therefore if we got the right offer we should let him go.'

But Madrid's first offer was derisory. Kenyon knew he had to create a market to make Madrid believe it had a rival, and here Barcelona came in very handy. A lawyer called Joan Laporta had long planned to overthrow the regime of Josep Lluis Nunez, the ruler of Barcelona. He had formed l'Elefant Blau (Blue Elephant), and back in 1999 this organisation had been in touch with Andy Walsh as Walsh orchestrated the protests against the Sky takeover. In *Not for Sale*, the book Walsh co-authored with Adam Brown about their fight against the Sky bid, a few pages were devoted to Laporta and his group and there was even a photograph of Walsh and his colleagues with Laporta. The Laporta story had developed since then. His five-year campaign to remove Nunez and his cohorts was reaching its climax. Now, in the summer of 2003, he was standing to become Barcelona's president and he saw Beckham as a sure election winner. At the end of May, a few days before the launch of his two-week campaign, he contacted Kenyon. Kenyon says: 'To be honest, we'd created a market for Beckham by talking to Barcelona on the back of the Laporta election. Because Madrid was offering 15 million euros and Laporta required a major name, I did a pre-election deal that got the money up to over 25 million. Then Madrid had to come in. Despite, at the end of the day, the player saying I don't want to go to Barcelona, at least we had created a market.'

Madrid had been watching what Barcelona and United got up to with great interest. Shimon Cohen was a prominent City PR man with long-established interests in football who had acted for many in the game – originally a Cardiff City fan, he now went to Arsenal. Not long after news began to emerge that Beckham was bound for Barcelona, he took a call at his London offices: 'About May I got a phone call from a dear friend of mine, Jose Angel Sanchez. Jose had been managing director of Sega, the Japanese games company, in Spain. He left to become marketing director of Real Madrid. He said, "I need to see you in Madrid tomorrow."'

Cohen went. Arriving at Barracas airport at Madrid, he was taken by car to an old Spanish restaurant. There in the corner sat Jose. 'We chatted for a while. Then he said, "We have signed David Beckham."

'I said, "No, you have not. Barcelona have got him."

'"Just ignore everything you read in the paper. We got him."'

It was made clear to Cohen that Madrid did not get involved in bargaining or competition with other clubs. Certainly not Spanish clubs, and especially not Barcelona. 'We will announce the signing of David Beckham when we are ready to announce,' he was told.

'When will you be ready?' he asked.

'The first thing that has to happen is the British media have to start saying what a great tragedy it is that Beckham is leaving Manchester United. Where can the England captain go to play football after Manchester United? There can be only one club in the world – Real Madrid. When the British media start saying that then we will announce we have got him.'

Madrid, says Cohen, saw this as the most amazing opportunity. Why should they go to war with English football fans, stealing the England captain? Spanish football was on British television, a lot of British football fans had their favourite Spanish team. Everybody who owned a no. 7 red shirt could also own a no. 23 white shirt. But it was never going to happen if it was felt that the rich Spaniards had turned up and stolen the England captain. 'It had to be the other way round. It had to be the guy's career at Manchester United was over. Where do you want him to go? There is only one club he could go to, the greatest club in the world.'

The lunch finished with a fat cigar, a fee for Cohen's services having been quickly agreed, and he returned to London to set the Madrid plan in motion. He brought not only his PR skills into the campaign but also his experience of working in football. His clients had included Rupert Lowe's Southampton, Sampdoria, Deportivo La Coruña, St Etienne and ENIC. He had done project work for Arsenal and Newcastle United and run David Sheepshanks' campaign to be chairman of the FA. 'I had to start getting the fans to sing along the lines Madrid wanted. We had to start working on the fans, changing their minds. You go into fans' websites. Where would an Englishman want to see the England captain playing? However patriotic you might be, Leeds, West Ham or even Arsenal did not have the same international magic as Manchester United. We fed this to people. With some direction it began to take a life of its own.'

Then there were conversations with the press. 'Beckham is leaving, so where do you want him to go? I didn't have to tell people where I thought he should go because people immediately realised where he should be going. In all my years I have never not told the truth. But I wouldn't have said I was acting for Madrid. The conversations would have started on other subjects. I would have conversations with sports writers and put forward this view. The whole thing lasted only a few weeks. Quite soon I told my client I had to make it clear who I was acting for because it was beginning to leak out. I knew too much.' But by now everybody was talking about Beckham going to Real Madrid.

Only one thing spoiled this brilliantly orchestrated campaign. A secret meeting between Kenyon and Jose Angel Sanchez in Sardinia leaked out. Cohen says: 'Somebody from the *Sun* was following Kenyon and took a picture of the four people who were at that moment getting into the car. They saw the flash or the lens. I got a phone call from my client saying they had a problem, there was going to be a picture in the *Sun*. That is when I had to put my head above the parapet and call Stuart Higgins [the former *Sun* editor, now in PR], who I had been told was acting for Manchester United on the deal.' Cohen told Higgins an explanation had to be found for the meeting. 'We agreed the marketing director of Madrid was meeting with the chief executive of Manchester United to discuss matters relating to the Champions League and the possibility of joint ventures regarding the marketing programme. Everybody who got that line knew they weren't going to get anything else.'

Higgins' involvement in the deal shows how many strands were involved in this transfer. His client was SFX, the company Tony Stephens worked for, but with Stephens closely involved in arranging the Madrid deal Higgins was also involved in helping out Manchester United. Cohen got the impression he was working for United when the reality was he was working for Beckham's agent. The Cohen–Higgins spin kept the deal hidden for a few more days but in reality, as Cohen says, the Sardinian meeting was to finalise Beckham's transfer to Madrid. 'There were concerns about his own private sponsorship deals with other products like Vodafone and Siemens [shirt sponsors of United and Real Madrid respectively]. They had to be squared off, all of those issues had to be talked about. Essentially the deal had been done.'

So did Kenyon get Barcelona involved in order to make Madrid pay more? Cohen says: 'Madrid does not care. They don't chase people down. The price was the price. The Madrid people will tell you that when it became apparent to them that David Beckham was available to them there was a price, there was not a haggle. That is how Madrid operate.'

But although the fine points of the deal had been sorted out in the Sardinian harbour, it could not be announced immediately, for at that time the elections in Barcelona had not taken place and Madrid wanted to score a political victory over their deadly rival. Cohen says: 'There was no way Madrid was going to announce the signing of David Beckham until Laporta had been elected. He would not have been elected had the truth come out. He looked a complete Charlie afterwards because he got elected on that platform and then it proved not to be true. So although the deal was done, the announcement was held back until after the election.'

In his book Beckham describes his anger when he heard that United had done a conditional deal with Barcelona. The news had surprised Stephens and the anger seems genuine. However, he seemed to have spun the story of his relationship with Real Madrid when he describes how on Sunday 15 June he rang Kenyon about his future at Manchester United, followed by a call to Perez. Kenyon told him, 'Well, David, if I'm honest with you, it seems to us that the relationship between you and the manager might never be the same again.'

Beckham concluded the call by saying that given what Kenyon had said, particularly with regard to Ferguson's feelings, it was time for him to move. An hour later he rang Perez for the first time. In a throwaway line he says, 'Although Tony had met Senor Perez before it was the first time I'd ever spoken to him.' By the end of the call, as Beckham puts it, 'I knew what David Beckham the footballer needed to do next.'

On the following Wednesday morning Manchester United confirmed to the London Stock Exchange that they were selling Beckham to Real Madrid for a fee of £24.5 million. They had been hustled into the announcement because the news leaked on Tuesday night in Madrid and from early evening it dominated the 24-hour news channels in the UK. A statement from the club said:

> David Beckham has agreed personal terms with Real Madrid and expects to sign his new contract with the club on completion. The deal is expected to be completed in July, conditional upon approval by the boards of Manchester United and Real Madrid, and on the provision of satisfactory payment guarantees. The proceeds of the sale will be used to support Manchester United's business development, including continuing to maintain its playing success at the highest levels of the game.

Kenyon's public comment was: 'While we are sad to see David go after so many great years at Old Trafford, we believe this is a good deal for the club, and we now look forward to building on the success of last season's championship title. We wish David all the best in his new career in Spain and thank him for his fantastic contribution to the team's achievements in the last decade.'

United had got a good price but like all deals it had many ifs and buts. United would get £5.25 million on completion of Beckham's transfer, £12 million in instalments over the next four years and £7 million based on Real's performances in the Champions League (£875,000 every year they qualified, £875,000 every year they reached the quarter-finals).

Beckham in his statement said, 'I recognise that this is an amazing opportunity for me at this stage in my career.' The statement and everything he has said since has presented this as the classic story of the footballer who does not want to leave but decides to go, having been told by his club that the manager is no longer keen and another club is very interested. The truth, as we have seen, is more complicated.

The Irish story was also becoming complicated. In the month following the boot incident Cubic had been buying Manchester United shares. For Cubic this had nothing to do with Ferguson, this was business. Manchester United was underpriced. In the previous months the share price had dipped to 93p, having reached £4 two years earlier. Although it was now climbing again, the club's value of around £350 million was a third of its peak of £1 billion. United were also about to announce interim results which the City expected to be very good.

In any case the fallout with Ferguson affected only one half of Cubic. McManus was not involved, although he supported the stance taken by his partner.

Heavy trading in United shares had taken place on 6 March 2003 and Cubic became the biggest shareholder with 10.37 per cent, surpassing BSkyB's 9.9 per cent stake, having spent £14 million acquiring their new packet of shares. At this stage the public were not aware that Ferguson and the Irish had fallen out. Newspapers headlined the purchase in terms of 'Two friends of Ferguson are now the biggest single shareholders'. Paul Hince, a former Manchester City player who had never concealed his love for the blue side of Manchester, wrote in his weekly Wednesday column in the *Manchester Evening News* that it would be a good idea if the Irish took over Manchester United. Compared to the suits in the boardroom they would at least be people with sporting backgrounds, and what is more friends of Ferguson.

Hince was noted for his witty, funny columns but this one did not amuse United. The day it appeared Paddy Harverson rang him and decided to tell him the facts of business life. Hince, said Harverson, had been unfair to the board, he clearly did not understand share ownership or business practice. Harverson thought he was speaking off the record, but this was not clear to Hince who reported Harverson's comments in full:

'We do not believe the two Irish racehorse owners you mentioned in your column are preparing to launch a takeover bid for this club. Our feeling is that they view the shares they have accumulated to be a shrewd investment because the club is currently undervalued on the Stock Exchange. But, in light of the figures I have presented, I would ask our rank-and-file supporters this question: should a takeover bid materialise from Messrs McManus and Magnier, would you like your club to be under the control of two Irish racehorse owners who know absolutely nothing about running a football business or would you prefer the club to remain in the hands of a plc board with a track record in all fields which speaks for itself?'

The next day other papers picked up the story, reporting Harverson's comments in some detail – in particular his dismissal of Magnier and McManus. A report in *The Times* by Oliver Kay described Harverson's comments as coming in an 'open letter'. He noted that this was the first time Manchester United officials had spoken on the possibility of a Irish takeover, leaving 'little doubt about the United plc board's hostility towards the so-called "Coolmore Mafia", two friends of Sir Alex Ferguson who are now the biggest shareholders in the company'.

Harverson would regret that he had not been clearer that his comments were off the record. But what stuck in the throats of Magnier and McManus was being described as 'two Irish racehorse owners', ignoring their wide business interests. The fact that this was described as an 'open letter' from the head of communications at Manchester United meant only one thing to Magnier: the board knew of their quarrel with Ferguson and were on the side of their manager and against their biggest shareholder. Cuttings from *The Times* and other papers on Harverson's comments were carefully preserved in the growing Coolmore file on Manchester United.

In the weeks leading up to Cubic's purchase other investors too had been buying Manchester United shares. Kenyon recalls, 'at that stage, we went to pitch with John de Mol [the Dutchman who had created television's *Big Brother*] and he came on board. We actually targeted various investors and that included de Mol.' De Mol spent £8.6 million to buy 2.9 per cent and the Glazers also bought a similar amount, their first packet of Manchester United shares. But while these were very welcome shareholders, at the same time the United board had been scouring the share register to find out who was buying in the name of nominees and had issued a number of Companies Act section 212 notices, a device which allows companies to force investors who had bought through nominee companies to disclose their real identity.

Others with Irish connections were also buying United shares, and all of them would soon be seen as part of the Irish web round the club. Harry Dobson, a Scottish millionaire who had made his fortune in mining, bought 6.5 per cent, almost all of the last shares owned by Martin Edwards. This considerably puzzled the board, who could not make out how he fitted into the Irish scheme of things. But in many ways the most intriguing Irish investor was Dermot Desmond, a director of Celtic and its largest shareholder. A billionaire in his own right, he had masterminded Dublin's International Financial Services Centre. In a sense he was the third member of the Irish troika that was often referred to as the Coolmore mafia. All this meant was that Magnier, McManus and Desmond were linked together as friends and occasionally as business partners, as in their investment in the Sandy Lane Hotel in Barbados. As regards Manchester United shares, Desmond's buying was completely separate and not part of anything that the City would consider a concert party – a group of shareholders whose shares might be held separately but who were secretly linked together. As owner of Celtic he could not hold too large a stake.

Also, unlike his two Irish friends, his interest in football was well known and his views on how the game should be run even more explicit. He made no secret of his desire to see Celtic and Rangers break away from the Scottish League and become part of the Premier League. He believed the European Commission should act against the Premier League's collective television selling rights, as he felt this curbed the power of the bigger clubs to earn money yet at the same time did not help spread the money to the smaller clubs.

Desmond had closely studied the ownership of football clubs and had followed United and its shares for many years. In November 2001, seeing that United's share price was low, he had commissioned Goldman Sachs International, the firm that employed Sir Alex Ferguson's son Mark, to carry out a study into converting Manchester United from a company owned by shareholders into a mutual trust. In the style of such merchant bank reports, United was not named; instead the name Mandolin was used, although it would not have taken long to work out the real identity of Mandolin. The 51-page document included details of recent share buying, listing names from United such as Kenyon, Gill, Gardner and Yea as well as Cubic. In October 2001 Gill and Kenyon had each bought £20,000 worth of shares, Gardner and Yea £10,000, each, while Cubic had bought £5.97 million worth. The document examined the debt required to buy out the existing shareholders in order to convert United into a trust. It envisaged having ten trustees each serving a three-year term, promising that Alex Ferguson, Bobby Charlton and 'other popular choices' would be considered. Nothing came of it, but it showed the thinking of at least one important member of the Irish clan.

Desmond had also developed a special relationship with Ferguson. When he was looking for a manager for Celtic he had asked Ferguson's opinion. Ferguson mentioned three names: David O'Leary, Alan Curbishley and Martin O'Neill. Approaches were made to O'Neill, but in vain. Desmond rang Ferguson and asked him whether he would speak to O'Neill. He did so and O'Neill agreed to come to Celtic. While the relationship between Ferguson and Magnier dissolved into bitter acrimony, Desmond maintained his friendship with Ferguson and remained an important link to Cubic. In the summer of 2003, when Ferguson was no longer welcome at Coolmore, Desmond could still be used to communicate with him.

Through the spring and summer of 2003 Magnier and Ferguson gave hints of the breakdown of their relationship. Shortly after the Beckham boot incident the *Daily Mail* reported that Ferguson's next horse was not to be trained at Coolmore but by Mick Channon, although the paper like everyone else did not know that the break had taken place and reported without comment that the Rock was 'now earning him around £16 million a year from stud fees'.

There were still moves being made to settle the dispute. Martin Hannan talks of two offers, one around May 2003 when Magnier offered four nominations a year, two each in Ireland and two in Australia where the Rock was due to go for covering mares. At 2003 prices this meant £240,000 a year. There was also a 'final' offer either the same month or in June, where Ferguson would have got £300,000 a year or £7 million if he took it all at once. But that too was rejected, although Magnier took comfort from the fact that Ferguson was now claiming not 50 per cent of the horse but only 20 per cent.

If this suggested that the Ferguson camp was playing a sort of poker game, that impression was bolstered for the Magnier camp when they heard rumours that Mark Ferguson had once said about the ownership of Rock of Gibraltar that they were on a 20-1 shot but those were the sort of odds the Fergusons loved.

Mark Ferguson was Sir Alex's eldest child, and a much-loved one. By the time Rock became an issue Mark was a great success in the City, having had well-paid jobs at Schroders then Goldman Sachs, and having been voted the Fund Manager of the Year in 1999. He could be expected to be a shrewd judge of such bets.

Magnier would also learn from Desmond, who would meet Mark many times to discuss the issue of the horse, that if the Fergusons could get even 5 per cent of what the Rock was worth that would be enough. Desmond formed the distinct impression that it was Mark, along with Jason who encouraged their father to demand the money. Jason was always the most enterprising of Alex's sons. When his father won his first trophy for Manchester United, the 1990 FA Cup, Jason got on the pitch and was chased by the stewards and the police before Ferguson intervened to tell them who he was. Now he was involved in the football business as an agent and had a very definite opinion on the Rock's worth.

The whole issue was now moving into the hands of lawyers. Ferguson appointed L. K. Shields, a Dublin firm, to act for him as the case would have to be brought in a Dublin court. Magnier instructed his own Dublin lawyer, William Fry, to defend his position.

By August 2003 newspapers for the first time began to report that Ferguson and Magnier were in dispute. It was 'a major fight', said the *Sunday Telegraph*. The *Daily Mail* reported Ferguson as being 'very disappointed at the behaviour of John Magnier and the Coolmore team', comments that rankled with Magnier, while the *News of the World* quoted a 'friend' of Ferguson (sometimes a device used in political journalism when politicians who do not want to be identified reveal their thoughts through 'friends' who often turn out to be themselves) as saying that 'he doesn't want to say anything at this stage as this is likely to be settled in court. The Magniers have offered him a one-off settlement of £10 million if he walks away. But compared to Rock of Gibraltar's stud earnings potential it's a pittance. All Sir Alex wants is a fair deal. He is half owner of the horse and should at least get half the stud fees.'

The media were nearly unanimous in expressing sympathy with Ferguson. After all, he had been identified as the half owner, the horse wore his colours, he had paid for it. So why should he not have breeding rights? Magnier was presented as the man trying to go back on a deal. Only later did it emerge that Ferguson had seemingly not paid anything for his half share. The quarrel was over a gift and the vastly different recollections of a verbal agreement between two men who had once been friends.

Ferguson had drawn first blood in the PR battle, but although Magnier never broke cover, Coolmore did get its PR act together, hiring a London consultant to help their Dublin operation. The battle, as the *Daily Telegraph*'s then racing correspondent Richard Evans says, 'got very vicious. The two men should have sat down after the 2,000 Guineas but they didn't and it became the most vicious I have seen in racing.'

And the more vicious it became, the more United shares Cubic bought. In July 2003 Cubic paid a further £5 million to increase their holding to 11.4 per cent. The board seemed to watch these developments as if the quarrel between Magnier and Ferguson did not concern them. This was clearly when the board should have intervened. Had Roland Smith still been in charge they might. But Smith was long gone.

And within a month so was Kenyon, the one member of the board Irwin and Power had liked. Here, as with Beckham, the night of the match against Real Madrid was to prove crucial. That night, when many felt Beckham was bidding goodbye to United and Beckham felt Ferguson had indicated he had no place at Old Trafford, quite unnoticed there slipped into Old Trafford the man who would change the face of English football in a way no one has done before. The visitor was a Russian called Roman Abramovich. He had been brought to the match by his friend Pini Zahavi and was introduced to Peter Kenyon. Nobody knew him, his name meant nothing and there was no indication of how wealthy he was. But he was looking to buy a football club. Soon he approached Tottenham and when that did not work out he settled on Chelsea.

Kenyon had given no thought to leaving United. But in July, he received an offer which initially shocked him. As he told me, 'the day that Roman bought Chelsea I was approached at a meeting at Les Ambassadeurs. He had just bought the club and we had a general chat about football. It was extremely polite, not specific: where is football going, what's happening in football, various issues. The day after that I got a call saying: would you like to come and work for me?' Busy with transfer deals at the end of the season, he told Abramovich he would give it some thought but could not enter into any negotiations until the year end, after the transfers were completed.

Among those transfers were Chelsea's purchase of Veron from United and United's purchase of Cristiano Ronaldo. The call for this deal came at half-time in the final match of the US tour and Kenyon had to hurry to Lisbon to make sure Ronaldo was not missed as had been Ronaldinho, who was all set to come from Paris St. Germain when he was allowed to slip through United's fingers, eventually moving to Barcelona instead. United had wanted Ronaldinho for £10 million, they ended up paying £12 million for Ronaldo. 'We contacted each other just before the start of the season. We had another couple of chats, dinner, meetings and we finalised the deal at his house.'

Back in 1998 when I was first writing about Manchester United at length, Kenyon, born and bred in Manchester, growing up to support the club, explained his move from Umbro in these terms: 'Manchester United was the only football club I would work for. Not from a fan's perspective, but from a business and commercial opportunity, an immense heritage in the football club and a huge international opportunity.'

But now Abramovich was the future and held out such an alluring prospect that Kenyon could not refuse. On 31 August Kenyon watched Manchester United play Southampton. The following Friday, 5 September, he rang Roy Gardner and asked if he could come and see him. 'He said "What subject matter?" I said "I just need to see you. I am in London." But we could not get together on Friday.' They arranged to meet early on Monday. 'I went to see him on Monday and I said, "There's no easy way of saying this, I have been offered another position and I'm going to take it." He looked really shocked.'

Gardner said, 'Can I ask you who it is?'

Kenyon replied, 'It's Chelsea.'

Gardner responded, 'We don't want you go.'

Kenyon said, 'I've given it a lot of thought.'

Gardner asked, 'Is there anything we can do?'

Kenyon answered, 'It's a career move, because I actually want to do this type of job. I've had a great time but you can't match the package.'

As Kenyon explains, Gardner 'was upset in terms of it coming as a shock, one of surprise. But he was extremely professional and we got on well. We had a chat about the next step, how it would be managed. Part of the discussion we had was a discussion about my successor. I said "At the end of the day you are going to have to give Gill a shot at it. He is ambitious. So you have to go down that route. He is different to me. But that will be my advice." Maurice was in London. I'd arranged to see him later on and I met up with him. At that point nobody else knew.'

United held a impromptu board meeting that Monday afternoon where they quickly moved to install Gill. Kenyon had hoped that would be the end of the matter, but soon legal complications arose. Kenyon's contract specified a year's notice and United were determined to hold him to that. They insisted he could not join Chelsea until the following September and put him on gardening leave. He was not allowed to go back to his office or anywhere near Old Trafford although he was paid, kept his company car and even his mobile phone. After more than a month, fairly late one evening, when everyone else had left Old Trafford, Kenyon was eventually allowed back into his office to clear out his effects. When he moved to Chelsea he took with him Pauline, his secretary, who had worked for both Louis and Martin Edwards. 'We then negotiated, through lawyers, through the Premier League. They went to the Premier

League and Bruce [Buck, chairman of Chelsea] led the negotiations in this case.'

The situation was unprecedented in English football. Poaching players was against the rules but such a situation had never before arisen with other employees, although the rule had been brought in when Stoke City hired a groundsman from Port Vale. But now the stakes were much higher; a chief executive had been poached from the world's richest club by football's richest man, engaged in building his own football empire. For months the talks dragged on. In the end United relented and Kenyon's employment came to an end on 31 January 2004. He had already received £61,000 until 9 September; for the period of his gardening leave he was paid £173,876, and a further £9,000 was paid as the company's contribution to the money purchase scheme run by the club. But as the accounts coyly noted, 'emoluments and pension contributions paid in respect of Peter Kenyon covering the period 9 September 2003 to 31 January 2004 have been fully offset by monies received by third parties'. They were more than offset; compensation was said to amount to £1 million and Kenyon was prevented from taking over at Chelsea until the January transfer window of 2004 had closed.

Kenyon himself benefited hugely in personal terms. The year to July 2003 had seen him earn a basic salary of £385,000 which with bonuses took him to £710,000, his salary being higher than that of most football chief executives but not in a league of its own. Moving to Chelsea brought him well over £1 million. And for 2005, the last year figures are available, Kenyon earned £2.67 million, over £1.5 million more than his closest challenger Gill, although this included £2.4 million described as compensation for leaving Manchester United.

Gill's remuneration nearly doubled in moving from No. 2 to the job he had always coveted, his salary increasing from £487,000 in 2002 to £909,000 in 2004. In 2005, which as a result of the Glazer takeover was a eleven-month period for United as their year end was changed to 30 June, Gill finally entered the millionaires' club, earning a total of £1,009,000.

The man most upset by Kenyon's departure was Martin Edwards, who felt Kenyon had let him down. From that moment Edwards let his friends know that appointing Kenyon as his successor had been his biggest mistake, the main charge against him being that he was far too soft with Ferguson and had given in to every player demand for more money. The man, who had tried to keep Ferguson on a tight leash, and who had brought Kenyon to Manchester United as his successor, was now his biggest critic.

Six weeks after Kenyon's departure it was announced that Paddy Harverson was leaving to be press spokesman for Prince Charles. It was suggested both men had left because they could not stand the strain of the increasingly bitter fight between Ferguson and Magnier. The speculation was well wide of the mark. Both men left for jobs they could not possibly turn down.

Kenyon dismisses any idea that the Irish had started investing to put Ferguson in power. He had always got on with the Irish and in particular with Irvin and Power. 'I have to say, my dealings with all the connections, the people who ran their operations, were always fantastic. We used to see them after the results announcements. They gave the impression of having the most rigorous understanding of the business. I think they were very good investors for Manchester United in a plc environment. I found the Irish unbelievably supportive because we were getting great investment returns for them. We were doing what we said we would do as a business.'

In many ways the most immediate effect of Kenyon's departure was on the Premier League's television deal. At his last Premier League meeting as Manchester United's representative, Kenyon had tabled an audacious plan for United to become a television company and screen Premier League matches. 'We'd been evaluating the whole television deal. I had done a lot of work on it. In fact, we'd got to the stage where Manchester United was bidding for one of the packages, the Sky package Premium Plus. One full game and a whole raft of others where you have twelve minutes each of a match. We put a bid in.' Kenyon had spoken about it to Richard Scudamore, chief executive of the Premier League. 'Richard,' he said, 'this is not about breaking away but about paying for more content in a positive manner. It works for Manchester United and it could work for other clubs.' Scudamore, says Kenyon, was supportive, seeing such a bid as neither disruptive nor breaking away from the League's collective selling. 'We got through the first round. We even spoke to Sky about it. It was received well by the rest of the clubs, received well by the Premier League. As soon as I left that all collapsed.'

Gill had barely got the job he always wanted when Manchester United were faced with a crisis that pitched the club against the Football Association and indeed the whole country. For a time it seemed United might even be responsible, albeit indirectly, for a strike by the England players.

Three weeks after Gill had taken over, on 23 September, two drug inspectors from UK Sport, the government quango that administers anti-drug policy, arrived at the Carrington training ground to carry out tests. They selected four United players out of a hat, Nicky Butt, Ryan Giggs, John O'Shea and Rio Ferdinand. They were all told by Mike Stone, the club doctor that after training they must give a urine sample. The other three did but Ferdinand left without doing so. Efforts were made to contact him but they failed. Ferdinand went to Harvey Nichols in Manchester city centre and then had lunch with Eyal Berkovic, an old West Ham colleague then at Manchester City. When Ferdinand realised he had missed the drug test he offered to return but it was too late; the drug inspectors had left. Two days later he did a drugs test and passed, which he assumed settled the issue.

But under sport's anti-doping rules, missing a drug test is no different from failing a drug test and attracts the same punishment, a two-year ban. However, England were due to play Turkey in the final qualifying match for Euro 2004 on 11 October, a match they had at least to draw. Ferdinand was a certain choice and the FA was placed in a terrible dilemma.

One FA insider who was intimately involved in the discussions recalls: 'We would have been informed by UK Sport within a pretty quick period of time. That would have gone through to the compliance division of the FA, which is entirely separate from the England team and its administration. Initially this was not seen as a major thing. This was Manchester United and their high-profile player. It was still expected at that time there was to be a reasonable explanation. Manchester United or Rio would come forward and say yes, we did miss it but these are the reasons. A footballer of that profile in a club of such repute just does not do things like that.'

This insider talked off the record to other clubs to find out how they managed drug tests. 'One well-known club [Arsenal] said, what we do is man mark the players concerned. One member of the medical team will follow, let us say, Bergkamp if he has been selected for a drug test. Bergkamp would come off the field. They would say "You have been selected for a drug test. Have a shower, then come to the medical room where the test will be done and then you are free to go." Up to that point the medical staff assigned to him would stay with him. They would go with him to the changing room, to the shower, back to the changing room to get dressed and then from the changing room to the medical room. There he would give the sample and then away.' But Manchester United did not operate in that way.

There was no suggestion that Ferdinand had taken anything and missed the test deliberately but the fact remained that he had missed it. 'We had to tread a very thin line. The practice in other sports is that if you miss a drugs test you face a two-year ban immediately. And what had happened up to that point was a unique case in football. From the moment the test was deemed missed, it was considered not appropriate for him to be selected for the England squad.'

But the decision met with fierce resistance from United and total bemusement from Sven-Göran Eriksson when told he could not select Ferdinand for the match. He responded, 'You are not saying he has taken drugs?'

'No.'

'You are not saying he takes drugs regularly?'

'No.'

'He has taken drugs at all?'

'No, not at all.'

The only issue was that Ferdinand had failed to take a dope test. Eriksson could not understand why that should be a hanging offence. For days he protested, arguing that it was his job to pick the strongest possible team for such a crucial match. Mark Palios, who had recently taken over as chief executive of the FA, maintained that he had to uphold standards and the integrity of the game.

Eriksson in the end very unhappily accepted that he must follow what his bosses were saying. But United were incandescent with rage and fought to the last minute to overturn the decision. A bizarre teatime meeting in a small Worcestershire village took place on the Sunday afternoon before the match at the home of David Davies, the FA's international director and the man who liaised with Eriksson. While the top brass of the FA met the top brass of United in Davies's drawing room, Ferdinand sat in the kitchen with Davies's wife Susan drinking tea and eating Battenberg cakes which Susan Davies had hurriedly rustled up for this most impromptu meeting. For Davies the Ferdinand saga was the last straw before a match he had been dreading for almost eighteen months.

Davies recalls how, because of the history of problems between the two countries, they had fought to prevent England having to play their crucial last game in the Euro 2004 qualification campaign against Turkey in Istanbul. 'Tord Grip [Eriksson's assistant] and I had attended a fixtures meeting deciding the matches in a group which included Turkey, Macedonia, Finland and Liechtenstein. We never wanted the last game to be either England–Turkey or Turkey–England. It was obvious that Turkey was the strongest of the opponents. We didn't want the climactic game to have that edge to it if we could possibly avoid it. We sat in Istanbul for five hours in the fixtures meeting trying to arrange a schedule of fixtures and, in the end, we had to abandon it. Then we had the drawing of lots, and, lo and behold, the one thing we didn't want came up – Turkey. It's Sod's Law, and that has happened to us too often.

'So we had to go to Turkey. My first memory is hearing ten or eleven days before that there had been a problem and that a player had missed a test. Even I hadn't experienced that one before. I didn't know the name at that stage but ultimately I was called in and told.' He and Palios immediately realised the implications if the story emerged when the match was about to start. 'It was clear pretty quickly that we couldn't run the risk of having this coming out when we were trying to win a crucial qualifying match.' But on the other hand, England would have to do without one of their star players. 'A number of us had a huge affection for Rio and had done since he first came into the ranks. He's a good bloke, Rio. All I knew was that he failed to take a test at that particular stage, we didn't know why.'

For days beforehand there had been phone calls galore. There was even some talk that Ferdinand could feign an injury, although this was never seriously pursued. Eventually a meeting was organised at Davies' home, selected because it was in the centre of the country. Davies recalls:

The meeting was fixed for the Sunday afternoon but there was another complication that even I hadn't thought about. This was that my road was blocked at one end. So Susan had to go out and meet everybody, in a lay-by off the M42. Susan then had to lead them cross country to come back down the other end of my road and eventually to our house,

Thus it was that on that Sunday September afternoon the leaders of Manchester United and the Football Association sat round the dining-room table of the Davies household. 'To begin with we had a conversation – just Maurice, David Gill, Nick Coward, (then the in-house legal expert at the FA) and myself.' Ferdinand was not involved at that point. 'Susan and he may have gone for a walk in the garden and then they sat in the kitchen. They would have had some tea and cakes.'

It was decided that Davies should tell Ferdinand he could not be selected. Manchester United's view was that by leaving Ferdinand out the FA were pronouncing him guilty. 'But we weren't doing anything other than say that we can't have this, we can't put the whole team expedition, if you want to use that expression, at risk. There was going to be a huge circus around the Istanbul game. It had to be dealt with at home before the match. Remember, there was a lot of talk about not taking any supporters to Istanbul because of what had happened before. There was already enough controversy around that game without adding another level of controversy. I think there was some talk of trying to bring the hearing on Rio forward and involving Gordon [Taylor, chief executive of the PFA]. Our argument was very clearly that whatever we did, however we did it, in the next few days this was going to come to a head. And we couldn't have that jeopardising the match.'

After half an hour of discussions Ferdinand came in. Davies says: 'I think he knew by that stage that it was pretty serious. I think he came in hoping that it wasn't as serious as he thought, but I had to tell him. That was when he first realised the mess he was dealing with. He was upset.'

Ferdinand never told Davies why he missed the test. 'I still don't know the truth. But it was one of the most difficult things I ever had to be involved in.' In his autobiography *Rio My Story*, Ferdinand describes how on getting to the Davies house he was upset not to find Mark Palios, the FA chief executive, and tried to contact him at least ten times but failed. Then when Davies told him he would not be selected for Turkey Ferdinand lost his cool and started shouting as he protested his innocence, 'I've not been found guilty of anything. I've not taken drugs and now you're going to make it seem like I have. I've been forgetful and that's it.' He then suggested the FA say he was injured rather than reveal he had missed a drug test which the FA rejected. It is clear from his memoirs, ghostwritten almost three years later, that Ferdinand just cannot understand that missing a drug test is an offence on a par with failing one and the FA had no option in the course of action they followed.

But if Ferdinand accepted the situation, United were not prepared to give up. Sometime on Sunday David Gill rang Paul Barber, head of communications of the FA. Barber was in his office at Soho Square.

Gill said to Barber, 'Look Paul, I have got Alex here and he wants to speak to you.'

'Fine.'

Ferguson took the phone and said, 'Paul, this is a fucking disgrace. You are killing the boy's reputation. You don't know what you are doing.'

'Alex, there is one issue here and one issue alone. That is Rio Ferdinand was selected for a random drug test and for whatever reason – and I don't know the reason – he missed it. Because of that we cannot have a player called up for the England team having recently missed a drug test for no apparent reason. That is unacceptable and the chief executive, backed by the international committee, has taken that decision. That is all there is to it. So tomorrow we will be announcing the squad minus Rio Ferdinand.'

Ferguson's reaction was to give Barber the sort of hair-dryer treatment he meted out to players who upset him. He screamed down the telephone at what he felt was a monstrous decision although he also kept saying, 'Paul, this is not personal. It is not your decision alone, but you are the representative of the FA.'

At the end Ferguson did switch off the hair dryer and told Barber again, 'Paul, let me reiterate, this is not personal. I am sure we will speak when you come to Old Trafford, but you must understand what this will do to the boy's reputation.'

'Alex,' said Barber, 'this is not about killing Rio's reputation. I understand this is going to look bad. But he has admitted to us he missed the test. You must ask him why. Eventually the investigation will ask him why. At this point in time he has admitted missing it. It is a massive problem for us. And we can't select him for the England team.'

Gill then took the phone back and thanked Barber for trying to explain matters to Ferguson. 'You can see we are not happy. We think you are doing this the wrong way round. This is not right. He is innocent till proven guilty. You are hanging him out to dry.'

'David, the last thing we are going to do is hang Rio out to dry. You are not going to hear from us tomorrow that he has done anything other than missed the test. That is all there is to it.'

The announcement of the team, already delayed by a day, was again delayed, leading to wild speculation in the newspapers. However, on Monday evening the facts began to emerge. On Tuesday morning, as Palios and Barber drove down to St Albans where the squad was assembling, Gill made one last attempt to dissuade the FA from announcing the squad without Ferdinand. He spoke to the pair on the car phone but it did not work.

However, nor could the FA convince United that by not selecting Ferdinand they were not prejudicing his case, that what they were doing was the routine procedure for a missed drug test. The United players in the England squad refused to accept that and threatened a strike, which was averted after long negotiations just before England flew to Turkey.

During the whole affair United formed the view that the FA were gunning for them. They contrasted how Ferdinand's missed drug test had been dealt with compared to the identical case of a Manchester City player, Christian Negouai. When brought before an FA disciplinary panel Negouai faced a similar charge and escaped with a £2,000 fine. What is more, his name was kept secret and did not emerge until the Ferdinand story broke. To United this seemed an example of double standards.

Coincidentally Ferdinand's lawyers, Watkins's firm James Chapman & Co., had also represented Negouai. That fact, and the fact that the FA panels in both cases were headed by the same man, Barry Bright, the Football Association councillor from Kent, emphasised how small and incestuous the world of football administration can be. But the Negouai case gave Ferdinand and his team from James Chapman a sense of deep grievance. They developed a siege mentality which had echoes of the attitude displayed by Millwall fans: the world's against us but we don't care. This drove United on as through the winter months they fought hard not to have a ban imposed on Ferdinand.

A week before Christmas at Bolton's Reebok Stadium came the final blow. Most observers had anticipated that, if he was punished at all, Ferdinand would get a three-month ban. Instead, after a two-day FA hearing that had lasted the best part of eighteen hours, with the verdict delivered at 8 p.m., an independent commission banned him for eight months from 12 January 2004 after finding him guilty of misconduct. This ruled him out of England's Euro 2004 campaign as well as the run-in to United's season: at least seventeen League matches, along with Champions League and FA Cup games. He would not return until the first month of the 2004 season. Ferdinand was also fined £50,000 and ordered to pay the costs of the hearing, which were estimated at around £100,000. Along with his legal costs, this left him poorer by £250,000 – although that was perhaps the least of his worries.

The verdict from the three-man disciplinary panel shook many in the world of football. It was denounced by Maurice Watkins, who said an appeal was inevitable. Ferdinand, standing next to Watkins, said nothing but looked shell-shocked.

The decision was all the more stunning because throughout the hearing United had exuded the air of a team who could not possibly lose. Nicky Butt,

Ferdinand's team-mate, Eyal Berkovic and Ferguson himself gave evidence. Although privately United's explanation for Ferdinand's failure to provide a urine sample was that he forgot, at the hearing they went in hard on the FA and tried to make much of their imprecise drug-testing regulations.

The first day of the hearing had been taken up by the FA's case. The second day, until the verdict, was United's day. In the morning Ferguson had breezed in and out of the Reebok Stadium, saying nothing to the waiting press but looking extremely pleased with himself. He had earlier told the media, at his regular Friday press conference, that Ferdinand was definitely in the team to play Tottenham the next day. It seemed like a gesture of defiance.

In the afternoon came the main defence, presented by Ferdinand's QC, Ronald Thwaites. He is believed to have made much of the fact that at no stage had there been any direct contact between the testers and Ferdinand. On the day of the test all communication with Ferdinand had been carried out by Mike Stone, then the United doctor. Under the FA's rules, clubs are allowed to decide the precise procedure for unannounced tests. In the case of United, Stone, who gave evidence, had always been the contact man and Thwaites is said to have argued that such opaque procedures meant Ferdinand could not be blamed.

The plea dismally failed to impress the tribunal. The councillors reached their verdict at about 6 p.m. Then they heard pleas of mitigation, which clearly did not sway them.

The verdict raised yet more controversy. Dick Pound, chairman of the World Anti-Doping Agency, was not happy, calling for the ban to start immediately: 'The FA are sending out a bad message by allowing him to carry on playing. He has done very well with what he has got. He should be careful about his appeal as his sentence could be increased.' However, Sepp Blatter, the FIFA president, who had criticised the FA and United for their handling of the issue, had more reason to be pleased. Before the verdict was delivered Ferguson had attacked Blatter, saying: 'It's very unfortunate that a man in his position would want to interfere and I don't think there is anyone happy in England with what he has been saying.'

Ferguson was soon embroiled in further controversy on this issue, although this was partly due to the way the press reported his comments. The Sunday papers reported him as saying that he had suggested Ferdinand might take the matter to the High Court. That was not quite how it happened. Ferguson's comments were made on the Friday morning at his normal pre-match press conference, during which he responded to a series of hypothetical questions put to him by Sunday newspaper journalists. This was long before the verdict was delivered and before Ferguson had even given evidence at the hearing. But his remarks were reported in the Sundays as if he had made them in response to the judgment.

United had to spend some time making it clear that Ferdinand was extremely unlikely to take his case to the High Court if he failed to reduce his suspension through the appeals process. Should an appeal to the FA fail, Ferdinand's team would consider whether to take the matter to the Court of Arbitration for Sport in Lausanne. But the matter would be unlikely to go beyond that because of the perceived risks of pursuing what could become a drawn-out affair. Watkins, a well-respected figure in sports law circles – at that moment he was actually representing the FA in another case – would not have wanted to be in a position of challenging the norms of the sport, which require issues to be settled within established sports tribunals and not the general courts.

Sources close to Ferdinand were also keen to emphasise that Ferguson, Manchester United and Gordon Taylor, the chief executive of the Professional Footballers' Association, who had at various stages been presented in the press as driving the issue, did not speak for the player. While the support they had given Ferdinand was appreciated, the legal case was the sole responsibility of Ferdinand's lawyers. That explained why the short statement issued by Watkins after the judgment thanked United and the PFA; it was a way of distancing the player from the two.

The ban clearly played a huge part in Manchester United's season. Having been top of the League since early December and going into January, they slipped away and finally finished third. But the whole episode also showed how the country's biggest club was not only on the wrong side of the country's ruling football body but also most of the country and the media. On the Ferdinand issue the media supported the FA, a rare display of solidarity for the often beleaguered supreme body of English football, and were firmly against the country's biggest club.

As one FA insider explains, Manchester United and its players just did not get it: 'It was a classic bit of misinformation. I do not know who was advising the Manchester United players, Neville, Butt, Scholes. They didn't agree with our decision to drop Rio. They knew he had missed the test. We told them what the situation was. They said "yeah, but you are hanging him out dry. He is innocent till proven guilty." We said "no, no, all we are saying he is guilty of is missing the test, which is an offence in itself." It was one of the great mis-communications of all time. Whoever was advising them, whether it was Gordon, whether it was Alex or whether it was his agent, I do not know. A missed test is an offence as great as a negative test.'

United had been on the wrong side not only of the FA and much of the nation on the Ferdinand issue but also of their biggest shareholders, Cubic. The Irish had carefully followed what had happened to Ferdinand and, as they would later put it in a letter to Roy Gardner, they did not like the way United had handled it. A whole paragraph of the letter would be devoted to the issue:

The Suspension of Mr Ferdinand

We share the general concern in relation to the current suspension of Mr Ferdinand and the problems that have arisen because of his failure to attend for a drugs test. Is this a breach of his contract? We are anxious to know what steps have been taken to ensure that this type of problem does not occur again. Are we to understand that the Board has authorised the continuation of his full salary (which we understand to be £70,000 per week) as if he is playing while he is, in fact, suspended as a result of a disciplinary action taken by the FA? Will he also be in receipt of any bonuses? If so please explain the reason for the payment of such bonuses and salary?

For the board, matters with the Irish were reaching crisis point. As with the Ferdinand affair and the FA, here too there was a vast gulf of miscommunication and misinformation, complicated by the fact that it involved their manager and their biggest shareholder. Within days of the Ferdinand verdict Gill was flying to Ireland to see if something could be done to repair the damage.

18

THE SEARCH FOR A WHITE KNIGHT

ON SUNDAY 14 September 2003 the *Observer* led its front page with a story headlined: 'Overseas billionaires in battle for Manchester United. Three in £600m bid for Britain's richest club'.

Sports stories do not normally lead the front page, unless recording a major English sporting triumph, and it was hardly a slow news day. But this one relegated both a story on the Iraq dossiers and how Sweden was swinging in favour of the euro following the stabbing of its foreign minister. Denis Campbell, the sports news correspondent, who had written the story and done a much larger analysis of Manchester United inside, was not exactly happy with editor Roger Alton's decision to lead the front with it; he felt the story was rather 'uncooked'. The three predators were not identified and he was surprised when Alton became so excited by the story; it was an indication of how football, and Manchester United in particular, sells.

The paper claimed the three predators, 'said to be at least as rich as Abramovich', were a Russian oligarch, a Middle Eastern billionaire and a European. It also reported speculation that the European could be John de Mol. His wealth and status was mentioned and a photograph of him was used to illustrate the story.

Campbell wrote:

> The trio have recently independently sought expert advice from City financiers about how much buying United would cost, which shareholders might be prepared to sell and how long it would take. It is thought that they are not aware that other entrepreneurs are conducting inquiries into United. They are understood to have been told that many of United's biggest shareholders would sell if the price was right, that getting hold of all 260m shares would cost around £600m and that, once acquired, the club could prove a lucrative investment. United insiders believe the increasing likelihood of a change in ownership at Old Trafford helped prompt Kenyon to make a move that, apart from a huge rise, many struggled to understand.

Campbell went on to say that, unlike Abramovich's purchase of Chelsea which was a plaything, 'the predators now stalking Old Trafford see it as a profitable business that, with a more aggressive commercial strategy, could yield yet more cash'. But in some ways the critical passage in the report was this: 'The trio's inquiries into the viability of the takeover have been confirmed to the *Observer* by senior United figures, some of whom would welcome the move.'

Campbell did not name these senior United figures and even now, three years later, he would not tell me. But he did say they were at board level. This could mean either Gill or Gardner or both. (I tried to contact both men when researching this book, but neither responded.) If they were indeed Campbell's sources, it would suggest that the purpose of the story was to broadcast to the world that United's board was looking for a white knight. Indeed Campbell quoted an insider as saying 'getting hold of a big English club isn't that difficult'. The story also made it clear that if the price was right the Irish would sell.

No invitation to bid could be clearer. That United was ripe for bidding had been made clear by many in the City. That month, Merrill Lynch, United's own stockbroker, had accused the club's directors of hoarding cash. They suggested that the habit 'could make United attractive to a predator'.

The day before the *Observer* story appeared Keith Harris, whose investment bank Seymour Pierce had helped Abramovich's Chelsea takeover, had told BBC Radio Five Live that United could return to private ownership soon if a bidder with enough money appeared. Harris, speculated Campbell, could become 'involved in any takeover or moves to oust the board'.

Over the next eighteen months, Harris, who had been at the heart of the United board's plans to sell to Sky, featured in almost every story suggesting some predator or the other was looking at United. He would be in touch with the Glazers, then would seek to organise fans against Glazer – driven, perhaps, by his desire to play a central role, possibly as chairman of the club he loved. In the end he would fail. The coupling of his name with stories about a bid for United would only cease in the summer of 2005 when the Glazers finally won control.

The three unnamed bidders for Manchester United never materialised. It was an American, whose presence was noted in the *Observer* story but was not highlighted, who from now on was to became the star player, wooed by the board, in particular Gill and Gardner, as an alternative to the Irish.

An initial stake in United of around 2 to 3 per cent had been bought by Avram Glazer on behalf of his father Malcolm. On 25 September 2003 Glazer increased his stake to 3.17 per cent. As this meant going above the 3 per cent limit, the holdings became notifiable to the Stock Exchange for the first time.

Around this time Sir Roy Gardner, having already changed his financial PR team, also changed United's City advisers. He brought in Cazenove, the City's most powerful broker and a firm that over the years had been involved in many a takeover battle, most notably the infamous Distillers takeover by Guinness in the 1980s. City analysts, however, played down bid talk. Andrew Lee, leisure analyst at Dresdner Kleinwort Wasserstein, said, 'We feel that a successful takeover of the club is highly unlikely both at this price and given the structure of the existing shareholder base.' DKW downgraded its recommendation on Manchester United shares from buy to hold following a period of sustained increases in the share price. Shares closed that night up 6½p at 195½p.

In October 2003 Glazer made three separate share purchases, taking his shareholding to 9.66 per cent, or 25.22 million shares. On 28 November he spent a further £30 million to raise his stake to 14.31 per cent. Less than a week later Gill flew to meet the Glazers in Florida, a meeting the board considered vital.

The board had wanted to meet the Glazers for some time now and Gill carried with him an important proposal. This had been prompted by the moves made by the Irish and reflected the great fear that had gripped the board about how to deal with the Irish menace. The Glazers were now being seen as potential partners who could help United form a special transatlantic relationship and rescue the board from the awful Irish. Having spent the autumn watching developments in the ongoing fight between Ferguson and Magnier, where an open declaration of war was imminent, the board clearly yearned for a saviour.

The autumn had started with an announcement about Sir Alex Ferguson's future which considerably alarmed the Irish. On 30 September, just before the Champions League match with Stuttgart, Ferguson made an important revelation. It was done in a certain Ferguson style. His control of the press, what he told them and who he spoke to, was well established by now. However, on United's European trips journalists could often have a few words with him while they all waited for their bags. On this occasion, at Stuttgart airport, Ferguson, responding to a question from Daniel Taylor of the *Guardian*, let it be known that he was negotiating a new contract. His contract was due to run out in 2005 but now there was talk of a new four-year deal. With the first year backdated, it would take him to 2007 and the retirement age of sixty-five. There was even the suggestion that he might stay on after that. Although Ferguson was guarded, speculation was that the new contract would be worth more than £12 million. It seemed that he had shaken hands on a deal with Kenyon before he left but only now were serious negotiations taking place with Gill.

Ferguson did not often talk about his contract. The fact that he had even lifted the veil was clearly a calculated move and one that was well timed. Journalists got the impression that by making it public he wanted to put pressure on the board to do a deal quickly. That was also the day United accounts for July 2003 were released, showing record turnover of £173 million, up from £146.1 million the previous year, group operating profits of £50 million and profits before taxation of £39.3 million.

A week later a mystery buyer was said to have bought BSkyB's 10 per cent stake for £62 million, the company offloading 26 million shares for 239p, just a penny short of the price it was willing to pay in 1998 when it wanted to buy the club. BSkyB had got a good price; the shares had been as low as 85p the previous November and with BSkyB no longer looking to buy football clubs it made sense to go out when the shares were again rising. Then it emerged that the mystery buyer was Cubic, which took its stake to 21 per cent making it the biggest shareholder in the club. All this fed further bid talk. United shares jumped 8 per cent to 254p, their highest level since December 2000, valuing the club at around £600 million. 'They are definitely in play now,' said Stan Lock, broker at private client stockbroker Brewin Dolphin. 'The Russians are still in the background, the American is still picking them up, and now it looks like the Irish are picking them up. It could be a free-for-all.'

Soon the Irish were buying more. By early November 2003 their shareholding had grown to 23.15 per cent. Glazer was the next biggest shareholder with 9.6 per cent, followed by Harry Dobson with 6.5 per cent. Hedge fund Lansdowne Partners held 5.2 per cent, John de Mol 4.1 per cent and Dermot Desmond 1.5 per cent.

At this stage, while it was known that Ferguson had fallen out with Magnier, the sheer intensity of the battle had not emerged publicly. During the summer there had been yet another final offer package from Magnier, estimated at around £7 million, but this had not been accepted. Letters were flying back and forth between the two men's lawyers and clearly the next step was a writ. But the long-threatened Ferguson writ had not yet emerged. Some in the Coolmore camp were now suggesting that Ferguson should either put up or shut up.

All this meant that the United board prepared with some trepidation for its annual general meeting. It was to be held on Friday 14 November and that weekend would turn out to be a significant one both for the board and Ferguson. Before the meeting Shareholders United made it clear they would be asking some tough questions of the board. Oliver Houston told the press, 'We didn't go through that epic battle [against Murdoch] only to see the club snatched away from its fans five years later by another rich megalomaniac or international corporation. United is a 125-year-old community asset, not some stock market plaything. We will be putting any potential bidders on notice that we will not give up our club without a fight. We'll also be urging the club to do more to flush out the intentions of any would-be predators, be they from the existing crop of large shareholders such as the club's two largest, Cubic Expression or Malcolm Glazer, or be they the "mystery" Russian oil tycoons, American media barons or Arab princes who are apparently circling like vultures.'

It was David Gill's first AGM as chief executive, and as it began he robustly dismissed talk of takeovers. 'We don't need a sugar daddy. We have a well thought out strategic system in place producing results. Our turnover is £173 million and we have £29 million cash currently in the bank. We also have a strategy in place to increase our revenue and the future is positive. The investment resources are now there for players because spending on assets such as the ground and training ground is now finished.'

With Chelsea and Abramovich on everyone's mind, Gill told the meeting that the club had tried to sign Damien Duff, who moved to Chelsea in the summer, and intended to sell goalkeeper Fabien Barthez at the end of the season. 'The assessment of the manager and the executives was that Damien wasn't worth that money. We had sufficient cover and other possibilities to chase at the time.' He praised Ferguson, saying 'We have a manager who has proved over sixteen years he has an eye for talented players.'

Gill also told the shareholder fans that the club was in regular contact with McManus and Magnier and he did not think Cubic Expression intended to launch a takeover bid. 'As far as the Cubic Expression group is concerned we believe they are long-term value investors.'

But even as Gill finished speaking and the shareholders began to ask questions, it became clear that some people in the room were acting on behalf of Cubic and out to embarrass the board and the manager – or at least this was the very strong impression that Michael Crick and some other fans got. A group of well-informed shareholders, who it later turned out were actors and actresses, had come to the AGM armed with detailed questions about the conduct of transfers. Their questions were so pointed that Crick's antennae were alerted. He claimed they were plants put there to try and embarrass the manager. Crick acknowledged they asked some excellent questions but it was, he said, a bit too obvious. Clearly they were acting for Magnier.

Crick's claims were denied by Andy Terrington, a television producer who specialised in undercover programmes and claimed this was part of a programme which was meant to look at what exactly happened at an AGM. There were also suggestions that it may have been part of a *Sunday Times* operation. The paper was soon to write articles dealing with United's transfer dealings, stories that reflected Irish concerns. When these stories emerged the strong suggestion was that Coolmore's PR had fed the paper information.

If the Irish did put up the actors and actresses, it is interesting to compare their tactics with those the Glazers would follow exactly a year later. Then, angered by the board, the Glazers were to use their votes to vote off three directors. The Irish challenge was not so direct. Indeed, before the meeting they had voted their proxies in favour of the board. That action too was to have repercussions a year later.

What, however, was not in dispute was that Magnier had hired Kroll, which specialised in corporate investigative work, the idea being that he wanted to know everything he could on United and Ferguson ahead of a possible court action. If it came to a court case, judgment might be based on the truthfulness of Magnier and Ferguson. Where better to look than at Manchester United? So Kroll began to look at transfers and how United had handled them.

Issues regarding transfers had been in the public domain for some time. Many of the issues concerned agents and, at Old Trafford, the role of the manager's son. In 2002, one chapter of Crick's biography of Sir Alex Ferguson was entitled 'Jason and the Larger Noughts'. This detailed Jason Ferguson's involvement with agencies such as L'Attitude and Elite Sports who had acted for United in several player transfers. L'Attitude Sports Consultancy had been founded by two of Ferguson's friends, Andy Dodd and Kieran Toal. Jason, widely considered the most problematic of Ferguson's sons, had tried many things. He had made an attempt to become a footballer, then worked for Granada and Sky as a journalist and in 1999 became an agent, joining L'Attitude. In August 2000 the agency helped United get rid of Massimo Taibi and were paid £25,000 for their work. The payment was fully justified but Jason Ferguson was a director of the company and Crick says officials at Old Trafford were nervous about making the payment. Jason left the company at the end of the year and the company, finding transfer business difficult, folded.

Jason acted for a time effectively as his father's agent, negotiating his post-retirement package. He joined Elite as director in the spring of 2001. That summer Elite got involved with the transfer of Jaap Stam to Lazio and were paid by Lazio. According to Harverson, Elite played a leading role in the transfer. There were also other agents involved in the deal but Paul Stretford, who would later become Wayne Rooney's agent, would tell Crick that 'Jason was the absolute key to the Stam deal'. Jason, he says, would have known from his father that Stam was available. 'That means Elite could operate as the only people who knew Stam would be going in a big money move, and find a suitable buyer.' Estimates vary as to how much Elite made from the deal, up to as high as £1.5million. The fee was paid by Lazio but arguably reduced the figure Manchester United got. Roland Smith was not happy about the number of agents involved in the deal, or that one of them was Ferguson's son. He is believed to have given Ferguson a warning in the autumn of 2001 that a plc must be like Caesar's wife, above suspicion.

The Irish had made a careful note of this chapter, as they did of Tom Bower's book *Broken Dreams, Vanity, Greed and the Souring of British Football*. Bower wrote, 'Agents discovered that Sir Alex encouraged Manchester United players seeking transfers in and out of the club to abandon their established agent and engage Jason Ferguson for transfers to clubs of the manager's choice.' Bower suggests that in the Stam deal 'Sir Alex had tipped his son about his desire to sell the defender, and Jason had activated other agents'. Jason was also involved in United's purchase of Stam's replacement Laurent Blanc and the transfer of Roy Carroll from Wigan to Manchester United for £2.5 million.

For the Irish, questions had been raised of corporate governance and how it affected shareholder values. The issue of corporate governance had come up almost as soon as Cubic started buying Manchester United shares. Some of United's other institutional shareholders had similar concerns and there had been meetings between these shareholders and the Irish to discuss the issue. There was much talk of the information the club released to investors, payments to agents and players' transfer fees. So even before the Rock of Gibraltar affair (privately the Irish used a stronger word when referring to the dispute), the issue of corporate governance had been raised. Now, as the board offered a long-term contract to a manager involved in a dispute with the club's major investors, Cubic decided to have a look at the whole thing. Hence the hiring of Kroll. Not that Cubic would ever admit, or even comment on any link between them and Kroll, a policy they have continued to adhere to until now.

In many ways the most interesting comments Gill made at the AGM were in relation to Malcolm Glazer. He said United had so far failed in their attempts to arrange a meeting with Glazer but intended to sit down with the Tampa Bay Buccaneers' owner soon. Gardner emphasised how keen the board were to see him: 'We are pretty confident that we will be meeting him in the near future. We are doing everything we can to understand the intentions of our major shareholders.'

At the AGM Gardner had said no approach for the club had been received, but the possibility that he was looking to life after a takeover, hopefully a friendly one, had been raised in that morning's *Daily Telegraph*. An item in the *Telegraph* City diary, edited by Simon Goodley, read as follows:

Sir Roy Gardner, chairman of Manchester United and chief executive of Centrica, is already making preparations for a takeover of the Premiership champions. Sources at United tell me he asked a senior director if the club rules allow him to secure his seat in the directors' box for life – or even beyond. Sir Matt Busby (d. 1994) still has his, so what was the answer? Apparently, the director dodged the question. A spokesman denies that Gardner ever asked, and blows the full-time whistle.

Footnote: former chairmen Martin Edwards and Sir Roland Smith both have lifetime seats.

Rumours of such a move by Gardner would persist for many months and were never convincingly denied.

All this clearly indicates that the board knew they had to find a heavyweight investor to match the Irish. This could only be the Glazers. A meeting with them became even more urgent following developments in Dublin forty-eight hours after the AGM.

Late on Monday 17 November, a dank, miserable evening in Dublin, Ferguson's writ against Coolmore and Magnier was finally lodged and news of it reached Magnier's lawyers. That evening Murray Consultants, Magnier's Dublin PR advisers, issued the following statement:

> Coolmore Stud has today been advised that legal proceedings have been initiated against Mr John Magnier by Sir Alex Ferguson alleging certain ownership rights to the stallion Rock Of Gibraltar. Coolmore Stud and John Magnier consider the action to be without merit and it will be vigorously defended.

Open war had finally been declared.

Ferguson's Statement of Claim, lodged in the High Court of Dublin, specified the damages he was seeking. But Coolmore were fascinated to find that this Statement of Claim was quite different to some of the earlier claims made in letters from Ferguson's lawyers. He was claiming half the value of Rock of Gibraltar, but he was not saying he was entitled to it because he had paid half the cost of the horse but because he felt he had added value to the horse by having his name associated with it.

Publicly United reacted as if this was nothing to do with them. A spokesman said he was aware of the legal action but that it was a private matter between the individuals concerned. But privately they knew they had to do something about the Irish. Two weeks later, as the Glazers raised their stake to 14.31 per cent, Gill decided to fly out to Florida.

Insiders have told me that at this stage, near the end of 2003, the Glazers had given no thought to mounting a takeover of United. The idea was planted in their heads when they first met David Gill. It was at this meeting that they realised how much the United board felt under siege from the Irish. At their meeting with Joel and Avi Glazer, Gill and the board made it clear they saw the Americans as their saviours. They told them that if they offered £3 a share to the Irish they would sell, and that such a move would be welcomed by the board with open arms. There was not much doubt that in the eyes of the board the Irish were the bad guys. The price of £3 a share was to prove an important figure, for when in May 2005 the Glazers finally made their move this was the figure they offered the Irish. That figure, and the seeds of the bid, were sown by Gill and the United board at this meeting. I understand that such a line had been agreed with Sir Roy Gardner and the £3 figure had actually been Gardner's idea. My information is that at this meeting Gill gave the Glazers the firm impression that the board would see them as white knights, come to rescue the board from the Irish.

None of this, of course, was revealed. United's official explanation was that this was a routine meeting, the kind the chief executive of a well-run plc would have with any major investor. A week later Gill would say, 'We had an excellent meeting with Malcolm and his sons. He sees the shares as a good investment and that was the end of the discussion.' The meeting had clearly gone very well. When asked if he was worried about the Glazers buying shares he said very confidently, 'I'm not worried.' And why should he have been, if he had invited the Glazers to bid and even suggested the price that could buy out the Irish?

Gill's public comments came on 1 December, when at Claridge's in London, United launched the club's new sponsorship deal with Vodafone. Ferguson sat next to Gill and dominated the press conference. It was evident at the launch that Gill and the board were caught between the Irish and Ferguson. The story I co-authored with Sam Wallace, then the *Daily Telegraph*'s northern correspondent, was headlined 'Ferguson in box seat for new contract':

Sir Alex Ferguson forced Manchester United into a public assurance that they would offer him a new contract as manager yesterday, despite his continued legal action against the club's major shareholder and speculation that the Premiership champions were ripe for a takeover.

The United manager was in the opulent surroundings of Claridge's, London to launch the club's new £36 million four-year deal with Vodafone when he was asked how talks over his new contract, expected to keep him at the club until 2007, were progressing. Turning to chief executive David Gill, Ferguson said: 'We're not far away, are we?' The pressure of his lawsuit against multi-millionaire John Magnier, over the stud rights to race horse Rock of Gibraltar, as well as the interest in United shares shown by American tycoon Malcolm Glazer, means it has suited Ferguson to make his new contract a very public issue. Privately there are fears in the Ferguson camp that Magnier's Cubic Expression investment company, who own 23.1 per cent of the club, have reservations about offering the Scot a new contract while their dispute is continuing. Glazer would also have to deal with the Irish investor if he wanted to take control of United. However, Gill, who travelled to America to meet Glazer and his sons last week, said that he would not allow any 'outside influence' to stop him from signing the man who had brought United eight Premiership titles and a European Cup to a new deal. 'Alex has been very successful and we're moving ahead to finalise the contract to make sure he stays with us to deliver more success for many years to come,' Gill said. 'Neither party has set a deadline date, that is something suggested by the media. We're working on it and both parties want it to happen.'

Gill became very twitchy when I asked him if the Irish had asked for seats on the board and conceded that the club would have to consider any request for such representation.

Two days later the issue of Ferguson's contract became more complicated when the manager experienced a heart murmur and had a pacemaker fitted. Ferguson revealed he had kept Gill fully informed and stressed that he was in excellent health. He even made a joke about it, telling one of his favourite journalists, 'The first thing they [the players] told me was that they'd had a real scare this morning – they discovered I had a heart.'

For the board this was no problem, or at least that is how the spokesman presented it: 'Discussions over the terms and conditions of the new deal are progressing well and no problems are foreseen.' But for the Irish a manager with a heart problem being given a new four-year contract raised fresh issues of who was really running Manchester United. Who made the crucial decisions at Old Trafford? The board or Ferguson?

Cubic were so concerned that they took time off from addressing the wider issue of corporate governance to write to the board about Ferguson's contracts. As a subsequent letter from Cubic to Gardner would put it, 'our attention was distracted by the announcement of the Company's intention to award an extended contract to the football club manager'.

As the letter setting out their concerns makes clear, this was not the first time the Irish had written to the board. There had been a whole series of detailed, well-argued letters raising pointed questions about how Manchester United was run. The Irish were keen to emphasise that the plc was not just for the benefit of the staff and the players. Shareholders had a legitimate right. They had paid money to buy shares and had been told they would receive returns in the form of dividends. These were issues that would not have been exceptional for any plc. The board had struggled to answer them and the answers they had provided had not impressed the Irish, who had begun to form the impression that some of those answers, whether deliberately or otherwise, may have been rather misleading.

The board and the Irish had to meet. It was decided that Gill would go to Ireland to see how these so-called horse owners worked. In Christmas 2003 Gill came to Tipperary to see how Coolmore was run. The visit went well and both Irwin and Gill got on, with Gill being quite helpful.

Gill was different to Kenyon. That was very evident. Kenyon was a marketer, Gill very much an accountant and much more hands on. But he was without Kenyon's sweep of marketing ideas, which the Irish had quite liked.

In one of their discussions there was some talk about Kenyon's proposal to bid for Premier League television rights. The Irish found this very interesting, a forerunner of the time when United might be able to bid on their own for television rights – which was something their friend Dermot Desmond advocated. However, when it was raised with Gill, he was not up to speed about the issue, although it had been a board decision.

If this somewhat surprised the Irish, on the whole the Coolmore Christmas meetings went well. But this all changed when Gill came back. As 2004 began Gill told the Irish that he had consulted the board and that what the Irish were doing was less raising the legitimate concerns of a shareholder and more getting at Ferguson.

This greatly perturbed the Irish. Early in January 2004 Irwin flew to Manchester and met Gill at the airport. The meeting was a disaster. Gill made it clear the board was not willing to be co-operative; they saw the Irish as being vindictive to Ferguson, raising questions about the governance of Manchester United in pursuing a personal vendetta. As far as the Irish were concerned the board could not have shut the door more emphatically. They knew they had to do something. The result was what has since become known as the infamous '99 Questions' letter, although it actually contained sixty-six questions which became ninety-nine only when subsections were included.

The letter, dated 16 January 2004, marked strictly private and confidential and addressed to Sir Roy Gardner, was sent by fax, with a copy to Philip Yea, chairman of the United board's audit committee. In it a gentleman signing himself as G. Picter, writing on the letterhead of Cubic's registered office in Torotola, British Virgin Islands, delivered one of the most devastating broadsides against the board of a football club:

As you will be aware, we presently hold in excess of 24% of the issued shares of the Company. The extent of this holding has increased over the past year. Over this period we have become more aware of the way in which the Company operates. This has led us to address in more detail the manner in which the Company conducts its affairs, how it reports its business to shareholders and its corporate governance processes. We have concerns that these should be improved and the purpose of this letter is to raise these issues and concerns with you directly in the best interests of the Company as a whole. In particular, we wish to draw the Board's attention to areas where we consider the supervision of the Company's affairs appears to be falling short of best practice in corporate governance as established by the Combined Code and accepted industry standards.

The letter went on to say how Ferguson's contract had 'distracted' matters, but having already raised their concerns on that subject in an earlier letter, they now raised much broader issues. Those issues were listed in the eight-page letter under several headings, such as:

Accuracy and Completeness of Presentation of Financial Data and Statements in Annual Accounts
Conduct of Player Transfers by the Company
The Company's Approach to Compliance with the Combined Code
Commissions Paid in Relation to Large Transactions
Conflicts of Interest
Internal Audit Function
The Suspension of Mr Ferdinand

A Further Information heading referred to the schedule, where the ninety-nine questions were listed.

There was, said the letter, 'insufficient detail about certain key transactions and . . . a lack of transparency in relation to a number of material payments of significant sums', particularly in relation to 'significant payments by way of player transfers and commissions paid to football agents'. It went on:

there is no transparency on player transfers. All transfer, agent and signing on fees are aggregated over all transactions. This is of particular concern when these are not all individually similar. There are some individual transfers where the fees and payments made to players and agents are particularly large and material and in the accounts no explanation is provided in relation to these particular individually material transactions. The topic receives little coverage in the Directors' Report . . . We well appreciate that the purchase and sale of players within an international marketplace may, in certain instances, require the Company to engage professional agents to procure the services of particular players or to find buyers for players who are surplus to the Company's requirements. However, what we cannot understand is the necessity for the relative secrecy in which the Agents conduct their role and also the astonishing fees which have been charged to the Company on the completion of transfers.

In the annual report the board had said it approved 'significant player transfers and contracts'. What was meant by that, asked Picter. 'Can you please explain the Board's current test as to "significance"?'

The Board will no doubt be aware of recent press allegations concerning transfer activities. We would like to know what steps the Board is taking to investigate these allegations as a matter of urgency and whether pending the outcome of such investigations the Board will scrutinise with care all transfer transactions and not merely those which it would previously have regarded as significant.

What about 'significant payments made to Agents by way of commission'? Surely if Manchester United counted itself as the most successful and profitable of all listed Football clubs, it 'should take the lead in respect of this matter'?

As regards agents, what were the internal controls and code of conduct 'when an agent is deemed necessary who the Company will retain as an agent and how much it will pay by way of commission. These points are of particular relevance at this time as we understand the Company is about to engage a number of additional players for the squad.'

With Jason Ferguson's links with agency business already in the news (having first been aired in Michael Crick's biography of Ferguson back in 2002), although no mention of him was made by name, a whole page of the letter was devoted to probing how United policed such matters, concluding with suggestions to ensure everything was above board. These included:

the full disclosure to the Board of any interest, whether direct or indirect, in a contract or proposed contract with the Company, by any director or officer concerned in a manner analogous to section 317 of the Companies Act 1985;

the prohibition of payments for player transfers to agents or agencies whose members or directors have a close personal connection with the Company or any officer or employee of the Company;

the prevention of the possibility that any officer or employee of the Company might persuade or seek to persuade any player to engage as their football agent an individual, firm or company which is associated directly or indirectly with that officer or employee;

the full disclosure to the Board of the names of football agents (and their associated companies) who represent, whether directly or indirectly, players involved in any transfer so as to ensure the interests of any such agent (or company associated with him) whether direct or indirect, in any transfer are known to the Board;

and due consideration of the value that would be derived from any proposed transaction, e.g. the production of a business case including an assessment of the reasonableness of a transfer price given market conditions, suitable alternatives and the position of the other parties involved in the transaction.

Given that Maurice Watkins' firm was not only the company's legal adviser but also acted for other football clubs on sport-related matters, the section on conflict of interest seemed to have been written with him in mind:

> Please can you assure us that no member of the Board, or any firm associated with him, is acting in a professional capacity for any third party who has any dealings with the Company or who is a competitor with the Company. We would be grateful if you could explain what steps are made to identify and deal with any such conflicts of interest at a Board or executive level.

The detailed schedule to the letter listed all United transfers in the last few years, along with pointed questions such as 'Please can you inform us if there is an outstanding sum owing to the Company from Lazio in relation to the transfer fee for Mr Stam. Where is this outstanding debt referred to in the 2003 Accounts?'

Another series of questions asked: 'Please outline the extent of the Board's consideration of the following transfers and provide details of the analysis or due diligence undertaken in each case.' The transfers cited were the purchases of Juan Sebastian Veron from Lazio, Rio Ferdinand from Leeds, Diego Forlan from Independiente and Jaap Stam from PSV Eindhoven; also those of Tim Howard from New York Metrostars, Kleberson from Atletico Paranaense, Cristiano Ronaldo from Sporting Lisbon, Roy Carroll from Wigan, Laurent Blanc from Inter Milan and David Bellion from Sunderland; and the sales of Veron to Chelsea, of Stam to Lazio, of Jonathan Greening and Mark Wilson to Middlesbrough and Massimo Taibi's transfer to Reggina. It was asked: 'When were these deals bought to the attention of the Board? How long did the Board have to consider the transactions? Did the Board make any changes to the transaction from the terms initially presented to them?'

Many of these transfers were suspected to have had some connection with the Elite agency, either directly or through associates. It was clear what the Irish, well coached by Kroll, were driving at.

With regard to the commission paid to agents in relation to the big transfers, the Irish asked:

> Please identify the person on behalf of the Company who conducted the negotiations with agents in the purchase or sale of the above players.
>
> Who signs off on the value of agents' commissions? What approval procedures are in place?
>
> Does the Company have a select few agents it retains? Please identify those agents. Are these the only agents the Company will use? If so, how has the company identified or approved these agents?

In relation to each of the above transfers, what were the services provided by the agents engaged on behalf of the Company?

Even as United reeled, a further letter was sent on 21 January 2004 dealing with Ferguson's contract. 'Can you inform us whether you have complemented legal advice with medical advice, in light of the executive's [Ferguson's] recent health concerns and his age?' And given Ferguson's health, it asked how the new contract was being negotiated: 'We do not understand how the board can reach a conclusion that the executive will remain of central importance for the course of any extended contract. It is quite possible that the executive could suffer ill health during the course of any extension period, such that he would no longer be of central importance.'

The 16 January letter having raised issues of corporate governance and conflicts of interest which had indirectly alluded to Watkins, there was in this letter a more direct reference to him: 'Can you advise why the company believes it is appropriate to obtain its advice on the employment contract from a firm of solicitors whose senior partner is a member of the board and which has, we understand, represented the executive in separate legal proceedings?'

Magnier and McManus were out to prove that they were not just a couple of Irish racehorse owners, comments which rankled deeply and which they saw as racist. The letters were intended to impress on the board they faced a formidable corporate enemy in their biggest shareholder. They certainly served that purpose.

The board realised they needed help to deal with the letters. Mark Rawlinson, who had already been seeking involvement with United, was hurriedly brought in as an adviser to deal with this written menace. Rawlinson recalls being summoned to an emergency meeting with board members late one afternoon at Gardner's Centrica offices: 'It was really with the Irishmen where I got heavily involved. It was when the Irish started to cause all the trouble, when they had their falling-out with Ferguson over the racehorse. This was a period where perhaps the board were trying to keep a sort of engagement with the Irish, trying to keep them on side.' He had several meetings with the board in relation to the Irish situation. 'I think one was at Centrica's offices in Windsor. They would phone up to say we had to meet and discuss the latest Irish letters.'

Rawlinson had only to look at the letter of 16 January and earlier letters to see they were not easy to deal with. Some of the points raised tested even a lawyer of his calibre. 'A lot of them concerned the running of listed companies, based around concerns about the Blue Book, the listing rules, things like that. The Irish letters were very well drafted. They'd clearly got advice. I was impressed by their questions. The whole list of questions were designed, in my view, to be as much of a nuisance as possible to the board. The legal side of things was pretty straightforward, there were just a lot of them. But there were a couple of things that were just awkward. The agents' area is a difficult area.'

Having got nowhere in meetings with Gill, the Irish decided to let the world know what they were doing. So Cubic's London PR leaked the stories of the ninety-nine questions to the *Daily Mail*. Soon everyone realised that this was no longer a dispute over a horse but something that went to the heart of Manchester United.

Ferguson had to react. He told a press conference that he had never abused his position in his seventeen years at the club. He also gave public expression to the fears he had revealed to Colin Gibson that his family was being targeted, in particular Jason. He alleged that Jason's rubbish bins had been searched.

The Irish quickly drew blood over Ferguson's contract. In the schedule to their letter of 16 January they had asked, 'What length of service contract is usually offered by the Company to its senior executives? Why is the standard 12-month rolling contract (which the Report indicates is applied to directors) not applied to all senior executives?' This was clearly a reference to the fact that the talk was about Ferguson getting a four-year deal. Twelve days later, when United announced a new contract had been signed, it emerged that Ferguson had indeed been given a rolling contract and not a four-year deal, although the money was said to put him on a par with Sven-Goran Eriksson, at between £4 million and £5 million a year. Ferguson expressed happiness, saying this was exactly what he wanted. But the Irish knew they had scored.

In their letter about top executives' salaries Cubic had also asked, 'Please clarify the role and input of The Audit Committee on these issues and the preparation of the Annual Accounts.' This put people like Yea, chairman of the committee and a prominent City man and chartered accountant, on notice that Ferguson's contract could not just be a deal between him and Gill.

Until now the fans had watched the battle between Ferguson and the Irish from the sidelines, although their sympathies were with the manager. But now the public storm over the '99 Questions' letter meant they could say the Irish were targeting their manager. This was one issue the fans could latch on to, their beloved manager being threatened by the Irish who having started off as friends were now ready to be demonised. For fans with nothing else to hold on to at the club, the manager was the rock they clung to. And while the more established supporters' groups, such as Shareholders United, formally stayed out of the war, there now emerged new groups to champion Ferguson, including the Manchester Education Committee (MEC) and United 4 Action. One person whose identity was never revealed daubed obscenities on the Magnier family home in Cork, except it was not John Magnier's house. These groups once again employed actions similar to those used by animal rights groups. Coolmore's phone numbers and addresses were printed on leaflets and widely distributed.

Soon the idea of targeting Magnier and McManus's horses on racecourses was formulated. There was a small-scale protest at Hereford, but with Cheltenham on the horizon the fan protestors had a wonderful opportunity to hit the Irish. The idea was for Sean Murphy, leader of United 4 Action, and 150-odd demonstrators, to picket the course.

The plans worried the racecourse and angered the Irish. Hannan says at that stage 'Manchester United were just days away from complete disaster':

> I have been told that, had the protest gone ahead and had trouble occurred at Cheltenham, Magnier and McManus would have acted to try to remove Ferguson, or perhaps themselves, from Old Trafford ... But a course of action involving Ferguson was much more probable. Either the board would have been forced to act against Ferguson or an Extraordinary General Meeting would have been requisitioned to make public certain accusations against the manager and directors. Coolmore's owner had become convinced by then that 'sources close to' Ferguson were either tacitly aware, or complicit in, the protests against the club's major shareholders. He was also suspicious that leaks against Cubic Expression had emanated from Old Trafford.

This was averted when Ferguson issued a statement:

> The reputation of Manchester United is paramount to my thinking. The private dispute I have is just that and I don't want to exacerbate the whole thing. Cheltenham is such a great festival and I don't want it marred in any way. There is a lot of concern about what could happen and I would ask supporters to refrain from any form of protest. I am strongly opposed to any violent, unlawful or disruptive behaviour which may reflect badly on the club and its supporters in general.

The United board, who the Irish had often felt had done nothing to deter the wilder fans, now spoke backing Ferguson: 'Sir Alex also knows that this is the view of the Manchester United board, who have previously urged fans not to participate in any disruptive or criminal activities.'

Sean Murphy, was to tell Hannan how he had said to Sir Alex that Cubic were 'bullying our manager and destabilising our football club'. He felt betrayed when Ferguson stepped in to stop the protest and was left wondering if Ferguson himself had not destabilised the club through the horse.

During their conversation Ferguson had told Murphy that 'the case was nearly at an end'. The early spring of 2004 was to see a settlement thanks to Dermot Desmond, who had continued to be a conduit between Ferguson and Magnier. It meant that the matter never reached court, Mike Dillon never gave evidence as to what was the exact agreement between Ferguson and Magnier, and Ferguson walked away with £2.5 million tax free for his share of the stud fees Rock of Gibraltar might earn. It was much less than what he wanted – indeed, than what he had been offered in 2003 – but it was not a bad settlement for a horse for which he had paid nothing. Both sides signed confidentiality agreements which meant the settlement was never disclosed, nor the court papers filed by Ferguson or Magnier.

As Hannan says, Ferguson got the money for acting as the owner:

> which, it must be said, he did to Oscar-winning proportions. He deserved to be rewarded for helping the horse's profile, and it could be argued that he became the highest paid cheerleader in history. Coolmore's people can also argue till they are blue in the face that Ferguson did not add a penny to Rocky's worth, but that is not the point – Coolmore was happy to use the Ferguson name and the manager's considerable presence as it suited them, and they also concealed the truth about the ownership situation, which was a sin of omission. Coolmore did eventually acknowledge that Ferguson had played a role in Rocky's career, and that realisation – not the threat of court action – is what led Magnier to eventually make his payment to Ferguson.

Manchester United also moved quickly to deal with the transfer and corporate governance issues raised by the Irish. Nick Humby was asked to make an internal assessment of the whole situation and prepare a report. They contacted the Irish, admitting that in the past certain things had not been done properly and there had been a lack of documentation.

When, soon after, the club presented its half-year results for 2003–04 it took the bold and innovative step of revealing payments to agents involved in transfers. There was a new schedule to the accounts entitled 'Payments to Agents', listing each player purchase and the fees paid. No club had ever opened its books in this fashion and Manchester United remains an exception. For good measure the club also banned Jason Ferguson's Elite agency from acting for the club.

In June 2004, after Humby had produced his report, there was a meeting in the Old Trafford boardroom between the Irish, represented by Irwin and Power, and Gill and Humby. Gill did not give the Irish the report – it has never been made public, being an internal document – but Gill and Humby talked them through it. No wrongdoing had been found but Gill assured them that things would change. His predecessor Kenyon was not a details man, he said, and did not keep records. But he, Gill, came from a financial background. He was in charge and things would change. The Irish for their part afterwards sent to Old Trafford a response to Humby's report. They had done substantial research on a lot of football clubs and went through with Gill and Humby how things should be run.

By then the Irish storm had abated. Ferguson had got his money, Magnier had not had to go to court and the Irish had forced through the biggest changes any single investor had imposed on a public company, let alone a football club. The Irish war was over but Manchester United and its board had paid a very heavy price. The Irish were no longer fighting the board, but they were a very unfriendly neutral. They had no love for this board. And this at a time when the United board needed all the love it could get.

For by this time the white knight that Gill and Gardner had wooed so diligently at the turn of the year was no longer coming to the rescue of the board. It was now out to take over the club, whether the board liked it or not. And if the board did not like it, it would devour the board in the process. The board had played its Irish game so ineptly that it had been holed under the waterline with little chance of saving itself. A year after Irwin and Power met Gill and Humby in the United boardroom to discuss the famous Humby report, that boardroom would host the Glazer brothers, who had come there not by invitation but by right as owners.

PART FOUR

The Knockout Strategy

19

THE CHRISTMAS BREAKTHROUGH

ON THE AFTERNOON of 23 December 2004, Robert Leitao, an investment banker with Rothschild, and head of its Mergers and Acquisitions Department, received a call on his mobile phone. It could not have come at a more inconvenient moment. He was in an Oddbins store in central London buying some champagne to take home, where his wife had organised a Christmas drinks party. Leitao was feeling more than a little harassed. He had promised his wife he would get the drinks, then forgotten all about it and was now trying to make amends on his way home. The moment his mobile rang he had just got out his wallet and was fishing for his credit card. Leitao says, 'I was trying to juggle my credit card and things, and it was a bit confusing as to what was going on, who it was.'

The caller was someone he had never met and did not know. It was Joel Glazer. He was calling from Florida and wanted Leitao and his team to fly out immediately to discuss the Glazers' plans for buying Manchester United. It was now six weeks since the Glazers had given the United board a bloody nose at the AGM of November 2004 and, despite the general belief that the subsequent loss of their merchant bank and their PR adviser had meant they could not possibly bid for the club, their dream was intact.

But while the call was a surprise, and momentarily confusing, it was a call Leitao was 'half-expecting'. As he says, 'The story goes back to the previous summer when they [the Glazers] were clearly looking to appoint some advisers. We were contacted by Allen & Overy and asked whether we wanted to put our name forward, which we said we would do. But then nothing happened. J.P. Morgan were involved in providing the financing base, the Glazers had been using JPM as an adviser and as funder. JPM had two or three previous attempts and when that failed, having already had the name put in front of them, they picked it up again, contacted the people they had asked before. I think there were a couple of other people they contacted.'

Leitao could not just leave his drinks and board a flight to Florida. 'I explained to Joel that I couldn't come out before Christmas and New Year. He said he understood, he had small children himself, so we flew out on 3 January.'

One of the first things Leitao did later that evening was ring his colleague Majid Ishaq, who was still in the office. Leitao himself had not much interest in football, although he had vast experience acting for football clubs including Tottenham and Arsenal. Majid Ishaq was a season ticket holder, steeped in United's history and proud to call himself a Red. A season ticket holder at the Stretford End, he had been a fan since 1976. This was something of a surprise, for he had been brought up in West Yorkshire in the heyday of Leeds United and had lived surrounded by Leeds supporters. But Manchester United had claimed him due to two brothers who, perhaps because they wanted to be different, had chosen to cross the Pennines in their search for a football team. His brother had been a season ticket holder since the late 1970s and Majid himself got one in 1998, the season that was to end in such triumph for the club. Working in London meant he did not always get to games but his wife was from Manchester and a visit to Old Trafford meant staying with the in-laws. Majid was fond of joking that this was the downside of going to the Theatre of Dreams.

For both Leitao and Majid, that the Glazers should turn to Rothschild was very natural. Just as Majid felt he supported the best club in the world, Rothschild's Mergers and Acquisition (M&A) team, which has about twenty people, prides itself on being the number one in the UK, France, Germany – in fact in Europe.

As deals went, a near £900 million takeover of Manchester United was not massive by City standards, but it was big enough, and all sorts of other considerations made it both challenging and exciting. As a season ticket holder and member of a number of fan websites, Majid was well aware of the feelings the bid aroused among some of the fans. After Joel's calls, Leitao and Majid consulted the bank's hierarchy about working for the Glazers. While there was concern, they were comfortable.

Interestingly Majid Ishaq knew all about bids for Manchester United; what is more, he had worked on them from the inside. When BSkyB made their bid Majid was working at the HSBC team that advised United, and while not a director as now at Rothschild he had been an important part of Rupert Faure Walker and David Blake's team. Like many fans he had initially queried the bid, wondering about Rupert Murdoch's motives, but then decided it was a good thing. Since then Roman Abramovich had come on the scene and all football fans judged a potential buyer against him. However, if the Glazers were not an Abramovich they were willing to put their own money into the club. They had already invested more than half a billion dollars in buying 28 per cent of the club, the biggest investment anybody has made in English football. (Abramovich has spent more overall, but his actual investment in buying Chelsea was much less.)

This is how Majid saw it:

The fact that the Glazers were prepared to spend so much of their own money even before they bought the club meant here were potential owners who had every reason to make sure it was a success. They would surely want performance on the pitch to deliver financial performance, otherwise in the long term the Manchester United brand and business would decline. It could also be argued that a person with such a personal investment would have a much bigger financial interest in the business, making sure the money was properly spent in getting the best players and being much more emotionally involved than a financial fund manager in the City, managing an investment for several pension funds. The Glazers as businessmen would want to protect their investment and everything indicated that there had to be a direct linkage between performance on the pitch and financial performance.

Joel Glazer had suggested to Leitao that he come over to Florida for lunch. He had also told Majid to get in touch with William Sondericker, who worked for the Glazers, to sort out the details of the assignment and this was done on 31 December as Majid stood outside the church at Newick Park in Kent where his secretary was due to get married. Andrew Ballheimer of Allen & Overy also spoke to Robert Leitao between Christmas and New Year and on 3 January 2005 Leitao, Majid and Richard Bailey, head partner at the Rothschild office in Manchester, flew to Florida to meet the Glazers.

The Glazers' choice of Donald Trump's Mar a Loga Club as a place to select a merchant bank to advise on a bid was a surprise. Lunch was served by the pool, an unusual place to have an investment banking M&A lunch. Nor was the food the best. And the way Joel Glazer conducted the meeting was different to any normal meeting between a client and an M&A firm. Joel wanted to know from each of the three about their background, whether they had any interest in football and where they all came from. It was altogether more personal than a normal City M&A pitch. Both Majid Ishaq and Richard Bailey could tell the Glazers of their lifelong support for the club. Bailey like Majid was a season ticket holder, although he had to put up with ribbing that it was easier for him as he lived in Manchester. And being in the South Stand, he was one of the prawn sandwich brigade that Roy Keane had complained of.

If Joel Glazer's approach was unusual, then it was in keeping with the family style, which was very different to that of others with similar money. Although the Glazers live in an ocean-front mansion in Palm Beach, near Jim Clarke, the founder of Netscape, a computer services company best known for its web browser and now part of AOL, and Rod Stewart the rock star (and a Chelsea supporter), they do not mix with Palm Beach society. Thom Smith, the society columnist of the *Palm Beach Post*, recalls visiting the Glazer house for a fundraiser for an Israeli technical college. The guest of honour was Jehan Sadat, the wife of assassinated Egyptian president Anwar Sadat. Smith is one of the few media men to have been inside the house and says, 'Malcolm stayed in the background, he seemed downright shy.'

At lunch Joel mixed a distinctive personal style with some hard business talk. All the issues were touched on, such as the positions of the Irish and of the board, including the individual members. The Glazers' past dealings with the board were discussed and Leitao formed a very definite impression of how the Glazers saw them: 'My own view is that the board gave out some encouraging signals at the beginning to the Glazers. I wasn't around in the early days to know how encouraging it was but I certainly know that the Glazers, who, once you know them, are pretty straight up and down people, knew they were being encouraged to buy Manchester United. But then the board changed their position. I don't know whether it was because the Irish's position was perceived to be different from what it was effectively or whether because the fans started getting restive – of course it was a small minority of fans who caused all the noise. But my perception is that the board changed their position from one of welcoming the Glazers to frankly a bloody battle. Some members of the board would have hell freeze over before they put the company in other hands.'

Right from that first lunch it was clear that financing would be an issue. Anyone wanting to own Manchester United would have to buy out the Irish. But the key was not to approach the Irish unless the money was there and an unconditional offer could be made for their shares. The feeling was still that at the end of the day they were Irish horse traders. 'Tell them you are going to come back in two months' time with the money and they are not going to entertain you. But if you turn up with the cash and say I want to buy the shares it would be very different.'

That meant taking the City takeover route designated Rule 9. Under City takeover rules a shareholder who gains 29 per cent or more of the shares in a company must make an offer to buy out all the other shareholders. The rule was devised to prevent a situation where a shareholder held a huge block of shares, yet did not own the company or make any effort to own it, but could be seen by its very presence to be threatening the board and its ability to run the company. With the Glazers already having 28.11 per cent, any move to buy the Irish and their near 29 per cent would inevitably trigger Rule 9 and compel them to bid for the entire company.

Leitao, Majid and Bailey flew back to London discussing these options. A week after their return their appointment was finally confirmed with Allen & Overy. By then Leitao had worked out his strategy: 'What was clear to me from the very beginning was that there was only one way to do the deal. We had to devise an entire strategy around the fact that if you can get to the Irish and say here's the dosh, give us your shares, they would accept. That was the strategy from day one, my knockout strategy.'

Leitao knew he was flying in the face of conventional wisdom: 'The conventional strategy would have been to get the Irish to sign a piece of paper saying they would accept the offer and then go to the board and say the Irish want to accept the offer, hope that the board will open up and help us take over the company.' But that wasn't going to work with the Irish. 'Before I was involved, J.P. Morgan, acting for the Glazers, had been in contact with the Irish through intermediaries – you never speak to them directly, you always speak to intermediaries – and solicited their support for that proposal. But the Irish didn't want to get involved, they didn't want to be seen to be the people who would make it work. So when J.P. Morgan went public with that support Cubic put out a statement saying "Hold on, we've never had an offer made to us." '

This could not be a conventional takeover. 'It was riskier in the sense that when you mount a takeover you offer a certain amount in order to get to 75 per cent or 90 per cent or 51 per cent, whatever your hurdle is. So you don't commit more than the money required in clearing your hurdle. In this case you were committing to buying the Irish shares, regardless of what other shareholders might do and whether you succeeded in taking over the company. But the risk was reduced by the fact that the Glazers already had 28 per cent. They already had a lot of money invested. They might as well go double or quits. But secondly it also meant that in getting to the 75 per cent threshold (crucial because then no other shareholder can block you), once the Glazers had added the Irish shares to the ones they had already accumulated, it would be very straightforward.'

The problem for the Rothschild team was that it would not be easy to convince the banks and finance houses offering the money that this was the correct approach. The banks' horror scenario was that the Glazers would pay out a huge chunk of money to the Irish and would get over 50 per cent, which meant they had to make an offer to everyone. But they would fail to reach 75 per cent, and so would not be in total charge of the destiny of Manchester United.

However, while the Rule 9 bid route would cause problems for the Glazers with their financiers, it held enormous advantages in dealing with the Irish. Long before a formal bid was launched the Irish would have their money and would have got out of Manchester United, even before the fans knew what had happened, let alone be able to put them under pressure not to sell to the Americans. So given the take-over was being launched against a background of determined resistance by some fans who were pledged to stop it at all costs, the Glazers would have neatly outflanked these fans and presented them with a cold hard reality that the Glazers had the Irish shares, the Irish had the Glazers money and there was nothing anybody could do to alter that.

In appointing Rothschild as their M&A experts the Glazers had come a long way since that July day in 2002 when Avi Glazer had walked into the New York offices of Allen & Overy and spoken to Andrew Ballheimer about making an investment in European football. The journey had been a steep learning curve for the Glazers.

The first lesson was the very different way takeovers in the UK work as compared to the USA. In the USA takeovers are initially handled by lawyers, in the UK a merchant bank is always involved. Sometime from August 2003 Allen & Overy were giving the Glazers advice about UK takeovers and how they worked.

The Glazers were still without a British merchant bank when the first story of a Glazer bid surfaced – except there was no bid. The story mystified the Glazers.

On 12 February 2004, the Glazers increased their stake to 16.3 per cent, using Commerzbank to buy shares. Around this time they were visited by Keith Harris. The *Financial Times* reported that the Glazers had consulted Harris and the *Sunday Times* would later say, 'Keith Harris, the former chairman of the Football League, who heads the investment bank Seymour Pearce, is also expecting to be retained as an adviser to Glazer on any possible bid.' Harris himself said nothing publicly and has maintained his silence since, but my understanding is that his contact with the Glazers came after he sought them out. Sources close to the Glazers have told me that he flew to Florida to see them and expressed great keenness to work with them in order to help them buy United.

The Commerzbank story had broken soon after the '99 questions' letter was leaked to the press and just as militant fans' direct action against John Magnier and his racing interests was gathering force. The arrival of the Glazers on the scene gave the fans a new enemy to target. A legend was born when the *Sunday Times* on 15 February 2004 headlined an article, 'The Leprechaun – will this man buy United?'

The article narrated the story of how Malcolm Glazer had told the New York *Village Voice* newspaper that while his son Bryan wore $200 Hugo Boss trousers, he himself wore trousers costing $19.95. 'And you know something? I like my pants more than he likes his pants.' For the first time British newspaper readers were told a little of Glazer's background. Son of Orthodox Jews from Lithuania who had migrated to the States, he was born in Rochester, New York. He had inherited his father's watch-making business and then worked hard to make his first million, eventually moving from trailer parks to shopping malls and then sports franchises. He now lived in a $25 million palace in West Palm Beach, Florida, with another home in New York. The *Sunday Times* explained that his nickname, 'the Leprechaun', had been given to him by Tampa Bay Buccaneers fans despite the fact that he is not Irish but, said the paper, 'because of his short stature and ginger beard'.

The paper doubted whether Glazer had either the money or the guts to buy United. Oliver Houston of Shareholders United was quoted as saying, 'Someone like Malcolm Glazer is not going to want to take on 35,000 pesky fans who are all asking questions.' The paper said, 'There are also question marks over whether he truly has the resources to mount a full bid.' The strapline on the piece had said Glazer was 'small potatoes' compared to Roman Abramovich and the *Sunday Times* quoted a City insider as saying. 'He simply hasn't got Abramovich's wealth, Abramovich can buy £110m of new playing talent with loose change. Glazer would struggle to spend £10m after buying United.' 'Perhaps', concluded the piece, 'the story about the cheap pants doesn't seem so ridiculous after all.'

The paper did not mention that Glazer had proved himself a very skilful businessman who, like Carl Icahn or T. Boone Pickens, was a corporate raider. These were investors with money who targeted companies they felt had under-valued assets. They threatened to take them over and often walked away with a great deal of money. In 1989 Glazer had been involved in litigation when targeting Harley-Davidson. The company sued, accusing him of chicanery. The judge in the hearing called him 'a snake in sheep's clothing', but ten months later when Glazer sold his shares he made a large profit.

The *Sunday Times* was not alone in thinking the Glazers could not be considered serious buyers of Manchester United. At this stage most people, none of whom had any contact with the Glazers, concluded they were punters and not looking to own the club. Their share buying, however, had alerted the City takeover panel, as it led to United's share price rising to a three-year high of 290p.

The Glazers were not the only ones buying. The Irish were even more hectic buyers. In the previous three months Cubic had been steadily buying shares, taking their holding from 23 per cent on 2 December to just under 29 per cent on 11 February. This had raised speculation of a bid and the share price movement was watched anxiously by the Takeover Panel.

Within days they were on to Allen & Overy, and a number of extremely fraught conversations followed. The Panel demanded to know what was going on. Were the Glazers going to make a bid? This in turn led to calls between Avi, Joel and their advisers. These were uncharted waters for both the Panel and the Glazers. It was only as a result of these conversations that the Americans began to understand the very different way the British conduct takeovers. They had come up against the Panel's strict rules about who it talks to about takeovers. Under City takeover rules the Panel do not talk to the principals, the Glazers, or their lawyers, not even an international firm like Allen & Overy. In such situations they deal with what under the Takeover Code are called Rule 3 advisers, which means only financial advisers and bankers. As the Glazers did not have a merchant bank adviser at this stage, the Panel had to talk to Allen & Overy. But they did not like it and it made their conversations with Allen & Overy somewhat surreal.

The Panel was also interacting with Manchester United, but along more conventional City lines. Cazenove, the club's merchant banking advisers, handled discussions in just the way the Panel liked and understood. United were very keen to find out whether the Glazers were bidders. The Glazers would not rule out a takeover, but had no plans for bidding at this stage; a bid would only come with the consent of the board. The Panel initially wanted to put the club under a six-month offer period, but this was negotiated down to a month. It was, perhaps, the most curious offer period any public company has ever been subjected to. As far as the Glazers were concerned this was an offer period under a false pretext, as they were not at this stage bidding for the company nor had made any plans to do so. Throughout this period they kept insisting that the story that a bid was being mounted in the conventional sense was untrue, although they were looking at the possibilities. Eventually, advised by Allen & Overy, they issued a statement to that effect.

Mark Rawlinson had no doubts what this meant: 'My immediate reaction was that they were a potential bidder.' The Glazers' share buying, admits Rawlinson, had caused great uncertainty among the United board. 'The company was in a complete state of panic. We weren't quite sure what would happen.' But despite the fact that Manchester United was now a target company it decided its best course was to wait and see what happened.

But while inaction suited Manchester United, that was not an option for the Glazers. They knew they had to find a merchant bank adviser if they were to seriously contemplate a takeover. Not long after the talks with the Takeover Panel, and as a result of contacts through the Glazer family, J.P. Morgan were appointed as bankers. They brought Brunswick with them as PR advisers. Merchant banks generally employ their own advisers, and Brunswick had been involved with J.P. Morgan in many of the bank's deals. In the media Brunswick was presented as the Glazers' PR firm. This was strictly not true, although there was some interaction between the Glazers and Brunswick and its representatives went to Tampa, saw the stadium, took in a game and met all three of the Glazer brothers.

The choice of Brunswick was to prove significant. They, of course, had been Manchester United's first PR advisers when Glenn Cooper had floated the company. Started by Alan Parker back in the 1980s, they had an awesome reputation as a City PR firm, but the call from J.P. Morgan had come at a crucial time. The firm was just recovering from a bruising sporting encounter.

In July 2003 Barbara Cassani, leader of the London bid for the 2012 Olympic Games, had brought in Brunswick as PR advisers. But the experience of working with sports journalists had not proved a happy one. When Mike Lee joined the Olympic bid as leader of the communications team, one of his first jobs was to get rid of Brunswick. In his book *The Race for the 2012 Olympics*, he describes this as one of his crucial decisions: 'I saw very quickly the limitation of the PR agency. They were excellent in the City but in my view had limited experience of the cut and thrust of the sports media.' Lee describes how Brunswick did a less than satisfactory job of launching Cassani as bid leader; the event was hijacked by a group of residents of London's Coin Street who made anti-Olympics protests. Instead of selling the Games to Londoners, Cassani had to field hostile questions about a British bid being led by an American.

The whole London 2012 experience had a profound impact on Brunswick. Keen to make sure they had sporting expertise for the Manchester United job, it was decided to bring in Paul Ridley, the former sports editor of the *Sun*. The hope was that Ridley, who had of course also helped launch MUTV and could therefore claim to know United, would make sure J.P. Morgan's and the Glazers' side of the story got a fair run on the sports pages.

So from the moment J.P. Morgan took over, journalistic callers to Brunswick found Ridley returning their calls. The strategy was, as one Brunswick source told me, that 'They wanted to neutralise Shareholders United and the hardcore fans opposed to the bid.' Ridley tried hard to influence the back pages, but was far from successful. United fans committed to stopping the Glazers so loaded his mobile phone with calls that it crashed. He had to change his number and, moreover, keep it a secret; given he was a PR adviser, this was not much use. As we have seen, J.P. Morgan and Brunswick had to cope with all sorts of other nastiness ranging from angry calls to deliveries of tons of pizzas, tampons, used condoms, the unexpected arrival of taxis at their doors and attempts to subvert their computer systems.

For militant fans, any association with the Glazers was death. The daubing of Maurice Watkins' car with paint by the Manchester Education Committee after he sold a packet of shares which was then bought by the Glazers demonstrated that. Ironically at this stage Watkins had not even met the Glazers; he, like the rest of the board, only met them when in the summer United went on a tour of the USA.

It would seem that, around this time, fan pressure began to have an impact on the United board. Previously friendly to the Glazers, eager to encourage them to come in and make a bid, even suggesting the price of £3 which they felt the Irish would accept, the board now started getting anxious about any bid. But whatever their private fears about the Glazers, for the moment the subject did not surface publicly. On 31 March 2004 United announced its interim results for the year, but there was no reference to the Glazers when the *Manchester Evening News* interviewed David Gill. United's financial results were better than expected and all the talk was about the lessons of the Rio Ferdinand affair and why United were not competing in the transfer market with Chelsea. United had missed out on Arjen Robben, who went to the London club. But Gill said, 'Arjen Robben would have liked to come to us. We made what was a very significant offer (£8.5 million) for a player of nineteen who had great potential. Our scouts had assessed him. Unfortunately that wasn't enough for PSV. But we move on.'

Gill went on to say how United had spent £12.8 million for Louis Saha and £12 million for Cristiano Ronaldo. Although Gill did not go into the details of Saha's transfer it had required the intervention of Philip Green. Always keen on football, and a Tottenham supporter at heart, he had got involved when the deal ran into problems. With United very keen but Fulham's owner Al Fayed proving difficult, and Fulham accusing United of destabilizing the player, it was Green who asked Gill to be at Northolt airport on a Friday afternoon where he took his weekly jet back to his base in Monte Carlo. His yacht was berthed next to that of Mohammed Al Fayed and that lift on Green's jet meant Gill at last had the chance to do the deal in face to face negotiations with Al Fayed. On that Friday 23 January, Saha was signed.

There were other signings that Gill spoke about with much pride. Gill described the purchase of Tim Howard as 'a great buy'. Howard had cost £2.5 million and a further £5 million had been spent paying off Fabien Barthez's contract. Gill spoke of how happy Ferguson was with both his goalkeepers, Howard and Roy Carroll. Within a year, both Gill and Ferguson would be singing a very different tune.

The way Gill presented the story to Manchester's local paper, everything in the United garden was rosy. Ferguson's rolling contract was great as it meant the manager could go on and on. 'The rolling contract was designed to specifically take away some of that retirement talk.' He dismissed ideas that Ferguson might go and work for another Premiership club. He also spoke of plans to expand Old Trafford so it would seat another 7,500, taking the capacity to 75,000. He was not asked about the Glazers and made no mention of them.

But while the United board publicly pretended the Glazers did not exist, the Glazers pumped more of their own money into buying United shares. Their shareholding increased to 18.25 per cent in April and 19.1 per cent in June. By this time they had also met other people who had been associated with United, including Greg Dyke. The meeting with Dyke took place in April 2004, a couple of months after he had been forced out of his job as BBC Director-General and while he was considering his options. He gave the Glazers the impression he might quite like working with them.

The United board watched these developments with mounting concern. Rawlinson explains the mood in the board: 'There wasn't any opposition per se to somebody taking over the company, you can't do that. The difficulty was trying to find out what they had in mind in terms of price and structure. The position of the board was that if they had the financial muscle, if their first proposal had been three times the offer, and lots of equity, and not much going into debt, I think David [Gill] would have got a recommendation for them from the board. I think the problem was you have to know what people have in mind. Eventually, the board, in September 2004, laid down some ground rules, saying we need some certainty in this process. At this stage they [the Glazers] had not made an offer, it was only indicative. They had not put a business plan to the board.'

That month, September 2004 had seen Gill and Nick Humby fly to Florida for another meeting with the Glazers. Publicly the board did not want to give any hint of the panic the Glazers' buying of shares had caused. While their private thoughts may have been dominated by what the Americans might do, the official position was that this was a meeting where the two principal executives of the club were to outline United's plans in order to keep one of their major shareholders briefed, just the sort of meeting any well-run company holds. In fact, Gill and Humby were keener to find out what the Glazers' intentions were.

The board, says Rawlinson, 'told the Glazers that first of all they needed to sort it out'. The Glazers listened to what Gill and Humby had to say but, like the board, they could play a double game and did not reveal their entire hand.

In retrospect the September meeting was a crucial one and in many ways the turning point in relations with the Americans. It would ultimately lead to the breakdown in relations which culminated in the AGM of November 2004 when the Glazers voted the directors off and demonstrated who really yielded power at Old Trafford. Until then the Glazers were under the impression that the board were friendly to them and would back a bid provided the price was right. But after that it became clear that the board would do no such thing. However, given that the Glazers were offering to pay £3 a share, an exceedingly generous if not grossly overestimated price for the club, the board could not just knock it back. So they began to devise a strategy whereby they would never strictly be seen as rejecting the Glazers out of hand, while taking a position that kept them on the right side of fans opposed to any bid. The board were helped in their strategy by the way the Glazers played the game.

Despite public talk that the Glazers were making a bid, they did not come to the board and table an offer. Instead they made what may be called an indicative offer, saying they would be prepared to offer £3 if the board backed them. In a conventional bid situation, the board of a public company would have listened to the Glazers and said 'The price looks right, we can recommend it to our shareholders', or 'We do not think it is enough, we want more money for our shareholders.'

But the Manchester United board, desperately keen not to be seen as selling out to the Glazers, did not do that. Instead they told the Glazers to find out what another shareholder thought. It was a neat passing of the buck, clearly designed to make sure that the board avoided any flak from hostile fans. It helped the board that there was another shareholder, the Irish, who did not want to be kings but were the real kingmakers of Old Trafford. The board's position is well summed up by Rawlinson: 'The board knew that for a bid to fly the Glazers needed the support of the Irish. The Glazers were never going to get their bid going unless the Irish were prepared to accept it. We said, don't come back to us until you've got the Irish.'

This advice took the form of a letter. Not long after Gill and Humby had returned from Florida, Rawlinson started drafting the letter, a process in which David Anderson of Cazenove and David Gill joined. The final draft was circulated round the board and then sent to the Glazers: 'Yes, a letter went out to the Glazers saying, tell us where you are on Cubic, tell us where you are on financing structure. They had not indicated how they were going to do their financing structure. We wanted information about what the conditions of the offer would be, what their future intentions in respect of the company were.

'Then there was more press speculation. In early October 2004 we had to confirm the Glazers had made an approach and we had sent a letter asking for clarification of their proposal. The Takeover Panel was jumping up and down. We talked to the Takeover Panel and told them we'd had preliminary discussions about a possible offer. But there was currently no definitive proposal for the board to consider, which was true.' They also told the Panel of the board's understanding that the Glazer family and their advisers were currently in discussions with Cubic, and that those talks were ongoing. 'And then we said that the Glazer family could proceed if it considered all of its options. So what we told the Panel was that they hadn't gone away, but there were no ongoing talks.'

According to Rawlinson, the Glazers 'made various attempts to get Cubic Expression on side. We don't know what was said between the Irish and the Glazers. But they could not get the Irish on side and we got the message back that the Irish weren't happy about what the Glazers had proposed. I can't say how we heard this. It reached me second or third hand. The fact is discussions between the Irish and the Glazers broke down.'

It was J.P. Morgan who, on behalf of the Glazers, tried to contact the Irish, although this by all accounts was a very curious affair. One source close to the Irish told me: 'There was telephone contact sometime in October 2004, two phone calls in an hour. No offer was made, no price discussed. They tried to talk to the Irish about a conditional offer and for the Irish to put pressure on the board to give due diligence. The Irish only wanted an unconditional offer and were not saying whether they would accept or reject such an offer.'

A source close to J.P. Morgan said, 'J.P. Morgan always worked on the principle that this would be an agreed deal. They had to persuade the Irish. They needed to be careful with the Irish and the board. But the way it worked out was the board did not want to go for the deal unless the Irish wanted it and the Irish did not want to go for it unless the board approved.'

The Irish were left bemused by the calls and the United board were exultant that their strategy of forcing the Glazers to turn to the Irish had worked. The Glazers had not forced open the Irish door, which would have placed the board in a very tricky situation.

The board announcement to the Stock Exchange on the Glazers was made on 15 October 2004. The board may have hoped that, having failed with the Irish, the Glazers would now go away but that is not what happened. It was the Glazers' reaction to the announcement that inspired a new nickname for them. Says Rawlinson: 'The next thing the Glazers did was increase their shares from 19 per cent to 25.5 per cent. At that point we really realised they were like the Terminator, that keeps on reforming from nothing. It smashes itself into smithereens, it goes into lots of silver pieces and reforms itself. It was clear that the Glazers just carried on whatever happened. You knew they weren't going to go away, they were seriously there. We then thought we had to try and find out exactly what they had in mind.'

Detailed discussions took place with J.P. Morgan and Cazenove. The discussions led the Glazers to present their plans for buying the club and their vision of how Manchester United could run the business. However, they left the presentation to their advisers and did not feel it necessary to make the journey to London. Keeping in touch via telephone and e-mail, they were, says a source, 'very methodical, very calm, very even tempered'. J.P. Morgan presented the Glazers' plan in late October, at meetings held in the London offices of Cazenove between the board and its advisers and the Glazers' advisers. According to Rawlinson, 'That is when the club began to understand a bit more about the proposal that they had in mind. And the area we got into is the proposed capital structure for the bid. This was the first time we had really understood them, how they were going to finance their purchase of the club.'

J.P. Morgan valued United at just over £800 million and said the Glazers would contribute £365 million of equity. J.P. Morgan would lend £500 million of bridge finance which would be refinanced through £150 million of junk bonds and £150 million of senior debt – debt that would have priority for payment in a liquidation. Later J.P. Morgan also presented a business plan of sorts, which spoke of aggressively increasing United's sponsorship income to £15 million a year, possible sale and lease back of the stadium which would bring in £175 million with lease costs of £12.5 million, player purchases capped at £10 million a year and an increase in season ticket prices. The plan showed the bank would receive fees of around £30 million. According to a report in *Legal Business* some months later, the document is also believed to have said that if one part of the plan failed the club would struggle to pay its debt and could go bankrupt. The sale and lease back proposal would come to haunt the Glazers for many months. Rawlinson says: 'We didn't get a formal business plan. That came much later. What they showed then was the details for the first time of their financing structure, how they were going to finance it rather than what they were going to do for the club going forward.'

In return for presenting their plans the Glazers now wanted due diligence, access to the books of account, the management accounts and other details that are not publicly disclosed but which someone wanting to buy a company needs to know. The board knew the money being offered for the shares was fabulous. Any shareholder offered £3 a share – apart from fan shareholders who hated the Glazers – would immediately grab it. So if the board were to deny the Glazers access, they had to come up with a very convincing argument that would not lay them open to action by shareholders.

This is when Rawlinson came up with what came to be known as the Scottish strategy, an attempt to legally thwart the Glazers and stop them from looking at the books. In essence it argued that the directors of a company are not responsible merely to the shareholders but have wider interests. Rawlinson says: 'It was legitimate for the board to worry about the financial structure and the effect it might have on the club going through. Support for that view came from the fact that when you are directors of a company, you are supposed to act in the interests of the company. You are there as a custodian of the company's interests. Football clubs are pretty unique in that.'

The Scottish case that he relied on was Coats Paton versus Dawson International. Rawlinson explains: 'There's lots of authority, loads of authors backing such a view. In case law relating to directors' duties, it is absolutely clear that directors owe their duties to the company, not just to shareholders. I think the duty of the directors is to act in the best interests of the company, not in the best interests of the shareholders.

'I'll give you one example of how this can happen. Suppose the Premier League say that if you get taken over by an overseas bidder, an American bidder, you get booted out of the Premiership. Not inconceivable. And let us suppose Glazer had been offering £10 a share, not just £3. Now, the directors of the company would have been in breach of their fiduciary duties had they recommended that offer because it would demonstrably not be in the interests of the company to get booted out of the Premier League. Fantastic for the shareholders, they get £10 per share. But actually, as directors you owe duties to the company, and not to the shareholders. You have to advise shareholders on the takeover situation – directors have to advise shareholders what to do – but they still owe their duties to the company.'

Rawlinson advised the board over a period of time, through various meetings in October. Most of these were held in the evening at Centrica's offices in London although later meetings, round about the time of the AGM, usually took place at Old Trafford. Rawlinson took the board through the Scottish strategy, giving board members notes, talking them through drafts, showing them slides. Rawlinson liked giving each board member a series of slides printed on paper – each slide having a number of bullet points, normally six to a page – and then talking to the slides.

The crucial meeting took place sometime in the last week of October 2004. The board had to be sure that in denying the Glazers access to the books their action could be legally justified. Rawlinson's assurance that in well-established case law they had backing for refusing the Glazers was immensely comforting. It meant that in rejecting the Glazers the board would not lay themselves open to civil action by shareholders. They could not have taken this step without Rawlinson's legal advice.

On 25 October the board made public its opposition to the proposed Glazer capital structure. The statement pointed out that financial returns were very closely correlated with performance on the pitch, that there was a strong relationship between the special capital structure the Glazers were proposing and performance on the field and that the board had decided to inform all shareholders that it would regard an offer at this level of borrowing as not being in the best interests of the company.

Rawlinson is very proud of the advice he gave and sees the board statement as 'a very clever, pre-emptive strike against the Glazers'. However, he knew that with the Irish and the Glazers between them owning well over 50 per cent the game was already over. United could no longer remain an independent company. The refusal to deny Glazer access to the books had merely bought time: 'At this moment the United board was facing quite a difficult situation. They knew they had the Irish out there and they could put Glazer in control tomorrow. The board had no cards to play at all. In other words the game for the control of Manchester United was over in October 2004. In a normal takeover, the game was over then. If they could afford to there was no reason why the Glazers could not have bought the shares there and then.'

The only strategy was for the board to fight a rearguard action, in the hope that either the Irish would not accept the Glazers or their financing would not work out. It was like a match which had gone to extra time and where the golden goal was to decide the outcome. If the Glazers came up with the money and the Irish accepted, a golden goal would have been scored and the match would be over.

As we have already seen it was this rejection by the board, and the refusal to grant the Glazers access to the books of United, that led the Glazers to teach the board a lesson at the AGM of November 2004.

There was also another internal problem for the board. They had begun to feel less than happy with Cazenove. Sir Roy Gardner was almost apoplectic about what he felt was a terrible conflict of interest. Just as the battle with the Glazers was heating up, Cazenove had linked up with J.P. Morgan to form a J.P. Morgan/Cazenove joint venture. Words were exchanged between Gardner and David Mayhew. Gardner, who had brought Mayhew's Cazenove in as the club's adviser, was more than a little peeved that United's adviser was now formally tied up with the merchant bank which was helping the Glazers take over the club. Cazenove tried to reassure Gardner that if there was ever a question of the Glazers making a hostile bid then they would step down. It would seem J.P. Morgan too now made it clear that they would not be involved in a hostile bid. Gardner's less than friendly words with Mayhew showed how in his eyes the Glazers were now a very hostile shareholder.

The board's rebuff of the Glazers, however, pleased the fans. When, within hours of the AGM, J.P. Morgan and Brunswick resigned, these fans convinced the media that the Glazer threat was over and the Americans had been repelled. This helped spin the story that the Glazers' victory over the board was in fact a victory for the board. But insiders like Rawlinson knew that was far from true. And, as we have seen, little over a month after J.P. Morgan's withdrawal the Glazers had employed Rothschild.

The experience of J.P. Morgan and Brunswick at the hands of hostile fans did, however, have an impact on how Rothschild tried to handle any public exposure they had working for the Glazers. Just as J.P. Morgan brought in Brunswick, so Smithfield came in with Rothschild. John Antcliffe, a former merchant banker who had spent twelve years with Rothschild, had gone into PR and it was only natural he should look after his old firm. A source at Smithfield told me: 'We at Smithfields are long-term advisers to Rothschild. John Antcliffe, having been an investment banker with Rothschild, has a very close relationship with the bank. Our association on the Glazer account started in January 2005. Some of us are football fans and John isn't a football fan. We asked him "Are we really sure this is a wise thing to take on?" John's response was, "You know where Rothschild originates from, don't you? Manchester. That's Rothschild bedrock. And if Rothschild believe in the family and in the takeover, that is good enough for us." We submitted a strategy to the client soon after the appointment back in January. Our strategy was one scenario in case it leaked, another scenario maintaining radio silence until a bid was announced. Then we provided advice on how to best break the silence.'

An appointment like this cannot be kept silent, but Smithfield and

Rothschild did prevent it leaking out for a month. The *Mail on Sunday* first had the story. The paper's Lisa Buckingham rang Leitao who, well aware of the problems the public outing of J.P. Morgan had caused, asked her not to write it. John Ancliffe and Smithfield got involved in negotiations with the paper and, according to one source, 'John Ancliffe said please don't print that, I would appreciate it, it is a very sensitive time. They duly didn't. The paper was given something else on some other deal.' But then a few weeks later the *Standard* got hold of the story and broke the news.

This was on 28 January 2005. But neither Rothschild nor Smithfield faced anything like the harassment that J.P. Morgan and Brunswick had endured. Rothschild did face a backlash from some fans, although one attempted action went wrong. As a result seventeen Manchester United fans were stuck in the lift in the Manchester office of Rothschild on a Saturday, when nobody was in. They might have stayed there for much of the weekend but for a fortunate alarm call. There were also other attempts to disrupt the bank. Leitao recalls: 'There was some really boring stuff that was mildly irritating. Like screeds of deliveries, Ann Summers catalogues, Rentokil sent round the houses – mildly amusing but after a while a bit irritating. But there was some amazing stuff.

'Clearly among the small minority of supporters there were one or two IT people. They were very good, they tried to bring down our e-mail system. They did bring it down one Sunday afternoon for an hour and a half. They took our New York office down and got us in London for a couple of hours.' The fans came near to closing down Rothschilds' system on a number of other occasions. 'Actually the activity of these people always went up on weekends, so people were doing it from their basements, as it were, rather than whatever employment they had. They were quite good at that apparently. But our guys were pretty good too. But to counter against such activity is expensive because you need loads of IT people running around buildings. I don't know how these things work, but basically when someone starts an attack you've got to respond and react. It lasted about two or three weeks and then I think they got bored, so that stopped.'

The Manchester United fans organising the direct action had picked up the names of the partners and directors from Companies House. Like Allen & Overy, Rothschild, after applying to the Secretary of State, were able to remove the addresses. They put in additional security at the office and at certain people's homes, but Leitao was not worried.

One reason was that he had done his own personal deal with the papers, convincing them that because of the security threat posed by some of the fans it would not be right to reveal the names of the Glazer advisers. 'I was probably the best kept secret. No one knew. It was an unwritten rule with all the newspapers that I'd speak to them but they weren't allowed to print my name, because I didn't want the papers turning the hostility generally directed at everyone to just me.' Smithfield also came to the same arrangement. John Ancliffe led the dialogue with a selected group in the media on the assurance that Smithfield would not get any publicity. Three other members of Rothschild's M&A team took on assumed identities. Roland Oakshett became George Jefferies, Edward Halfon became Bruce Cohen, and Marco van Oord signed on fanzine websites as Marco van Dermeyde.

No attempt was made to counter the image of the Glazers, who at this stage had no direct contact with Smithfield. Here the Irish factor came into play. A spokesman for Smithfield explains: 'The last thing we wanted was to antagonise the biggest block of shareholders, John Magnier and J. P. McManus. How the Irish reacted was integral to Rothschild's strategy. The thinking was not to do anything to upset them.'

The media were faced with two problems: the Manchester United board were saying very little and there was no access to the Glazers. The vacuum thus created was filled by fans hostile to the bid, who succeeded in setting their own agenda. However, in the process they grossly overestimated their power to influence the bid. They pictured it as a replay of the Sky bid – it was now part of United fan folklore that fan power had stopped Murdoch. As we have seen, the reality did not quite match the myth. And to add to the fans' problems, there was a new, very unhelpful factor. Against Murdoch the various fan groups had shown remarkable unity and worked well together. Now there were divisions in the ranks and although these divisions did not become public they had an impact on the anti-Glazer strategy to be followed.

THE FUTILE SEARCH FOR MERLIN

ON 5 NOVEMBER 2004 Gary Wilder, managing director and co-head of the Asset Finance Group of the City merchant bank Nomura, wrote a four-page letter offering to help the supporters buy out the Irish and the Glazers. The letter, marked 'strictly private and confidential' and 'subject to contract', was addressed to Jules Spenser, chair of IMUSA and Nick Towle, chair of Shareholders United, with copies to Keith Harris and Harvey Alexander, another member of Shareholders United. The letter to Towle was sent to his London office at Crowell & Moring, a legal firm where he was a partner.

Nomura headed the letter Project Merlin; this was the name given to Manchester United, whose name did not appear in the letter. Interestingly, both the Irish and the Glazers were identified, although for much of the letter they were abbreviated to C (standing for Cubic) and G.

Wilder outlined a plan to buy out G and C. They would be offered £3 a share. He assumed that a small premium of 5 per cent to the current share price would be 'required to persuade G & C to agree to our proposal'. This, said Wilder, would mean raising £450 million. Nomura would provide £230 million of secured long-term debt finance, the balance being funded by a rights issue of £220 million:

> Under this strategy, Shareholders would be presented with a package that includes both an orderly exit by G & C, and a financing proposition that would be of long-term benefit for the company. It is assumed that a board of Merlin would come to the view that this proposal is in the interest of Merlin and that they would be satisfied that the benefit to the company of arranging an exit for G and C by way of buy-back is sufficient to justify the company incurring the required level of debt to effect the buy-back and to pay the potential premium that may be required.

The scheme that Wilder presented was a leveraged buyout and complicated in the extreme. It involved several scenarios. It would require board approval. However, if this was not forthcoming the letter discussed issues such as removing the board or replacing directors who did not agree, which would mean calling an extraordinary general meeting. There would also have to be a court-approved 'scheme of arrangement' whereby a new holding company was formed and superimposed on the existing one. This would be necessary since, under the Companies Act, a company can only buy back shares from distributable profits. Manchester United had £95 million for that purpose. Given that it would require £450 million to buy out Glazer and Cubic, this meant a further £355 million would be required. The rights issue would provide £220 million of this, but Nomura also suggested that it would be necessary to increase reserves to be used to buy shares. This would come from a reduction of capital, requiring the scheme of arrangement and the formation of a new holding company. The new company would agree to a reduction of capital so as to create a total of £135 million of distributable reserves. As an alternative, Nomura also proposed forming an unlimited liability company, or a company registered abroad, which could then issue preference shares at a subscription price of £135 million to an 'orphan' company that would be financed by Nomura. All this would mean a shareholders' meeting, with 75 per cent of those present voting in favour if the scheme was to go ahead.

The Nomura letter indicates the extraordinary lengths to which fans opposed to Glazer were prepared to go in order to stop him. It is fascinating that, in order to get rid of the Glazers and the Irish, the fans had discussed with Nomura a plan to load on United a debt only slightly less than the level of debt that the Glazers eventually loaded on to the club. Equally fascinating are the meetings between the supporters and Nomura that had led to this letter. Wilder's letter began by saying, 'Further to our previous discussions', and it was clear from the letter that he had been given the impression by the supporters he met that both Glazer and Cubic might want to sell and that supporters, while keen on increasing 'their influence on Merlin', were not 'interested in acquiring the company as a whole'.

The fact that one of the people Wilder sent the letter to was Keith Harris was hugely significant and the subsequent fate of the offer provides a fascinating insight into the way the fan activists worked. And the interaction between Harris and the various fan groups reveals that, despite the public façade, the response to Glazer created deep divisions in the various fan groups, even those listed at the top of Wilder's letter.

The victory over Murdoch, as we have seen, was claimed as a huge fan victory, a demonstration of what fans can do when they are united. After the victory the two main organisations – IMUSA, which had existed for some years before the Sky bid, and Shareholders United, which was born as a result of the bid – decided it made more sense to go their separate ways. Andy Walsh, who had led the IMUSA campaign against Murdoch, says, 'It was decided that we needed to split our resources. IMUSA decided to hand over all dealings with the plc and the business side of things to Shareholders United, a sister organisation. We would encourage fans to become members of Shareholders United to build up their membership. IMUSA should turn back to match-day issues: ticketing, prices, standing issues and things like that.'

Walsh, himself a computer technologist who had given up his job during the Murdoch campaign and made his front room an office, needed some income. After remaining active for about a year following the bid, he decided to take a back seat in IMUSA. 'The Murdoch campaign sapped the energy of a lot of people. It was a very intense campaign.' This split of responsibility between the two main fan groups worked reasonably well for some time. 'Shareholders United were able to open a dialogue with the board,' says Walsh, 'that the board would not open with us in IMUSA. The board could not ignore Shareholders United, who represented supporter shareholders, in the same way it ignored other fans.'

Ferguson's problems with the Irish revealed the limitations of these two main fan groups. They could not claim to represent all shades of opinion, certainly not groups that preferred illegal methods of protest. The Irish problem saw the rise of previously unknown groups such as the Manchester Education Committee. By then IMUSA and Walsh's relationship with the board, which had been blossoming after Martin Edwards left, had turned sour. Walsh says he warned Peter Kenyon and David Gill that there were darker forces around. 'I had arguments in fans' forums with Peter Kenyon and David Gill and I said to them, "If you think that I'm being unreasonable, then you ought to see the people I have to deal with when I go to IMUSA meetings. People are making demands and I have to moderate those demands to be able to come to these meetings and put forward an agenda which I think you can sign up to. If you are not happy with what I'm saying now, you want to see the extremities of the arguments that are currently being put." But having started the dialogue with IMUSA and raised the hopes of supporters, they then dashed it by shutting the dialogue down.'

The board's point was that all matters of the sort IMUSA raised should be dealt with by the fans' forum. While Walsh gives credit to United for sending high-powered representatives to the forum – in contrast to most clubs who, he says, send 'underlings and junior managers' – he is convinced 'IMUSA was cynically used by the board to try and derail fans.'

But, if the board was cynical with the fans, then the two main fan groups also played a cynical game when dealing with extreme groups such as the Manchester Education Committee. They had nothing to do with them but they never wholeheartedly condemned them. Jim White has acutely summed up the relationship between these two main groups and the extreme ones as 'football's equivalent of the Sinn Fein–Provisional IRA relationship. Publicly, like Sinn

Fein, they were against any violent illegal acts, but privately they were glad somebody was doing it.'

The board's decision to shun IMUSA had already made it re-examine its strategy and the arrival of the Glazers on the scene made this even more urgent. So, despite the fact that shareholder matters were supposed to be the exclusive domain of Shareholders United, IMUSA also began to take an interest in who owned their club. According to Walsh, sometime in 2004 they opened a dialogue with the Irish to find out their intentions. The dialogue lasted for over a year, well into 2005: 'There were indirect contacts with Cubic. Through an intermediary. I can't name him. We spoke to somebody who we know is Cubic's person. It was genuine. And in all the discussions we had with Cubic they constantly reiterated the point that they were in for the long term. We were led to believe that if anybody came to them with signs of an offer and they were willing to sell we would be the preferred buyer for their shares.'

These discussions with Cubic, or someone claiming to know Cubic's mind, led IMUSA to look for a merchant bank. Walsh says, 'We were in negotiation with Nomura to obtain sufficient funding for buying the Irish out.'

At the same time Shareholders United were also getting in touch with Nomura, although neither Walsh nor Nick Towle of Shareholders United would tell me who put them in touch. Walsh says, 'It came about through contacts we have at Nomura. Mutual contacts. Through the fanzines and IMUSA, we have an extensive range of contacts with United fans throughout the city. One of the benefits of supporting a club like United is that there are United fans everywhere and we make sure that we find the right person in the right place. It was a mutual friend of one of our key activists, who was a key activist during the Murdoch campaign.'

Towle told me, 'We got introduced to Nomura via a guy who is in the background and who, I think, will want to remain so. This person knew Gary Wilder.'

It is normal in such fan organisations, which often have the characteristics of small political sects, to jealously guard their secrets. But it is significant that well after the Glazer takeover neither Walsh nor Towle should disclose who put them in touch with Nomura. The reason may be that the groups' main conduits to Nomura were actually David Bick and Keith Harris. Certainly Bick has provided the clearest explanation as to how the Nomura contact came. He told me: 'The fans wanted me to investigate a possible method for countering Glazer so I approached Keith Harris. It was in effect IMUSA but it also involved Shareholders United at that point. Conversations had been going on between me and the fans' groups going back two years, even before Glazer became a problem. I had an established relationship with Shareholders United and IMUSA.

'Then when the Glazer threat came along, the question was: what could we do to counter that threat? This was around September or October 2004, before the AGM. I spoke to Keith Harris about it and he suggested that we went to Nomura. The result, first of all, was that a representative of Shareholders United and a representative of IMUSA met Keith, Oliver Houston and Nick Towle for Shareholders United and Jules Spencer from IMUSA. Nomura then separately held a meeting with representatives of Shareholders United and IMUSA and from that emerged that letter saying this is what we can do. Shareholders United in particular say that they spoke or could speak for about 18% of the equity. Keith was sent a copy and we waited for a response from Shareholders United.'

But when I asked Towle whether Nomura was Keith Harris's doing, his response was interesting. 'No, funnily enough, it wasn't. He sort of piggybacked it. Richard Kurt [the former IMUSA press officer who had been forced to resign after he made critical comments about Alex Ferguson over the Paul Ince issue] had been speaking to Keith Harris for a while but he [Harris] never talked to us. Richard Kurt, if you like, kept him away from the mainstream fans' group. So we didn't know. Keith Harris had originally been working with the Glazers. I think he had some connection with Commerzbank, helping the Glazers or someone connected with their initial share searches, their borrowing of money from Commerzbank. People found out about it and obviously contacted Keith and he got rather worried and started talking to them. He didn't want any aggro from the heavy mob.'

By the time of the Nomura offer, Harris had been involved with supporters' groups for about a year, 'purely because he wanted to keep the channel open with the people, the wilder side of the United supporters. He wanted to be involved and he wanted to lead. He was popping up all the time. He would love to be chairman of Manchester United. Keith Harris was involved in the Nomura discussions but the actual introduction to Nomura had come via somebody else. I'd better not say who it was.'

Interestingly, Towle is fulsome in his praise of Bick: 'David Bick was a classic operator. He's very good. You can't get better really. He's one of those guys who gets the job done.'

The reluctance of Walsh and Towle to acknowledge Harris's involvement, despite the fact that Wilder sent a copy of the letter to Harris, shows that some of the fans just could not forgive him for being on the other side during the Murdoch bid and also, perhaps, his subsequent flirtation with the Glazers. Bick says, 'There was clearly, initially, at Shareholders United a huge suspicion of Keith Harris. He'd been an adviser to the board on the Sky bid, he was a suited Manchester United supporter. The sheer ignorance that some of these people displayed was breathtaking. Because of having that suspicion they did not realise that when we said Keith was prepared to get behind their endeavours, he meant it. They then dallied for too long. After the Nomura letter went off Keith waited for a response, essentially from Shareholders United, who were leading the charge on it. Nothing happened for months. In the end they came forward and said we accept that Keith is doing this for all the right reasons. It was too late by then. They spent too much time pursuing their own agenda, forgetting where the cause lay, suspecting people of things that never existed. In my opinion they effectively wasted six months that could have been put to use in finding a real solution to combat the invaders.'

Towle rejects this charge. 'That's wrong. The first offer of financing from Nomura was unworkable. The offer was dependent upon passing a special resolution and a form of financing which involved the club borrowing money and basically doing what the Glazers have done. But on the day after they sent the offer through Glazer was on 28 per cent and therefore, we lost any possibility of getting the special resolution passed which would have required a 75 per cent majority.' So the offer lay dormant. 'But we kept up a dialogue with Nomura all the way through. They were very helpful and they really wanted to help.' However, this help would not surface again until April 2005. By that time the whole landscape of the bid had changed.

If Bick is right that Towle and Shareholders United wasted time over Nomura, part of the explanation may also lie in the fact that in the months preceding the letter the board had held out the prospect to Shareholders United that they could finally have the sort of real boardroom influence that all fan groups dream about. In a way that had happened at no other Premiership club, for a few short months in 2004 the United boardroom door had been tantalisingly opened. Although by November 2004, when Wilder was writing his letter, the door had once again closed as a result of the various offer periods following the Glazers' buying of shares, Towle and his colleagues had reason to think that it was not shut completely, but left slightly ajar.

It is easy to see why at this stage Shareholders United would have every reason to feel pleased with how far they had got with the board and congratulate themselves that years of perseverance had finally overcome initial suspicion. All supporter groups would like to influence their board; in the lower reaches of the League they do exercise much influence and some even own clubs. But in the Premiership no fan group of shareholders had established quite the relationship that Shareholders United managed with the United board by the summer of 2004.

It had taken much effort to open the boardroom door. The relationship had started in a very hesitant way soon after Martin Edwards left. Towle says, 'Under Martin Edwards we had no relationship with the board. We didn't even try for it. But when Kenyon came in he wanted to open things up. He was about marketing and satisfaction. So we got the fans' forum, we got the charter, we got him to come to our meetings every year, we had an open meeting with questions and answers. It was a good dialogue but nothing really came of it.

They obviously didn't see us as any kind of threat but they thought it was a useful thing to talk to us, a useful sounding board. We also got an automatic place on the fans' forum and all that was progress.'

As they tried to prise open the boardroom door Shareholders United were also building up their membership. 'We had about fifteen hundred members in the early days. In the summer of 2003, when Kenyon went, we probably had five to eight thousand. By May 2004 we had ten thousand. Our objective was for Manchester United to remain under independent ownership, not owned by any single person or company but with the supporters having a share stake, so that it would never be taken over by somebody like Glazer or the Irish. No one person would be in control.'

The relationship blossomed once David Gill replaced Kenyon. 'When Kenyon left and Gill came in it got much better because David Gill and Nick Humby were much more open. Gill and Gardner quickly realised because of all the takeover speculation that we could be very useful. Gardner was very different to Roland Smith. Roland Smith was another one who really did not give us the time of day. He didn't see us at all. Possibly that's where Kenyon did run up against a genuine barrier. We'll never know. But by 2004 we had reason to think that our voices were being heard.'

It was the autumn of 2003 which Towle feels marked the turning point in the relationship between Shareholders United and the board, following the shareholders' meeting where Michael Crick spotted that certain shareholders asking questions were plants. 'Michael worked it out and raised the questions at the AGM. That was the turning point for us because Jonathan Michie [then chair of Shareholders United] stood up and said that with all this speculation about shareholdings they should talk to Shareholders United, the independent shareholders' group. Both Gill and Gardner stood up at this stage and said yes, they were very happy to talk about that. That publicly signalled for the first time that they were ready to talk to us about co-operating. That was it, the door had opened. We left the meeting pleased that the board had finally recognised that the supporters had a legitimate interest and there was a dialogue to be had. So we set up a meeting with Gill and Gardner in December 2003.'

A morning meeting over tea and biscuits was held in the boardroom of Centrica's Mount Street office in London's West End. Both Gill and Gardner were present as Towle and his colleagues outlined their plans: 'There was myself, Jonathan, Duncan and Theresa, my wife, who was at that time vice-chair of Shareholders United. I was just a legal adviser although I was on the committee. We did a PowerPoint presentation, which took about fifteen to twenty minutes, about what we would like to see from them. It was the history of how we got started, how we'd got to where we were and how we thought that having a supporters' trust with a chunk of shares collectively held by supporters would be beneficial to the club because we're the long-term, emotional stakeholders. We weren't going to sell out our shares to financial speculators. We were not there for the dividends.

'We asked for things like a link on the website, a mail-out to all the United members. All the things that they could do to help us spread our message and get more members in through the club's official distribution centre. Until that meeting we'd always had a problem. There had been mutual suspicion and everything we'd suggested to either Kenyon or Gill came back: "You can't do that." But, at that meeting, finally we were getting signals that things were moving in our direction. They said, "We'll get back to you. We've got to talk to our lawyers and we will talk to Cazenove." There were legal issues about how far they could go to favour one shareholder against another. We realised that things had changed. We still didn't quite believe what we were hearing. But we came away from the meeting very happy.'

Gill and Gardner had told Shareholders United, 'We'll get back to you by the end of January.' But before they could do that the first Glazer offer period intervened. This was ironic, given that the Glazers felt that period was a bogus one, but its consequences could not be avoided. Towle says, 'We had to shut down communications. They weren't allowed to talk to us and we couldn't talk to them about share ownership, for obvious reasons. However, the signal we got was that they wanted to continue the dialogue. By the end of the first offer period Shareholders United had doubled their membership. It had been around five thousand in the summer of 2003, now it was ten thousand.'

The board kept its promise to talk again once the offer period had ended. Early in May 2004, talks resumed. If the first meeting had been with Gill and Gardner, subsequent meetings were mostly with Nick Humby and David Beswitherick. Towle recalls: 'We started a series of meetings with them. All over the place. At Old Trafford. One in London at Freshfields – the first one. That was in early May. Then every month or so, or every few weeks we were meeting. We held meetings all the way through 2004, five or six meetings which were very friendly. A mix of people from our side attended. Myself, Jonathan, Theresa, Duncan and Oliver. It was a rolling group of people who attended these meetings, during which we developed our ideas.'

Initially at these meetings Towle and his group were like missionaries in front of heathens. They found that many of their ideas – and they were brimful of ideas – had never been considered by the board: 'We had all sorts of ideas that they hadn't thought of. I have to say, they're fairly unimaginative, the directors of Manchester United. They're good guys, but they aren't connected to the fans and they don't understand. They look at it in marketing terms. How can you market to the fans? How do we sell to the fans? They don't understand they've got to deal with the fans on their own ground and treat them properly. Fans are different. They don't like being patronised, sold down to, talked down to. A lot of them don't anyway.'

The basic idea Shareholders United wanted to sell to the board was the setting up of a supporters' trust that could hold a block of shares which would never be sold and would mean that the club effectively became bid proof. It could never be bought by one person: 'What we were talking about was the establishment of what we called an independent supporters' club. We had explained in our initial presentation about the concept of the industrial and provident society [a cooperative run for the benefit of the community and registered under the Industrial and Provident Societies Act 1965], how in the lower leagues many clubs were now owned by their trusts and by the fans and how it was a beneficial thing for football generally. But, of course, it hasn't permeated up to the Premier League in any way at all. So the board was really learning about it for the first time.

'The trust we were talking about forming would be an independent group – independent from the club and in a way independent from us. The board wanted it to be seen to be a new thing. By the end of our meetings we had agreed a set of rules for a trust where Manchester United would encourage fans to buy shares. It was dissimilar to our share scheme in that this was a collective pot so that shares were not held in individual fans' names. It would be held in the name of the trust, a genuine collective holding on behalf of all fans everywhere, basically locked in for ever, not to be sold.'

By the summer of 2004 such was the degree of understanding between these two once mutually hostile groups that, although Shareholders United's website still bragged about how it had stopped the board selling to Murdoch, the board now offered money to help them build up this independent supporters' trust: 'We asked for money and they agreed to give us funding to set it up and get it going. They were being absolutely, genuinely co-operative and Gill made a public statement at that time saying that supporters having a collective stake would bring stability to the shareholder base. By August 2004 we had got to a point where we could move forward. We'd agreed but the only thing we didn't have was final agreement on how we would get to our objectives.'

Towle was realistic that even if the supporters' trust was formed it would initially have only a very small percentage of shares. 'We didn't really have a target but we all realised that it wasn't going to grow suddenly, it wasn't going to get to 10, 20 per cent within a very short time. But that was our long-term project.'

But just as Towle, who had become chairman in May 2004, was thinking that his group had gone where no supporters' group had gone in a major English club, events intervened. To borrow Rawlinson's phrase, the Terminator had re-formed and was attacking United again. All the discussions with the board became irrelevant. 'In August 2004,' says Towle, 'everything changed. The

Glazers made their first serious approach and we went back into an offer period. The conversations stopped completely. And they never resumed.'

It was after this that the approach to Nomura came. We have already seen how sensitive Shareholders United and IMUSA remain to Keith Harris's involvement in the Nomura affair. The whole issue also revealed the deep divisions within the supporters' ranks. Towle admits with great reluctance that there were differences of opinion between Shareholders United and other Manchester United supporters like Richard Kurt on the issue: 'There was a little bit of a power thing going on there between the *Red Issue* people, Richard Kurt's people and us. They didn't get on with Oliver [Houston]. Oliver's a spikey character. He's a fantastic attack dog, the sort of person you would expect on a political campaign. Exactly like James Carvill [Bill Clinton's 'attack dog' during his two successful US presidential campaigns]. I've had my own problems with Oliver, I'm not going to go into them. Oliver is very in your face.'

But if Oliver Houston's personality was a factor, other more fundamental differences on the planned strategy led to a great deal of tension not only between Kurt and Shareholders United but between the two organisations that had bonded so well against Murdoch.

Like Towle, Walsh and others at IMUSA are reluctant to talk publicly about these differences, but it is clear talking to Walsh that he does not hold the activity of Shareholders United in the highest regard. When I mentioned Shareholders United's discussions with the board about forming a supporters' trust, he credited the initiative to IMUSA: 'IMUSA had been pressing Shareholders United for some time to establish the trust. One of our number has been pecking away at this idea for over ten years. We had been involved with Supporters Direct [a government initiative funded by public money to help supporters play a responsible role in their club]. I was an adviser to Supporters Direct where they were talking about trusts. I wrote a paper on Northampton Town Football Club for the government. And we'd had discussions with Andy Burnham who was, at that time, special adviser within the Ministry of Culture, Media and Sport [he has since become a minister]. We were looking then to see how that could be achieved. Shareholders United took all that on board.'

When I asked him, 'So did everything not flow smoothly between Shareholders United and IMUSA?' his answer was the sort you get from a politician: 'In any hard-fought and intense campaign there are tensions, and there have been tensions. I'd be wrong to deny it over the course of the last couple of years. I think there should have been a different strategy.'

When I asked him for an example, Walsh replied, 'I'm in some difficulty here, because the battle's not finished and I'm not willing to be divisive in any critical comments. There are different strategies that could have been adopted and there were different strategies being discussed at the time.'

However, a source high up in IMUSA, who did not want to be identified, told me: 'There were discussions about the need to make contact with people who had large shareholdings. Those people needed to be brought together as a group. But a number of those larger shareholders were reluctant to get involved with Shareholders United. They weren't willing to hand over the voting rights of those shares because they wanted to have that influence themselves. They didn't have confidence in Shareholders United. Comments made in the press by Shareholders United spokespeople like "it's time for United fans to come forward and be counted" were not helpful.'

In fact, according to this source, they showed an absolute lack of respect. 'People don't gather wealth by squandering it and throwing it before swine, do they? Those comments were distinctly unhelpful to the efforts that were being made by a number of United fans to pull together. Those efforts were hampered by some of the more crass comments being made in the press by certain individuals. There were people around, if they were spoken to and approached correctly, who may well have been willing to get involved, but they weren't. What Shareholders United did was megaphone campaigning rather than con-structive campaigning. It pushes people away. There are plenty of philanthropic Manchester United fans, rich fans who have done a lot for football in this area who would be willing to do something for Manchester United if they felt that it was actually going to help regain the club. You don't want to antagonise them. Shareholders United were looking to field a mass base membership when really you don't need to, to be honest.'

These differences, while hidden from view, became even more acute when on 13 March 2005 the *Sunday Times* had a full-page 'Special News Focus' on how Shareholders United might be able to thwart the Glazers. The Glazers had come back with revised proposals and all the fans' groups were searching for some way to fight them off. The law firm Weil, Gotshal & Manges was by now providing Shareholders United with pro bono advice. Will Rosen, one of its partners, was part of The Legal Reds, a grouping of Manchester United lawyers formed in the days of the BSkyB bid back in 1998. In February 2005 *Legal Business* had quoted him as saying how important it was for United to remain independent, which is why his firm was doing this pro bono work. The magazine had predicted that while at the moment Rosen was peripheral, he could be 'a major asset to the team if Glazer manages to get back in the game'. Now Glazer was back and Shareholders United were busy trying to figure out how they could get back into the game, which really meant getting media attention.

Just then Jonathan Northcroft, a *Sunday Times* sports writer, rang Oliver Houston. Northcroft explains what happened: 'Will Lewis [then business editor of the *Sunday Times*, now editor of the *Daily Telegraph*] had done a story saying Shareholders United were well informed about Manchester United. I rang up

Oliver to do a story. Will's story had got Shareholders United excited. Oliver said he had something for me. If I was prepared to wait for a week it would be a much better story. I am a football journalist and I brought Will in, who helped me hugely to understand the business side. Will and I met Oliver and Nick at a pub near Wapping called the Pepperpot, which I believe was owned by a Shareholders United supporter. Nick knew the guys there. Grimy, smoky, dingy, sawdust on the floor, but it served Thai food.

'At the meeting they told us about some of their plans. Shareholders United had done a big mail-out to every shareholder in the register. They found 10 to 15 per cent of the shareholding were people who had been left shares, like widows and descendants. They felt that if they could get half of them they could get to 10 per cent. If they got 12 per cent then one of the City institutions would give them the money to acquire 12 per cent by going to people like Harry Dobson and other large shareholders and persuading them to sell to Shareholders United, rather than the Glazers. They were talking to various institutions but would not tell us the names. They had also had discussions with the Takeover Panel. Oliver works for the TUC and you got the hard sell with him. He said Shareholders United could claim to speak for 10 to 15 per cent.'

What Houston and Towle presented to the *Sunday Times* that day was what Towle admits was a 'cocktail of ideas', some of which had been kicking round for months: 'We thought the *Sunday Times* would make a good platform for these ideas. So we cooked up the idea and Oliver spoke to the *Sunday Times* and gave it to them. And they did a very nice piece on it, on how we could finance ourselves.'

The newspaper ran three stories that Sunday under the headline: 'United against the Enemy'. Jonathan Northcroft wrote the lead story and also what journalists call a write-off on the main sports pages. In addition there was a picture-bylined article by Houston.

At that time the *Sunday Times* did not know of Nomura and its name did not appear. The reference was to 'several City institutions with whom they [Shareholders United] are in talks'. The only City firm mentioned was Weil, Gotshal & Manges. Houston's article was meant to rouse the fans to oppose Glazer; it touched all the right United buttons, even quoting Eric Cantona who had declared, 'If Glazer were to come here, we would lose everything.'

In a box in Northcroft's article headlined: 'How the fans can block Glazer' the *Sunday Times* explained the scheme Houston and Towle had outlined in the Wapping pub:

The fans' groups, Shareholders United, are therefore targeting a stake of 25 per cent. They already have 'loose' control over as much as 18 per cent of United stock and 'firm' control over at least 10 per cent, meaning they may need to buy as little as 7 per cent more of United shares – which would cost them £50 million. Here's how the plan works. Shareholders set up a tender bid vehicle to borrow £50 million from one of several City institutions with whom they are in talks. The debt is spread between individual members who take out personal loans. It is hoped that the average loans would be over five years and cost individuals £25 per week. The personal loan can be split in two. One part is used to purchase shares. The carrot for the fans is that the other part can be used to buy five-year United season tickets at fixed prices based on current season ticket price plus inflation. It has been indicated to fans that the club will agree to this. The personal loans are secured against the season ticket and the shares purchased. Using the £50 million loans fans acquire their extra 7 per cent through a tender bid process which involves offering to match or exceed anything Glazer will pay for the shares. The beauty for them is that because Glazer is bidding for a far greater number of shares he has to raise far more money to keep pace with the fans. So if the fans exceed his bid by offering 310p per share they only have to find an extra £1.5 million. Glazer would have to find an extra £18 million – and he is already borrowing almost to the max.

The article made just the impression that Shareholders United wanted. But were their claims justified? Did they indeed control 18 per cent, albeit 'loosely', and 10 per cent 'firmly'? And had the United board agreed, as they told the *Sunday Times*, that part of the personal loan could be used to buy season tickets and part to buy shares? In reality both were wishes rather than the sort of hard reality they had made out for the benefit of the newspaper's readers.

In August 2005, four months after the article appeared, I asked Nick Towle about how many shares Shareholders United could speak for. He said, 'Between us, with Shareholders United and members like me holding shares privately and also through our share scheme, at that time probably just over 1 per cent. Some of the shares were held individually and some held for the trust.' And of how much of this was held by the Shareholders United trust he said, 'A small amount. We never built it up. At the very end [i.e. by the time the Glazers had taken over the club] the Trust had about 0.3 per cent.'

So how could the claim be made in the *Sunday Times* that Shareholders United had 18 per cent? Towle's explanation is that this was media spinning. 'The media kept speculating. The press always quoted 18 per cent. At one point, the FSA said, "You mustn't say anything about how many shares you've got because it's confusing." We tried to make it clear, 18 per cent was the percentage of shares held by fans individually, not through Shareholders United.' That was the general number of shares held by individual shareholders. 'But with our members' private holdings, which we assumed would be effectively pledged, we could get up to 2 per cent at the end.'

However, given that the *Sunday Times* article was written after a briefing by Towle and Houston, chair and vice-chair of the organisation, this explanation seems somewhat disingenuous.

And the idea of combining season ticket sales with share purchasing, of which it was said that it had been 'indicated to fans that the club will agree to this', was merely one of a cocktail of ideas that had been discussed months earlier when Shareholders United were meeting with the board, ideas about which the board had doubts. Towle explains: 'We'd been discussing some ideas with Nick Humby and the club people about encouraging the fans to take out loans to buy shares as part of a package. We had a very good idea, which I think the club was going to steal, where the Manchester United finance would offer a loan to fans, half of which would be to buy a season ticket for, say, three, four or five years, locked in at last year's price. The other half of the loan, £2,500, would go to buy shares to be put into the collective. The club were certainly interested from the season ticket viewpoint but they thought there might be financial or fiscal problems with the shares.'

However, as far as Shareholders United was concerned, all that did not matter. They saw themselves in a war with Glazer and clearly took the line that in such circumstances truth is the first casualty. For them what was more important was the tremendous impact the article had – as they had hoped it would. Towle told me, 'The article got a good reaction. We had a lot of members enquiring because an article like that goes out all over the world. We had a lot of calls from abroad.'

The *Sunday Times*, too, was keen to follow up the story. Towle says: 'They called us up because they liked the first article and said: "Is there anything else we can do?" We were talking about a follow-on article about how we were going to write to shareholders and how we were planning to bring all the shares under a collective hat. I suddenly had a thought. We were scheduled to see Nomura in the following couple of days. I said hold on guys, I might be able to give you a better story than the one we're talking about now. We had this idea that if all the 18 per cent of individual private shareholders were under the control of one entity, you'd be almost there, blocking any deal. You don't actually need 25 per cent because the way voting works you're pretty much there with 18 per cent.' (On the very reasonable theory that 100 per cent of shareholders are never going to vote, 18 per cent in almost every conceivable situation would effectively amount to 25 per cent.)

'Even the club had said to me, "Nick, why don't you just gather together all these 18 per cent of shareholders?" This was at one of the early discussions. I had said yes, and we had thought of finding an investment bank or some financial institution who would help us bring these shares together and a vehicle to do it. It would be effectively an investment trust where individual shareholders have their Manchester United shares, but the shares are locked into the trust. People hold their shares in the trust vehicle and can buy and sell and trade. You're liquidising effectively but you're locking in the underlying assets. It's really a simple thing. It's a single service managed fund. It was a very, very good idea and the club said this is what we should be doing.

'But we hadn't been able to interest anyone in it because it needed money and investment. We estimated a quarter of million initially to get it up and running and meet the fees of lawyers, accountants and other costs. You need serious money and we didn't have that sort of money. We're a volunteer organisation, all our money goes on basic costs. So it was very difficult to get it off the ground and my only regret is that I didn't take it to Nomura earlier. They had proposed one thing that wasn't workable and they were waiting for us to get back to them with a way which could be workable. Our mistake was not to go back to them with the idea earlier.'

This led to an April meeting with Nomura, who came up with proposals which were very much more workable than their previous idea of trying to raise £450 million to buy out the Irish and the Glazers: 'At the meeting with Nomura in April they said if you do this managed trust we will leverage it for you. For every pound worth of Manchester United shares you can get into the trust, we will lend that trust another pound to buy more shares. So the 18 per cent could have turned into 25 per cent. After that we had an ongoing dialogue with Nomura about how we could do this. The plan was that we would write to Manchester United shareholders and invite them to pool all their shares into an investment trust, because clearly part of the exercise was to get as many as possible of the 18 per cent of private shareholders together and on our side. That's what the second *Sunday Times* article was all about. Nomura agreed to go on the record for that article.' The second article had a tremendous reaction. 'From around the world, people were saying wow, fantastic, we can win. It was very realistic. Suddenly people thought there was a way to stop the Glazers.'

However, one group of fans were less than impressed. When I asked Andy Walsh about the *Sunday Times* articles, he said, 'I was not aware the articles were going in the *Sunday Times*.'

'Were you surprised they went in?'

'I don't want to comment on that.'

'Did that help?'

'I'm not going to comment on that.'

In contrast, Towle was so convinced that the scheme would finally work that he felt it might even tempt the Irish: 'I wrote a letter to the Irish two days before the *Sunday Times* article came out, telling them it was coming out. I said, we're asking you please don't sell your shares because what we are offering is this. We are intending to do this, it's going to be in the newspapers on Sunday. I explained the situation to them. I didn't give the name of Nomura because it wasn't public. I said, we have an investment bank, an investment trust, we have a fund holding the shares, we have leverage. But the story was leaked to Matthew Garrahan of the *Financial Times* the same day. He did a simple spoiler on Saturday but didn't manage to spoil it completely.'

Garrahan emphatically denies that he wrote any sort of spoiler or that he got the story from the Irish. He himself was chasing the Nomura story but when he rang Towle he was told Shareholders United was working with the *Sunday Times*.

Towle's desire to reach the Irish emphasises that, like the Glazers, the fans knew they were the key. Like Walsh, Towle and his group had what he calls 'our own back channel to the Irish'. What this channel was he will not say but it kept reassuring Shareholders United, just as Walsh had been reassured, that they would not sell. Indeed, when Houston and Towle had met the *Sunday Times* back in March 2005 for their Thai meal, they had confidently told the journalists that the Irish would not sell. Northcroft recalls, 'They were very optimistic. They thought the Irish were not going to sell under any circumstances. They were relying on the backing of David Gill and the board. They also said J.P. Morgan would not press on with a hostile takeover.'

But even as Shareholders United celebrated having secured Nomura's backing for a scheme they felt would work, and cocooned themselves in the comforting but false sense of security that the Irish would not sell, Leitao and Rothschild were ready with their plans. The *Sunday Times* article appeared on 1 May. Ten days later, on the evening of 11 May, Leitao picked up the phone and made a call to John Power of Cubic. What he told Power, and Power's response, would make all the fan group calculations meaningless.

Jim White has brilliantly summed up the dilemma of Shareholders United which led them to following their ultimately flawed strategy: 'Shareholders United in their triumph [over Murdoch] assumed they had greater potential in stopping future takeovers than they did. The problem is when Glazer came on the scene the assumption was we will do the same thing. We will organise the shareholders. Shareholders can stop him. The trouble is that there was no exterior element to Glazer's takeover. There was no competition element, no media involvement. It was a straightforward takeover, therefore adopting a pure Shareholders United approach was not going to work. He was going to outflank them. All he had to do was buy the Irish and he had bought the company. The Irish were solely interested in money. They were not interested in Manchester United. They had never been interested in Manchester United. The trouble was the Irish had absolutely no sympathy whatsoever with the Manchester United supporters. Because Manchester United supporters had taken Ferguson's side over the racehorse.'

21

THE BURDEN OF WAYNE AND THE CURSE OF LIAM

IN THE SUMMER of 2004 Manchester United signed two players. One was on a free transfer, the other was potentially Alex Ferguson's greatest purchase since his capture of Eric Cantona. Both transfers would have important consequences for the club, the free transfer in particular causing such a rift with an Irishman that it would play a vital part in making sure that within a year Manchester United was no longer an independent company.

The great buy was Wayne Rooney, who was unlike any young player Ferguson had ever bought. Ian Ross, a well-known football journalist based on Merseyside, who had joined Everton as head of press and communications in 2001, says of Rooney, 'He is not a Alex Ferguson type player. A wild boy from Liverpool – that is not the sort of personality Ferguson goes for. But I believe that by then, having missed out on Paul Gascoigne and then on Alan Shearer, not once but twice, Ferguson was determined to get this, the greatest player Everton has produced and perhaps one of the best we have ever produced in these isles.'

Everton knew Rooney was a sensation long before he had played for their first team. Ross says, 'I had heard of Wayne even before I joined the club just as we had all heard of Michael Owen. You hear of young players who are going to be world beaters and they never make it. But when I came to the club people like Colin Harvey, Walter Smith, Ray Hall, who is head of our academy, had told me that this lad was exceptional.'

By the time Rooney was ready to make his debut for Everton, others beyond the club had picked up how gifted he was. His original agent had been Peter McIntosh, a small-time agent in Liverpool who spots up and coming players and had players like Francis Jeffers on his books. But Rooney's potential reached Paul Stretford, based in Wilmslow in Cheshire, not far from where Ferguson lives and whom Jason Ferguson had consulted before he joined L'Attitude. Stretford is the founder of Proactive UK Ltd (now part of a listed company, Formation Group) whose website describes itself as 'one of the world's leading football representation agencies, providing management services and expert advice to over 100 professional footballers across the globe'. Rooney's move to Stretford was not without controversy. Stretford alleged that

McIntosh's business partner John Hyland had intimidated him in a Cheshire hotel room. Hyland and two others were charged but the case collapsed after five days of hearing at Warrington Crown Court. Nigel Bunyan, reporting the collapse of the case in the *Daily Telegraph*, wrote:

> Yesterday it emerged that the head of the Proactive agency had misled the court about the date he took control of the striker's career. He told a jury at Warrington Crown Court that he had not represented Rooney before December 2002. But two documents disclosed over the weekend proved that he had poached the striker three months earlier.
>
> John Hedgecoe, prosecuting, told the court his team had decided to offer no further evidence. He said: 'In the circumstances, and having seen those documents, in particular that one dated Sept 19, we do not feel able to rely on Paul Stretford as a witness in this case.'
>
> Judge David Hale passed not guilty verdicts on Mr Hyland, 42, and two co-defendants, Christopher Bacon, 34, and his brother, Anthony, 38. All three had denied demanding money with menaces from Mr Stretford.
>
> The nub of the blackmail trial was an incident at the Lord Daresbury Hotel, near Warrington, Cheshire, in June 2003. Mr Hyland wanted his rival to sign a contract that would have given him 50 per cent of the agent's earnings for Rooney for the next decade and had sent a subordinate to negotiate. Mr Hyland burst into the meeting unannounced and began banging his fist on the table and shouting. The Bacon brothers stood nearby. All three, the court was told, were intimidating.
>
> Mr Stretford insisted in the witness box that he had not poached the footballer and had acted entirely honourably. The disclosure of the new document yesterday proved that he had been representing Rooney while the player was still under contract to his previous agent, Peter McIntosh.'

The court case led to an FA investigation against Stretford and he was charged with misconduct. Stretford challenged the charges in court and at the time of writing the matter was still unresolved.

Aged sixteen years and 298 days, Rooney made his Everton debut in the opening match of the 2002–03 season against Tottenham, which ended in a 2–2 draw. He was substituted after seventy-seven minutes and Everton clearly wanted to introduce him slowly. Walter Smith, their previous manager, had resisted calls to play him. If Everton insiders knew Rooney was a great talent this was not a match that made it obvious, although he did lay on Everton's first goal. The game was more notable for marking Everton's 100th year in the top flight of English football and the 125th year of the club's existence, an event marked with special commemorative souvenirs.

But his talent was to become obvious on 19 October 2002 when, as Ryan Giggs marked his 500th appearance at Fulham, Rooney in the last minute scored a spectacular winner against Arsenal to hand them their first defeat of the season. He became the youngest player ever, at sixteen years and 360 days, to score in the Premiership.

Rooney had arrived and this was recognised by Everton in January 2003 when he was awarded his first professional contract, a three-year deal which meant he went from being a trainee at £75 a week to £8,000 a week. However the contract also had an image rights clause written in, which meant Rooney would get a percentage of all commercial rights sold by the club which used him. Rooney in his autobiography boasts that these must have been the first image rights for a seventeen-year-old. Along with that came signing-on fees, bonuses which meant he was probably on around £13,000 a week. Ross has a vivid description of the young Rooney as he signed his professional contract.

'Rooney even at sixteen produced tremendous media interest. We would get calls from Canada, Nigeria, Paraguay – the word had got round that we had a world-class player. We shielded him from all media enquiries. His first professional contract was going to be broadcast live on Sky and I felt we should give him some idea what to expect. I said to David Moyes, the manager, that I would talk to Wayne about the sort of questions to expect. David told me, "You can try but I must tell you Wayne does not do talking." I found that out soon enough. Before the Sky broadcast I had an hour with him in our boardroom. For that hour he sat there, listened to me but did not say a word. At the end of it he took out his gum and walked out of the boardroom. He was very polite but he was clearly petrified.

'At the press conference I was on the platform with David Moyes and Bill Kenwright [Everton's chairman]. I was sitting next to Wayne. The first question was, "Wayne, you must be delighted." He answered "Yes, I am very delighted." I looked across; he was white as a sheet as he answered. He was simply terrified.' In front of Rooney was a big bottle of water and some glasses. As is his habit he took a swig from the bottle but heard Moyes whispering, 'Use the fucking glass!' Rooney ignored him, not understanding why he should change a lifetime's habit just because he was live on television. The whole experience unnerved him and clearly still rankles; when he came to write about it in his autobiography he described it as 'a nightmare' experience and feels Everton milked the occasion to promote the club. Yet later when Rooney wanted to explain incidents on the field he alleges he was not allowed to speak to the press.

Ross says, 'There is a dichotomy in Wayne. On the field with a football he is like an English bulldog, he frightens the life out of defenders. Off the field he is terribly shy. I would see him leave the dressing room, he would have his head down and he would be looking only for Coleen. She is the only one he communicated with.' Coleen McLoughlin, of course, is Rooney's fiancée.

It was this complicated youngster that Ferguson had decided he must have. It helped that the youngster was keen to get away from Everton. Bill Kenwright had just taken over as the club's chairman; despite being desperately short of cash, let alone success, he had no desire to let such a prize go. But Rooney was determined. Ross says, 'Even today our supporters have not forgiven us for selling Rooney, but the fact is we could not keep him. Wayne had decided he wanted out. Maybe his agent Paul Stretford encouraged him but he was also not getting on with David Moyes. The relationship had broken down. He was by now the leader in the dressing room although only eighteen, the man everyone looked to for leadership. David can be a bit of a disciplinarian and Wayne did not like that. He did not want to take it from somebody who had not played at the highest level. We did everything we could to keep him but in the end he had made up his mind.' Rooney's autobiography included a whole chapter called 'Trouble with Moyes', which made a number of allegations against the manager. Reference to them by the *Daily Mail*, whose sister paper the *Mail on Sunday* had serialised Rooney's book, considerably upset Moyes and there was talk of legal action.

That summer Euro 2004 put Rooney on the world stage for the first time. For a time it seemed he would drive England to finally bring home a trophy, their first since 1966 – until he broke a metatarsal bone in his right foot on 24 June in the quarter-final against Portugal. After Rooney limped away England, leading 1–0 at the time, lost in a penalty shoot-out, their traditional manner of exit from tournaments.

A week earlier Rooney had made history by scoring two goals in the victory over Switzerland and for a brief period he was the youngest ever scorer in a European championship at eighteen years 236 days (the record was broken a few days later by the Swiss Johan Vonlanthen, who was ninety-five days younger). The Swiss match illustrated the contrast between the dominance Rooney can show on the field and his hesitant, dreadfully shy, almost childlike behaviour off it. Named man of the match, he was dragged in for a press conference. Afterwards Helen Wood, then a press officer with UEFA – she is now head of press at Portsmouth – called me to one side and asked if I could help a Swiss and a Swedish journalist. They had been at the press conference; their English was good, but they had great difficulty making any sense of what Rooney had said. Asked to describe how he had scored the first of his two goals, he had replied, 'Michael put it on me head.' One of the journalists asked me, 'Who is this Me Head? He is not listed on the English team sheet.'

I explained Rooney meant that Michael Owen had crossed the ball on to his head and he had scored. That Rooney should speak with a heavy Scouse accent was not surprising, but he also spoke in a thin, hesitant voice which almost seemed to be unbroken and was quite a shock after his magisterial performance on the field. The giant with a football was really a boy without it.

Euro 2004 made the Liverpool boy a star. Now his every deed was on the front pages of the newspapers. Soon after he returned from Portugal, Rooney and Coleen went to New York and their activities there, particularly their shopping trips, were reported with much glee. The tabloids had found a new football couple to match Posh and Becks. But with glitz comes dirt, as many a celebrity knows. The tabloids dug up the fact that as a sixteen-year-old he had visited prostitutes and reported that the revelation of this story had led to a crisis in his relationship with Coleen, who was said to have thrown Rooney's engagement ring away. In his autobiography, published in the summer of 2006, Rooney denies she did any such thing. But he admits Coleen was very upset after it emerged he had visited massage parlours, more so as she had heard the story from a friend whom she had refused to believe. Rooney's explanation is that the relevant incidents had happened two years previously, when he was sixteen, not long after he had met Coleen and was still hanging round the chippy with his old mates:

> On Saturday evenings, they would sometimes go on to a massage parlour and, now and again, I went along with them. I'm not saying it's OK to do it, or it's justified, it's what a lot of lads have always done – regardless of where they are from – when they go out with their mates and enjoy a few laughs. I never expected this story from my past to come out – which it wouldn't have done had I been just a nobody, another ordinary lad – and this had happened before me and Coleen had become serious. But after my success at Euro 2004 the papers were keen to dig up any dirt about me, even if years old. They didn't make that clear in the articles, of course – people thought I was still doing such things at that time, or had done so recently.

The publicity badly shook the youngster, and Everton insiders believe that is when he finally decided he must leave Merseyside.

Until then Everton were feeling confident that they could persuade Rooney to stay. Both Kenwright and Moyes had had several meetings with Stretford and they had decided that they would break the bank to keep him. A new five-year contract offered him £50,000 a week, more than three times what he was then earning.

A week after this offer Newcastle approached Everton for Rooney. In the second week of August, Freddy Shepherd, who knows Kenwright well, had rung him to say he must come and see him. He travelled down to London to tell him Newcastle wanted to buy Rooney. Kenwright told him, 'You could not afford him, Freddy.'

Shepherd said, 'I will take out my cheque book and write out a cheque for £20 million here and now.'

Kenwright's response was, 'I don't want to sell him.'

However, within two weeks Rooney made it clear he definitely wanted to go. The season had already started and on Monday 30 August, the day before the transfer window closed, Everton were due to visit Manchester United at Old Trafford. On the Friday Kenwright got a call from Stretford. He was ringing from the Everton training ground and told him Rooney had had some terrible publicity and wanted to go. He then put Rooney on the phone. Rooney told Kenwright in a tearful voice, 'Please Mr Kenwright, you have got to let me go. I have got to go.'

Kenwright said, 'Wayne, you know how I love Everton. I will do the best for Everton football club and for you.'

Within an hour Rooney had met Moyes and slapped in a transfer request. The die was cast. According to Rooney he had also had a major training ground bust-up with Moyes in front of all the players which had led him to say he could not play for him any more.

However, at this stage Manchester United had made no move for the player. Instead, on the Saturday it was Freddy Shepherd who was back on the phone to Kenwright, and Stretford confirmed that Rooney would be prepared to go to Newcastle. While Rooney was clearly keen on Manchester United, he had told Ross he would move to Newcastle, they were a bigger club than Everton. It proved to Everton how keen he was to go. It was only on Saturday morning, two days before Manchester United hosted Everton, that David Gill rang, telling Kenwright 'We would like to speak to you about Rooney.'

With the two teams meeting in a lunchtime kick-off on the following Monday, it was decided to have a meeting after the match. The match itself resulted in a 0–0 draw, a better result for Everton than United.

After the match, Kenwright, Moyes, Gill and Maurice Watkins trooped into Sir Alex Ferguson's room at Old Trafford to begin negotiations. Kenwright knew United were the only game in town. There had been talk of Chelsea being interested – they were then talking to Steven Gerrard – but in fact they showed no such interest, having just signed Didier Drogba for £24 million. But Kenwright also knew how fraught a deal would be and how much hostility had been generated among Everton fans at the prospect. Some of them had taken to making anonymous, threatening calls to his home number late at night.

Manchester United had a money problem. They had spent their transfer budget during the summer. Apart from £12.8 million on Louis Saha in January, in May they had bought Alan Smith for £7.05 million and then in July Gabriel Heinze for £6.8 million. It had long been agreed that Rooney should be bought, but the initial thought was that this could be done in the next transfer window in January, or even perhaps the following summer. In mid August Gill had been quoted as saying it would be 'bad business' to sign the player for £30 million.

Newcastle's interest altered matters. Having lost Gascoigne to Tottenham back in 1988, and then in the 1990s twice lost Shearer, to Blackburn and then to Newcastle, Ferguson was not keen to lose Rooney.

Ferguson remembered seeing Rooney chip the United keeper from the halfway line in a youth game at Old Trafford. He had also proved a real handful for United's defenders when coming on as a substitute for his first appearance against United. Ferguson would later say, 'When a player of that potential becomes available you have to be alive to the situation and do something about it. The twists of fate can be strange because if Newcastle hadn't gone in for him Wayne would still have been an Everton player. Once we knew that Everton were talking to another club then we had to do something. If a player like Wayne Rooney had escaped our clutches when he is only thirty miles up the road it would have been a terrible shame for us.'

The answer the money men at Old Trafford came up with was that Rooney would come out of the following year's budget. In a sense this could be justified as the accounting year was over, but normally clubs buying in the summer see their purchases as one packet. It also meant that in the January transfer window and the following summer there would be hardly any money left for new players.

United's initial offer was £18 million. Kenwright was determined to get as near as he could to £30 million. At one stage he broke off negotiations to say he had to go for a walk, and spoke privately to Moyes. It was clear Ferguson was keen on Rooney: he said several times how much he wanted the player. After a couple of hours of intense negotiations it was agreed that United would pay £20 million. A further £3 million was guaranteed, with a conditional £4 million more: £1 million if United won the Champions League, £500,000 if they were runners-up; £500,000 if they won the Premiership, £250,000 if they finished second; £150,000 if they won the FA Cup. There would also be £1.5 million if Rooney extended his contract with United, £500,000 if he earned twenty England caps in competitive games while a United player and £500,000 if he played a further twenty times for England. Above all there was a 25 per cent 'sell-on' agreement, under which Everton would receive a quarter of any excess sum over all amounts paid in this agreement.

Rooney's agent Paul Stretford did not do badly, as United revealed in their accounts. The agent's fee was £1.5 million, more than the levy paid to the Premier League on the transfer deal.

Manchester United had signed the player just before the UEFA transfer deadline. Kenwright says that as the deal was finalised, 'I felt awful. Absolutely drained. He is without doubt the greatest player I have ever seen, not just for Everton but anywhere. But we could not keep the boy. He wanted to go.'

Rooney made all the right noises as he signed. 'It was a tough decision to leave Everton, the club I've supported and played for all my life, but I'm excited to be joining a club as big as Manchester United. I feel this can only improve my career, playing with top players in top competitions like the Champions League, and I can't wait to meet up with the team.' The bitterness he felt against Moyes and indeed against Everton would only surface when he published his autobiography two years later.

United fans had to wait another month before they saw Rooney play, but it was worth the wait. On his debut against Fenerbahce he scored a hat-trick in a 6–2 triumph. The performance had the club's anorak supporters looking up the record books, for this was only the second time in the club's history that a debutant had scored a hat-trick. (On the previous occasion it had been one Charlie Sagar, on 2 September 1905 against Bristol City.)

A month later Rooney scored the second goal as United ended Arsenal's 49-game unbeaten run, and then a couple at St James's Park sent Newcastle to defeat. On welcoming him to Old Trafford Ferguson had said, 'I think we have got the best young player this country has seen in the past thirty years.' He had reiterated his familiar desire to protect Rooney, as he had done with other young players. 'Wayne understands, as Ryan Giggs understood and Cristiano [Ronaldo] understands, we will not ask him to climb the mountain tomorrow. The important thing is that Wayne is a major player in five years' time. The big danger with young players is always that you ask too much of them too quickly. We will let him mature and develop as easily as we can.' But despite his plan not to overuse Rooney, with Ruud van Nistelrooy absent the young player was now an integral part of the manager's starting eleven. By January he had scored fifteen goals in thirty-three games, including the winner at Anfield against Liverpool.

But off the field Rooney could also make waves. Unlike Ryan Giggs, Ferguson and United have been unable to shield him from intrusive media interest. If Rooney was a handful for opposition defences, he has also put United and its management on their mettle several times in his short career at Old Trafford.

This became most evident in the run-up to the 2006 World Cup in Germany, when after Rooney injured his metatarsal in the match against Chelsea the nation agonised for weeks over whether he would be fit. This soon turned into a near re-run of the Rio Ferdinand affair, although with a curious twist. In Rio's case United was outraged that the FA wanted to drop him from the Turkey match because of missing a drug test; in this case United were less than happy that the FA, and in particular the England manager Sven-Göran Eriksson, was desperate to take Rooney to the World Cup when United's medical advice was that he was not fully fit. The disagreement between the national association and England's premier club inevitably developed into a Manchester United versus the country battle, with Ferguson seen as not wanting his star player to go to the World Cup unless he was fully fit.

According to Manchester United's initial statements, Rooney would be out of action for six weeks, meaning he would certainly miss the World Cup. On 30 April Ferguson seemed to confirm this, saying, 'I doubt he'll take part [in the World Cup] because of the recovery time. At first, we didn't think it was too bad but when we sent him for the scan we realised what a blow it was for the boy and for England.'

Insiders have told me that during the course of this battle there were clashes between Ferguson and his bete noire Sven which were not far short of the hair-dryer treatment Ferguson's players receive from him. Certainly in his public statements Ferguson did not hide his unhappiness about Eriksson claiming Rooney would go to the World Cup even if he was not fully fit. Ferguson described this Eriksson plan as 'a wild dream, the kind of talk we don't want to hear'. His concern was to make sure that what he felt was the Beckham mistake of 2002 was not repeated. 'You cannot take anyone half-fit to a World Cup. I think that happened with David Beckham. People might think I'm selfish but Wayne is the most important player at United. We have to ensure the boy is going to be fit at the start of the season for us.'

Like the Rio affair, the Rooney one was marked by dramatic developments, including United suddenly parting company with their medical doctor Mike Stone, who had been at the club since 1996 and had been a key figure in the Rio Ferdinand drug test miss.

When news of Stone's departure emerged the press reported it as a result of 'a major falling-out' with Sir Alex Ferguson. According to the *Guardian*'s website:

> Given the cautious tone he adopted over the 20-year-old's chances of playing in Germany this summer, Ferguson has presumably grown increasingly unhappy at the number of positive bulletins being released on Rooney's condition. Although most of the statements have been attributed to the England doctor Leif Sward, Stone has been liaising closely with the Swede …

United, however, insisted the departure had nothing to do with Rooney. The club said, 'We can confirm Dr Stone has left the club. There was a difference of opinion on a non-footballing and non-clinical issue, as a result of which Dr Stone felt it to be in his and the club's best interests for him to leave.' In fact, Stone did fall out with Ferguson but not over Rooney. Stone wanted to carry on his work with the English Institute of Sports, and approached Ferguson who said no. He then approached Gill without telling him Ferguson had said no, and this led to a break between him and Ferguson which could not be healed.

Rooney in his autobiography does not mention Stone and skates over these events, but says that while Ferguson always wanted him to play in the World Cup he reminded him that Beckham had taken eight weeks to recover from a metatarsal and Gary Neville was out for four months. He also warned his young star that just because he did not feel pain did not mean he was healed. With the medical experts of the FA and Manchester United not always singing from the same hymn sheet over Rooney's recovery, a number of near-farcical situations ensued. Rooney flew out with England to Germany on Monday 5 June, but two days later he was back in Manchester to be scanned at the BUPA Whalley Range clinic in Manchester. In England's retreat in Baden Baden was a first-rate clinic, but the FA had promised United Rooney would be scanned in Manchester. Eventually, with medical opinion diverging, outside specialists were called in and their decision, with a final check on the morning of the Trinidad and Tobago match, the second World Cup group match on 15 June, led to Rooney eventually playing. But that was not the end of the problem.

In the crucial quarter-final match against Portugal Rooney was sent off for kicking Portuguese player Ricardo Carvalho between his legs when tussling for the ball. Rooney claimed it was an accident, but the Portuguese saw malice, and the referee agreed. England subsequently lost the match on penalties, as they normally do at this stage in major events. A predictable tabloid storm ensued, further whipped up by the fact that Cristiano Ronaldo, a United player in the Portuguese side, had encouraged the referee to send Rooney off, in return for which Rooney had given him an angry shove. The Rooney/Ronaldo spat was much exaggerated in the press (Rooney's autobiography made clear that no animosity existed between them), but the whole episode showed that United now had a player in Rooney whose combination of difficult temperament and iconic status in English football meant that Ferguson could not manage him as easily as he has managed so many other players over the last twenty years.

However, it was a free transfer earlier the same year that Rooney came to Manchester United that was to cause Ferguson and United much more of a problem. This was the case of Liam Miller.

Miller, a Celtic midfield player earning around £60,000 a week, was in the last year of his contract in the 2003–04 season. Celtic were desperately keen to keep him. Apart from his value as a player, he was the only Irishman in a side that identifies strongly with Ireland and is supported in the main by the Catholics of Scotland. Celtic worked hard to persuade Miller to sign a new contract; Dermot Desmond was very keen to secure him and at one stage even offered him his own plane to fly him and Martin O'Neill to Cork, Miller's birthplace, to try and sweeten the deal.

Under the Bosman rules Miller, as a player in a Scottish team, could sign a pre-contract agreement with a club in another country in January, six months before his contract with Celtic ended. Desmond knew the clock was ticking. But despite all Celtic's efforts the player would not sign. Then Desmond heard whispers that Manchester United had been tapping up the player, seeing him as the long-term midfield replacement for Roy Keane. Desmond was furious. He had always thought Celtic had a special relationship with United. The two clubs had never crossed each other. He decided to speak to Sir Alex Ferguson.

If the relationship between Celtic and United was special, Desmond had every reason to feel his own relationship with Ferguson was even more special. Ferguson, after all, had helped him secure Martin O'Neill's services as manager of Celtic. What was more, at the time of the Miller affair Desmond was trying to do a deal with Ferguson over the Rock of Gibraltar dispute. He rang Ferguson and, according to Desmond, the manager promised him United would not try to poach Miller. But then Desmond was told Miller was not signing and had already signed a pre-contract agreement with United. In some fury he again rang Ferguson, who told him he knew nothing and would check with David Gill. Desmond then spoke to both Gill and Gardner, but Gill brushed the matter aside. As far as Manchester United was concerned they had done nothing wrong. Under the Bosman rules, the player could talk to another club in the January of the season his contract ended, and United had acted within the rules of football.

Desmond was furious. He rang Ferguson back, cursing him and vowing to seek revenge. 'The curse of Liam Miller will haunt you,' he told Ferguson and Gill.

Miller was indeed to prove one of Ferguson's worst buys. He may have cost no money in transfer fees, although the agent got £100,000, but the player did not solve United's midfield problems. Miller made his debut two weeks before Rooney was signed, coming on as a substitute in the eighty-seventh minute against Dinamo Bucharest on 11 August 2004, in the Champions League qualifying round. In the two seasons since he managed just twenty-two first-team appearances. Despite the huge number of senior players missing, he was still only a substitute in the opening game of the 2006–07 pre-season tour of South Africa. The twenty-five-year-old had spent the latter half of the previous season on loan at Leeds as the Yorkshire team tried to make it back to the Premiership. But Leeds' failure to overcome Watford at the Millennium Stadium scuppered any chance of Miller making a permanent move to Elland Road.

Ferguson soon accepted that it would be better for all parties if Miller did move on, and not long after the 2006 season started this is exactly what happened. One of Roy Keane's first moves as Sunderland manager was to sign Liam Miller. For all the expectations of Miller when he moved south from Celtic, he had achieved virtually nothing and from the moment he set foot in Old Trafford he seemed overawed by his surroundings.

But more significantly, the signing of Miller from Celtic made a permanent enemy of Dermot Desmond, the only one of the Irish with whom United had good relations, or any relations at all. This was to prove crucial when the Glazers came calling again.

22

HOW ROTHSCHILD RESCUED THE GLAZERS' DREAM

ON THE AFTERNOON of 12 May 2005, the Glazers' takeover of Manchester United was just fifteen minutes from crashing down in flames. The Irish had agreed to sell their shares to the Americans; all that was needed was for the money to be paid and the shares would change hands. But a crucial tranche of money from one of the hedge funds backing the Glazers had failed to come from New York. If it did not come in fifteen minutes the deal was off.

Then the two merchant bankers from Rothschild stepped in. Taking on a huge financial burden on behalf of their bank, without any consultation with their bank's credit officers, they said they were good for the money. The Irish were paid, the deadline was met, the deal done, the storm passed. The knockout blow that Robert Leitao had been aiming to deliver on behalf of the Glazers since the previous Christmas had landed.

What they did was unusual, risky and extremely bold. It was not written in any City mergers and takeover handbook. But for the Glazers it was extremely beneficial. Had they not done so, Leitao's entire strategy for buying out the Irish and then buying Manchester United could have collapsed in a heap. By then the Glazers had come so near their dream. The Rothschild men, who had plotted and worked so hard for months to help them realise that dream, and in the process come to like Malcolm Glazer's sons, could not let it turn to nightmare.

The fact that on 12 May the Glazers had come so close was itself remarkable. In the previous six months it had been by no means certain that the Glazers would get anywhere with their bid. During this period the Manchester United board had several chances to stop them, but they had failed to seize those chances.

The first moves had come when, about a month after United's AGM in November 2004, David Gill and Nick Humby went to Florida to meet the Glazers. Mark Rawlinson recalls: 'Gill and Humby were thinking this can't go on, we can't live with this uncertainty. They had sponsorship deals to do, all sorts of things. People want certainty in a public company, they don't want things up in the air. So they knew they had to shake it out. And so at the back end of 2004 Gill and co. went to see the Glazers to find out what the hell was going on. The Glazers made it clear that they were thinking about revisions to their proposal but they were still there. They hadn't gone away. The Glazer document somehow or other got leaked to the press.'

One Glazer source told me, 'Joel Glazer gave David Gill details about their plans, a few pages showing a leveraged bid, a fairly short working document. It was a piece of paper with five numbers on it. This showed much reduced debt compared to the plan in October. Gill said he would look at it. Days afterwards it appeared in the paper. It was leaked by a journalist in Tampa.'

One consequence of the leak which the Glazers could not have foreseen was that it brought the takeover panel back into the game. United were back in an offer period. A Glazer source says, 'The panel came down on the Glazers and said, "Did you make the proposal or not?" They said "No." Then they seized this piece of paper – quite a pathetic piece of paper if you think about it – flourished it front of the Glazers and said, "Well, you gave them this piece of paper, that's tantamount to a business plan" and pushed them into the offer period.'

Rawlinson says: 'As soon as there were press rumours, the takeover panel was on the phone to Cazenove. So we put out a short announcement, saying that the board did not intend to open discussions on this matter unless it received a definitive proposal from Glazer.' The Glazers were told to go away and sort out their advisers, put together a properly financed proposal. Then United would be prepared to talk. 'So they went away and they came back in February with a definitive proposal.'

For the third time in less than a year Manchester United were in an offer period, although on none of the three occasions had the Glazers made anything like a proper offer. Both David Gill and Sir Roy Gardner would later publicly complain about these various offer periods, Gardner saying how they had proved 'very disruptive to the smooth running of the business, creating considerable uncertainty for all our stakeholders'.

Gill himself was in turmoil over the various Glazer overtures and around this time he would give strong indications that he wanted to support fans opposed to Glazer. Sometime in December 2004, not long after he had met Joel in Florida, Gill had a revealing telephone conversation with Nick Towle. Towle says: 'We had each other's numbers and I'd been talking to him on and off. He called me up and said, "Nick, I want to exercise some share options and obviously I don't want [the shares] to fall into unfriendly hands." He hedged around a bit but he clearly did not want them to fall into the hands of the Glazers.'

Gill realised that this was a sensitive time to sell shares. He told Towle, 'I'm in no hurry but I would like to know if Shareholders United would be comfortable with that.' By asking Towle it was clear he wanted Shareholders United on his side so they wouldn't say he was selling out. Towle told him, 'David, that's fine. The most important thing is these shares don't fall into unfriendly hands.' Gill replied, 'I understand that [the bankers] think that they can finesse that.' The shares had to be sold on the open market, but presumably the bank would be able to ask potential buyers to identify themselves.

Gill went on to say 'I want to offer to donate £25,000 to Shareholders United,' adding, says Towle, 'Nick, if I wasn't where I am now I would be behind the barricades.' That phrase made a great impact on Towle, who described it as 'priceless'.

Towle could hardly believe what he was hearing. 'I got in touch with a friend of mine who had contacts with rich red knights and we came up with a buyer. At that time the share price was about 275p. Our buyer would have taken the whole lot but only wanted to pay 250p or 255p, at a discount to market value. It looked as if the takeover wasn't going to happen. Against that background these people did not want to pay top price, which is fair enough.' But Gill insisted on receiving the market price. He eventually sold to Jim O'Neill, the Manchester United non-executive director who had been brought on the board after the AGM of November 2004, at market price.

If there was a touch of gesture politics on Gill's part, particularly in his avowed intention to 'man the barricades', his position was difficult. He wanted to keep on the right side of Shareholders United, yet at the same time cope with the Glazers. Sir Roy Gardner, his chairman, was also indulging in gesture politics, or at least that is how the Glazer camp saw it. The Gardner gesture came two months later, in February 2005, when the Glazers finally came back with a definitive proposal. Rothschild had told the board that they were now representing the Glazers. After some discussion and the exchange of a number of e-mails, along with an advance list of questions and a business plan, it was agreed that the Glazers should meet the United board in the first week of February. Or at least that was the idea until Gardner intervened.

The chairman made it clear that if any one of the Glazers personally attended the meeting, then Manchester United would not attend. He absolutely pro-hibited their presence. The Glazers' advisers were dumbfounded, but decided it was just one of Sir Roy's peculiarities. The effect of the ban was curious. He seemed to be saying it was perfectly all right for United's directors to meet the Glazers' advisers but not the Glazers themselves, the people who really wanted to own the club. It was as if he was endorsing fans' portrayal of the Glazers as the personal incarnation of the devil. Sir Roy was treating the Glazers much as high-caste Hindus in India had treated the untouchables for centuries – any touch, even their shadow, was polluting.

United were also paranoid about meeting any representative of the Glazers at Old Trafford. So the club proposed that everyone should gather in the hotel at Manchester airport. United would book a conference room in the hotel under the name of Smith.

At 9.30 on a cold February morning Robert Leitao, Majid Ishaq and Andrew Ballheimer flew in from London where they were joined by Richard Bailey. Waiting for them on the Manchester United side were David Gill, Nick Humby, Mark Rawlinson and David Anderson, along with Patrick McGee of Cazenove. On arrival at the hotel all of them had to go to reception and ask for a conference room booked in the name of Mr Smith. The secret was nearly blown when, halfway through the meeting, somebody walked in saying they were looking for a travel agent. A travel agents' meeting was indeed going on in another conference room and the person had clearly come to the wrong room. For a few minutes United were worried that 'Mr Smith' would be rumbled, but the person concerned did not recognise anyone and United's blushes were spared.

Although nobody from J.P. Morgan was physically present, their contribution to the meeting was immense. Their corporate team may have walked out on the night the Glazers voted out the board, but their relationship with the Glazers had not ended. If anything it was strengthened. If J.P. Morgan's corporate operation had not covered itself in glory during the Glazers' first takeover attempt, the bank's debt finance side had risen to the challenge and put in place all the money to fund the takeover, including organising the hedge funds. This was led by Edward Woodward and Andrew Honeymen with a particular mission to get hedge funds to lend the Glazers money. (Hedge funds are lightly regulated funds which often have unconventional, rather risky, investment strategies.) Woodward's success in getting the finance and in particular the hedge funds would make a terrific impression on Joel Glazer, so terrific that less than a year later the Glazers gave him a job.

J.P. Morgan's help in raising finance was valued by Leitao, who jokes that he 'might have an unpronounceable name but I have a big reputation' – in Manchester United circles it was common to refer to him as 'the foreigner'. He recalls, 'J.P. Morgan essentially provided the debt entirely themselves and also arranged the hedge fund money. On that side they did a very good job. We at Rothschild helped bring order on the structural side.

'Why had the club turned down the previous offer? The reason they gave was too much debt. It was an excuse, but it could not be ignored if the Glazers were to get the backing of the board. So the central part of the new structure was to put less debt in the club. The Glazers were going to put more money in. But there was also a layer of capital in the middle. That was not debt loaded on to the club, that was essentially the Glazers borrowing against the shares of the company. If the Glazers couldn't pay them back, they'd have to hand over the shares. All these borrowers would end up owning the club.'

A diagram was drawn that United described as the Leitao diagram. 'It followed the presentation I put in front of the board to show the debt on the club. There was a dotted line and everything above was not a debt on the club, it was simply debt against the Glazer family. That is not Manchester United debt, it is borrowing against their shares in Manchester United. The new structure was absolutely crucial.' According to the diagram, the debt for which United would be liable was only £265 million. The rest was the responsibility of the Glazers.

The Glazer debt was borrowed from hedge funds. But Leitao, worried that hedge funds had a certain reputation, did not tell the board at this February meeting that such funds were involved. His tactic was clear – make it impossible for the board to refuse due diligence, which was vital if the banks and hedge funds were to be persuaded to lend the money. 'The whole presentation was done on the basis that they would let the Glazers have due diligence. The Glazers could have possibly gone to law to force due diligence but the strategy was to get them to give due diligence without forcing the issue. The key was to have different proposals that the board couldn't immediately reject. It was a sort of cornering of the board and forcing them to say, "It's too dangerous for us not to hand over the due diligence material."'

Before the meeting Leitao had spoken to several institutional investors and, although he did not speak to the Irish, there was contact with Dermot Desmond. 'You've got to give Desmond ammunition, basically saying to the board give them the due diligence material.'

The layer of debt above the line in the Leitao diagram did, admits Leitao, 'cause much confusion and comment'. One of those present at the meeting recalls: 'There were a couple of moments when it got quite heated around whether the preference shares were debt or equity.'

The meeting was a long one, lasting over three hours. This was the third time the Glazers had asked for due diligence. The board had refused twice before and on both occasions their refusal had been fortified by Rawlinson's advice that they were on sure legal ground in saying the board had responsibilities beyond those to its shareholders. But now, in February 2005, things were very different.

The board was concerned that shareholders might sue. Here was a potential bidder prepared to pay £3 a share and the board was not even prepared to let him make a bid.

But, more than being taken to court, what worried the United directors was that if they did not give the Glazers due diligence, this time they might simply be removed as directors. At the AGM the Irish had handed the Glazers victory by staying away. What if they now decided to join forces? The board desperately wanted to know what the Irish were thinking. Soon after the Manchester airport meeting, David Gill rang John Power. One Irish source told me: 'When the Glazers asked for due diligence in February they asked us to respond. Gill rang. Our response was "It is up to you." If it was a bona fide, fully funded bid then it is the duty of the board to do so. But the decision was that of the board. At no stage did we even threaten to sue them if they did not allow the Glazers due diligence. We think they rang us so that if we had said yes, they could have told the fans "What can we do? The Irish said we must let the Glazers in".'

Like that classic put-down of the press administered by Stanley Baldwin to Lord Beaverbrook, the board wanted all the privileges of the harlot: power without responsibility. The Irish had no love for the board and no desire to humour this particular harlot. The board, however, interpreted their words as implicitly saying 'Let the Glazers have a look at the books.' Rawlinson says: 'The thing that had changed since the last time we'd had to take this decision was that the Irish had indicated they wanted due diligence to take place. The message had been communicated indirectly, to the board. Smoke signals had been received. The message had got through.'

Rawlinson will not say, or does not know, how this was done. It is possible that, in addition to Gill's conversation with Power, Jim O'Neill played a part. He was by now on the board; he knew the Irish and it was well known that his appointment had been made after it was checked that he was acceptable to them. They may even have suggested his name and passed on some message through him.

Here Dermot Desmond and the curse of Liam Miller came into play. As Cubic's Magnier and McManus had no relations with the board – they never formally met in all the years they were shareholders – Desmond was almost a surrogate spokesman for the entire Irish block. His fury with the Liam Miller affair had not abated and he was eager that the Glazers should have due diligence. He made this abundantly clear. While he too might not have sued, he might have considered calling a extraordinary general meeting to remove the entire board.

This was the fear that now gripped the board, a fear that had haunted Rawlinson even before the AGM: 'The board was faced with the situation that over 50 per cent of the shareholders were saying "We want to see this proposal." In such a situation it would have been wrong to deny it. Was there a threat of legal action? That was said in the press. But I think what determined the board's decision was that if they didn't allow this, they could allow control to pass by the back door. If the Glazers and the Irish were operating together, and they both wanted due diligence to take place, then they could get together and change the board. So all the protection Manchester United had, the only protection the club had, which was the current board, would have gone out of the window. They had no practical solution other than to allow due diligence. But we made it clear that we still didn't like the level of debt, we still weren't inclined to recommend it as being in the best interests of the company.'

However, before the board spoke, the fact that the Glazers had made another proposal leaked. Andrew Murray-Watson of the *Sunday Telegraph*, who had consistently been ahead of the field, broke the story on 6 February 2005.

The leak embarrassed United and dealt a grievous blow to the Glazers, further souring their image with the fans. But for both of them these wounds were self-inflicted. Right from the moment the Glazers had arrived on the scene a decision made by David Gill had meant the United PR machine, both externally via Finsbury and internally, was placed in a very difficult situation. One source close to United's PR told me: 'David felt he didn't want to fight it out in the press. Throughout the battle with the Glazers we had never been on the front foot, we were very much on the back foot. The problem in constructing a PR campaign was that the Glazers never made a formal offer, so there was nothing like a proper offer to announce to the Stock Exchange. All we could say was they had a conversation, but they had not made an offer. It was a bizarre situation for any plc takeover.

'They were bizarre characters. It was very much driven by Joel. We never met him. Everything was done very secretively. The impression we got from Manchester United was that he was a nice guy. But how much did he know about football and the football model? How much was this just a passion for him? But they were offering £3. It was a very good offer for the business.'

The mole who leaked that talks had been held was timing his leak to cause maximum damage to the Glazers. The date 6 February is one all Manchester United fans remember. It marks the anniversary of the Munich air crash. No sooner was the story in the *Sunday Telegraph* confirmed by United than fan groups led by Shareholders United were berating the Glazers, accusing them of leaking the story and of being so crassly insensitive as to do so on the anniversary of Munich. The Glazers had nothing to do with the leak – which in all probability came from an anti-Glazer fan working in the City – but they had shot themselves in the foot by insisting that they would not do any PR. Early on, when one of their advisers had suggested a PR strategy to them, they had said, 'See you in two years' time.' Their PR men could do nothing except watch helplessly as yet another huge black mark was registered against the foreign invaders.

Murray-Watson was not the only journalist causing problems. In February 2005 *Legal Business* magazine caused Allen & Overy some headaches. That month's issue carried a big feature article by James Baxter entitled 'Theatre of Hate'. It revealed for the first time some of the details of the October financing proposal, but its main thrust was the various legal personalities involved in the takeover battle, including Maurice Watkins, Mark Rawlinson and Nick Towle. It was clear that the magazine had spoken at length to Rawlinson, who was much praised for his tactical acumen. All the lawyers mentioned were profiled with a picture – except one. Against the name of the lawyer from Allen & Overy was mentioned in brackets 'Anonymity Requested'. Iain Rodger, then head of

PR at the firm, says, 'It started with Jim Baxter of *Legal Business*. They printed an article showing all the lawyers but with Andrew's face blanked out. I had worked out a deal with him to keep Andrew's name out.'

However, it was not difficult for a good journalist to work out the man's identity. Jason Nisse did just that and rang Rodger. According to Rodger, 'Nisse said give me a scoop or I shall mention his name.' Nisse's demand, if that was what it was, was not unusual. The relationship between PR and journalism is full of such stories.

For the first time Andrew Ballheimer's name was out in the open and blazoned across the fanzines. *Red Issue* clearly identified Ballheimer as the Glazers' lead lawyer. For almost three years he had kept his identity secret; now he received death threats by e-mail, saying 'Leave Manchester United or die'. Ballheimer had to have a bodyguard and special protection.

On 11 February Manchester United announced that the Glazers were to be given limited due diligence. The statement, carefully crafted after advice from Rawlinson, read in part:

> Glazer is willing to make an offer of 300p per share in cash with a minimum 75 per cent acceptance level. The pre-conditions, which could be subject to change, currently include due diligence and a public recommendation of the offer by the Board. The financial structure of this revised proposal of 300p has been restructured since the proposal considered by the Board in October. The proposal involves a lower level of senior debt than the previous proposal with the equity in the bidding vehicle being supplied by Glazer and an issuance of preferred securities. These preferred securities would be issued by a holding company above the bidding vehicle, such securities only being secured upon the shares in that holding company. The Board believes that the nature and return requirements of this capital structure will put pressure on the business of Manchester United, particularly if Glazer's business plan was not met. The Board continues to believe that Glazer's business plan assumptions are aggressive and that the direct and indirect financial strain on the business could be damaging. Glazer's financing is supported by commitment letters and the proposed offer is at a level which if made, the Board is likely to regard as fair. The Board believes that the proposal may be deliverable and that a majority of shareholders would want the Board to permit its development. Against that background, the Board has concluded that it now must provide limited due diligence, following which Glazer will be able to determine whether he wishes to put an offer to shareholders. If the current proposal were to develop into an offer – and there can be no certainty that this will occur – the Board considers that it is unlikely to be able to recommend the offer as being in the best interests of Manchester United, notwithstanding the

fairness of the price. However, it is ultimately for the shareholders to determine whether an offer will succeed.

If this was an exercise in climbing Everest, then Leitao and Rothschild had reason to feel that they had reached base camp. The Glazers were well aware they had won the first battle of this long war and were confident of taking over Manchester United. On 10 February they had formed Red Football Shareholder Ltd, the shelf name of which was previously Alnery 2486; it would become the parent company for the club. A week after United allowed due diligence, on 18 February, the Glazers set up a company specifically formed to take over United and borrow the money from the banks. It had the strikingly original name of Alnery 2505, changed to Red Football Ltd on 13 April.

United fans puzzled long and hard about what was meant by limited due diligence. In a sense due diligence is a sort of game. The person seeking it wants to gain as much information as he can about a company so that he can decide whether to buy it or not. United were, in effect, telling the Glazers, 'You can ask for a limited amount of information. You ask for loads of information, we are not going to give it you. We are not going to allow you to pick any document. We are not going to let you trawl over the company. So you come up with your list of what you regard as really material information that you need to decide whether to make this offer, and we will give you that for a defined period of time.'

The Glazers put together a list of what they wanted to see: management accounts, sponsors' contracts, players' contracts, information needed to perfect their financial model so they could get their numbers correct and keep their financiers happy.

Due diligence was carried out in a second-floor office of Freshfields at 65 Fleet Street, where a data room was set up. David Beswitherick brought down the information required, between ten and twenty lever arch files. Keen not to let the files out of sight, he put them in the boot of his car and drove down to London. The room could comfortably accommodate six. The Glazer people could take notes. But they could not photocopy, could not dictate to a Dictaphone, could not bring in laptops – this was old-fashioned notetaking with pen or pencil. The visitors were given tea and coffee, but this was business and pleasantries were kept to a minimum. And none of the Glazer men and women were left alone with the documents. There was always someone from Freshfield, usually a trainee or a para-legal, watching them as they inspected the documents.

The rules had been defined after Freshfields spoke to Manchester United. The general pattern was that the Glazers' people would ring to say what documents they wanted to see and Freshfields would then provide them.

One source intimately involved with the process told me, 'When the club said limited what they meant was that we could see everything on the business, but nothing to do with player contracts. The club said there was some special information they would not show us, such as players' contracts, management contracts, individual names in the club. The contracts of Ferguson were excluded. They were in the super-sensitive class of information.'

But limited or not, a chance to look at the Manchester United books created a sensation among the Glazers' advisers. One source told me, 'Due diligence normally is boring, nobody wants to go. But when we had to choose we had to hold a huge meeting, everyone wanted to go. There was a scramble.' Ten senior partners and associates of Allen & Overy wanted to take part. Deloitte, appointed by J.P. Morgan and the hedge funds, sent in ten people. United had imposed a rule of one person per funder. There were not enough seats in the room. The real-estate documents were held at James Chapman and staff had to go to Manchester to view them. 'Normally to carry out such due diligence you would struggle to get a junior. Now the real-estate partner of Allen & Overy himself wanted to go to Manchester.'

The due diligence was essentially in two parts. There was a two-week period where the lawyers and accountants obtained certain information. Then there was what City insiders call the seventh-veil material, the sensitive information Rothschild needed to finalise their plans and documentation. One of them told me: 'Manchester United rightly felt that somewhere in Rothschilds, J.P. Morgan, the hedge funds, all those communities, someone was not necessarily sound. I think they were right to be worried. Some of the newspapers did get hold of information about the contracts. In the end they did give the Glazers all the sensitive information, all the players' contracts and the managers' contracts. But only to a certain number of named individuals. To Joel [Glazer], to the chief credit officer of J.P. Morgan. But not to Rothschild because they did not need it. It was not only normal and understandable, it was correct.'

The credit officer of J.P. Morgan was a crucial figure. He was the official who would recommend whether Morgan's would lend the Glazers the money to buy Manchester United. But before this happened, the whole process was very nearly derailed by the sudden illness of Joel Glazer.

Some time in late February, with due diligence having commenced, Glazer was on his way to London – actually in the taxi on his way to the airport – when he experienced acute pain. It turned out to be appendicitis and he was taken to hospital. There he suffered blood poisoning. Doctors forbade him to fly and he was out of action for three to four weeks. The illness was serious enough to threaten his life. For a time his advisers in London were completely in the dark. Assuming he had caught the flight, Rothschild had sent a driver and security guard to Heathrow, only to find he was not on the plane. For a short time there was real worry about what had happened – at Rothschild there was banter that

Majid Ishaq's brother-in-law, a supporter opposed to the bid, had abducted him. Then came the news from Florida. While Joel recovered the whole process came to a grinding halt. One source says, 'Joel's illness definitely was a real issue. It delayed everything.'

Joel was eventually able to fly to London. United provided the seventh-veil information some time in late March. This was vital for the banks and hedge funds. They did not want to discover after they had agreed to lend that a player's or manager's contract would mean a lot of money being given away. At this stage the borrowers lined up by J.P. Morgan had not yet committed irrevocably. They had imposed preconditions prior to making an offer and these included having proper due diligence.

United provided the seventh-veil information to a select group of named senior individuals from the banks and hedge funds, and to Joel Glazer. The information was again provided in a room at Freshfields. Joel went there accompanied by Majid Ishaq, who was not allowed into the room. Once inside, Joel was watched every moment by a Freshfields para-legal and not allowed to take notes. All he could do was read the contracts and come out of the room. It was the same with the hedge funds; in each case United had specified that only the head of the hedge fund would be allowed in.

This applied equally to J.P. Morgan's credit officers. They were Ray Doody and Renee Pouisson who had to say yes, lend the money. As one source told me: 'J.P. Morgan had to have a credit officers' meeting in there because they couldn't bring the information out, they couldn't take notes, they were not allowed to tell anybody in their organisation about the information. The credit officers of J.P. Morgan had to attend, and they were allowed to discuss it between themselves but not with the credit committee. The two people who went in, Doody and Pouisson, in essence, formed the committee.' Nobody was allowed to come out and tell anything; nor were they permitted to commit information to memory. Everything had to be forgotten when you came out of the room. 'In fact such due diligence had never been seen before in the City, it was altogether a most unusual transaction.' Despite these efforts, information about Ferguson's contract and those of players such as Roy Keane still leaked out to the papers.

The information uncovered by due diligence made the Glazers' advisers change their plans. They were surprised to find that United's figures were not quite what they had assumed. The profile of the business, its cash flow and assets, were much less favourable than they had thought. There would therefore be problems in both the first and second financial years after a Glazer takeover. Leitao says, 'We would make less money in Year 1 and even in Year 2 it would take a bit longer, so we had to rejig a little bit. J.P. Morgan lent less, the other funders lent less and the Glazers put in more of their cash.'

In addition, Rothschild were faced with problems in holding together the lenders arranged by J.P. Morgan, in particular the hedge funds. The problems with the hedge funds were particularly acute. Four funds had been involved in the initial discussions. But in February, as due diligence began, some of the lenders began to get very nervous and one of the funds pulled out. Leitao says: 'We had four hedge funds, then we had two, then we had three, then we had one, then we went back again to four and then one cried off. Why did they cry off? I don't know. I suspect in the end they called the deal too difficult.'

The Glazers finished up with three hedge funds: Citadel Horizon Ltd, Perry Capital and OZ Management LLC, all of them American. But although Rothschild dealt mainly with their representatives in London the fact that their head offices were across the Atlantic came close to scuppering the bid on the day it was launched.

The other major problem with the financing, one not solved until days before the takeover was launched, was the condition set by the providers of the funds that the Glazers had to reach 75 per cent of all United shareholders. This is a normal condition for banks and other lending institutions in a leveraged takeover. The 75 per cent threshold is set because a bidder who owns that proportion of a company can use the company's assets as security with which to borrow money. In other words, United's assets would be charged as security against the loans taken out by the Glazers. However, the adoption of Leitao's knockout strategy, to get the Irish first and go down the Rule 9 route, meant that the bid became unconditional once the Glazers had crossed the 50 per cent threshold.

The banks and hedge funds were not happy about this. It meant that, while at 50 per cent the Glazers controlled the company, they could not charge United's assets against the loans the banks and hedge funds were giving them. So they insisted that they would only lend if it was agreed the bid become unconditional at 75 per cent, a condition which under Rule 9 Leitao could not accept. Rothschild's task in convincing the banks they could get to 75 per cent without making it a condition of lending was immensely sensitive. As Leitao conceded, 'One of the most difficult discussions was convincing the funders that we could get 75 per cent and that they did not have to make it a condition of their lending. We had to get them to drop 75 per cent because of Rule 9.'

Majid Ishaq says, 'We were really struggling to get there. Not just with the banks but also the hedge funds. For the hedge funds in particular this was not their business. Their big concern was being left somewhere between 50 per cent and 75 per cent. Getting the financing sorted out and committing the financiers to Rule 9 was very difficult.'

At the first crucial meeting of all the lenders, the banks and hedge funds, called by Leitao at Rothschild, around thirty people gathered in one of the bank's main conference rooms. According to those present it proved to be Leitao's most difficult moment of the entire exercise: 'He was trying to explain how easy it was going to be to reach 75 per cent, and he was clearly expecting it to be an easy meeting. But it was difficult to explain to all the hedge funds and banks what Rothschild was trying to do. They lend money for a living and they were worried about not getting it back. Leitao had to come back and do it a number of times before he got them comfortable. This was perhaps one of the most difficult parts of the funding exercise, made more difficult by the gap between what he was expecting and what happened.'

One of the reasons why the banks were reluctant simply to accept Rothschild's word that the Glazers would get to 75 per cent was that they had been affected by the media talk that Shareholders United controlled 18 per cent of the shares and were aiming for 25 per cent. If that was the case, the banks feared, then how could Rothschild be sure that, after they had the Irish, triggering Rule 9 and making the offer unconditional, they could achieve 75 per cent? Could the anti-Glazer fans not form a road block? This worry had already made the Glazers' advisers look constantly at the Manchester United shareholders' register to try and find out how many shares were held by anti-Glazer fans. In the end they were satisfied, as one source says, that 'the anti fans had at most 0.5 per cent, certainly well below 2 per cent. Towle had 50 shares.'

But in order to convince the banks Rothschilds agreed to do something special. They hired a specialist firm of stockbrokers who would coax people to sell their shares to the Glazers. One source told me, 'In order to convince the banks that we could get to 75 per cent we agreed to employ a brokerage firm that wouldn't be an institutional brokerage firm. Somebody who goes out there and knows how to find and buy stock and keep knocking on the door till they get a sale. So we started using Teather & Greenwood. Some would say that was bizarre, because they are small. But they are very good at getting stock. They are very active, they are a traditional stockbroker in that sense. They will speak to every shareholder three times a day and say sell, sell, sell. So we told the banks we would use them. And also that we would build a bridge to 75 per cent by analysing the register to death, trying to see where the shares were – who were likely to be sellers, who would get out, who couldn't sell.'

Here matters were helped by the fact that among the investors in Manchester United were index funds, passive investment funds that buy a proportion of each and every company within an index, say the FTSE 100. Majid Ishaq says: 'An index fund can only sell their shares to a bidder when the bid is unconditional. If you go down the Rule 9 route the bid is unconditional at 50 per cent. So these index funds could accept our offer once we had bought the Irish. We totted up the index funds and that brought us to 72, 73 per cent. We presented it to the banks to show how easy it would be to get from there to 75 per cent. That was critical. The agreement with the banks and hedge funds was finally done on the day before we launched the bid.'

The J.P. Morgan–Cazenove connection also played a role in shaping Leitao's strategy. Sir Roy Gardner had already made his feelings known to David Mayhew of Cazenove about J.P. Morgan providing the Glazers' finance. Others in Cazenove echoed how Gardner felt and were not happy about the deal, including, I am told, some senior people. This introduced a wholly novel element in the takeover, one that not many City takeover specialists encounter. A note by a Glazer adviser put it like this: 'Given the potential for newly merged J.P. Morgan–Cazenove to face a real conflict of interest in the event the deal became hostile it was imperative to Red [Football Ltd] that the deal did not become hostile. Clearly if it had J.P. Morgan would have been forced to step down leaving Red without financing and no time to find alternative sources of funding.' J.P. Morgan had promised Gardner that it would not provide money for a bid where the board was recommending against it.

This dictated Leitao's strategy. He told me: 'In an ideal situation we wanted the board to say that they were going to recommend it. But what we absolutely needed them to say they weren't going to recommend against it. That statement was very important.' If the board said simply that they could not recommend it, it would be an 'unfriendly' bid but not a 'hostile' one. As long as the negative was not there, the banks and hedge funds would stay and the bid was on – this was the condition attached to the senior debt provided by J.P. Morgan. 'That was a bit of skulduggery on our part. We needed that because some of the funding was conditional on it not being a hostile bid or a hostile offer.'

So the United board could have killed the Glazer bid stone dead by saying they were hostile to it. That was what fans opposed to the bid wanted; even some board members led by Sir Roy Gardner may have felt that way. But the board could not take such an enormous step. Having said £3 was a good price, they feared what the Irish and Dermot Desmond would say. They never had the courage to brand Glazer a hostile bidder.

With Joel Glazer well again, and joined by his brothers Avi and Bryan in London, Robert Leitao was ready to stage the second act of the drama. Due diligence, his first act, had made him revise his figures, making £3 even more attractive; now he would try to convince the board that they should recommend the offer to their shareholders. Over three days, 13 to 15 April, the Glazers met Manchester United. These meetings were some of the most crucial in the history of the club and, in effect, decided that United would not long remain a public company. In keeping with this story they took place not at Old Trafford but at Moorgate in the City of London, the boardroom of J.P. Morgan. Some within United might have felt they were playing away from home, but the meeting place could also be seen as a neutral Cup final or semi-final venue. J.P. Morgan's alliance with Cazenove meant this was also Cazenove's turf; indeed these were the old offices of Cazenove, now renamed J.P. Morgan/Cazenove. However, by this time United had decided that they could not rely merely on Cazenove's advice. They brought in another adviser, a small boutique firm called Tricon Partners. Guy Dawson of Tricon was present throughout the meetings.

The background for the meetings could not have been more sombre for United. It was over a month since they had been dumped out of the Champions League and they had slipped to third in the Premiership, with no chance of catching Chelsea. Their only hope of a trophy was the FA Cup. To add to the misery of United supporters like Majid Ishaq, the night before the first meeting Liverpool, who had just managed to qualify for the Champions League by finishing fourth, had reached the semi-final by drawing 0–0 at Juventus, winning the tie 2–1 on aggregate. Gill and the United team looked far from happy as they trooped in to the boardroom.

The first meeting on 13 April was purely with the advisers. The second, the next evening, brought in more people, along with the lenders of the money. All three Glazer brothers were present, as well as United's executive directors led by Gill and Humby, representatives from Cazenove, Freshfields, Allen & Overy, Rothschild, and the debt finance side of J.P. Morgan. This included Edward Woodward, Andrew Honeymen and the credit officers Ray Doody and Renee Pouisson. There were also representatives from the hedge funds and Guy Dawson of Tricon. To fit everyone – there were around twenty people representing the Glazers alone – the boardroom of J.P. Morgan had been made available.

In explaining the financing Leitao had decided against a slide presentation. Instead, in front of everyone was a bound book containing a number of documents around which his presentation was based. Leitao recalls: 'There was a formal big table, they were on one side, we were on the other. We said this is what we're presenting, this is what we're going to do, this is how we're going to make money, this is how the funding structure works. The first meeting, which was just me and the Glazers, was magic.'

In effect this was the third time the Glazers had presented a business plan to the United board. In a normal takeover such repeated presentations to the board by a bidder would mean the price had changed. But not now.

Glazer's cash offer of 300p still valued Manchester United at £790 million. Given all the talk of debt, Leitao emphasised that the Glazer family had spent £222 million buying a stake of just below 29 per cent. They were putting in another £50 million of cash, the additional sum that Leitao had introduced after the due diligence results. For the rest, £265 million would be secured loans, senior debt being provided by J.P. Morgan. Then came the Leitao diagram again, with the dotted line and the explanation that the remaining £275 million was not debt at all which was being loaded on to United but preferred securities against the shares the Glazers had in United. It was clear this money was coming from the hedge funds, but Leitao insisted once more that it should not be regarded as debt as far as United was concerned. It was not chargeable to any member of the United group; it was solely the headache of the Glazers, who would pledge United shares against it.

Rawlinson has summed up very well the Glazer financing package: 'His financing was basically one third equity, one third senior debt and one third securities – the hedge funds. If those hedge funds are not paid back within 63 months of the takeover, the hedge funds get 30 per cent of the club.'

The debate about these securities was to become somewhat heated, to say the least. As Leitao had spoken about them, David Gill, who had started the meeting looking depressed – which, given Liverpool's success and United's failure in the Champions League, was understandable – looked up. Then, some time after Leitao had made his presentation and after J.P. Morgan's two debt officers Doody and Pouisson had made their contributions, Gill spoke. Leitao recalls: 'There was an explosion. The argument was about debt and whether this little thing [the money from the hedge funds] was debt or not. The debt officers of J.P. Morgan basically said that as of today there was no way they would lend their money if this was regarded as debt. It should be regarded as equity. At which point David was very upset, physically, probably the first time he'd been upset. He said, "Hold on a minute, Cazenove advised me it is debt! How can you two people work in the same organisation and disagree like this? Forgive me, but the difference between debt and equity is a very important point."'

During the course of the meeting others joined in the debate. One Glazer source said, 'David Gill had always been told the preference shares were debt and we had a legal debate about whether they were debt or equity. Our lawyer gave his view and their lawyers gave their counter view.'

The hedge fund managers sitting round the table must have listened to this exchange with interest. They knew the money they were providing the Glazers was what is called 'fingers crossed' debt, about which the Bank of England would later express concern. Known as payment in kind (PIK) debt, it could be left to accrue interest for years. The holders of such debt demand abnormally high interest because of the risk attached and because they get paid only at the end of the term of the loan.

Under the agreement the Glazers would sign less than a month later with the three hedge funds, the preferred securities would mature in April 2020, fifteen years from the lending date. The exact terms of the preferred securities have never been revealed, but the debt was said to accumulate interest at around 20 per cent, up to £54 million a year. The hedge funds' agreement with the Glazers spoke of a 'test period' from August 2005 until July 2007; if Red Football failed to achieve 85 per cent of its target operating profits in that period, the hedge funds would start to accumulate 'extraordinary powers', such as the right to appoint 25 per cent of Red Football's directors.

As far as fans opposed to the bid were concerned, it was all debt. They argued that it was debt loaded on to Manchester United, at that time free of debt. The resulting interest burden provided much grist to the media's mill. At that time, to treat all the £560 million the Glazers were borrowing as debt on Manchester United was incorrect, although ironically within a year that would indeed prove to be the case. However, as far as Leitao and his objective in getting a recommendation from the board were concerned, the meetings in April were not the time for details of hedge fund lending to be discussed, let alone what might happen to those loans in the future. The board had rejected Glazer because he was borrowing too much; now he was absolutely determined to prove that the debt had decreased.

If at the meeting of 13 April Leitao did most of the talking, the next day's meeting was more Joel Glazer's show. These meetings were very important for Joel and his brothers. Gill and Humby had met Joel many times, but this was the first time many on United's wider team had met Joel or any of the other brothers. It was the first opportunity for them to project to the board and explain why they wanted to buy the club, what they would like to do with it. This was their big moment.

Rawlinson describes his first encounter with the Glazer brothers: 'They all wore suits and ties, they were very polite. All three brothers had big, golden Superbowl rings. They did not try to impress anyone with their knowledge of Manchester United but tried to come across as being very interested in football. The other two brothers didn't say very much. Joel did most of the talking. Joel was medium height, balding, affable. He sounded very American and comes across as a perfectly nice, normal human being. A normal American.'

However, at one moment something Joel said led to another explosion, a very sharp, if brief, argument between himself and Gill. Stressing that the Glazers were offering a very generous price of £3, Joel spoke of the need for the directors to understand their duties to shareholders in the matter. Incensed, Gill visibly bristled and retorted sharply, 'You don't tell me about my duties. I understand my duties only too well. I've taken advice on them, I know exactly where I am. Don't you tell me.'

Gill's reaction shook the meeting. For a few minutes everyone round the room looked at each other before the discussion resumed. The feeling in the United camp was that Joel had made a very unfortunate comment and Gill had reacted against it.

There was actually a second argument involving Joel, this time with one of his own side. Robert Leitao suddenly said, without having consulted him, that there should be a third meeting, this time with the full board including the non-executive directors, led by Sir Roy Gardner. Leitao says, 'Without Joel's permission, I offered them a separate meeting with the non-executive directors, out loud in the meeting. My suggestion upset Joel.'

The meeting on 14 April had been a long one. At the end of it there was a buffet dinner organised by J.P. Morgan, and the Glazer camp felt they were getting somewhere. They were much encouraged by United's readiness to have a meeting between the Glazers and the full board. A Glazer source says: 'We had told Gill and co., "You have said to us in writing the price is a good price. You would run for the hills for that price. We have sorted out the financial structure. We have shared with you our business plan, now we want a recommendation from you." The executive directors of the board and their advisers had sat through our presentation. Now if they had come away thinking that it was a load of bollocks and disagreed with it, they were not going to bother getting us up in front of the whole board the next day and saying come on, play it to us again. So we went into the meeting with the full board expecting that we could get a recommendation. But we were surprised.'

The surprise was caused by Sir Roy Gardner, with some help from Ian Much. Perhaps the Glazers should have been forewarned. As one source says, 'This third meeting was again in the evening. An immediate tell-tale sign was that no buffet had been organised, only some tea and coffee.'

In some ways, of course, Sir Roy's mere agreement to meet the Glazers was a concession. It was only two months since he had banned them from coming to the Manchester meeting. Now, on the evening of 15 April, here he was in the same room as all three brothers. But while he could physically bear to be in the same room, if anything his attitude to the Glazers and the bid had hardened. That shaped the meeting, making it very different from those of the two previous days. It proved to be one of the most tense and fraught meetings the Glazers had in all their talks with the club.

Before they met the Glazers, the board had a meeting with their advisers. They had a long discussion about the bid, Rawlinson giving them advice about their duties. For this meeting David Mayhew was also present, although as Rawlinson says he could not 'imagine him a football fan'. Rawlinson gives a vivid portrayal of the entire United board as they readied themselves to formally meet the Glazers for the first, and as it turned out, the last time: 'The whole approach of the board throughout had been that they didn't want it to happen. They recognised that they had a duty to the company and that they shouldn't obstruct it. But neither did they want to facilitate it. They recognised that it might happen and that they shouldn't take steps which would frustrate that, particularly once they knew that the Irish wanted it to happen as well. So that was the way that they approached this meeting.'

Before the meeting David Anderson, the Cazenove partner, had spoken to Robert Leitao. It had been agreed that the presentation made to the executives would now be repeated to the entire board. In addition to the three Glazer brothers, the American team also included Leitao and Majid Ishaq, along with Andrew Ballheimer. J.P. Morgan were represented as the main financier but there were no hedge funds. One source says, 'There was a level of the usual pleasantries. The introductions were done and then Joel gave the family history. We had some good questions from O'Neill about why the Glazers were doing it and then it was Much and Gardner.'

And it was Gardner, as the Glazer camp immediately noticed, who made this meeting so different to the others. Rawlinson explains: 'I think the difference in approach was that Sir Roy regarded it as a totally bad thing. At the meeting Sir Roy gave them a hard time. On more than one occasion he was quite hard. Gill had already told them that he did not like the business plan. But he was less aggressive.' Even Gardner's aggressiveness was not outspoken: 'It was in terms of the tone Sir Roy used. He didn't shout at them. He's a gent, but he came across as being not in favour.'

The Glazer camp was very surprised by Gardner's attitude: 'At times it felt a little bit more personal than it should have been. They were not saying anything antagonistic, not directly of that nature. Just the tone wasn't friendly. I don't know whether it was that he was the chairman of Manchester United and also a fan but there are other fans. He had a very difficult situation. Cazenove were advising the company, J.P. Morgan were lending on the other side. In the middle of all this these two businesses, J.P. Morgan and Cazenove, were coming together.'

It would have been interesting to know how Sir Roy, looking back, saw the events of April and his overall stewardship of Manchester United as he attempted to stop the Glazers, but when I approached him he felt unable to help.

Days after the Glazers launched their bid Gardner vowed to sever ties with J.P. Morgan and end Centrica's relationship with Cazenove, an indication of how unhappy he felt at J.P. Morgan's involvement in a bid he perceived to be hostile. There could be no clearer signal of his position.

It did not help that Gardner did not like the presentation the Glazers made. But then nobody on the Manchester United side did. Rawlinson says: 'The presentation by the Glazers to that board meeting was not very good. It was disappointing. It was deeply unimpressive, to be honest with you. It was a missed opportunity as far as they were concerned, and didn't really answer the non-executives' questions.'

The meeting, which had begun at around six in the evening, was over by seven. After they had sipped their tea and coffee the Glazers trooped away feeling very dispirited. One Glazer source says, 'We went to this meeting hopeful, but we came away thinking clearly we were not getting where we were thought we were getting. Our feeling was that we were not going to get a recommendation.'

There was, though, one major consequence of the tone Gardner used with the Glazers. They formed the impression that they could work with Gill but not with Gardner. So was a division in the board visible at this meeting? Rawlinson insists that 'there was definitely not a division within the board. I can tell you, I wouldn't say that if it wasn't true.'

So why did the Glazer camp think they could work with Gill? 'I think, probably because they reached the impression that David Gill was somebody they could do business with, although he didn't give many indications of that at the time.'

Rawlinson is backed by Leitao on this. He has no recollection of Gill saying anything in the April meeting which suggested he could work with the Glazers. 'Gill was in an impossible position. He had a difficult board, he had a job with a service contract and it was important to the Glazers that they understood Gill's position. That was that if Gill didn't want to work for the Glazers then they'd have to make alternative plans. Because they wouldn't want to grab the company and then have to bring in the management. They are owners, not managers with specialist skills.'

Much of the hour-long meeting had been devoted to the United board's rationale for not wanting to give a recommendation. In normal takeovers the question of recommendation centres round the price, but here the price was not an issue. Instead Gill and co. wanted assurances from the Glazers that they would state publicly they would not interfere in team matters, that their leverage in football matters would be limited. Also that they would limit the borrowings they might make. The Glazers sensed that this could be a useful bargaining weapon. If they gave such assurances, would the board recommend the offer? If so, they were willing to consider it and said they would be happy to look at the assurances Gill and co. wanted.

One source said, 'They were looking for reassurances for things like securitisations of the stadium, sale and leaseback, who picks the team, spending on players. In all honesty we would have given some of those, we were prepared to put that into writing, if we had a recommendation.'

Leitao says: 'There were discussions about what we were prepared to do to make it a recommended bid. They were looking for some form of trust arrangement. And we were saying, "Now, let's be clear on it, we will make Statements of Intent, but we wouldn't say anything about not doing this or that." There were drafts floating about but in the end, because they fought the takeover, nothing was done.'

The United board met immediately after the meeting with the Glazers was over. It was agreed that no instant decision would be made, but the Glazers would be told that after further board discussions they would be informed of what the board were prepared to say. Sir Roy's tone and the whole demeanour of the board suggested they might totally reject the offer. This alarmed shareholders like Dermot Desmond, who within hours of the meeting knew what had gone on. He immediately made it clear that if there was an outright rejection, the board might be taken to court by the aggrieved shareholders. As one source says, it was clearly an option for the board to reject the offer. 'Whether it was a serious option or not I do not know. I think they would have been on very tricky legal ground.'

The board waited until the weekend was over. It was a crucial weekend. United were meeting Newcastle at the Millennium Stadium in Cardiff in the semi-final of the FA Cup, the only trophy they could win that season. The match, billed as Alan Shearer's last chance to win a Cup final medal, resulted in a United romp as they won 4–1. Apart from a brief period when Newcastle equalised an early Ruud van Nistelrooy goal, Manchester United were in charge.

Two days later, the board tried to give the fans the impression they were also in charge off the field. They wrote to the Glazers telling them that, while they concluded that the price was fair, they could not support the offer as in the best interests of the company.

Before United issued the statement, Cazenove showed it to Rothschild. One source said, 'We told them we don't think you should say this, this or this, but they didn't change anything. Their statement said we are not going to recommend it but we are not going to reject it completely. In some ways we saw it as a victory.' In many ways Leitao had outfoxed the board. 'They thought we needed them to say they'd recommend. But our absolute ambition was to get them to say they were not advising the shareholders to reject the bid. What we really needed was [for them not to] come out against it.'

Now, with J.P. Morgan reassured that they were not funding a hostile takeover, the Glazer bid was finally on. The very next day Joel and Avi became directors of both Red Football Ltd and Red Football Shareholders Ltd. To underline their confidence the Glazers now told United they were going to bid. Leitao says, 'We said we want to bid anyway. They were quite surprised. I think they thought the statement would kill us on the basis that it was not a recommendation.'

Rothschild went so far as to give Cazenove the draft of a statement which would be issued when they made their bid. Majid Ishaq says, 'After they told us they liked our price but could not recommend we told them, "We hear what you are saying. This is what we will be saying in our announcement as and when we formally come in and make a bid." We gave them the alternatives, Rule 9 or a straight offer. We were not worried about showing our hand. And we were confident that the Irish would accept an unconditional offer.' Once again, like the Terminator the Glazers just refused to die.

But, if this indicated that the Glazers would bid, United had no way of knowing when they might bid; it could still be several months. So they decided to go to the Takeover Panel and ask the Glazers to either 'put up or shut up'. The idea was that the Takeover Panel would give the Glazers a certain time to bid; if they did not bid, then they could not do so for six months. Glenn Cooper had for some time felt the board had missed a trick in not demanding this earlier. But in fact the board had considered it for some time. They had not done so previously as they felt that it would only keep the Glazers quiet for six months. Then the whole thing would start again. As David Gill would later say, 'We wanted a resolution.'

Cazenove proposed to the Panel that the Glazers should be given eight days to come back with an offer. Rothschild asked for more time. It was while Rothschild was making this argument to the director-general of the Panel that Majid Ishaq heard the 'seventh veil' due diligence information regarding players. Ferguson's contract was now available and he took Joel Glazer to Freshfields for him to have a look at the contracts. He, himself, could not go into the room where the contracts were, only Joel Glazer was allowed in.

After some arguments Rothschild were given three weeks until 17 May, four days before the Cup Final, to make an offer. If they failed they could not bid for six months. Rawlinson says, 'They would have liked a bit longer and we would have liked a bit shorter. It's normally six weeks. I think you will find that it was the shortest deadline that the panel has ever imposed on a put up or shut up. Rothschild, I think, secretly welcomed the fact that there was a deadline for them to work to. We knew that they were going to try and buy the Irish stake. We weren't sure when they were going to approach the Irish.'

Leitao was not unhappy with the deadline, even though Rothschild had asked the panel for more time. 'We argued with the panel to make it longer, but I'm glad we didn't win in the end, because through our own inefficiencies we managed to take up nearly all the time! We went almost to the wire. Actually, if it had been eight days earlier we probably would have gone on to the wire, but we would have done it faster. This is about people, the lawyers, taking as long as they have.'

Leitao still had to get the banks and hedge funds to agree to dropping the 75 per cent clause of acceptance by shareholders. The hedge funds' representatives flew in from New York. Some time after the Panel had given them the 17 May deadline Leitao 'had this ghastly meeting, where I walked into a hostile audience, thinking it was going to be really straightforward. This meeting was with our banks! It surprised me how difficult it was to get our funders to agree to drop a 75 per cent acceptance.'

On 10 May Manchester United suffered a humiliating defeat at the hands of Chelsea, who beat them 3–1 at Old Trafford. The defeat added to the sense of gloom at the club, especially as United performed an embarrassing lap of honour in front of a near-empty stadium. The following night Rothschild and Allen & Overy finally sorted out the paperwork relating to the funding. Majid Ishaq went over to Allen & Overy where the financing documentation was signed. There were still issues to be resolved with the hedge funds and Citadel's representative asked some questions on the debt. There were a couple of other technical issues, which did not take long to sort out, and one of the hedge funds ended up by asking for a box at Old Trafford. The source says, 'that is when we felt the financing was in place.'

When the offer document was finally issued by Rothschild it showed that the agreements about financing with the hedge funds and J.P. Morgan Europe Ltd were signed on 11 May 2005. Majid came out of the meeting and rang Leitao to tell him the news. Now Leitao was ready to do what he had been planning to do ever since Christmas Eve, when Joel Glazer had rung him on his mobile phone while he was shopping for champagne for his wife.

This was the final act of the drama: ring the Irish. Leitao now called John Power.

Leitao knew Power and many of the people who worked on the investment side for Magnier and McManus. The call did not come as a surprise to Power, for a few days before this Leitao had called him to ask about Manchester United shares in order to sort out certain essential technical details. Leitao, who was trying to complete the deal before going on holiday, recalls: 'I had rung John Power some time back just to say hello, I'm working on the deal and I'll come back to you when I've got something to say. We both understood we wouldn't have any more discussions until I was ready. And then a few days before Wednesday night I had warmed up the Irish that they might get a call by ringing John Power again. The worst thing that can happen is if you get everything ready and all lined up and then you find a guy can't deliver the share certificates. So I warned him he might get a call, I needed to know where he was going to be.'

He had asked Power whether Cubic held their shares in one account. 'If they were held in two names it would create a technical problem. Under the rules a shareholder who already holds between 15 and 30 per cent of the stock of a company cannot buy more than 10 per cent unless it's from one shareholder. So if the Irish shareholding was in two names, one in Magnier's and the other in McManus's, then the Glazers could buy one of them outright, but only 10 per cent of the second one. They would have had to wait for seven days before buying the rest. This would wreck their plans of buying the Irish, which would take them to 58 per cent, and then immediately buying in the market which would get them to around 70 per cent of Manchester United by the end of day one.'

Power assured Leitao that the shares were all in one name, that of a person in Switzerland. Leitao also had to ask about the share certificates. Did the Irish have paper certificates or were they in Crest, the paperless trading system? To own shares and be able to start buying in the market the Glazers had to have completed the deal, have physical possession of the Irish shares. If the Irish had share certificates then the Glazers would need them and would have to physically collect them. If they were in Crest it was easier for, once the money changed hands, the paperless shares were exchanged at the push of a computer key.

Everything was set to go. Soon after he received Majid's call on Tuesday night Leitao rang Power again. 'I rang him on the Wednesday evening, offered to buy the shares unconditionally and trade on Thursday. He said he would have to phone me back. He phoned me back within ten minutes and said yes.'

The Irish had fooled everyone. For months the speculation had been that they would not sell. Fans opposed to Glazer were sure they would not; Walsh was convinced, as was Towle. Some claiming to be in the know said they would not accept anything less than £3.50. But in the end the future of Manchester United had been decided in ten minutes and the price was £3, the same price Gardner had suggested to the Glazers many months ago.

That night a three-way conference call took place between Rothschild's, the Glazers in Florida and Smithfields. This was the first time their PR advisers had spoken to their American clients and they found Joel and Avi lighthearted, very friendly, charmingly informal. There was much debate about how the media announcement was to be handled. What should the statement say? Should it make pledges to the fans about what the Glazers were proposing to do, a statement of intent and reassurance? The family were quite keen, but by the time the call finished at around one in the morning nothing was decided.

The Rothschild plan was to do the deal with the Irish at nine o'clock on the morning of 12 May, then start buying furiously in the market so that before the day was over they would have bought so much stock that United for all practical purposes belonged to the Glazers. But suddenly a wholly unexpected problem arose, which nearly torpedoed the deal with the Irish. Majid Ishaq told me, 'We didn't have all the money through from the hedge funds. They were wiring instructions from New York and one of them got a digit wrong.' The Irish shares were indeed held in the Crest system, and such deals had to be completed by two o'clock. 'We were worried what the Irish might think. The Irish might have wondered if the Glazers had the money or not. Who knows if the board would then go to the Irish and get them to reverse their decision to sell. We were very worried.' So worried that they could see the deal which they could almost touch slipping away.

John Power could not work out what was happening. Having been told he would get the money by nine o'clock in the morning, it was now midday and there was no sign of it. Power was beside himself. Every ten minutes for the next two hours he was on the phone to Rothschild, to both Leitao and Majid Ishaq. 'Where are you? Where is the money?'

By 1.45 in the afternoon Leitao and Majid knew they had to do something. There was fifteen minutes left, the money from New York had still not arrived and the exchange had to be done by two. That is when they decided to provide bridging finance and act as bankers. Without consulting anyone they told Crest the money was there, effectively buying some of the shares for Rothschild. They then went to Rothschild's financial arm and asked them to find the money, as they had done the deal. The money from New York eventually came forty-five minutes later, at 2.30. But had Leitao and Majid not acted the deal would not have been completed. Had the Irish been rebuffed in this fashion after agreeing to sell, the whole thing could have unravelled. Rothschild had organised half an hour of finance, underwriting the Glazer deal, in order to ensure the deal did not collapse.

Once the drama was over and the share buying started it was magic. Majid Ishaq says, 'I have been involved in a lot of transactions. The moment we bought the Irish and then started buying in the market was fantastic, the real buzz of Mergers and Acquisitions. We closed the day at 67 or 68 per cent. You do not see too many Rule 9 bids where somebody ends up with nearly 70 per cent on the first day, especially with the sort of sensitivity and hostility that surrounded this deal.'

Yet the drama with the New York hedge funds meant the Rothschild team were given a very black mark by Cazenove. This may have been a bruising battle but the civilities of the City were still being maintained, so Rothschild had promised to ring Cazenove and inform them the deal with the Irish had been done before the announcement appeared on the Stock Exchange screen.

Instead Cazenove and the United board saw it on the screen. When the call came to Patrick McGee, he was not best pleased and complained bitterly about broken promises. However, John Power soon rang Majid to apologise for being annoyed about the time it took to get the money. Elsewhere other Glazer advisers were keeping their counterparts informed.

Rawlinson says, 'Ballheimer rang me to let me know. All of a sudden it was out there and I knew it was game over.' Within twenty-four hours the Glazers were slightly short of 75 per cent – even in the most uncontroversial takeovers the figure rarely goes much beyond 60 per cent.

But fans opposed to the bid refused to accept it was all over. Much of the press, taking their cue from the enormous amount of material the fan groups were putting out, also gave the impression that the Glazers could still be stopped.

This resulted in perhaps the most bizarre twist to this story. For more than a month after 12 May there were two parallel accounts of what was going on at Manchester United. There was the fan version – an outpouring of raw emotions, much anger and some violence, allied with various ideas as to how the Glazers could still be stopped. And then there was the relentless logic of the Stock Exchange, where the Glazers just kept buying shares. The Glazers let the Stock Exchange announcements of their share purchases do their talking for them. In a normal City takeover there would in any case be very little further to say. But because Manchester United is also a football club which touched people's lives in ways other businesses do not, the story acquired several other dimensions.

On 12 May, as news broke of the Glazers' purchase of the Irish shareholding, about a thousand fans protested outside Old Trafford. There were five arrests and an effigy of Malcolm Glazer was burned. Some angry fans visited Rio Ferdinand's Cheshire home demanding to know whether the defender would sign his new contract with the club.

Shareholders United still publicly professed they could stop Glazer on the stock market, or at least prevent him from taking the company private. On 12 May their US branch's website urged fans to join saying 'There's still time to make a difference! It could be your share that saves our club.' Over the next month Shareholders United came up with several strategies. The first was to persuade fans not to sell to Glazer but instead to join their organisation and buy shares in the market to prevent Glazer buying 100 per cent. There was absurd speculation that the fans' group might be able to secure up to £50 million of their club's shares. The idea was to make sure Glazer could not take United private without having to call an extraordinary general meeting. If he was forced to do so 2,000 fans might turn up, making the meeting impossible; he might have to move it to Florida. Then there were calls for the Office of Fair Trading to examine the deal. This ploy was being urged even as late as 16 June, when Manchester MP Tony Lloyd chaired a Shareholders United meeting in the Attlee Room of Portcullis House at the Commons to argue there was a competition argument here, as with Sky. There was talk of a legal challenge to the takeover, which merely required fifty shareholders, and of using the fans' economic power to hit Glazer where it hurts most – by refusing to renew season tickets, not buying any United merchandise and even boycotting companies that sponsored the club.

But none of these plans were remotely realistic. As Rawlinson says, 'The OFT was nonsensical because there was nothing in competition law. The OFT looks at any deal over £70 million but that's a formality. There's no public interest involved. As for Shareholders United's efforts to form a sort of blocking trust, it was too late by the time they even announced it. They had precious little support. They talked about 17 or 18 per cent, but they never had 17 or 18 per cent.'

Even Towle, who led the Shareholders United campaign, agrees that the minute the announcement was made that the Glazers had bought the Irish shareholding, 'I knew it was gone. The game was over but we were still campaigning because the whole thing about this is keeping the continuity, keeping people's belief. It's a sort of religious exercise, absolutely. We had to keep the faith. We had to keep believing and we still have. Our major aim now is to keep enough people with us stop them thinking forget it, it's all over. We are there if and when Mr Glazer decides he's going.'

He gave up his season ticket, which he says 'was very easy to give up because I'd already made the decision that I could not put any money into his pocket to pay back his debt'. He still watches on television, still supports the team. 'I say to myself, I support the team, I don't support the debt or the new owner. I'm trying to keep the two completely separate.'

But as he admits, 'Many people couldn't give up the season tickets.' Exactly a month after the Glazers had bought out the Irish, Manchester United announced record ticket sales, with more than 40,000 supporters having either renewed their season ticket or bought one for the first time. Only 120 hardcore supporters were said to have cancelled.

The events of 12 May also inspired Andy Walsh, who had taken a back seat, to return to lead and chair meetings, first at the Methodist Hall and then at the Apollo, where plans were laid to stop Glazer and work for the future. Like Towle he was surprised when the Irish sold, and by how swiftly and decisively the Glazers had moved. 'We did not know the Irish were selling. The Glazers caught everyone by surprise.'

Even in February 2005, some months before the Glazers' Irish coup, there had been talk in the fanzines about the establishment of a new club, something that had also been talked about during the Murdoch campaign. Walsh says, 'Of course, since then Wimbledon had happened so there were new legs to that campaign idea. Then it was a question of how it fitted in. Is it part of the strategy to debunk Glazer or is it a breakaway, turning your backs on the campaign? It had to be a balance. If people aren't going to renew then they have to be kept together. That became a new strand of the campaign. This FC United idea was a way of keeping together disenfranchised and disaffected supporters.'

The breakaway club was formed in the image of AFC Wimbledon, whose chairman and other officials instantly offered support and help. AFC Wimbledon had been formed by disgruntled fans of Wimbledon in 2002, after the FA approved the club's planned move from its rented home in Selhurst Park, south London to Milton Keynes. The disgruntled fans refused to follow and set up their own club, their ambition being to qualify for professional status by joining at the bottom rung of the English football ladder.

FC United was soon elected to the second division of the North West

Counties Football League, putting the club at level ten of the English football league system, nine levels below the FA Premier League. The league had four spare places at the time, so no other club was denied promotion as a result of FC United's admission. The club then arranged to play their 2005–06 home matches at Bury F.C.'s stadium, Gigg Lane. Players were recruited and a manager chosen. Walsh, who became chief executive, told me: 'The formation of the new club was seen as being still very much part of the campaign. It's still Manchester United fans, and it's seen by Manchester United fans who are involved with Shareholders United as an extension of MU. It's been compared to a similar situation in the Second World War, where the Free French decamped to London while the Vichy were in power. My task is to try and keep all that together. It's two different strands of the same campaign.'

Walsh, Jules Spencer and others formed the club as an industrial and provident society in which members only receive one share regardless of the amount they have invested in the club. The original name for the club was FC United, but the Football Association rejected this as too generic. Those who had pledged money to the club were then asked to vote on a name from FC United of Manchester, FC Manchester Central, AFC Manchester 1878 and Newton Heath United FC. On 14 June 2005 it was announced that FC United of Manchester had been chosen with 44 per cent of the vote. FC United continues to be used as an abbreviated form of the club's name. Karl Marginson was appointed as manager on 22 June, and the club held trials for players on 26 June. Nine hundred players applied to take part in the trials, of whom 200 were selected to do so and 17 were chosen to play for FC United, although most of those have since left the club. By 8 July 2005, over 4,000 people had pledged money to FC United and the club had over £100,000 in the bank.

FC United played their first home match on 20 August, beating Padiham 3–2 in front of 2,498 people, a crowd higher than some League Two clubs attracted on the same day. FC United was to have a very successful first season, being confirmed as champions of the second division of the North West Counties Football League on 15 April 2006. FC United is proud of the fact that while the majority of the club's support comes from Manchester and the surrounding area, its supporters' club has branches in over ten countries including Poland, New Zealand and the United States of America.

During the 2005–06 season John Cassidy of the *New Yorker* went to one of FC United's matches:

> One evening, I drove to the stadium, paid an entrance fee of seven pounds, and found about two thousand people, most of them men between the ages of twenty and fifty, settling in to watch FC United play Eccleshall F.C. The FC United players, who include a plumber, a schoolteacher, a stock boy and a

window fitter, were wearing red and white-Manchester United colours – and in the stands a fan had unfurled a large banner that read 'FC United MUFC Exiles' Another banner said, 'FC UNITED, THE ONLY TEAM IN MANCHESTER THAT IS NOT IN DEBT'. The atmosphere was festive; despite the crowd's small size, the sound of its singing filled the stadium . . . Some of the team's supporters teased Eccleshall's goalkeeper, yelling, 'You fat bastard', every time he touched the ball. At Premier League grounds one can be arrested for swearing but here they could curse with impunity. 'Fuck off, linesman!', a middle-aged man sitting near me screamed, whenever an officiating decision went against the home team. 'Fuck off!' With each goal by FC United, the chants grew. Some were familiar – 'United, United, top of the league'. [FC United won 7-1.]

The first meeting that Walsh had chaired, at the Central Methodist Hall, had called for protests at the Cup final, where black armbands would be worn and customer power would be used to boycott Glazer and his business partners with businesses in Manchester urged to boycott matches. Much was made of Eric Cantona's comment about the takeover: 'It's a change in direction for the club, but a wrong direction.'

The calls for Cup final protests did have an impact on the Glazers. Following their 12 May coup, quick details of their offer were promised. But the Glazers were very reluctant to issue anything before the Cup final on 21 May. The fear was that Shareholders United might organise a mass burning of the offer document as part of the protests at the final.

By 16 May, five days before the final and a mere four days after paying the Irish, Glazer had reached his target of 75 per cent ownership. United lost the Cup final to Arsenal 5–4 on penalties after failing to score in a match they dominated. After coming third in the Premiership, behind Arsenal and eighteen points behind winners Chelsea, and having been knocked out of the Champions League at the second-round stage, this ensured a trophyless season. All this might have fuelled a lot of anger at Cardiff but protests in response to the Glazer takeover were muted. The inside of the stadium was dotted with many colours but there was not the block of black the protestors had sought.

Two days after the Cup final the Glazers finally issued their formal offer to remaining shareholders to acquire the 24.3 per cent of shares still owned by other parties. The issuing of the document had been marked by a great deal of internal debate as to what the Glazers should say. One source says, 'The bid document was slow to come out. There were lots of discussions between Rothschild, Glazers and Smithfields, conference calls galore. There was much discussion about a letter to all shareholders, but the question was who would sign it. After the Irish deal was done a PR plan put to the Glazers suggested having a media conference but they did not agree. The family was minded that less is more.'

So the offer document, which was in the form of a letter from Rothschild, did not include a single word from the Glazers. It would provide further ammunition for the anti campaign. Giving a further breakdown of financing for the takeover, it revealed a new potential liability of almost £109 million. The additional loans were expected to cover bankers' and lawyers' fees, working capital for the club – including a summer transfer budget – and the redevelopment of Old Trafford. Fans opposed to the bid added all the debt together and, in contrast to the Leitao diagram, contended that the club – previously debt free – might be loaded with £649 million of debt by the end of the year. The media made much of the Glazer debt burden. The *Independent* devoted its whole front page to a story detailing how much the interest would amount to, although on closer reading it turned out this was not the actual interest burden but a much more hypothetical figure conditional on all sorts of other assumptions.

The offer document required the Glazers to display certain other documents, and these were displayed at the offices of Allen & Overy. But with the lawyers worried about security it was decided not to use the firm's headquarters at Cheapside but an office in Canary Wharf which could be made more secure. The first day the documents were displayed, Allen & Overy's head of security Joe Greenan warned that there could be an attack. The doors were closed and security beefed up. What actually happened was that five people turned up with television in tow, more a show for the cameras than a real protest.

I myself went to see the documents in mid-June and found them displayed in Room No. 13 on the thirty-second floor. As with the due diligence I was allowed to take notes but could not photocopy, and on each visit I was closely watched by one of a pair of young men whose size and demeanour made it clear it would not be advisable to mess with them. Both men, it turned out, were South Africans – one a Boer, the other a black man. Some City journalists also visited while Shareholders United sent representatives to help them extract yet more ammunition. The result was a document titled 'Glazer's Financing: A Debt Mountain Threatens the Future of our Club'. This was issued on 15 June. Although by then the Glazers had taken control of Manchester United, it brought much media publicity for Shareholders United.

What was fascinating about the detailed plans on display at Allen & Overy were the promises the Glazers had made to the banks and hedge funds in order to raise the cash. No football club had ever made such detailed plans and certainly they had never before become public.

These plans showed that, until 31 July 2005, Manchester United could spend £6.25 million on players. However, for the year ending 31 July 2006 spending could rise to £26 million net, that is the figure after money received from player sales. This, promised the Glazers, would also be the amount United would spend in the year ending 31 July 2007. However, after that it would be a constant £25 million net until 31 July 2014.

This is how the figures looked:

Financial year	Maximum capital expenditure (£)	Net player capital expenditure (£)
31 July 2005	6.25m	6.25m
31 July 2006	31m	26m
31 July 2007	31.5m	26m
31 July 2008	31m	25m
31 July 2009	31.5m	25m
31 July 2010	32m	25m
31 July 2011	32.5m	25m
31 July 2012	33m	25m
31 July 2013	33.5m	25m
31 July 2014	34m	25m

United had rarely been big spenders; this spending could not match that of Chelsea but compared favourably with what United had traditionally spent on players and was much more than they had spent in the last couple of years. But, if Glazer had pledged to spend more on average than United's historic spending, his borrowing meant that he had to make several other promises to the banks.

The details of player spending were part of an agreement which Red Football Ltd had entered with J.P. Morgan Europe. The agreement made it clear that, on top of the United board, there would now effectively be a super board of bankers, without whose agreement United could do little. United promised to provide the bankers a monthly financial report setting out profit and loss, cash flow and comparison with the budget. Once a year, chief executive David Gill would have to make presentations to the bankers explaining United's performance.

United promised not to buy any other company, nor to invest more than £2 million in any new joint venture. The agreement specified the type of pension scheme United employees could enjoy, even named the four firms which could audit United's accounts. Should Sir Alex Ferguson or any senior employee leave, then the bankers had to be informed immediately. Nor could United change the plans to extend their stadium. The Glazers, however, agreed that whatever happened United would play at Old Trafford and nowhere else.

The Glazers had to make the document so detailed not merely to satisfy the banks and their other financial advisers, but also to reassure the existing United board. Leitao told me: 'It was partly trying to gain the support of the management of the club. It came about principally as a concession or an attempt to placate the management and the board – that we did understand the actual need for investing in players, that we had more capacity to invest than they had invested in the previous couple of years. But it's not entirely stupid in the sense that the lenders themselves would want to be satisfied, understand that it is necessary to invest in players if the club is to continue to be at the top of the Premier League. It also made sense from the owners' point of view. The Glazers wanted to make sure that the lenders would allow them to invest that money: £25 million a year, plus an extra £25 million somewhere over five years.'

On 6 June the Glazers took control of Manchester United. That was the day when Joel, Avi and Bryan joined the board and the non-executive directors, led by Gardner, resigned. Two weeks earlier, on 26 May, Gardner, announcing his imminent resignation, had advised minority shareholders in a letter that they would be better off selling their shares. The board was not recommending the offer, but reluctantly advised remaining shareholders to accept the bid. After this point, anyone still holding shares was doing so for nuisance value. Gardner had also confirmed that almost two million shares owned by the board – 0.72 per cent of the club – would now be sold. Gill too soon sold his 11,000 shares to Glazer. By the time of the first closing (the date specified on the offer document for shareholders to say whether they were accepting the offer), 3 p.m. on 13 June 2005, the Glazers controlled over 95 per cent of the shares, unheard-of even in recommended offers.

The actual parting saw Gardner fire a broadside, saying the Glazers' takeover of the club might lead to a 'downward spiral' on and off the field; he reiterated his view that the Glazers had an 'aggressive' business plan and used heavy borrowing.

Gill too had once called the Glazer plans 'aggressive', but he had made his peace with his new owners. On that day Andy Anson, the man Ballheimer had voted off the board at Joel's instruction the previous November, was reappointed. This was seen as an apparent concession to Gill, but in truth the vote against Anson had been merely a tactical ploy on the Glazers' part. The war was won and they never had anything against Anson personally. The decision of Gill, Anson and Humby not to quit made them targets for the anti-Glazer groups, Shareholders United describing them as 'the three stooges'.

On 22 June Manchester United ended its plc life after fourteen years. By then the Glazers already owned 97.3 per cent of the club; six days later they had 98 per cent. It was only at this stage that the three Glazer brothers decided to come to England to finally take possession of the trophy they had worked so hard and long to own. They had already been visited in Florida by Gill and Humby; now it was time to examine their estate.

23

A SLOW DECLINE OR A NEW DAWN?

ON 27 JUNE 2005, as the official announcement was made that Manchester United's shares had been delisted and the Glazers owned the club lock, stock and barrel, Joel, Avi and Bryan Glazer flew into London and were driven to the Ritz.

That evening the three Glazer brothers threw a party for their advisers at Nobu, the most famous Japanese restaurant in London's West End. Ballheimer led the lawyers from Allen & Overy, Leitao the bankers from Rothschild, who also included Majid Ishaq. Also at this celebratory party was John Antcliffe and Tehsun Nayani of Smithfield, the PR advisers, and the men of J.P. Morgan Europe who had played such a crucial role in raising the money, including Ray Doody, Renee Pouisson, Andrew Honeymen and Edward Woodward, who by now was beginning to attract the close interest of the Glazer brothers, Joel in particular, as a man they might like to be working for them full time. It was a night of celebration, a night of thanks, a night to recall the low moments when the deal appeared to be lost and the high moments when it all turned right.

The next day a series of meetings had been arranged for the three brothers. They started with lunch at the Premier League's offices at Connaught Square, carried on with afternoon tea with the Football Association at Soho Square and ended with dinner at the House of Commons in Parliament Square with Richard Caborn, the sports minister. This was the sort of welcome for foreigners the English can do well. If the cuisine still carried the hallmarks of traditional English food – although tea at the FA did not include scones, merely some nice biscuits – there was no doubting the style and dignity with which the great and good of the English game welcomed the new owners of Britain's biggest football club.

If the welcome was restrained and the English just a little curious to know who the Glazers were and why were they here, the brothers themselves were hardly the type of overbearing Americans that the English love to caricature. Indeed they were in many ways rather English, very restrained and understated, and impressed their hosts as low-key, reasonable men. The offspring of a man pictured in the British media as having two heads or sprouting horns either side of his ears proved a welcome surprise.

This was most evident when at lunch with David Richards, chairman of the Premier League, and Richard Scudamore, chief executive, the brothers were asked who among them would be chairman. The answer came that they would share the job and be co-chairmen.

At this meeting there was some discussion of the collective selling of TV rights. The Premier League had read newspaper speculation that the only way the Glazers could make enough money to pay back the banks was by trying to sell their own rights and break the collective selling arrangement which has been the basis of the Premiership's success. The Glazers firmly denied any such intentions.

Scudamore and Richards were clearly intrigued by the brothers. There was talk of managing a sports franchise in America and the culture of football. Both at lunch with the representatives of the Premier League and at tea with the FA, the one question that came up was the debt they had incurred in buying United. Could that debt be managed? The brothers had no doubt that the debt was manageable.

At Soho Square, where they met FA chairman Geoff Thompson, chief executive Brian Barwick and David Davies, then the FA's international director, there also arose the question that intrigued so many: why had they bought Manchester United? This gave the brothers a chance to explain how they had been fans for years, followed Manchester United and felt they could bring something of their experience of managing a sports franchise in America to the UK.

By 6.30 p.m. they were ready to meet the minister; indeed Joel and his brothers shared Caborn's car for the short ride from his office in Trafalgar Square to the House of Commons, where dinner was provided for them in the Churchill Room. They dined on steaks. Here again there were familiar questions about debt and why they had bought United. But, with Caborn about to leave for Singapore to try and help London secure the 2012 Olympics – the announcement was due to be made a week later – the wider question of sport, health and obesity arose. Caborn talked of a DVD dealing with fitness at school produced by Sport England.

The meetings could not have gone better. The next day the three brothers went to see Vodafone, the club's sponsors, then drove to Manchester to finally visit Old Trafford for the first time as owners. Here they were to confront the other, less welcome, side of their position.

Until then Smithfields had had every reason to feel very pleased. Tehsun Nayani of Smithfield had flown to Tampa after 12 May to help with the flood of media inquiries which had completely overwhelmed the Glazers' existing PR operation in Tampa. But that was a stop-gap operation. It was only when the

Glazers arrived in England as owners that the PR plan that had been drawn up kicked in and it appeared to be working perfectly.

The Glazers arrived at the ground around 6 p.m. It was a warm, balmy summer evening. Across the road at Lancashire's older sporting ground, the cricket ground, a match between Lancashire and Yorkshire was taking place. This is where the crowds had gathered. At the newer Old Trafford there was still a crowd of a hundred or so, but any day of the week there are always that many visiting the megastore or the museum. That day there was also a fair gathering of the media, excited at the prospect of recording the first time the Glazers set foot in Old Trafford.

The Glazers' first steps on the Old Trafford turf were something their PR team wanted to broadcast to the world. Smithfield, who had been talking to Joel for much of the day, had arranged that pictures of the Glazers as they first stepped out on to the ground would be beamed around the world. For the Glazers, given the bruising fight they had had to win control, this was an important statement.

Certainly the pictures were worth taking. As Joel first stepped out he could not help exclaiming, 'Wow, there is the ground.' Bryan expressed less astonishment, having actually seen games there in his younger days. It was clear the brothers were in awe of the club they now owned. This became more evident as David Gill and Nick Humby took the brothers for a guided tour lasting a couple of hours. Gill had also organised a lavish dinner with Manchester dignitaries to welcome the new kings of Old Trafford. It all seemed to be going beautifully well. All the anger and voices of doom that had preceded the takeover seemed to belong to another world. Then came the moment when the club realised they had a huge problem; they could not guarantee their new owners' safety.

Unknown to the Glazers, and certainly to the club, for much of the day the rumour mills had been churning, saying that the Glazers were on their way. As early as 12.30 p.m. an e-mail had been sent by anti-Glazer fans saying, 'Show him what you think. United fans are being urged to get down to Old Trafford to show their opposition to the Glazers in person. Meetings are believed to be being held at Old Trafford all day.'

The moment of truth occurred round ten o'clock at night. An eyewitness told me, 'By ten o'clock the tunnel leading to the Old Trafford ground and the asphalt outside were full of screaming, quite scary, crowds. Hundreds. It was a very angry crowd, very noisy, and it was quite frightening.' There were shouts of 'Die Glazer, die Glazer.' In the Glazer team was William Nusbaum, a legal counsel and an old friend of Joel and the Glazers. As he saw the crowds he felt frightened and would later confess he had never experienced anything like this before. As night fell and a mob threatened the Glazers' physical safety, the club could not figure how to get their new owners out of the ground. They rang the police in some panic.

But they had done nothing to warn the police the Glazers would be at Old Trafford. Andy Holte, divisional commander of the Trafford division of Manchester Police, takes up the story. He told me: 'We were not aware that the Glazers were at Manchester United. There was a Twenty20 cricket match for which we would have had minimal policing. There are always quite a number of people, maybe one, two hundred people at the club, visiting the megastores, visiting the museum. So it is always busy. On that day we had officers at the club most of the day, up to about five because of the considerable media interest. We then stood them down apart from one officer. If there were more press, or people came back in the evening, that officer was there as a trip wire.

'We then got a call from the club that they were concerned about getting the Glazers out of the club. This is the first we had heard they were there. We were faced with having to get officers down to the club. The problem is that people in the days of mobile phones can start to gather very, very quickly, everybody has mobile phones. Word had got out that they were there.' The officer who received the call from the club about the Glazers was watching the cricket with his family. At the same time the officer on duty at United was reporting that numbers of people had begun to arrive.

There can be no doubt that Holte was not best pleased by the club's failure to keep the police informed. It could have led to a very serious situation. He told me: 'It is fair to say there was a breakdown in communications over the visit of the Glazers to Manchester United. Because of the breakdown in communications I don't think we were able to police the whole event effectively. The club's view of why communications broke down is different from ours.'

The Glazers were finally taken out of the ground at around eleven in a police van. Given this was their first visit to a place they had paid £800 million and expended so much effort to buy, this must have been both a terrifying and sobering experience. And pictures of the brothers under siege were flashed round the world, gaining much more prominence than those the PR team had hoped for, of the Glazers walking on the turf in wonder and excitement. The day's events suggested that the anti-Glazer fans might have been right. The Glazers might have won the share ownership battle for the club, but they would never win the minds and hearts of the fans and would always be the besieged owners of Manchester United. In fact they were back the next day meeting Sir Bobby Charlton, who greeted them warmly. They held a management meeting, briefing employees, all of whom listened to a speech from Joel. One observer said, 'Joel stood up and, coming quite close to the audience, disarmed people by being extremely witty and courteous.'

Since then, while some of the early matches did produce cries of 'die Glazer', these have been fairly isolated. In general there has been no disturbance or untoward incident to upset the Glazers. Indeed, in more than a year since that first frightening night, the Glazers' presence at Old Trafford has not apparently provoked a response much different to that generated by other owners; if anything it is much more muted.

The Glazers appear to have played the game exactly as they wanted to. They have been a different kind of owner, the like of which the English game has not seen, but they appear to have stuck to their game plan pretty much as they always wanted to. With minor exceptions their actions have been below the radar, making sure their financial control of the company is strengthened. On the issues that concern most fans, events on the field, they have left almost everything to Sir Alex Ferguson. In the process they have so changed Manchester United that in the months since their takeover the focus has not been on the Glazers but almost wholly on Ferguson. By doing so they have neutralised another major factor that has been a feature of United since the 1960s.

Ever since Louis Edwards took over as chairman, depriving Matt Busby of what many fans felt should have belonged to him, there have been two parallel United stories. One is on the field of play, about players and manager, a story common to all clubs. The other is about the usurper in the boardroom. This alienation from the board became even stronger under the reign of Edwards' son Martin and his various attempts to sell the club. As we have seen, when the Irish first invested in United they were welcomed; they would finally rid the club of Edwards and install Ferguson as the new chairman. But now the Glazers have done a curious thing. United's owners are rarely seen, certainly do not speak and mostly act by stealth. Joel Glazer has only ever given one interview, to MUTV during his first visit as owner. Smithfield had drawn up plans for interviews with several in the media, including TV and newspapers, but, advised by David Gill, Joel decided he would only speak to MUTV. Since then he has spoken to no one and this interview is treated almost as the last word by the Glazers on the club. When in the summer of 2006 Manchester United published *The Official Manchester United Diary of the Season* they reproduced the Joel Glazer interview, by then more than a year old.

For British owners of a football club this is rare. The only other owner who has behaved in this fashion has been Roman Abramovich. But then he does not bring the baggage that the Glazers bring. In his case he came to a heavily indebted club and put in so much money that it reached heights it had never before reached in its history. Moreover, Chelsea's spending in the transfer market has put so much money in the hands of clubs like West Ham that it saved them from severe financial trouble. Abramovich in that sense is like a medieval king, who suddenly rides into a down-at-heel city and through his largesse makes it the greatest in the world. The Glazers, in contrast, look like carpetbaggers.

The other big difference is that while Abramovich is in some ways even more mysterious and secretive than the Glazers – mystery about his money has caused much headshaking in high European football circles – he is accepted as a rich man who knows and loves football. So when, in the summer of 2006, Andrei Shevchenko was finally signed by Chelsea for £30 million, there was much talk that the deal was done by Abramovich himself over cosy dinners. Shevchenko has since denied this as fanciful, but admits he had met Abramovich and knows him. The Glazers, in contrast, have kept away from football as if they are afraid that getting too close might reveal their ignorance of the game and its culture.

In this they are in stark contrast to other British football club owners who come to the game as virgins. When Sir Alan Sugar bought Tottenham in 1991 it was no secret that he knew little about the game. When I interviewed him at the start of that season and asked him if he had been attracted to the club because of its famous Double side, he replied, 'Double? What's that, something in the fifties?' The remark later provided a powerful weapon to his enemies. For a Tottenham owner not to know the club's 1960–61 Double-winning side is like a Pope not knowing the Holy Trinity. But this did not stop him signing Jürgen Klinsmann on his yacht in Monte Carlo, arguably the greatest player the club has had in the last twenty years, or successfully fighting the FA over an FA Cup ban and points penalty incurred by the club due to irregularities in giving loans to players. Or even, not long after he became owner, pontificating on the back pages about the game and its ills. The Glazers, in contrast, have shied away from all this and have left everything to the existing management and this has meant that Sir Alex Ferguson has now acquired even more power and prestige in the running of the club, power he certainly did not have under the Edwards regime or its successors.

For the latter half of Martin Edwards' regime, as we have seen, Ferguson was almost at war with Edwards. And while things improved at the personal level under Peter Kenyon and David Gill, Ferguson never stopped complaining about the plc and how it hampered his style. With the Glazers he cannot say enough to praise the new owners. Like the friendship that developed between Labour politician Aneurin Bevan, arguably the most charismatic socialist of the last hundred years, and the Canadian millionaire and press baron Lord Beaverbrook, Ferguson, our most high-profile modern day socialist, seems happiest with a rich foreigner.

This became evident almost from the moment the Glazers went to Portugal to meet Ferguson in late June 2005, following their visit to Old Trafford. At that time the anti Glazer fans were still trying to cause trouble for the Glazers. Rio Ferdinand was in the middle of negotiating a new contract which he had been told had been held up because of the takeover and Gill's preoccupation with such matters. He was getting abuse from fans for not signing, labeled greedy and suddenly one night twenty fans with baseball caps and hoods turned up at his house and told him, 'We're Man United supporters and we think the Glazers are taking over the club, taking our money. They're going to raise prices and you won't sign your new contract because they won't give you £170,000 a week'. Ferdinand denied this and in the end the contract was signed.

In Portugal, United had just started pre-season training and the meeting with the Glazers went so well that Ferguson commented, 'The meeting was very positive and relaxed and they made it clear they would back the team. This has been a difficult time for all involved but the most important thing now is to get back to football.' By the time United played their first home match in the Premiership against Aston Villa on 20 August Ferguson could have not been more candid as regards the takeover and the Glazers. In his programme notes for the match, shortly after a Champions League qualifier which United won 3–0, he wrote: 'Joel, Avram and Bryan Glazer were all in the directors' box at the Debrecen game and were treated with the respect they are entitled to as owners and directors of the club. I am sure all they ask is for our massive support to keep an open mind on their stewardship and give them a chance.'

Sometime that month John Cassidy of the *New Yorker*, writing an article about the Glazers and their ownership of Manchester United, went to Carrington to interview Ferguson. Cassidy wrote:

Last summer he laughed off suggestions that he should resign in sympathy with the supporters' protests against the Glazers. 'Prior to the club going P.L.C., that is when the fans should have complained, but they didn't,' he told me. 'They maybe thought it was going into the hands of the fans but you know fine well when you put a club into a P.L.C. anybody can buy it. I don't understand why there is so much emotion now.' I asked Ferguson whether the Glazers had offered advice about how to run the team. 'I think they are expecting me to come up with the ideas,' he snapped. 'I've been here for nineteen years, you know.' Chelsea now has two players for each of the eleven positions on the team plus a couple of talented backups to the backups. Ferguson conceded that United couldn't match Abramovich's spending. 'I don't think we can afford that, to be honest with you,' he said. 'We are working with a squad of about nineteen or twenty players. In the past it was a bit bigger, but keeping a squad of more than nineteen or twenty happy financially is very difficult. They are all on terrific salaries, so you try not to carry surplus players.' Ferguson insisted that he had no intentions of resigning. 'I'm not going to be here in ten years, or anything,' he told me. 'But I'd like to see this side develop to its full potential.'

There could not have been a better insight into Ferguson's thinking and how his relationship with the Glazers was developing. This became evident when for two weeks in November United faced a major crisis regarding Roy Keane. United had made an indifferent start to the season and the tactics employed by the team had attracted much criticism. Much of this focused on assistant coach Carlos Queiroz, a hugely influential figure who had become Ferguson's deputy in 2002, then gone off to coach Real Madrid before returning to Old Trafford. Fans had even begun to shout 'Give us back our 4-4-2', cries that had not been heard at United for years. Then the Keane crisis blew up suddenly like a gale, calling into question Ferguson's management style.

On 29 October United suffered their heaviest away defeat in six years, losing 4–1 to Middlesbrough. Keane, who was injured, watched the match in a pub in Dubai in horror. With his foot injured the club had asked him to take a break. Keane would later say, 'That defeat still hurts; not that we got beaten 4–1, but the way we got beaten. I didn't even bloody play, which was even more frustrating, because part of me is saying, "Roy stay out of if it, it's not your business," but I'm a player in that dressing room, and this affects the dressing room. I was seeing players doing stuff off the pitch, had the feeling it was affecting them, and it came to a head with that defeat. That feeling, I'll take it to the grave. And yes I nailed certain people.'

According to one story, on the following Monday Keane heard Kieran Richardson telling his team-mates in the changing room at Carrington about ordering a Bentley Continental. Keane felt this showed little commitment after such a defeat and told him off. The player is said to have cancelled his order for the new car. If so, it showed the strength of Keane's influence, even when injured.

Two days later Keane conducted a thirty-minute MUTV interview called 'Roy Keane Plays the Pundit'. Other players had 'played the pundit' on the channel before – indeed, the fact that the channel has access to the players is one of its selling points – but here Keane did so in a fashion the channel could not stomach. He severely criticised his team-mates: 'The players have been asked questions and are just not coming up with the answers. I am sick of having to say it.' During the interview Keane was shown Middlesbrough's goals and asked to comment, but within ten minutes it become clear that the interview was beyond editing. Keane was invited on numerous occasions to tone down his words but continued to criticise his team-mates. Astonished, the producers of the programme felt they had no option but to contact David Gill before the programme was aired. Gill decided that the interview was too strong and should not be broadcast at its usual time of 5.30 p.m. The decision was apparently endorsed by Ferguson, and a member of Manchester United's staff called Keane in his Cheshire home to inform him. A youth academy match was shown as a replacement. There are apparently only three videos of the programme – two kept under lock and key at MUTV, with Gill having the third.

On 2 November United lost at Lille and put themselves in serious danger of not qualifying from their Champions League group. Ferguson, clearly upset, left the field after the defeat without congratulating the Lille bench. The fans had been booing the team and chanting Keane's name during the game. That episode much affected Ferguson and he partly blamed Keane for it. Keane had been the rock around which Ferguson had built his team. He had fought hard to get Keane to Old Trafford from Nottingham Forest, snatching him from the eyes of Kenny Dalglish at Blackburn. In Keane's first season United won their first Double, embarking on a period in which they won the Premiership a further six times in the following nine seasons. In 2000 Keane launched his infamous 'prawn sandwich' attack on the Old Trafford faithful. For years the skipper had challenged everybody at Old Trafford to raise their standards. But now Ferguson felt Keane was challenging him.

For some time Keane had made no secret of his disenchantment with what he felt were falling standards at Old Trafford: players not working hard enough and not being made to work hard enough, Ferguson leaving too much to Carlos Queiroz. The manager's relationship with Keane did not improve at the pre-season Algarve training camp. Keane expressed his unhappiness about the training facilities and in particular the arrangements for families. And there had been heated discussions between manager and captain about Ferguson's inability to find a long-term midfield replacement for the ageing Keane.

As a result of the pulled MUTV interview, there was now growing speculation that Keane, who had already announced his retirement from Manchester United in the summer of 2006, might bring forward his leaving date to January.

The next day, 3 November, Keane met his team-mates for the first time since the interview and was allowed to address the first-team squad at Carrington. According to Ferdinand, Keane said, 'Listen, I still wouldn't mind the tape going on air. I would have been happy for it to be played. I think it should have been played. The papers had made a meal out of what was said on the video. I never mentioned anyone's wages and I didn't insult anybody. I judge performance honestly and if you are not criticising yourselves in the same way you shouldn't be at United.'

According to Daniel Taylor of the *Guardian:*

It was at this point that Ferguson intervened and after an exchange he led Keane and the rest of the squad to his office to watch the MUTV video. Ferguson's anger soon matched that of Keane. He accused him of ranting and of bringing the club into disrepute. It is believed an apoplectic Keane made a reference to Ferguson's legal case over the Rock of Gibraltar, a remark that the United manager would consider beyond the pale.

Keane was also to lay into Queiroz, describing him as 'a fucking waste of space' and his training methods as 'fucking boring' after Queiroz intervened to call for loyalty. This reflected the feeling that Queiroz had left United for Real Madrid then come back when he could not make it in Spain. According to David Walsh, writing in the *Sunday Times* magazine, 'To use an expression he likes, he than nailed Queiroz by reminding him it was he who ran off to coach Real Madrid, and only came back to United when things didn't work out in Spain.' That meant Queiroz could not as Keane saw it preach loyalty to others. Ferguson was not amused by this abuse of his chosen assistant in front of the players. It is notable that Ruud van Nistelrooy followed Keane with some significant criticisms of the club, though he delivered them in a more diplomatic fashion. 'This is the most difficult time I have known at the club,' he said.

That evening Keane called his adviser Michael Kennedy and told him he believed the time for him to leave the club had come. He wanted him to prepare a statement, but Kennedy persuaded him to sleep on it and next morning Keane did not ring. Soon, however, there were reports of a second Keane MUTV interview in which he was said to have strongly criticised Ole Gunnar Solskjaer. On Ferguson's orders, the tape was thought to be have been put under lock and key at MUTV. Ferguson insisted that he would not tolerate any criticism of players from within Old Trafford being made public. All this might still have blown over had Keane agreed to apologise, but he refused when asked by Ferguson.

Keane first realised Ferguson had decided they must part on Wednesday 17 November. Having recovered from injury and come through four training sessions, he expected to make his return for United's reserves against West Bromwich Albion on the Thursday. However, on the Tuesday one of the physios who works with the reserves told him he wasn't in the team. On Wednesday Keane spoke to Ferguson and asked why. He was told to speak to Kennedy. Kennedy had already taken a call from David Gill and it was agreed that all four men would meet at Carrington at 9 a.m. on Friday. Kennedy travelled from London to Manchester on Thursday evening and picked up Keane at eight the next morning. That evening Keane cleared out his locker at Manchester United.

Unlike Keane, Kennedy was still hopeful the row would blow over. But, soon after the meeting began, Ferguson made it clear that Keane had no future at Old Trafford. Despite Kennedy's efforts there could be no meeting of minds between manager and player. The anger and recriminations of the past few days had gone; now an overwhelming sadness filled the room. David Walsh of the

Sunday Times described Ferguson's demeanour as that of a father telling his 'favourite son he would have to leave the family home. Keane sat mostly in silence, knowing it was no time for argument. God knows, there had been enough of that . . . Ferguson explained how he felt Keane was no longer good for the club.'

It was quickly agreed between Gill and Kennedy that Keane's contract would be paid in full. If he joined another club the agreement would stand. Keane would also be given a testimonial. This was duly held in May, although by then another player Ferguson had fallen out with did not play in the match. Ruud van Nistelrooy would ring Keane to say, 'I wanted to be there to respect Roy but I have not been allowed to and that's the most painful thing of all.' Just over two months later he too was out of the club, blaming his fight with Ferguson as the reason for his departure.

As Ferguson conducted his weekly press conference at 11 a.m. on that November day, he was relaxed and good-humoured and did not let on that Keane had gone. United announced that later. Following the settlement Kennedy drove to Keane's house. 'It's for the best, Michael,' Keane said. 'It's the right thing. Time to move on.' Soon Keane had joined Celtic.

During this whole affair the Glazers said nothing. At that time there had been reports that United had been talking to Ottmar Hitzfeld as a replacement for Ferguson. In a *News of the World* piece headlined 'Is Anyone in charge at Old Trafford?' Martin Samuel observed that there was no word from the Glazers and wondered if it was they who had contacted Hitzfeld or Ferguson himself. Samuel was not being entirely serious, but his comments on the Glazers showed how their style of management was causing a problem for those used to the ways of English football. He wrote: 'The day the Glazers bought United, Joel should have taken up residence in Manchester. He might have needed to do it behind several tons of reinforced concrete but it would at least have sent a message of professional intent, of hands-on management via something more meaningful than conference calls.'

But that was not the Glazer style. Their PR people insisted the family did not interfere in what Ferguson and Gill did and were said to be 'quite pleasantly surprised' by the reaction of fans at Old Trafford. They were happy just to back their manager's judgement. Whether privately the Keane affair produced more of an internal crisis is not clear. According to one well-informed source, Joel learnt about it on the internet, which led to words with Gill. Bobby Robson would later say that at about this time Ferguson thought of quitting, before changing his mind and deciding to stay.

By early December the Glazers should have had cause for worry about his judgement. Two weeks after the Keane crisis the criticisms Keane had made about his fellow players were fully justified when Manchester United lost 2–1 to

Benfica in Lisbon and went out of the Champions League, one of their earliest departures from the competition since it took its new shape. It meant a potential loss of £15 million and raised further questions about the Glazer finances.

Yet just before Christmas Ferguson signed for £7 million the highly sought-after Serbian defender Nemanja Vidic from Spartak Moscow, the biggest single payout for a player since the Glazers assumed control. The New Year had barely begun before Gill flew to Monaco to complete the transfer of French defender Patrice Evra. In two hours of talks at the Louis II Stadium Gill agreed a fee of about £5.5 million. By the end of the January transfer window United had spent a total of £15 million on players since the Glazers took over. This produced more praise from Ferguson for the family. 'Without question, I have found the owners excellent. They have never failed in their promises and support in what we have done.'

In April 2006 it emerged that Wayne Rooney owed a large sum to a private bookmaker. That footballers bet is hardly news; Ferguson himself likes to bet. But in this case the situation was somewhat different. Rooney would later describe the incident in his autobiography. He had got the number of a private bookmaker from a fellow England player – he cannot say who it was but it was not Michael Owen, although Owen uses the same bookmaker. Rooney only knew his first name, Mike. He always bet by text, never met or spoke to Mike. He started betting in September 2005 and had soon run up a debt of £51,000. In February 2006, the night before United played Blackburn, Mike rang to ask Rooney to settle. A frightened Rooney rang his agent, Paul Stretford, who was horrified to find Mike did not have a licence when he took Rooney's bets. The next day Blackburn won 4–3, although Rooney says his game was not affected. The debt was eventually settled but it raised questions about how football clubs manage young players who are suddenly given lots of money. The *Sunday Times* was to estimate that Rooney, only twenty, was already sitting on a fortune of £20 million and placed him fifth on its Rich List of footballers.

Rooney writes in his autobiography that Ferguson spoke to him: 'It wasn't really a bollocking. He agreed players have always liked a bet, but said to keep it in moderation or I could lose all my money.' The Glazers said nothing.

As it happens, this was just about the time that United were themselves in talks with Mansion, a Gibraltar-based online betting company, to replace Vodafone as their shirt sponsor. The takeover had seen anti-Glazer fans target the club's sponsors. Vodafone, one of the major sponsors, announced in November it was ending its £9 million per year sponsorship two years early, at the end of the 2005–06 season. Both Vodafone and United maintained it had nothing to do with the takeover, Vodafone saying they were keen to get into the Champions League. The Glazers, in particular Bryan, were very bullish that they could do even better – so much so that the press announcement of the end of the Vodafone deal had to be toned down at the suggestion of the Glazer PR so as not to give hostages to fortune. One of the first things the brothers had done when they came to England for the first time after the takeover was to visit both Vodafone and Nike, the kit sponsor. Those visits showed where their priorities lay.

The Glazers' optimism was to be justified when in April 2006 they announced a new shirt sponsor, US insurance company American International Group. The four-year, £56.5 million deal pays £14 million a year, more than the £11 million a year Chelsea get from Samsung, and is the largest sponsorship deal in English football. However, United could have got much more. They had been having talks with Mansion for a £70 million deal, although this included an element of profit sharing. The way United broke the talks with Mansion angered David Kinsman, the company's chief operating officer, who accused United of 'double dealing' and 'unprofessional' behaviour. On 31 March he had boarded a flight from China to London confident that the final talks he was due to hold with Andy Anson and Gill would see the deal signed and sealed. Instead a call came from Anson first postponing the talks, then cancelling them. United had found AIG. United's defence was that they never have exclusive talks with anyone; they were sorry to see Mansion upset, but wished them every success in the future.

When Rooney and co. paraded the shirts it was Gill who fronted the show, speaking of this as a 'blue chip deal for a blue chip club' and saying 'It underlines our position as the world's leading club.' Although intimately involved in the deal, with Bryan Glazer doing much of the negotiating, the Glazers once more kept in the background.

On the back of that and the shirt sponsorship deal, and ever-improving terms on the leveraged finance markets, the Glazers refinanced their borrowing early in July 2006. Such a refinancing was always on the cards. Back in May 2005, even as the Glazers were taking control of the club, City experts were saying this is what they would have to do. Stephen Schechter, who has advised a number of football clubs, had told me at the time of takeover, 'There is little doubt that Glazer would need to refinance his debt quickly . . . I see no problem in Glazer getting City support to refinance this debt.'

The refinance was not expected for three years but thanks to the diligent work put in by Edward Woodward, who had now joined from J.P. Morgan and was described as the Glazers' chief of staff (he effectively runs their finances from London) it was done quite easily. He had helped J.P. Morgan raise the money to finance the Glazer takeover; now he helped Glazer re-arrange the loans he had helped them take out in the first place.

This meant that the dotted line on the Leitao diagram, which Leitao had made so much of in his presentation, was all but obliterated. At that stage Leitao had said the only debt of concern to the club should be the senior debt owed to J.P. Morgan Europe; the payment in kind debts were not chargeable against United but against the Glazer shares. If anything went wrong the club would not be burdened with debt. The Glazers would have to hand over control.

In the refinancing the PIKs, risky payment in kind notes where the high interest charged on them is rolled up on the original amount of the PIK, were reduced to £135 million. The rest of the PIKs, including the rolled-up PIK interest, a horrendous £54 million a year, plus an early redemption premium of £15 million, were put together with the £270 million of senior debt into a debt package of £525 million chargeable to the club. The £135 million of the PIKs was also chargeable to United but at a lower rate of interest. This made a total debt burden of £660 million, not far from the figure the anti-Glazer fans always claimed was the real debt. In keeping with the Glazers' style they made no comment on the refinancing except to say that Sir Alex Ferguson would have 'sufficient funds in the transfer market'.

But despite the fact that by 2006 they claimed to feel at home and liked by the fans, the Glazers did not list their home address at Companies House. Having obtained a confidentiality order, they preferred to give a service address in Cheapside. The fear of what the anti-Glazer fans might do still remained.

The Glazers always make their moves carefully, and they have continued to do so in making the changes needed to ensure control of the club. Back on 10 May 2005, the night before Leitao was ready to ring the Irish, Mitchell Nusbaum became a director of Red Football. The 43-year-old American attorney acts as counsellor for the Glazer family. On 10 October 2005 they amended by special resolution the articles of the Manchester United football club, the one that had been registered back in 1907, to specify that either Avi or Joel could be chairman. In May 2006, slightly less than a year after Joel, Avi and Bryan had joined the board, all the other Glazer children, Kevin, Edward and sister Darcie, became members. A few weeks previously David Beswitherick had been replaced as company secretary by Patrick Charles Donald Stewart, a Scotsman who had worked for TEAM, UEFA's marketing agency who helped Europe's governing body for football to launch their highly lucrative Champions League. With Manchester United no longer a plc there was little need for a company secretary. Stewart brought other qualities. His job was to act as an in-house lawyer, a need that had been identified by the old plc before the Glazer takeover, and he concentrated on marketing and sponsorship deals where his experience with TEAM was invaluable.

Not long afterwards, Nick Humby, as expected, had gone to become head of finance at a plc and Andy Anson – the man the Glazers voted out in the 2004 AGM – had also left. David Gill remains, but his role may be changing. In the summer of 2006 he won election to the FA board, defeating David Dein of

Arsenal, one of the legendary power brokers of English football who has long harboured ambitions to be chairman of the FA. United has rarely sought elective office in the English game. In the past year Gill has become something of a campaigning radical. He wants clubs, as he put it, to 'grab the initiative' and publish the fees they pay to agents. This has led to suggestions that Gill may be seeking a new role.

Where all this puts United under the Glazers is difficult to say. In 2005–06 they did win a trophy, the Carling Cup, easily overcoming Wigan 4–0. For most clubs this would be satisfactory, but by United's recent standards it counts for little. They need to challenge once again both for the Premiership and in Europe. The refinancing package says they must make the qualifying rounds, as indeed they have, but they will need to do better if the fans are to be happy and income levels are not to drop.

The fans, of course, are now split. FC United had caused some tension during 2005–06. Fairly early on in the season Ferguson fell out with some of the fans. At one stage he advised them that if they did not like what was happening at United they could go and watch Chelsea. This led to chants at FC United games:

> And Fergie said
> Go watch Chelsea
> Are you having a laugh?
> We'll be watching FC.

In many ways FC United is a family quarrel. When at the beginning of 2005–06 James Alston, a fan, decided to not to renew his season ticket and instead to join FC United he said, 'They [Manchester United] want my brother-in-law, who lives in Surrey and spends a fortune in the megastore. It's like the website said: Manchester United Glazer Supporters. Mugs.' But while for much of that season the relationship between the divided family members was friendly, there are some signs that it might become quite strained. Those who have remained loyal to Manchester United are beginning to call FC United supporters traitors and there has been talk on the internet and amongst some fans of planning to cause trouble at Giggs Lane. This would force FC United to employ security and policemen, something they did not have much need of in their first season.

Chelsea's emergence has meant that United and all other clubs can always be outbid, as the search for a midfield replacement for Roy Keane showed. Ferguson admitted as much. He had wanted Michael Ballack, but in the summer of 2006 the player found Chelsea more attractive – and with a salary of £135,000 a week, that was understandable. However, United did not seem to be competing with the rest.

The 2005–06 season began with only two major signings, Edwin van der Sar and the South Korean international Ji-sung Park, who moved from PSV Eindhoven for £4 million. The 2006 close season saw United chasing many players, in particular Owen Hargreaves, but netting only Michael Carrick from Tottenham for £14 million. The summer also saw the departure of Ruud van Nistelrooy, who was sold to Real Madrid for £10 million. All this suggested that, contrary to their frequent claims, United were no longer the biggest club in the world. On the last Saturday in July 2006, as United lost a pre-season friendly at Preston 2–1, fans shouted the name of van Nistelrooy and they also shouted anti-Glazer slogans, the first for many a long month.

However since then, beginning with their 5–1 victory over Fulham in the opening match of the Premiership season, both at home and in Europe, United have done little wrong, apart from an unexpected Carling Cup loss to Southend. As the season reached mid-point, the team Ferguson has put together has at times played the sort of flowing football that was a hallmark of Ferguson's great teams. Whether this will be enough to dethrone Chelsea remains to be seen.

What is clear is that Ferguson has got a new lease of life under the Glazers, and he loves it. Nothing exemplified this more than his comments in *The Official Manchester United Diary of the Season*, where he gushed with admiration for the club's new owners, presenting the new regime as a liberation from the dreaded plc which he felt had so shackled him. For good measure he was sharply critical of the anti Glazer fans and in particular those who had deserted United to form FC United.

He disclosed how IMUSA had rung him at home at the time of the takeover, suggesting he should resign. Ferguson did not say who rang him. I understand this was a call made some time in July 2005 by Andy Walsh who told Ferguson that, if he and Gill left, the Glazers would fall apart. Gill did not return Walsh's calls. Ferguson listened in silence to Walsh but as his comments on the takeover, reproduced in the published diary of the season, show, the fan's plea made no impression on him. 'They seemed to forget that I brought everybody here! . . . What happens to my staff if I go? I feel that I have a responsibility to them. Need them to stay in a job, not me. So, therefore, there was a lot of hot air and a lot of unfair criticism because nobody actually knew the people.'

Ferguson then went on to say how Manchester United had changed the moment it became a plc; that was the time when he felt the anti Glazer fans should have protested. (It is worth reminding ourselves that as Shareholders United campaigned against Glazer they argued that the plc was the best form of ownership for Manchester United; their target was for most of the shares or a blocking number in the hands of the fans.) Ferguson had never liked the plc or its effect on his work. When he wanted to buy players he had to go through too many hoops. 'Anything you did you had to notify the City and while I wouldn't say it was a handicap or anything like that, it was alerting people. Other people would know if you were after somebody. You could lose him at the last minute because of that.' In contrast the Glazers allowed Ferguson to operate just as he wanted to, without all this interference.

'In the main,' Ferguson continued, 'the Glazers have been far more flexible and easier to deal with than in the plc in that respect because so far anything I have asked for they have said fine. They have never interfered in any shape or form with anything. They have been great. They have just let us get on with it because they know we can manage . . . I am more than happy with the way things have gone and they have respected our [Ferguson and Gill's] position very well. The brothers come over from time to time and they are getting used to Manchester United.'

As if his earlier comments were not praise enough, he then laid into fans who had opposed the BSkyB bid, saying they had got ideas above their station thinking they had stopped the bid. 'Absolutely not true. They may have made their voice heard but they are not responsible, it was the Monopolies Commission which stopped that. Because of that it has carried on to the degree where they actually think they have a say in the running of the football club. That is the reason why a lot of them have quit.' Ferguson also felt the fans who had deserted the club were perhaps not real supporters. 'I wonder how big a United supporter they are. They seem to be promoting or projecting themselves a wee bit … it says more about them than us.'

Only Ferguson could have got away with making such comments; nobody else in football would dare, and his words certainly devastated the fans who had so vigorously opposed the Glazers and seen Ferguson as a sympathiser.

Ferguson's comments could not have been sweeter for the Glazers and as the 2006 season was starting Bryan Glazer told Tampa sports radio station WDAE, 'I think they [the fans] have [accepted us]. I think they've seen that we haven't turned the place upside down.' Glazer was speaking in Orlando as the Tampa Bay Buccaneers began training ahead of the NFL season in September.

What made Bryan speak to WDAE after several years is not clear. Maybe as executive director of the Buccaneers he wanted to reassure their fans that he could also be a non-executive director of Manchester United. He told host Steve Duemig that he does not mind the punishing transatlantic schedule that the two jobs entail. 'I have two loves, American football and European football.'

But European football, in particular English football, is very different from American football in its culture and traditions. This is particularly so in the case of Manchester United where for almost forty years the club, despite being a public company for over a decade, was in effect run by the Edwards family. For much of that time Martin Edwards was very publicly in charge, even when Manchester United became a plc. He had an office at the club, came to Old

Trafford every morning, working till the end of the day and did not give up the office until 2004. If this often made him the focus of fan hatred, at least the fans knew who he was. The Glazers, in contrast, revel in anonymity.

That the Glazers are successful businessmen cannot be doubted. But they have paid far too much for Manchester United. The idea that United could be worth £800 million, when not even Doug Ellis can claim more than £63 million for Aston Villa, is absurd. They bought United against the background of the rise of Chelsea, financed by a man with limitless wealth. In contrast they had to borrow to buy United and their club's on-field destiny is in the hands of a manager whose replacement, whenever it comes, will be their greatest test. It could prove as great a minefield as finding a successor to Busby proved.

So far the Glazers have given every impression of being shrewd movers in the money market, but if they understand the very special nature of English football they have kept this secret to themselves and are yet to communicate it to the fans of United, let alone the rest of the world.

The result is that it is hard to shake off the feeling United, having been England's leading club for so long, is now a work in progress. For all the great start the club has made this season there is no knowing what will finally emerge.

INDEX